The Triumph of Eros

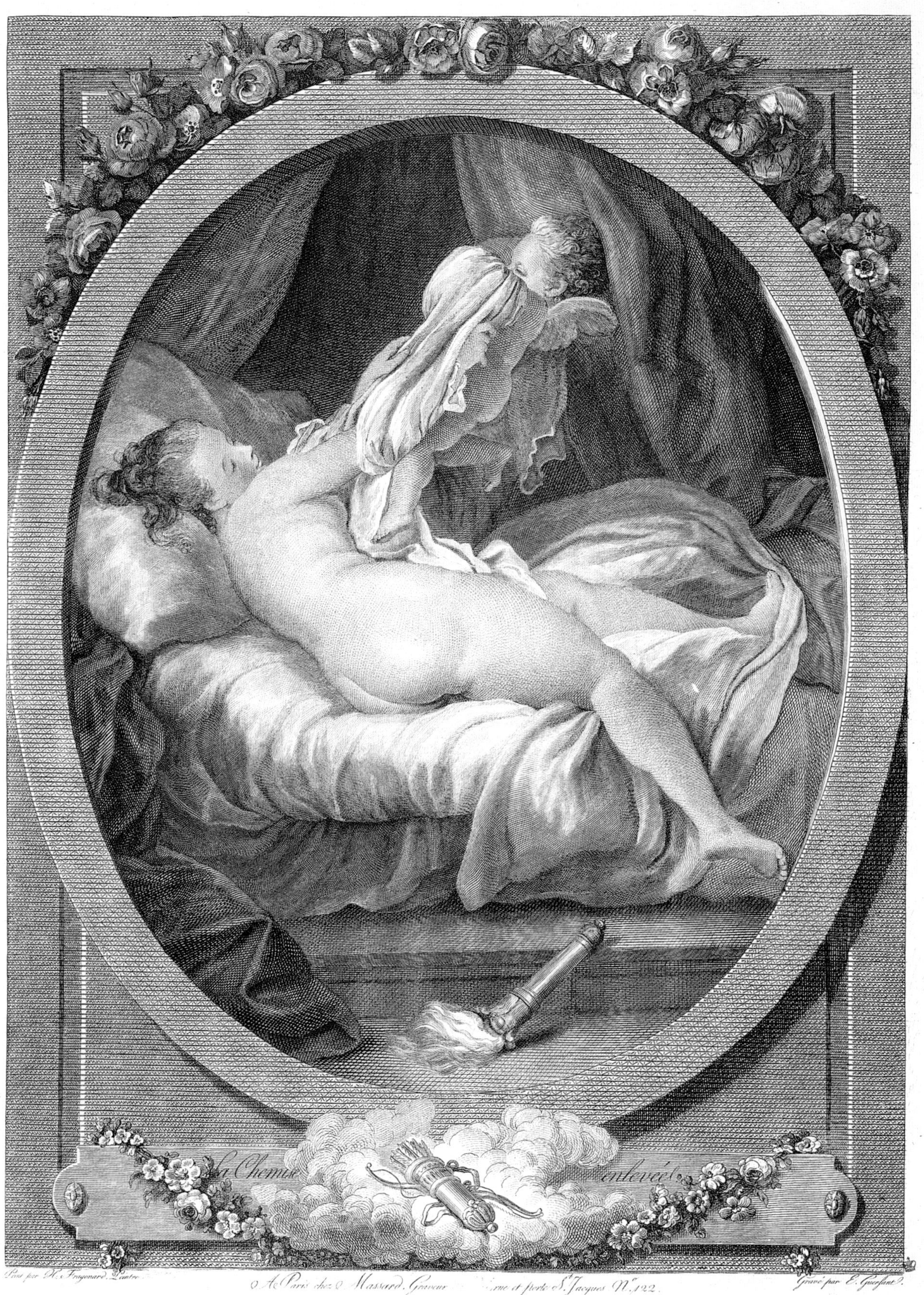

Peint par H. Fragonard Peintre.   A Paris chez Massard Graveur, rue et porte S.t Jacques N.o 122.   Gravé par E. Guersant.

The Triumph of Eros

Art and Seduction in 18th-century France

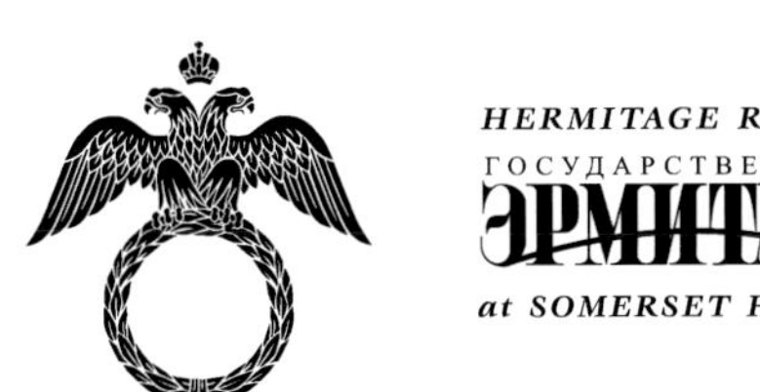

HERMITAGE ROOMS
ГОСУДАРСТВЕННЫЙ
ЭРМИТАЖ
at SOMERSET HOUSE

COURTAULD INSTITUTE OF ART

Published by Fontanka

This book has been published to coincide with *The Triumph of Eros: Art and Seduction in 18th-century France*, an exhibition held in the Hermitage Rooms at Somerset House, London, from 24 November 2006 to 8 April 2007, and jointly organised by the State Hermitage Museum and the Courtauld Institute of Art.

The Triumph of Eros develops the idea for the exhibition *Éducation de l'Amour. La gravure française du siècle galant dans la collection de l'Ermitage* (State Hermitage Museum, 2006)

Editors
Frank Althaus and Mark Sutcliffe

Design
John Morgan studio, London

Photography
Natalia Antonova and Inessa Regentova

Translation
Sophie Martin, Christine Barnard, Margaret Bradley and Sophie Edgley

Index
Hilary Bird

ISBN 0-9543095-7-X
    987-0-9543095-7-2 (hardback)
ISBN 0-9543095-8-8
    978-0-9543095-8-9 (paperback)

First published in 2006 by
Fontanka
5A Bloomsbury Square
London WC1A 2TA
info@fontanka.co.uk

Front cover: *Menacing Cupid*
Étienne-Maurice Falconet
After 1757
(cat. 85)

Frontispiece: *The Shift Withdrawn*
E. Guersant
After the composition by Jean-Honoré Fragonard
1787
(cat. 43)

Contents

The Triumph of Eros

Exhibition Acknowledgements

The Triumph of Eros: Art and Seduction in 18th-century France is a major collaboration with the State Hermitage Museum, bringing together more than a hundred precious objects which have never before been displayed together. As the Hermitage Rooms receive no public funding and all the exhibitions can take place only through philanthropic contributions, this fascinating exhibition would not have been possible without the significant support of a single donor who wishes to remain anonymous, for which we are extremely grateful.

We would also like to extend special thanks to Lord Rothschild. His dedication and personal support of this collaboration with the State Hermitage Museum plays a major role in enabling us to bring these unique exhibitions to London.

We acknowledge with grateful thanks ongoing support for the Hermitage Rooms at Somerset House by the Edmond J. Safra Philanthropic Foundation, The Deborah Loeb Brice Foundation and the Founding and Honorary Members of the Walpole Circle.

THE WALPOLE CIRCLE

Alpha Bank London
Mr Len Blavatnik, Access Industries
Mrs Abigail Bowers
Mr Theo Bremmer
William Browder, Hermitage Capital Management
The Marquess of Cholmondeley
The J.F. Costopoulos Foundation
Cycladic Capital LLP
His Grace The Duke of Devonshire
The Marchioness of Douro
Dame Vivien Duffield DBE
Nicholas and Jane Ferguson
Rocco Forte Hotels
The Sir Joseph Hotung Charitable Settlement
Lord Hindlip
Mr Georges C Karlweis
Professor and Mrs Nasser D Khalili
Mrs Marie Josée Kravis
The A.G. Leventis Foundation
Lord Moser KCB, GBE, FBA
Mrs Geraldine Norman
Ms N Parker
Professor Mikhail Piotrovsky
Mr Simon Robertson
Mr and Mrs S N Roditi
Lord Rothschild OM, GBE, FBA
SETE S.A.
William and Olga Shawcross
Mr Peter Simon
Mr John Studzinski
Mrs Charles Wrightsman

and others who wish to remain anonymous

The Hermitage Rooms opened with an exhibition dedicated to Catherine the Great, and thus to the eighteenth century; for the Russian empress was the most brilliant representative of the spirit of that age. Today the eighteenth century has come to life once more in Somerset House through marvellous pictures, fans, clocks and numerous other delicate and wonderful objects. All of them form the retinue for a series of magnificent engravings dedicated to Eros, the god of love.

Two themes dominated eighteenth-century discourse, lifestyle and activity: one was the Enlightenment, the other was love. Freedom of thought and freedom in human relations came together in an extraordinary way to lay the foundation of the European culture of which we are so proud today. Indeed, the freedom at the basis of our culture has reached such heights that many wish to limit it.

The French engravings on display here, dedicated to Eros and his education, are an important part of the Hermitage collection of graphic art. It is not long ago that their public display in Russia would have caused a sensation and no small number of protests. Now their display, which has already taken place in the Hermitage, troubles lovers of art, but does not cause a commotion that goes beyond the borders of art. Our world has changed, has become more normal. And the educational activities of a museum in particular help this process, as they help throw light on all the special features of the eighteenth century. It is true that there remain other drawings and engravings in the Hermitage which we have decided to put on show only next time – but that is another story, set in a different age.

Today we are telling the story of the eighteenth century, of its beauty, irony, audacity and gallantry – and of that eighteenth century in which Russia took special delight. For as always the Hermitage tries to tell both of important phenomena in world art, and of how they became phenomena of Russian artistic culture. Thus the rococo Eros is the Eros of imperial Russia.

It is a pleasure to note that an exhibition born in the Hermitage has been reworked as a result of the cooperation between the State Hermitage and the Courtauld Institute. I hope that in this way it will become a beautiful event in the art world of London.

Mikhail Piotrovsky
Director, State Hermitage Museum

The Hermitage Rooms has developed a strong reputation for its innovative and original exhibitions drawn from the unrivalled collections of the State Hermitage Museum in St Petersburg. The unique character of these exhibitions derives from the collaboration between the Hermitage and the Courtauld Institute of Art, whereby curators and academics from these two leading art institutions work closely together to look afresh at particular areas of the Hermitage's rich holdings of fine and decorative arts. *The Triumph of Eros: Art and Seduction in 18th-century France* is an exemplar of this approach: it combines current curatorial and scholarly research from both institutions to explore the themes of eroticism and aesthetics as expressed in masterpieces of French art from the Hermitage.

Whilst the exhibition includes some of the most famous works from the Hermitage's French eighteenth-century collections, such as Watteau's exquisite *Capricious Girl* and Boucher's sumptuous *Pastoral Scene*, at the heart of the exhibition is a group of previously unknown erotic engravings collected by Tsar Nicholas I. This group of prints recently formed the subject of a wonderful exhibition at the Hermitage, curated by Dr Dimitri Ozerkov, and our current exhibition is the first time that these fine and rare impressions have been seen outside Russia. For *The Triumph of Eros*, Dr Ozerkov has worked together with Dr Satish Padiyar from the Courtauld to produce an exhibition which displays the engravings alongside paintings, sculpture and decorative arts; together these works investigate the profound ways in which themes of love and seduction resonated in French eighteenth-century art across a wide range of media intended for both private and public consumption. A revelation of both the exhibition and this catalogue is how such imagery could carry a range of meanings during the period, from the pursuit of private pleasure to the interrogation of the cultural and political values of the Enlightenment.

The exhibition has relied upon the hard work, expertise and energy of many people from the Hermitage and the Courtauld. We are extremely grateful for all their contributions which have enabled us to bring this exhibition and catalogue to fruition.

The programme at the Hermitage Rooms would not be possible without the philanthropic support which enables us to mount these unique exhibitions. Exceptionally, *The Triumph of Eros* has been fully supported by a single, extremely generous gift, from a donor who wishes to remain anonymous. I would like to pay a special tribute and offer my warmest thanks to this individual for making the exhibition possible.

Deborah Swallow
Märit Rausing Director, Courtauld Institute of Art

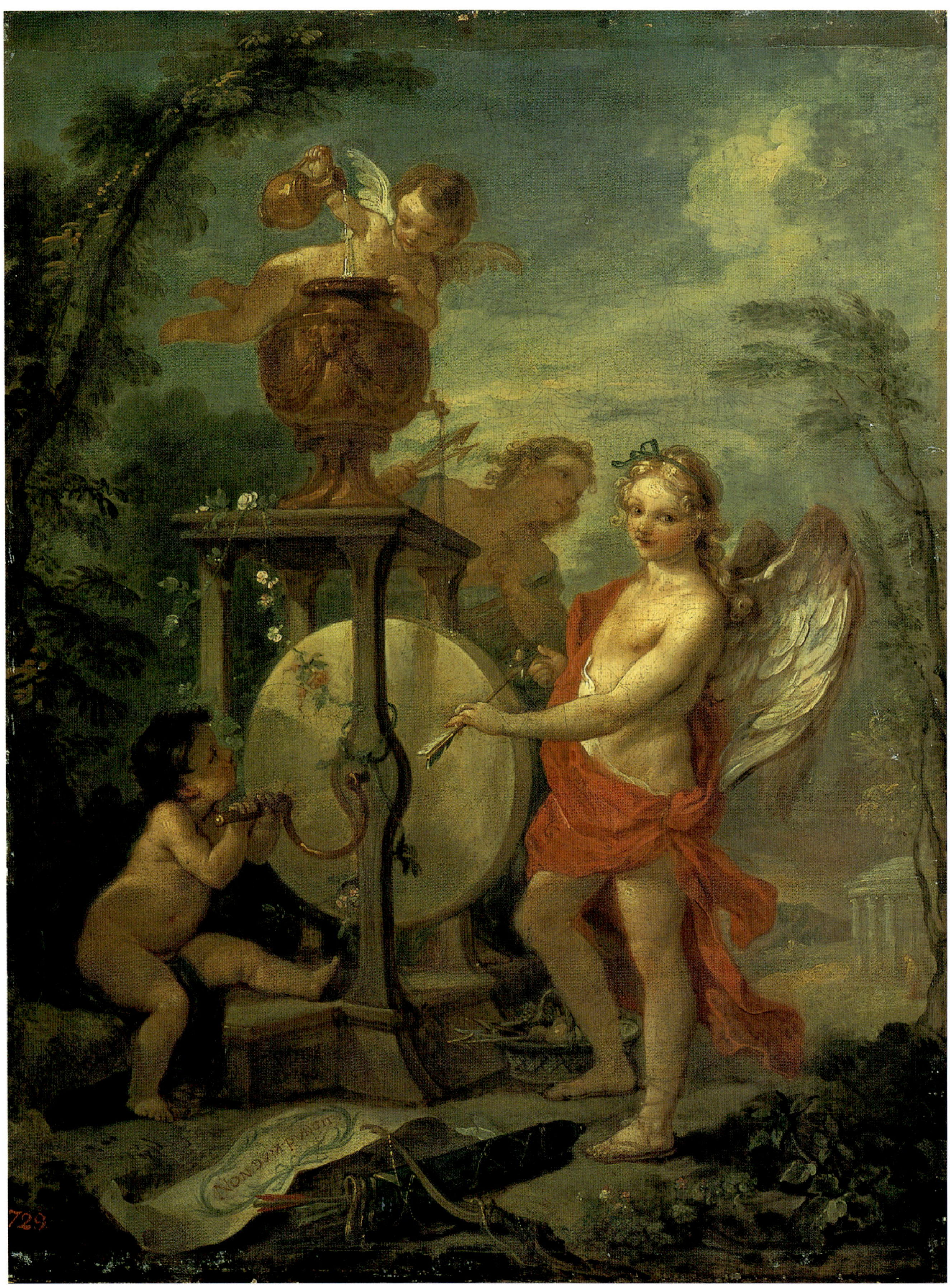
NONDVM PVNGIT
729

Dimitri Ozerkov *The Triumph of Eros*

In French the name of Eros, the god of love, and the word for love itself are the same: *amour*. The god *Amour* personifies the emotion *amour*; *Amour* creates *amour*. The interplay between these two meanings is central to French gallant culture of the rococo era. Thus 'l'éducation de l'amour' is at once the education of the god Eros himself, and the education of human emotions, or lessons in the 'art of love'. A playful attitude to definitions of love lies at the heart of artistic imagery in the eighteenth century, an age rightly referred to as 'gallant', when French attitudes dominated. Everything was expressed in the light-hearted style of the rococo flirt: not just the imaginary world of literature and myth, but also the real world of everyday conduct and forms of speech. Love and erotica were treated as an agreeable adventure without consequence, a droll way of passing the time. And the formulae to express love could be used to compile ironic dictionaries and catechisms, purely for amusement's sake. There are examples in novels of the age: in *Manon Lescaut*, published in 1733, the Chevalier des Grieux compiles a love commentary to the fourth book of the *Aeneid*,[1] while in *Les Liaisons Dangereuses* (1782) the Vicomte de Valmont composes a catechism of debauchery for his 'pupil' Cécile Volanges, where with delight 'he gives everything a specialist term'.[2]

In 1674 Nicolas Boileau wrote in his *Art poétique*:

Source of happiness, torture, heartfelt burning wounds,
Love has taken the stage and novel prisoner.
If you portray it thoughtfully and sensibly,
You will find the way to all hearts without difficulty.

A modern critic echoes him: 'Love became the outstanding myth of the eighteenth century. In the form of the impertinent flying Eros, he summons people not to the tragedy of grand passions, but to entertainment. Love in the eighteenth century is pleasure.'[3] Eros reigns over the French eighteenth century: he is its ultimate conqueror.

Cupid Sharpening his Arrow
Charles-Joseph Natoire
1750
cat. 5

In the ironic spirit of carefree giddiness that permeates the eighteenth century, tender sensuality is combined with witty wordplays. The nature of the god of love is dual: he is delicately simple and endlessly cunning; straightforward and sly; young and eternal. There is duality, too, in the gallant era's conception of love: it is passionate and platonic, all-consuming and short-lived. An awareness of the paradox of love is the essence of *galanterie* as a life philosophy, where life itself becomes one long sentimental adventure. In this way the dazzling eighteenth century, with its endless variations on the theme of love, represents the culmination of all love's previous artistic incarnations: the wisdom of Antiquity; the poetry of chivalry of the Middle Ages; the artistic formulae of the Renaissance; and the courtly love of Mannerism.

The gallant era, with Eros its chief symbol, openly made love fashionable. The emancipation of the emotion of love in eighteenth-century France marked the beginning of the assertion of sexuality in the European consciousness. Its echoes can be heard in the moral emancipation of the late nineteenth century and the sexual revolution of the twentieth. For eighteenth-century France introduced the logical approach which gave birth to the modern European idea of love. It now became possible to show interest in and comment publicly on subjects which had hitherto been taboo, or had existed only in scabrous forms in popular folk culture. High culture now turned eagerly to themes and subjects which had hitherto been only primitively reflected in folk art. The extolling of emancipated and cultured erotica helped 'amorous' themes to become a true reflection of contemporary morals; meanwhile the language of love, elaborated in artistic details, became an essential rational element of the eighteenth century. And Eros was the hero of the age.

In the second half of the eighteenth century in France the idea of love was reflected in abstract ethical formulae of philosophy, which were illustrated through a wide variety of literary and artistic examples. What is love? Wherein lies its essence? How does it come about? What are its signs? The answers to these questions were based on the creations of poets, novelists and artists. In order to express the condition of love, the nature of sexual relations, and the strength of feeling that gives rise to them, it became customary to draw on artistic examples, which in turn began to be categorised and treated as entries in a kind of lexicon of love. This was mirrored by the way in which *amour* began to be listed in artists' manuals and dictionaries almost as a technical term: definitions such as 'to draw with love' and 'to create through love' assumed particular importance. Thus, in the true spirit of the age, Watelet's *Dictionnaire des arts de peinture, sculpture et gravure* (1792) actually includes an article 'Amour', defining love in art as a mixture of desire and satisfaction: love is 'the miraculous effect of compatibility, which the soul constantly generates between parts of the body and with other souls'; it is 'the most delicate of inclinations'. The true artist must paint and draw with love (*peindre avec amour, dessiner avec amour*), and the very essence of his art is contained in this love. 'If you are lucky enough to find a wonderful model,' says the author addressing the artist, 'to meet a wonderful dawn or discover a wonderful landscape, if you forget about time and are dissatisfied when day draws to its close, you are by definition experiencing love for your art, you are happy, and rest assured that you will remain the same, for the reason for your happiness is the love which dominates over idleness.' [4]

Young Woman in front of a Mirror
Jacques-François Courtin
1713
cat. 32

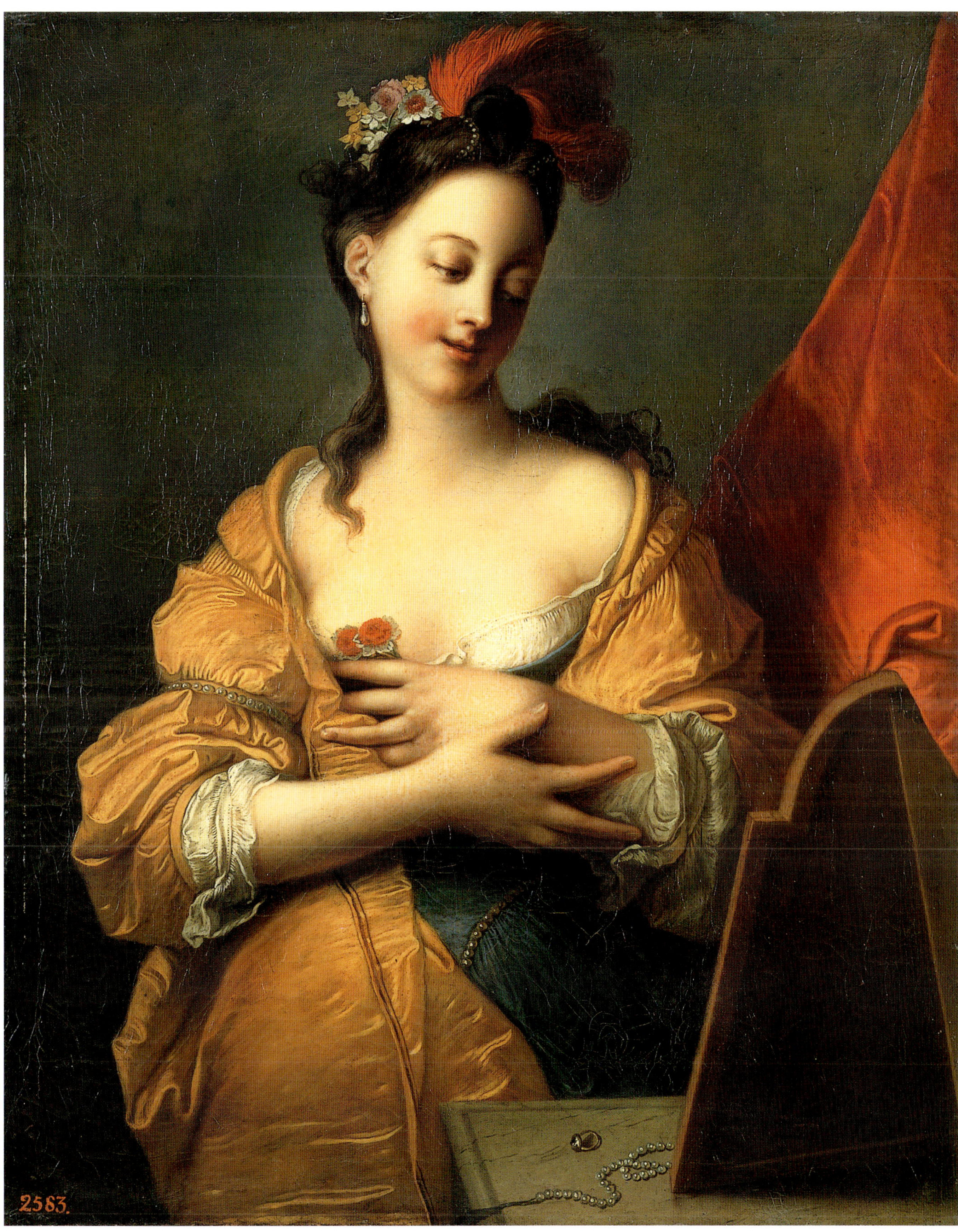
2583.

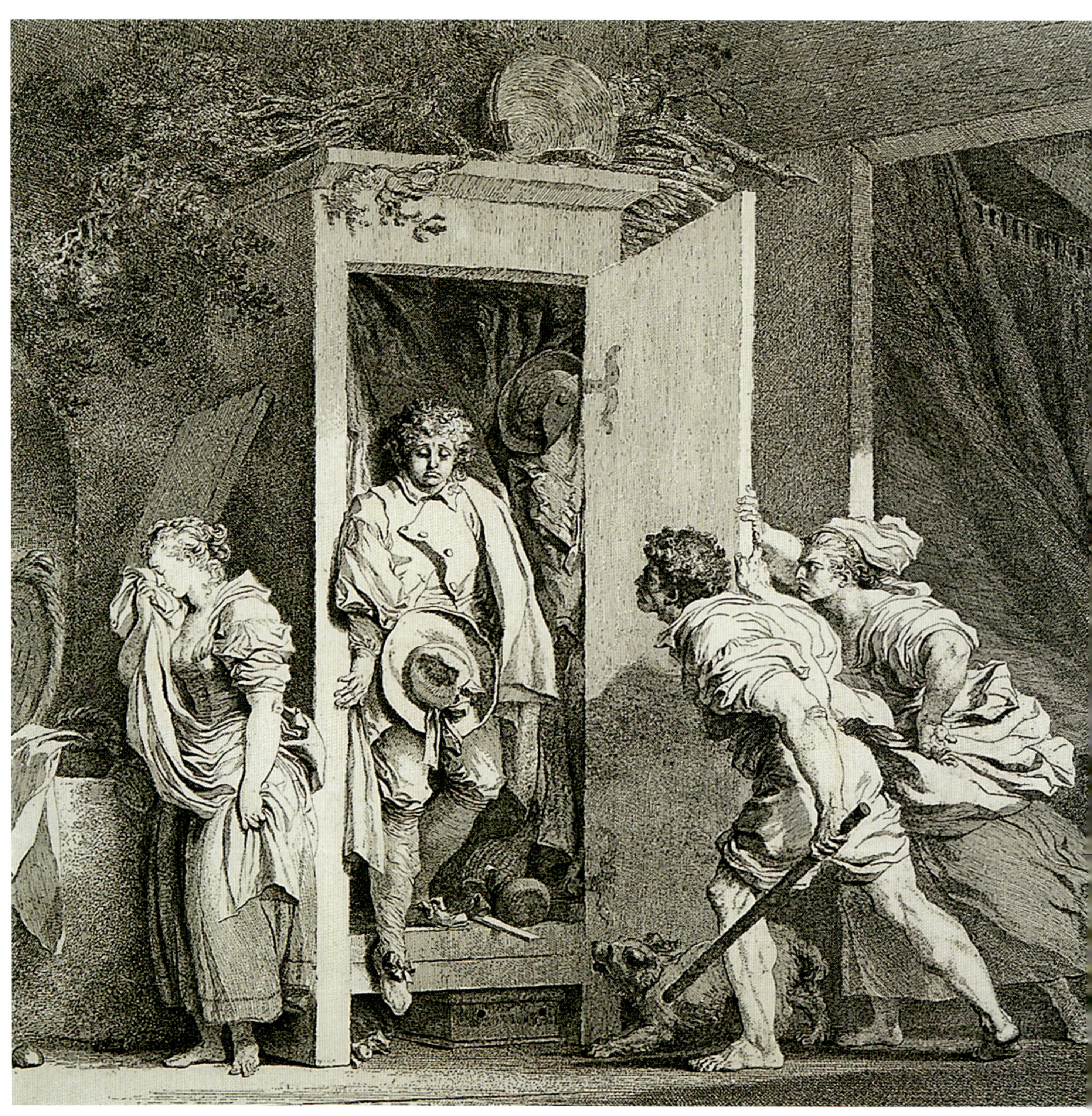

The Cupboard
Jean-Honoré Fragonard
1778
cat. 83

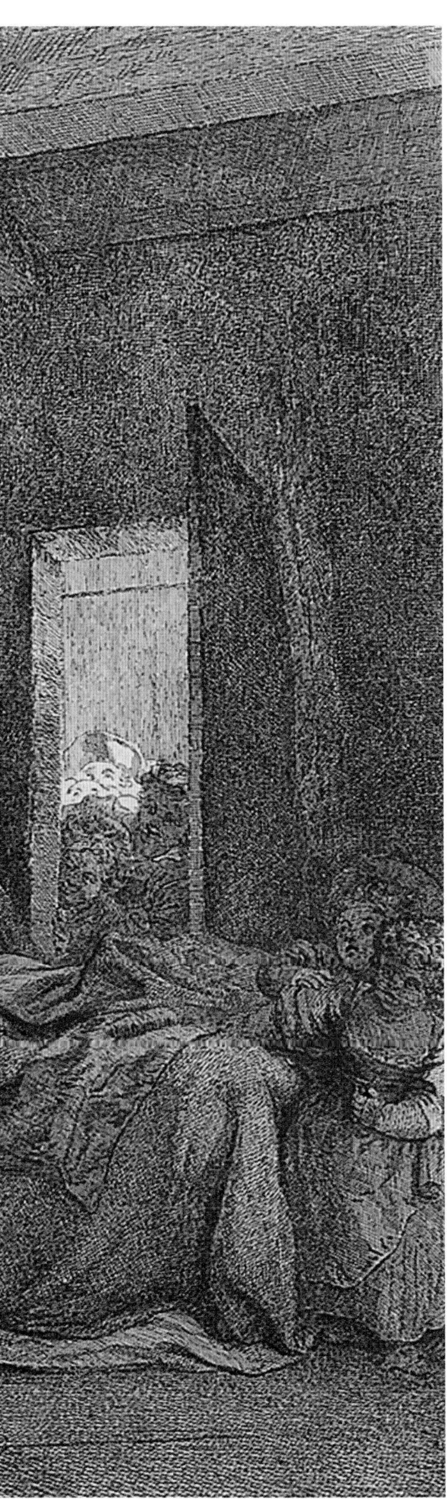

Love through art; love in art; love as art: ever more fascinated with the power of Eros, the French of the eighteenth century began to systematise and rationalise love. From then on love in its various forms, as well as the history of sexual conduct, morals and relations, were no longer merely matters of idle interest; they became accepted subjects for academic research. Ovid was foremost among historical sources, as love stories from *Metamorphoses* and two books about love, *Ars Amatoria* and *Remedia Amoris*, were constantly quoted in France. The idea that love could be 'comprehended' and systematised is expressed in a verse from *Ars Amatoria*:

Arte citae veloque rates remoque moventur,
Arte leves currus: arte regendus amor
(By art the swift ships are propelled with sail and oar;
there is art in driving the fleet chariots, and Love should by art be guided.)[5]

Love is presented as a complex collection of rules and formulae, of causes and effects. It is equivalent to other skills and areas of expertise, and as such proclaims itself subject to rational thought. This is the image of love that dominates in France from the late Middle Ages and Renaissance – from *Ovide Moralisé* (second half of the fourteenth century) to the essays of Molière (1622–73) and Racine (1639–99).

The nature of the 'knowledge' or 'art' of love was now a kind of philosophy, so-called 'erotology', which defined sexual feelings in scientific terms. Likewise, the form of behaviour unfettered by prejudice that was based on erotology was also treated as a philosophy. The publication of *L'Escole des filles ou la Philosophie des Dames* (1655), possibly the work of Jean l'Ange and Michel Millot, is the first chapter in the story of French philosophical erotology,[6] which then developed through the 'gallant-vulgar' philosophy of *Thérèse philosophe* (1748), probably by the Marquis d'Argens, to the Marquis de Sade's *La Philosophie dans le boudoir* (1795). These works are also concerned with the original philosophy of libertinism – a concept which since the eighteenth century has had fundamental significance both as an expression of the world-view of a particular kind of individual (a libertine is a sharp-witted free-thinker and Renaissance man), and as a description of human conduct in general (dissoluteness, 'the playfulness of the soul'). De Sade's description of the libertine Madame Delbène from *Juliette* is illustrative: 'advanced beyond her years, having studied all the philosophers, she had learnt to think like a philosopher herself'.[7]

It was not just writers, but also philosophers, who addressed the emotion of love. Luc de Clapier de Vauvenargue, touching on this theme in his discourse *Introduction à la connaissance de l'esprit humain* (1746), suggests that a man falls in love not with a real woman but with an image he creates of her. Love ought not to be confused with friendship, since the mind governs friendship, and love is a feeling, the inner quality of the soul. Voltaire's celebrated *Dictionnaire philosophique* (1764) includes three articles alluding to love: 'Amour', 'Amour nommé socratique' and 'Amour-propre'. The author believes that love is the highest emotion, embracing all others; and, with all the power of rationalism, he defines homosexual love as a fault of nature.[8] The first volume of Diderot and d'Alambert's *Encyclopédie* (1741) includes the article 'Amour', where love is defined as an attraction based on feelings, and investigates a whole series of its manifestations: love of society, love of glory, love for science and art, love towards neighbours, love between sexes, marital love, paternal love, filial

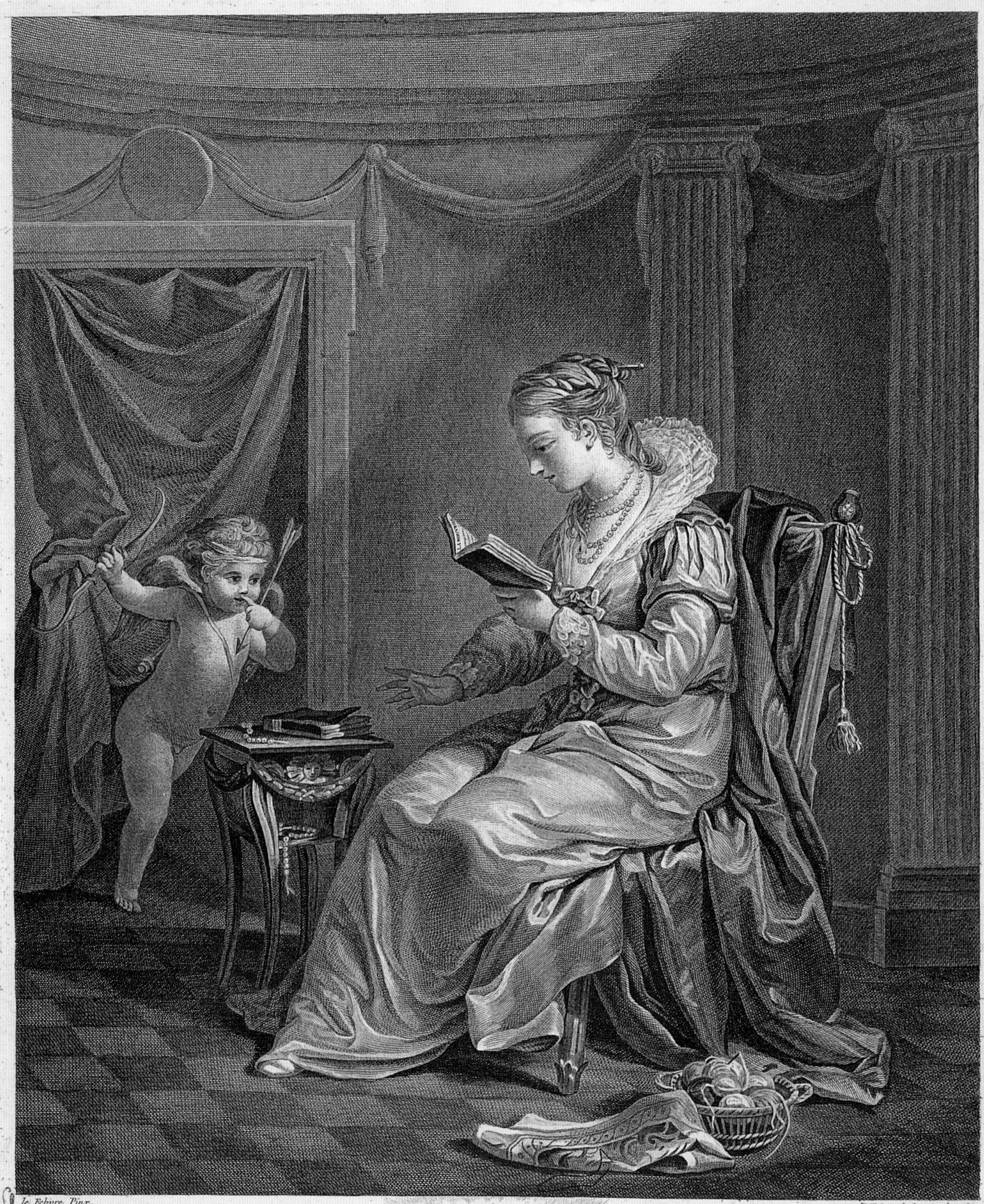

le Febvre Pinx.
F. Hubert Sculp. Année 1768.
LA NOUVELLE
HELOYSE
Dédiée a Madame
de Damery,
Le Tableau est au Cabinet de M.ʳ de Damery
Par son très humble et très
Chevalier de l'ordre Royal Militaire de S.ᵗ Louis.
Obeissant Serviteur Hubert
A Paris chez Beauvarlet Graveur du Roy,
Rue S.ᵗ Jacques vis-à-vis celle des Mathurins.

and fraternal love, love of honour, self love and others. Treated as an ethical category, love plays an important role in understanding the essence and defining the nature of human existence. [9] Another, shorter, article from the *Encyclopédie*, entitled 'Amour ou Cupidon', is dedicated purely to 'the heathen god, whose birth is interpreted in the most diverse manner and who is depicted in the greatest variety of forms – indeed, in almost every form that could conceivably relate to him'. [10] There may appear to be something paradoxical about the rational separation of the emotion of love from the god who represents it: outwardly the Enlightenment French laugh at Eros as if he were a superstitious hang-over from a previous age; inwardly, however, they are even a little afraid, as if he were about to play some sly trick on them.

For although the emotion of love is subjected to precise and often excessive classification in the literature of the age (as, for example, in the love geography of *Clélie*, by Madeleine de Scudéry (1654–61)), the god himself – cunning and changeable – remains beyond the grasp of logic. Illustrated in every possible way in mythology and numerous novels, his figure remains elusive and indefinable. It is, however, under his guidance that a whole procession of loving couples pass through the French literary Hall of Fame: Dorant and Sylvia, Valville and Marianna, Paul and Virginie, Orosman and Zaire, Tanzaï and Néadarné, Manon and des Grieux, Julie and Wolmar, Zadigue and Zemira, Mangogul and Mirzoza, Candide and Cunégonde, artless Annette and Luben. The very soul of the French novel is rooted in the love affair constructed (or contrived) by Eros. For ultimately it was novels and their plot-twists, rather than dry philosophical definitions, which defined the life morals of eighteenth-century readers. In response to a request for the hand and heart of his daughter Magdelon, Molière's Gorgibus tries to discuss things with her logically: 'Marriage is a sacred institution, and whoever offers their hand and heart at once becomes a civilised person'. But she responds that such simple logic contradicts the spirit of a novel; and consequently one must never be guided through life by such principles and immediately agree to marriage. 'O God!' she exclaims. 'If everybody thought the way you do, novels would end on the very first page. So it would be delightful if Quire married Mandan at once, and Arons, without further ado, wed Clélie!' [11]

A young girl would seek an explanation for her languor and feelings in verse and novels, where in certain episodes and metaphors she would find echoes of events and experiences in her own life. The plots of French novels of the age were based on the cunning intrigues of phoney heroes with their disguises and masquerades. New types emerged on the literary scene – Lovelaces and Courtesans. The thread of the novel would be woven with refined badinage: the elegant, witty language of fashionable salons. An interest in literary novelties and a desire to seek out and read the very latest works became a feature of eighteenth-century culture, and gave rise to a demand for new publications. For a young girl on the threshold of society the ability to read opened up the possibility of keeping up to date with the latest fashions – and the widest imaginable range of novels, verses and fables were on hand to help. Madame de Merteuil, preparing the young Cécile Volanges for her role as a victim of society, provides her with the books from which the girl will glean the answers to the questions that so interest her and of which she has learnt nothing from her years at the convent: 'The Marquise has merely advised me not to talk to Mama about these books, lest someone say to her that she has neglected my education, which might be

La Nouvelle Héloïse
François Hubert
After the painting by François (?) Lefèvre
1765
cat. 36

disagreeable to her. Oh, of course I won't tell her anything.'[12] Cécile might have
been referring to *L'Escole des filles ou la Philosophie des Dames*, which, as the
anonymous author writes in his introduction, was intended to enlighten girls in
what they need to know in order to satisfy their husbands when they come to them,
and to instruct them in how to arouse ardour even if they are not possessed of great
beauty. The text is in the form of dialogues between two girls, in the course of
which Susanna enlightens her cousin Fanchon in such matters.

By reading novels and works that examined society life, the young French girl
would complete her education in love, or 'l'éducation de l'amour'. And Eros, of
course, as was commonly held, guided the hands of writers and gave strength
to the voice of poets. This schemer and all-powerful teacher of young hearts,
whom Mercury instructs, whom the Nymphs raise, and whom Venus punishes
remorselessly for his mischievous pranks, is everywhere and has time for everything.
He will accompany a young girl throughout her life, and at a whim will turn his
arrows for or against her. One way or another Eros will always be the victor,
although he will remain unseen and indefinable.

This exhibition and book are dedicated to the delicate relationship between the
emotion of love and the various hypostases of the god 'responsible' for it. Essays by
Sarane Alexandrian and Satish Padiyar discuss the ways different eighteenth-century
artistic media dealt with these hypostases. The exhibition is principally concerned
with the central role of love in the life of a young girl as she emerges into society
under the guidance of Eros. It explores the subtleties of lovers' correspondence,
the peripeteia of the emotion of love and, finally, the triumph of love and the god
who represents it. At this key period in European cultural history – the mid- to
late eighteenth century in France – Eros triumphant is at once a survivor from
mythology and a divine personification of the most powerful emotion that can
affect art.

1. Antoine-François Prévost, *Manon Lescaut*, Paris, 1999,
   ch. III.
2. Laclos, *Les Liaisons Dangereuses*, Paris, 1964, no. 110.
3. P. Stewart, *Le masque et la parole*, Paris, 1973, p. 13.
4. M. Watelet and M. Lévesque, *Dictionnaire des arts de
   peinture, sculpture et gravure*, Paris, 1792, pp. 69–72
5. Ovid, *Ars amatoria*, Book I, vv. 3–4.
6. *Dictionnaire des œuvres érotiques*, Paris, 1971, pp.167–8;
   J.J. Pauvert and M. Pauvert, *Anthologie historique des
   lectures érotiques*, 1995–6, pp. 738–43.
7. Marquis de Sade, *Juliette*, New York, 1968, vol. 1,
   Book I.
8. Voltaire, *Les Œuvres complètes de Voltaire*, Oxford,
   1994, vol. 35, pp. 323–36.
9. *Encyclopédie ou dictionnaire raisonné des sciences, des arts
   et des métiers*, Paris, 1741, vol.1, pp. 367–74.
10. Ibid., pp. 374–5.
11. Molière, *Lesses ridicules*, Act V.
12. Laclos, *Les Liaisons Dangereuses*, no. 29.

The Cage Concealed
Louis-Marin Bonnet
After the painting by Noël Hallé
1769
cat. 91

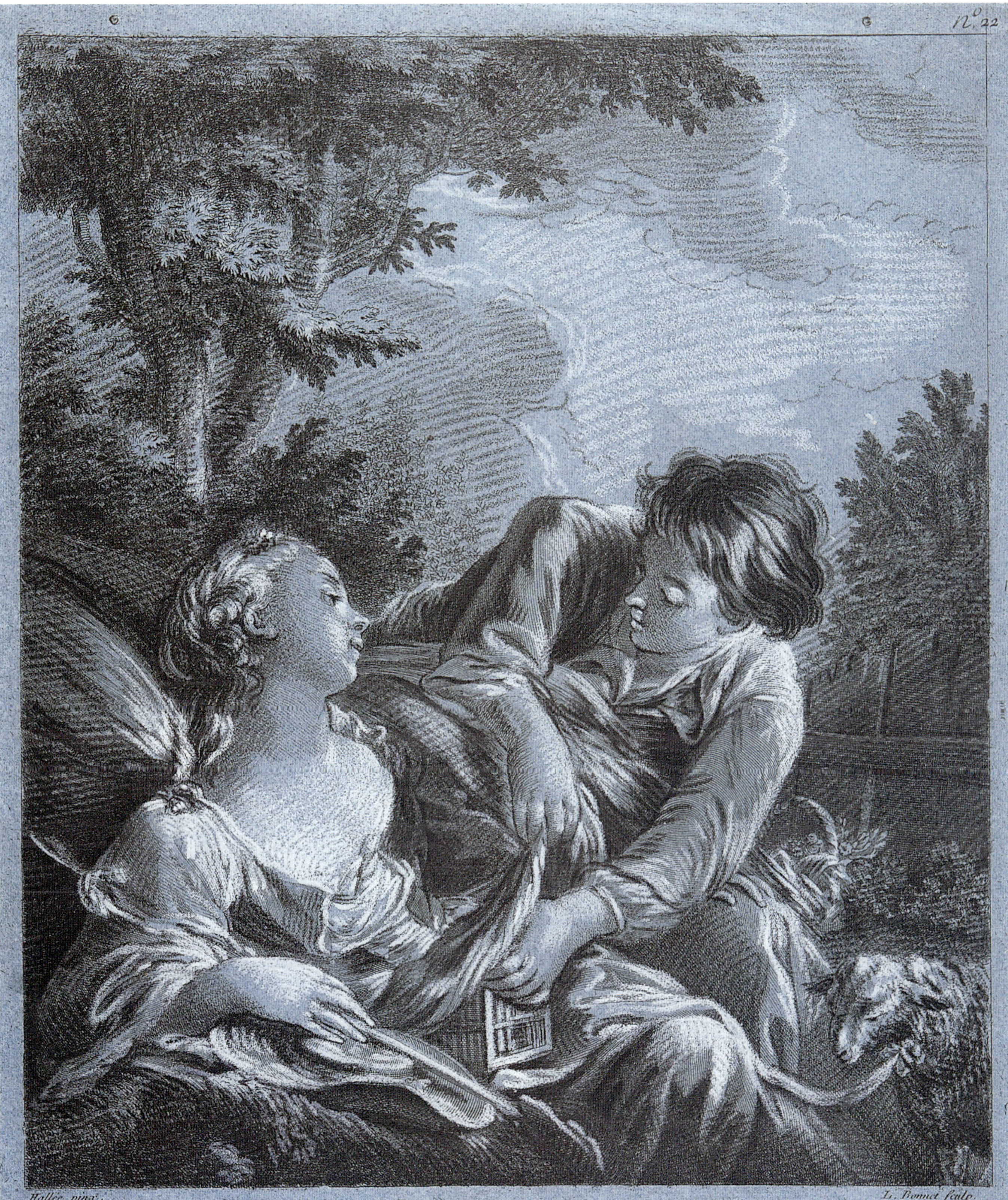

La Cage d'Erobée

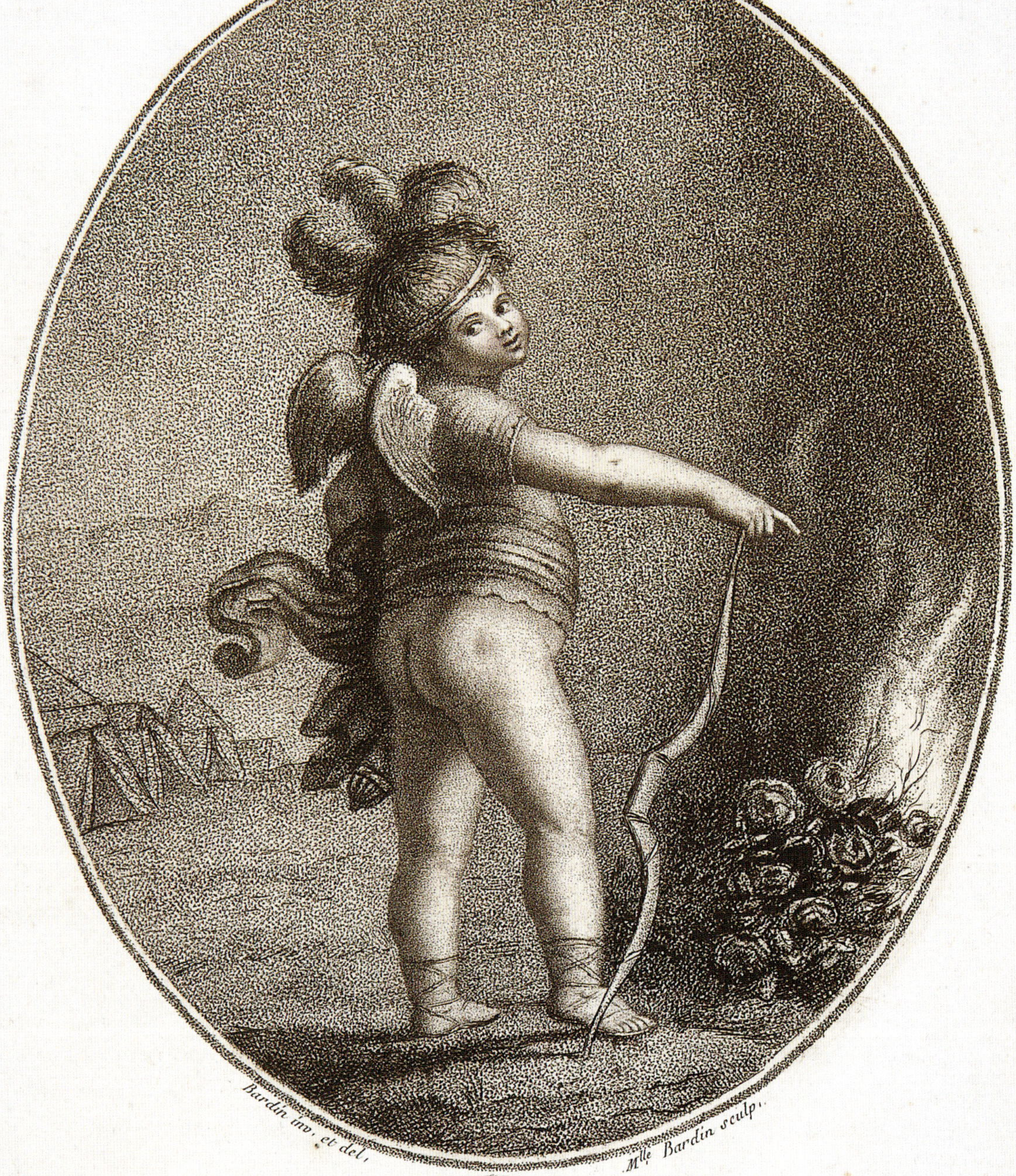

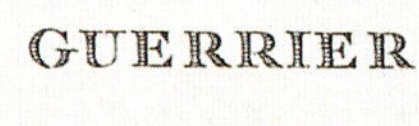

L'AMOUR   GUERRIER

Dedié à M^r le Comte   Auguste de Louvois.

Bardin inv. et del.   Mlle Bardin sculp.

Se vend à Paris chez Bardin Peintre du Roi rue du Foin S. Jacques

Satish Padiyar   *Menacing Cupid in the Art of Rococo*

Today, the body of the child is a focus of intense anxiety. The depiction of childhood nudity and sexuality, especially on the Internet, incites growing public concern. In recent years, this has only increased the pressure to censor images of childhood. In her 1998 study entitled *Pictures of Innocence. The History and Crisis of Ideal Childhood*, Anne Higonnet concluded 'no subject is as publicly dangerous now as the subject of the child's body'.[1]

Things were different in the eighteenth century. In the period covered by this exhibition the citizen was surrounded by images of naked babies and eroticized children. In fashionable Parisian aristocratic *hôtels* of the 1750s and 1760s fluttering putti, chubby amorini and busy cherubs were everywhere; in the material culture that survives they can be found on everything from decorative painted panels to furniture, candlesticks, fans and clocks (for example, cat. 29, 31, 47, 55). As early as 1767 the *philosophe* Denis Diderot lampooned this decorative taste in his description of Jean-Honoré Fragonard's submission to the Paris Salon of that year — the decorative ceiling panel *Groups of Children in the Sky* (Paris, Louvre) — as nothing more than a 'nice big omelette of infants'.[2] Related to this proliferation of children as mythological décor was a fashion in the art of the mid-eighteenth century — in paintings, engravings and small porcelain statuettes — in which the bodies of 'real' children were bizarrely co-opted into the two activities that define adulthood: sex and work. As for work, the pleasure afforded by these wildly popular, but to our disenchanted eyes alienating, *enfants de Boucher* (as they have come to be known, after their prime exponent) was twofold: on the one hand the viewer could take delight in seeing children playing at things they cannot understand, and on the other, could take solace in imagining 'serious' adult activities as forms of play.

They are innocent enough, one may think. But what about the co-opting of the childish body into sexual imagery? As any dispassionate inspection shows, the eighteenth-century infantile figure was frequently sexualized to a degree that might raise alarm in audiences at the beginning of the twenty-first century (*left*; cat. 9). Amongst themselves these children engage in sexual activity of various degrees of explicitness. Often they are seen in close conjunction with adult sexual activity, as procurers, facilitators or witnesses. One figure that is linked inextricably with the erotic appears frequently in this exhibition: the often overlooked, typically rococo child-boy god Cupid himself.[3]

One of the most famous of these boyish Eros figures in mid-eighteenth-century France is the Hermitage's *Amour Menaçant* (Menacing Cupid) by Étienne-Maurice

The Warrior Cupid
Ambroise-Marguérite Bardin
After the composition by Jean Bardin
1780s
cat. 9

Falconet (*right*; cat. 1). After first exhibiting it as a small-scale terracotta model at the Paris Salon of 1755, Falconet was commissioned by the Marquise de Pompadour to make a full-scale marble of it, which was completed in 1757. The marble was placed in her private quarters in the country estate of Bellevue. Madame de Pompadour also commissioned a copy to stand in the small garden of her Parisian residence, the Hôtel d'Evreux. The Hermitage version is one of five that we know Falconet produced between 1757 and 1770, and it was executed for Count Alexander Sergeevich Stroganov.[4] To this day *Menacing Cupid* remains an icon of the French eighteenth century, and is a central work in this exhibition.

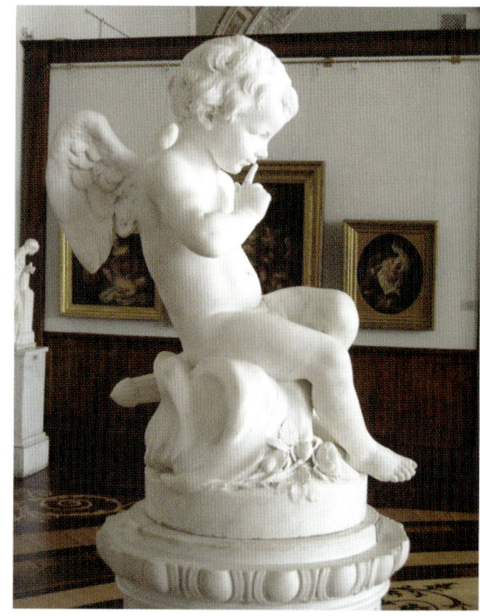

The sculpture depicts a small boy of indeterminate age (five years' old, maybe?), seated upon a cloud. The rose at the base of the pedestal, the finely detailed wings and above all the quiver with protruding arrowheads indicate that this is the god of love. The figure's crouching left leg and foot are nestled firmly into the cloudy substance; by contrast the right leg and foot extend provocatively – as if seductively goading – into the viewer's space. The subtle interplay of these legs, neither a crossing nor a crouching, succeeds in concealing the figure's genitals. The slightly chubby and creased torso forms a fleshy backdrop to the dominating gesture of the sculpture. This is the finger raised to the lips, propped up by the right arm, communicating the injunction 'Be Silent' (or does it? For all its apparent clarity the gesture is ambiguous: in the eighteenth century the sculpture was known variously as *L'Amour Silencieux*, *L'Amour Menaçant*, *Garde à Vous*, and *Soyez Discret*).[5] Crowning this body is the bulbous head, slightly lowered so that we can appreciate the beautifully chiselled tousled hair. With his half-smile and upturned glancing eyes, the boy's expression is playful and cunning. There is not the least hint of innocence in this glance. So if he is not innocent, what does he know?

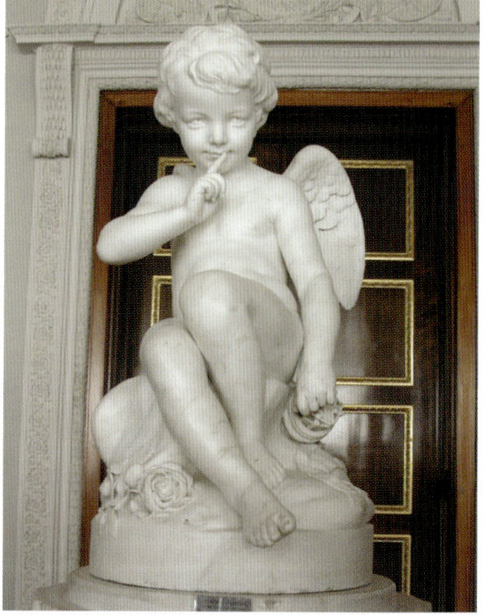

Moving around the statue something is revealed to us. If we stand to its left, the 'silencing' gesture in profile is remarkably clear. As we walk around the statue, the figure's left arm, which was hidden, begins to come into view. Echoing the extended right leg, it hangs casually, and yet it is more obedient than the leg, for it never deviates from the graceful line of the torso that it parallels. It is only when we can see over the projecting thigh of the right leg that we realise that something is ado concerning this left arm. Far from obedient, the boy's left hand is revealed to be extricating an arrow from his quiver. Matters immediately become more complex as the gesture that invokes silence is matched and doubled by this other more menacing one, which amounts to a preparation to strike out, to shoot an arrow at any target he may choose. This Cupid is ready to unfurl and discharge. The enigmatic smile now becomes complicitous, we share his secret as those still on the other side of the figure (across the room, where we were before) have not yet seen, and do not yet know, what threatens in this half-obscured fumbling. By seducing us into his secret (Latin *seducere*, to lead aside) the *Menacing Cupid* sexes the space around it.

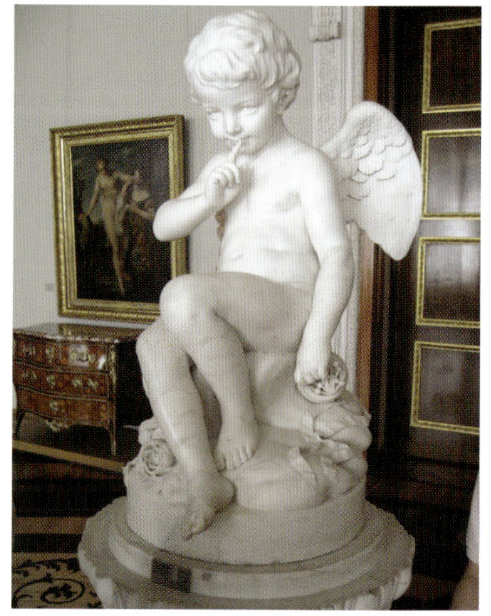

Who is this little boy who smiles and threatens, charms and menaces, and who entirely lacks innocence? First, we might consider where he comes from. And second, what is the nature of his menace.

As for origins, we cannot go back far enough. Hesiod, in the *Theogony* (7th century BC), puts the god Eros at the origin of the world. Eros emerges from a primal state of Chaos and flutters over the created heavens and earth, a winged being at the beginning of creation. Coming first, Cupid reigns over all other gods, as well

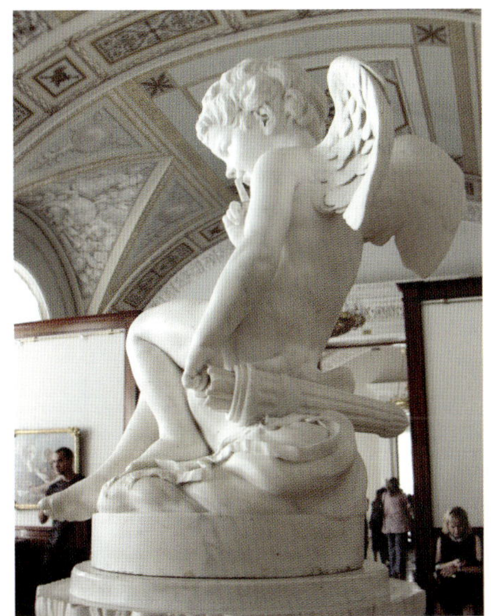

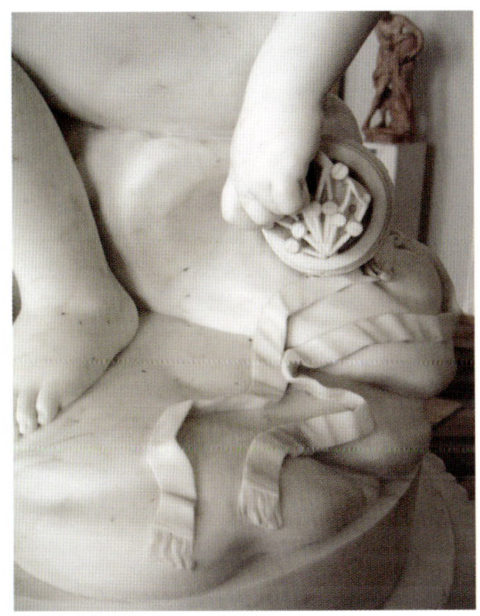

Menacing Cupid
Étienne-Maurice Falconet
After 1757
cat. 1

as men. And because he emerges out of chaos, Cupid pre-exists the constitution of any law or order, heavenly or terrestrial. He is beyond the law, and his existence is permanently fugitive. Perhaps it is this outlaw status, as well as narratives about the arbitrariness of his attacks (which are alluded to in the theme of Cupid as blind, unseeing in his targets), that have led to so many narratives that suggest the need to discipline his uncontrollable whims.

In its more rationalising and orderly mode the French Enlightenment is especially fond of 'containing' Cupid, which only attests to the power of his threat. Thus, on the one hand we find Cupid inserted into a family dynamic which is frequently very unhomely: now domesticated, Cupid becomes the child of Mercury and Venus, and he is variously encouraged, remonstrated with, scolded, or violently beaten (cat. 10, 11, 14, 16). On the other hand, by coercing him into union and heterosexual marriage (the ancient classical Greek Eros presided over homoerotic seductions), Cupid's sexual license and autonomy is diminished. This is done most famously through the tale of Cupid and Psyche, which was widely disseminated in eighteenth-century French art and literature. Cupid falls in love with Psyche, a king's daughter, and makes nightly visitations to her; eventually he marries. It comes as no surprise that Falconet capitalized on the success of his statue by producing, in 1761, a small-scale biscuit porcelain of the girlish *Psyche* as a pendant to that of his *Menacing Cupid*. They were subsequently sold in pairs.[6]

What for us most typifies the art of the rococo are its ubiquitous figures of putti, amorini and cupids. We speak of the late eighteenth century as a 'return to the ancients', but before the onset of a more severe neoclassicism these rococo icons of untrammelled pleasure attested to the persistence of a *different* antiquity in the eighteenth century. The archaic and classical Greeks had represented Eros as a lithe and beautiful winged adolescent. In later, Hellenistic, representations this ceded to the chubby child-Eros (depicted occasionally asleep amongst the flowers in order to suggest Love's regenerative powers). This infantile figure was transformed into the Roman 'Cupid' (*Cupido*: Desire, Latin equivalent of *Eros*), who might be seen embellishing Roman sarcophagi (leaning on his expunged, inverted torch Cupid is the very figure of death: cessation of passion).[7] It should be said that these representations of Eros/Cupid are simply different visual conventions that were made available to inheritors of the classical tradition. The difference between the infantile and adolescent Cupid did not indicate that the god of Love grows older, that his body matures, for he is in fact ageless. While eighteenth-century France deployed both versions, the neoclassicists generally preferred the more adolescent and homoerotic Eros (for example, the mantel-clock with Eros, cat. 30), while the rococo reinvented and played out every facet of the infantile Cupid.

The ancient erotic poetry of Anacreon, Sappho, Theocritus and Ovid continued to provide a textual representation of the power of Eros in the eighteenth century.[8] But what of its visualization? In Renaissance and post-Renaissance Europe the figure of Cupid as something more than just decorative marginalia (to which it had begun to be reduced in Roman art) was revived by Donatello in fifteenth-century Florence, and then reworked by artists such as Michelangelo, Caravaggio and Correggio in Italy, and Nicolas Poussin and Eustache Le Sueur in France.[9] But the image of Cupid was most effectively disseminated through prints. In seventeenth-century Europe a visual vocabulary to depict the chubby winged child circulated through the Dutch

classicist Otto Vaenius's *Amorum Emblemata*, first published in 1608 and reprinted
throughout the seventeenth and eighteenth centuries. This volume of emblems
anthologized ancient love poetry (mostly Ovid) for a post-humanistic European
aristocratic audience. Crucially for the visual arts it was also illustrated with a series
of engravings that depicted the adventures of Cupid on earth. The frontispiece says
it all (*right, above*). Here is the 'triumph of Eros', and it is total and devastating. Men,
women, animals and even, in its upper corners, the sun and moon, are struck down
by Eros, rendered insensible by his merciless, implacable arrows. Within the *Amorum
Emblemata* we discover Cupid roaming the earth, encountering strangers, getting
into trouble, and generally causing havoc and destruction. He can be seen arbitrarily
attacking a wanderer, felling him with a profusion of arrows. Elsewhere, he
crouches, incubus-like, over the body of a sleeping woman (*right, below*). Cupid
inserts his arrow into her flesh, rendering her dreams fevered. In another the god
himself suffers the maladies of love, writhing in agony. For a book about love
these images are unsettling in their violence and morbidity. There is a conspicuous
absence of the art of seduction. Vaenius's seventeenth-century version of Cupid
impels his victims into a state of subjection, and into a love-madness that is beyond
their choosing. Falconet's eighteenth-century *Cupid*, by contrast, properly *seduces*
us. It leads us aside with its soliciting glance and its promise of secrets shared
and maintained.

But just what are the secrets implied by this injunction to silence? When Madame
de Pompadour commissioned the statue in 1755, Paris was in the grip of intrigue,
gossip and secrecy. As the publicly acknowledged mistress of Louis XV since 1745,
Pompadour was especially vulnerable. A mistress in the stratified body politic of the
Ancien Régime, she was, not unlike the figure of Cupid, beyond the law. To make
matters worse, her sexual relations with the king had quickly palled: rumours about
this rapidly emanated from the court.[10] By 1750 a swift public realignment of her
relationship to the king became urgent. As a powerful patron of the arts in the years
around 1750, Pompadour could negotiate her altered status through iconographic
decisions, and attempt to take control of her situation. In 1755, for example, she
commissioned Falconet to produce a small biscuit of *Madame de Pompadour as the
Personification of Friendship*, which was clearly meant to signal her now platonic, yet
enlightened and continuing, relationship with Louis XV.[11] It is hardly surprising that
Falconet's powerful gestural command in *Menacing Cupid* to 'be silent' might have
seemed particularly apposite to her.

Yet neither Madame de Pompadour, nor the monarch to whom she was
dangerously close, could silence the critics. In the 1750s the monarchy was
increasingly subject to a political onslaught by the Paris *parlements*, who through
their pamphlets publicly remonstrated against the monarchical government's
'despotic' anti-Jansenist policies. Rife with suspicion and secrecy, Paris erupted into
violence in 1750, inflamed by rumours that the king had authorized the abduction of
children from the streets to be sold into slavery (the case of Deschauffours, in which
a 'pederastic' network was revealed to be operating in 1720s Paris, was still fresh in
people's minds). In 1757, as Falconet was completing the marble of *Menacing Cupid*
for Pompadour, these stirrings of discontent culminated in an assassination attempt
on the king by Damiens, a political dissident who claimed to be acting in the interests
of the parliamentary opposition. In a symbolic attempt to quell the threat posed by

Frontispiece (*above*)
Engraving to 'Nuit et Jour' (*below*)
Amorum Emblemata
Otto van Veen (Vaenius)
1608
Glasgow University Library, Special Collections

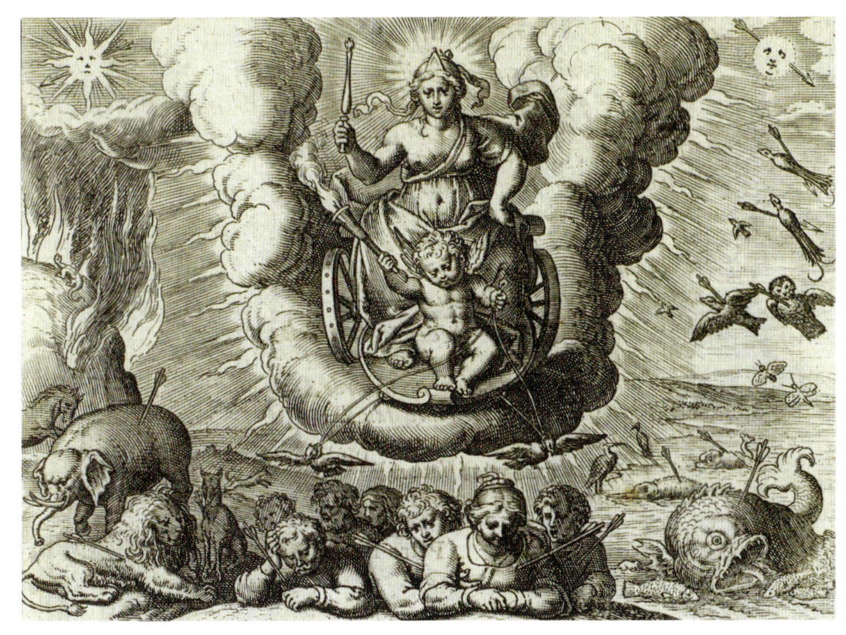

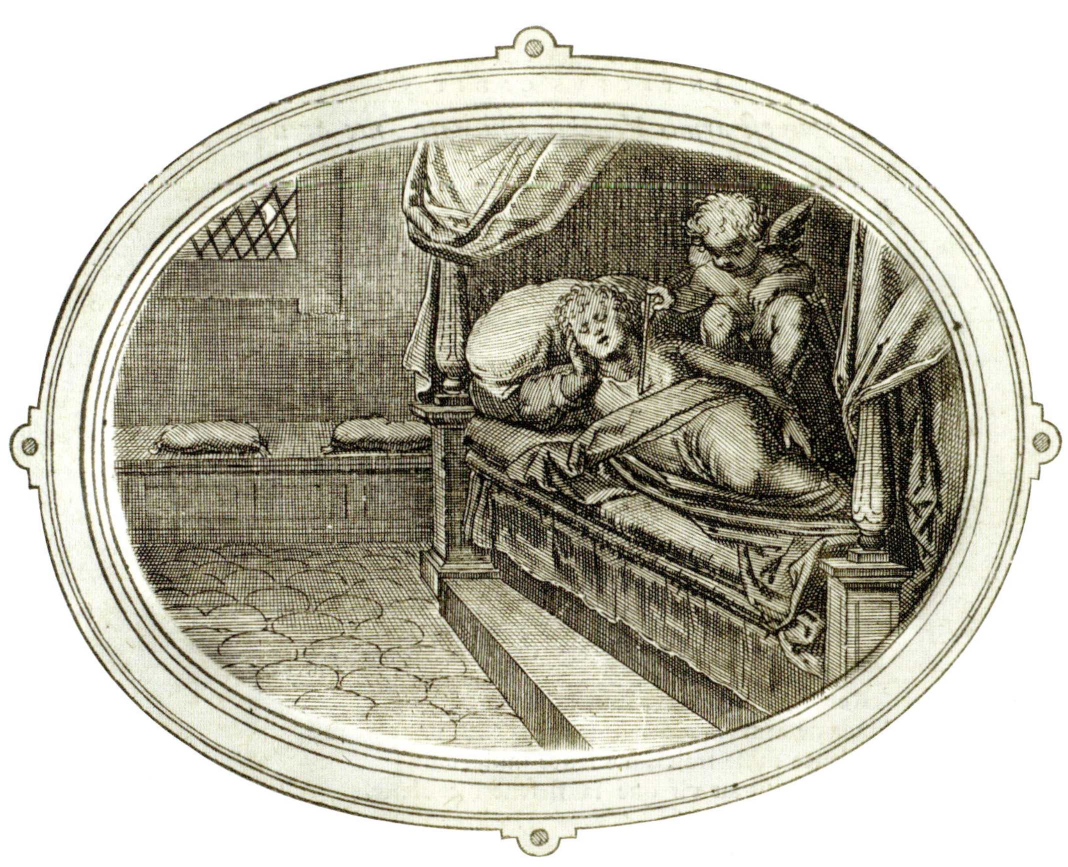

subversive speech and dangerous rumours, Damiens was publicly and horrifically
torn limb from limb and the remnants of his body then burnt. While *Menacing Cupid*
does not in any way allude directly to these dangers, it nevertheless springs from the
culture of a pre-Revolutionary city gripped by secrets and shocking disclosures.[12]

If there is a political – and sexual-political – dimension to Cupid's silencing
gesture, there is an erotic one to his gaze. Cultural historian Robert Darnton has noted
that sexual intrigue heightened through the voyeuristic gaze is typical of the seductive
strategies of clandestine erotic literature in eighteenth-century France. Pornographic
libertine novels such as *La Putain Errante*, *L'Académie des Dames* and *Vénus dans le
Cloître* were grouped under the category of 'philosophical', which is to say dangerous,
books. Darnton writes:

> If any teaching distinguished the category [of these books] it was voyeurism.
> Everywhere in the libertine tales, characters observed one another through
> keyholes, from behind curtains, and between bushes, while the reader looked over
> their shoulders. Illustrations completed the effects…the interplay of illustration
> and text multiplied the effect of mirrors within mirrors, giving an air of
> theatricality to the whole business. Sex in the *livres philosophiques* was rococo…'[13]

This obscene, pornographic dimension of *Menacing Cupid*'s glance is explicitly
articulated when the figure is taken out of the control of both Madame de Pompadour
and Falconet, and replicated by a different artist in a different context. In this
exhibition we can see, for example, how the artist Baudouin, in the 1778 engraving
of *La Nuit*, reconfigures the famous *Cupid* so that it now comes to preside over the
moment of successful night-time sexual contact between fugitive lovers (cat. 92).
The condition of sexual arousal with which the male viewer is invited to consume
this image is suggested by Baudouin's doubling of the body of the now leering
Cupid with the tree-trunk that rises from the base of the statue in barely-concealed
phallic fashion.

When Fragonard employed *Menacing Cupid* in the classically voyeuristic *Swing*
(*right*; Wallace Collection, London), on the other hand, it was to more foreboding
effect. Here, Cupid is no mere silent witness and accomplice. Indeed, his presence
actually undercuts this famous triangular situation, where, thanks to the unknowing
efforts of the curate pushing the swing in the background, the figure of the lover,
hidden in the bushes in the foreground, is able to catch the forbidden sight of female
genitals. In this work Fragonard seems to play with that other intonation of Falconet's
Cupid, 'Garde à Vous!', as a kind of divine warning. The marginal but luminous figure
of *Menacing Cupid* is the only indication in the *Swing* that these rococo seductions and
the deceptions they involve might end in disaster.[14]

If the figure of Cupid could presage disaster, more typically it was seen to be a key
motivator of literature and the fine arts. In this positive role Cupid could be
represented as the embodiment, progenitor and enabler of art; or as the divinity that
brings consolation to the beleaguered artist. In the Hermitage's *Allegory of Poetry* by
François Boucher, for example, with consummate charm a visual analogy is set up
between the arrow of Cupid and the poet's instrument of writing (cat. 3). The
diminutive figure of the poet is demonstrably frustrated – this is a putto suffering
from writer's block – and appears to be unconscious of Cupid, who is about to come
to his aid.

The Swing
Jean-Honoré Fragonard
1767
The Wallace Collection, London

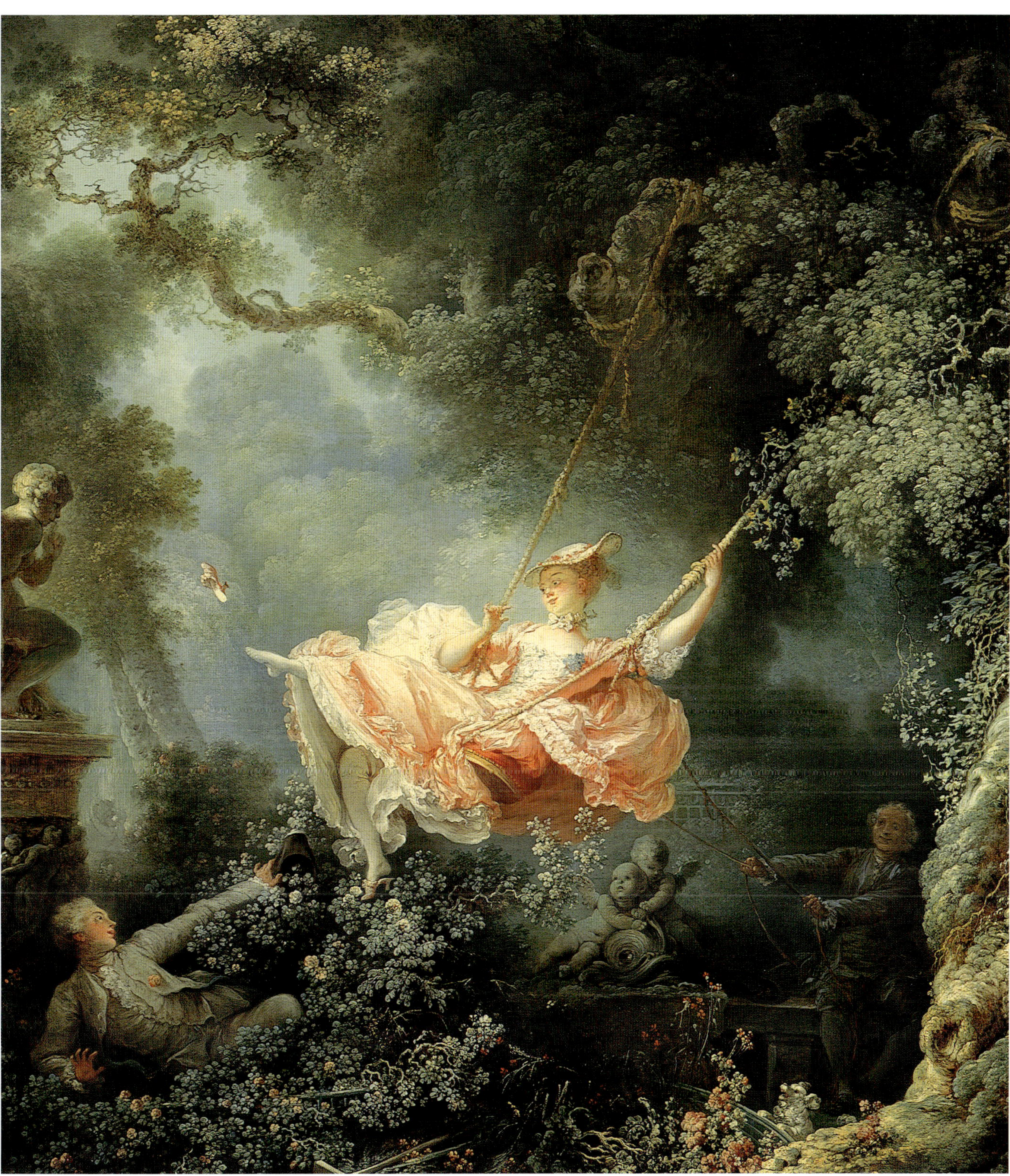

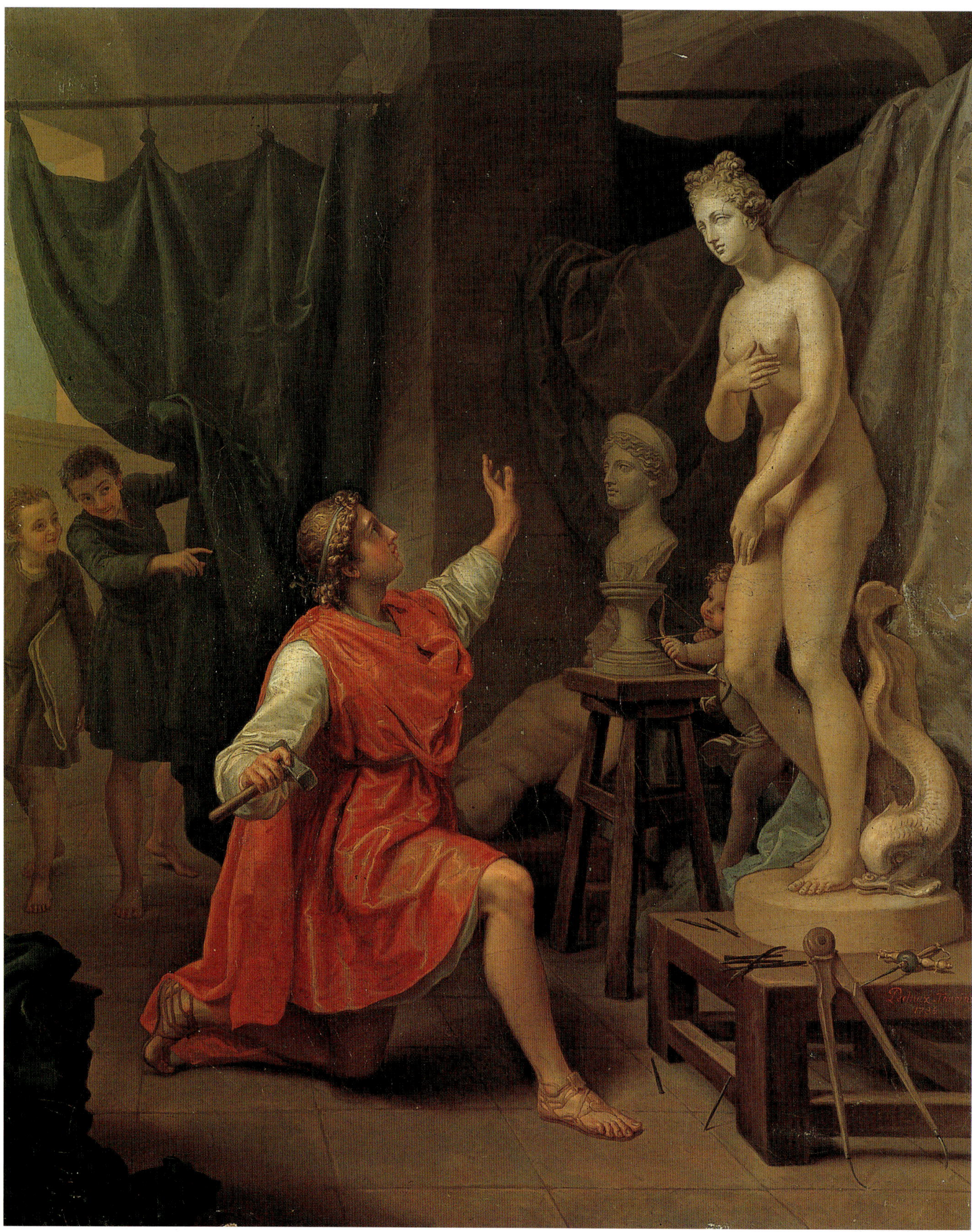

It could be said, indeed, that without the intervention of Cupid as the agent of Love – or what post-Freudians term libido – art would simply not take place. One of the most popular amorous fables in eighteenth-century France, that of Pygmalion and Galatea, dramatized the relationship between Cupid, the artist and the realization of a work of art. In *Metamorphoses*, Ovid relates how the Cypriot artist-king Pygmalion takes a vow of chastity: he is surrounded by 'fallen' women and is disgusted. He fashions a marble of a woman and becomes obsessed with the beautiful statue, bearing it gifts, decorating it, and taking it into his bed. Venus is touched, and on her name day she answers Pygmalion's prayer to give him a sexual partner 'just like my ivory girl'. The statue's ivory limbs turn into flesh. Ovid represents the moment of transformation as sex:

> Pygmalion, home, takes the statue of girl & lies
> on bed kissing it: hands feeling breasts;
> she seems warm; kisses again; the ivory,
> stroked, softens, yields to his fingers…
> the girl feels kisses; blushes; raises eyes
> timidly, sees her lover & daylight at the same time.[15]

In 1748 Rameau composed music for a ballet on the same subject, which was performed throughout the 1750s and 1760s. Jean-Jacques Rousseau's experimental short play *Pygmalion* of 1762 reinvented the story for a modern *sensible* audience, creating a profound impression. Boucher, Lagrenée, François Le Moyne, Carle van Loo and Falconet all essayed the Ovidian theme.[16] This exhibition presents two examples: Laurent Pécheux's neoclassicizing painting of 1784 (*left*; cat. 87); and Falconet's *Pygmalion and Galatea*, here in its reduced porcelain biscuit version (cat. 97). The full-scale marble of this was shown to great acclaim at the Paris Salon of 1763, and Catherine the Great made every attempt to purchase the artists' models, without success.[17]

Eighteenth-century artists appropriated the story of Pygmalion and Galatea for their own ends, seeing in it an allegory of the sculptor-artist's Herculean powers of transformation, and the proper attitude of fascination before the work of art (Pygmalion is both ideal maker and spectator). One of the reasons for this was that artists were becoming increasingly accountable to public judgement, and at a time of unprecedented scorching criticism the fable of Pygmalion could only bolster their wounded egos.[18] Yet it is perverse to understand Ovid's tale as a homage to the artist. In *Metamorphoses* it is not Pygmalion who is the agent of the realization of his sexual fantasies, of his prayer; rather, it is Venus, or – as we can see in this exhibition – her son and representative on earth, Cupid. In relation to his own sexual desires, the artist in this narrative is never actually in control.

Thus in his neoclassicizing version, Laurent Pécheux – a pupil of Raphael Mengs – attempts to secularize the tale by virtually removing the presence of divinity, and focussing upon the figure of the working artist. The scene of transubstantiation is characteristically taken out of the bedroom and into the studio, which is perfectly workmanlike (we are even treated to a couple of distracted students). The sculptor kneels before his Galatea, chisel still in hand, having just completed the final touches. Pygmalion's conventional gesture of astonishment is a little ungainly – too declamatory perhaps – but the passionate red of his cloak reveals the heat of his sexual excitement. On another plane, Pécheux invites an analogy between the parallel vertical forms of the central stony pillar and the figure of Galatea. The analogy is immediately undermined, however, as the statue softens, yields, and inclines towards Pygmalion's gaze, as it begins to free itself from its stony identity. At any moment 'her' eyes will open both to him and the daylight.

While the dominant focus of Pécheux's composition is this encounter between the lovers-to-be (they will marry and live in domestic harmony: anticlimactic), there is nevertheless a counter-narrative here, one that suggests the determining role of Eros in the miracle of sexual and artistic consummation. By Pygmalion's groin, and at the picture's central vertical axis, Pécheux has placed, at a suggestive angle, the fragment of a classical statue of a male nude. Like some thick swollen shaft, this hard, muscular torso shoots out from Pygmalion's groin in the manner of an extraordinary phallic protrusion. In fact it points to the figure of Cupid who stands, half-revealed, behind Galatea. This baby Cupid is ready to shoot a final arrow into the body of Pygmalion, who will then vibrate in unison with his work of art. To Cupid's tune. In other words the figure who is directing this theatre of seduction is the lingering, unseen presence of the god of love. Its slight visual presence in *Pygmalion and Galatea* belies its structural centrality in the narrative. But the very fact that Cupid remains in this 1784 picture suggests that the French Enlightenment could neither entirely divest itself of the divine, irrational aspects of sexual and artistic inspiration, nor rid itself of Cupid's ability to tamper uncontrollably with circuits of desire.

The Russian taste for amorous French imagery continued into the nineteenth century. Pécheux's *Pygmalion and Galatea* was purchased by the fabulously wealthy Russian art collector Prince Nikolai Borisovich Yusupov (1750–1831) during his time as ambassador in Turin between 1784 and 1789. In succeeding years Yusupov was to amass an extraordinary collection of French erotic, and homoerotic, art by painters and sculptors such as Greuze, Boilly, Canova, Prud'hon, and David.[19] Jacques-Louis David's ambitious *Sappho, Phaon and Cupid,* now in the Hermitage, was commissioned by Yusupov in the summer of 1808 (*overleaf*). It clearly shows how the figure of Cupid continued to haunt both French artists and Russian collectors beyond the rococo, and beyond the French Revolution of 1789.

The French philosopher Jean Baudrillard has suggested that the French Revolution – all revolutions – put an end to seduction.[20] Secrecy, intrigue and sexual playfulness ceded to public transparency, accountability and a sexuality that was disciplined within the bourgeois family. In many ways David's 1808 picture is a throwback to the eighteenth-century culture of seduction. The scene of the boudoir, the return to the conventional rococo symbolism of sex (the 'copulating' doves, the bed in disarray), the subject of the enamoured lesbian poet Sappho itself (a favourite in eighteenth-century literature and art),[21] all reprise a pre-Revolutionary sensibility. What is perhaps most obviously *post*-Revolutionary about this scene of seduction is the insistent manner in which the two lovers gaze out towards the viewer, accountable, transparent and exposed to the public. The adolescent figure of Cupid in this painting appears, by contrast, to inhabit a different space, and it is one that is half way between the private and the public. Cupid engages with his 'victims' within the picture – here is that *Menacing Cupid*-like glance again – but his face is also inclined towards the viewing public. In its state of semi-emergence, the figure of

Cupid cannot quite 'come out' in David's picture, in the way that those of Sappho and Phaon can; it seems unable properly to enter into the public sphere of modernity.

The figure of Cupid in art has always inhabited a marginal position; it has repeatedly been expelled into the supportive role, the decorative superfluity, the edges of pictures. Yet in his strange reprise of the language of eighteenth-century seduction, David does not deny Cupid's continuing power to disrupt. The handsome Phaon is enamoured of Sappho. Like Pygmalion, the artist Sappho experiences through every limb the thrill of a sexual rush. This time Cupid, the agent of these sexual pleasures, gently disarms Sappho, removing the lyre with which she composes, removing, that is to say, her brush. By this delicate action she will be delivered to her eventual abandonment by Phaon, and thence to her tragic leap into suicide. To remove the brush from the artist, to drive the artist into a self-destructive erotic frenzy, or, as in the case of sculptor Pygmalion, into satisfied domestication – would this not mean the end of art? Menacing Cupid, indeed.

1. Anne Higonnet, *Pictures of Innocence*, London, 1998, p. 133.

2. Denis Diderot, *Diderot on Art* (trans. John Goodman), New Haven and London, 1995, p. 255.

3. Little attention has been paid to the rococo figure of Eros in art histories. See, however, Katie Scott, 'Under the sign of Venus: the making and meaning of Bouchardon's *L'Amour* in the age of the French rococo', in Caroline Arscott and Katie Scott, eds., *Manifestations of Venus: art and sexuality*, Manchester and New York, 2000.

4. *Madame de Pompadour et les Arts*, ex. cat., Versailles, 2002, p. 311; Frits Scholten, *L'Amour Menaçant or Menacing Love: a statue by Falconet*, Amsterdam, 2005, pp. 45–6; Louis Réau, *Étienne-Maurice Falconet*, Paris, 1922, p. 190.

5. See Réau 1922, pp. 183, 185.

6. Svend Eriksen and Geoffrey De Bellaigue, *Sèvres Porcelain. Vincennes and Sèvres 1740–1800*, London and Boston, 1987, p. 313.

7. *Éros Grec: amour des dieux et des hommes*, ex. cat., Paris, 1989.

8. On Eros in ancient poetry see Anne Carson, *Eros, the bittersweet: an essay*, Princeton, 1986.

9. Charles Dempsey, *Inventing the Renaissance Putto*, Chapel Hill and London, 2001.

10. Jean-Pierre Guicciardi, 'Between the Licit and the Illicit: The Sexuality of the King', in Robert Parks Macubbin, ed., *'Tis Nature's Fault: Unauthorized Sexuality during the Enlightenment*, Cambridge, 1987, p. 90; Scott, 2000, pp. 274–5.

11. See Katherine Gordon, 'Madame de Pompadour, Pigalle, and the Iconography of Friendship', *Art Bulletin* 50, no. 3 (September 1968).

12. See Arlette Farge and Jacques Revel, *The Rules of Rebellion: child abductions in Paris in 1750* (trans. Claudia Miéville), Cambridge, 1991. The Deschauffours affair was another area of secrecy and sexual scandal. In late 1725 Paris police had rounded up some two hundred men, suspected of having taken part in 'pederastic' sex parties at the home of Deschauffours. On 25 May 1726 Deschauffours was convicted of 'sodomie' and burnt at the stake on the Place de Grève. The painter J.-B. Nattier and his academic 'reception piece' of 1712, *Joseph and Potiphar's Wife*, was implicated in this gay sex scandal, the most famous in eighteenth-century France (see cat. 71). Nattier was arrested in the company of a 'tout jeune homme' and thrown into the Bastille with Deschauffours. He committed suicide on 27 April 1726 by cutting his own throat. The Académie des Beaux-Arts stripped him of his academic status, returned *Joseph and Potiphar's Wife* to the artist's family, and threw a veil of silence over his name. Ironic, that the key painting in Nattier's life and tragic death should be on the subject of chastity. See Edmond-Jean-François Barbier, *Chronique de la Régence et du règne de Louis XV*, Paris 1857, I, pp. 424–7; and Ernest Raynaud, 'La Mort de J.-B. Nattier', *Mercure de France*, 15 July 1928.

13. Robert Darnton, *The Forbidden Best-Sellers of Pre-Revolutionary France*, New York, 1995, pp. 72–3.

14. On catastrophic endings in rococo narratives of seduction see Pierre Saint-Amand, *The Libertine's Progress: Seduction in the Eighteenth-Century French Novel* (trans. Jennifer Curtiss Gage), Hanover and London, 1994.

15. *Ovid's Metamorphoses* (trans. Charles Boer), Dallas, 1989, p. 214.

16. See Andre Blühm, *Pygmalion. Die Ikonographie eines Künstlermythos zwischen 1500 und 1900*, Frankfurt am Main and New York, 1988.

17. *Falconet à Sèvres, ou l'art de plaire*, ex. cat., Paris, 2001, pp. 171–2.

18. On artists, critics and public see Thomas Crow, *Painters and Public Life in Eighteenth-Century Paris*, New Haven and London, 1985.

19. Lioubov Savinskaïa, 'La Collection de Peintures de Nicolaï Borrissovitch Youssoupov', in *Hubert Robert et Saint-Petersburg. Les Commandes de la Famille Impériale et des Princes Russes entre 1773 et 1802*, ex. cat., Valence, 1999, pp. 35–6, 76–7.

20. Jean Baudrillard, *Seduction* (trans. Brian Singer), London, 1990, p. 1.

21. See Mary D. Sheriff, *Moved By Love. Inspired Artists and Deviant Women in Eighteenth-Century France*, Chicago and London, 2004.

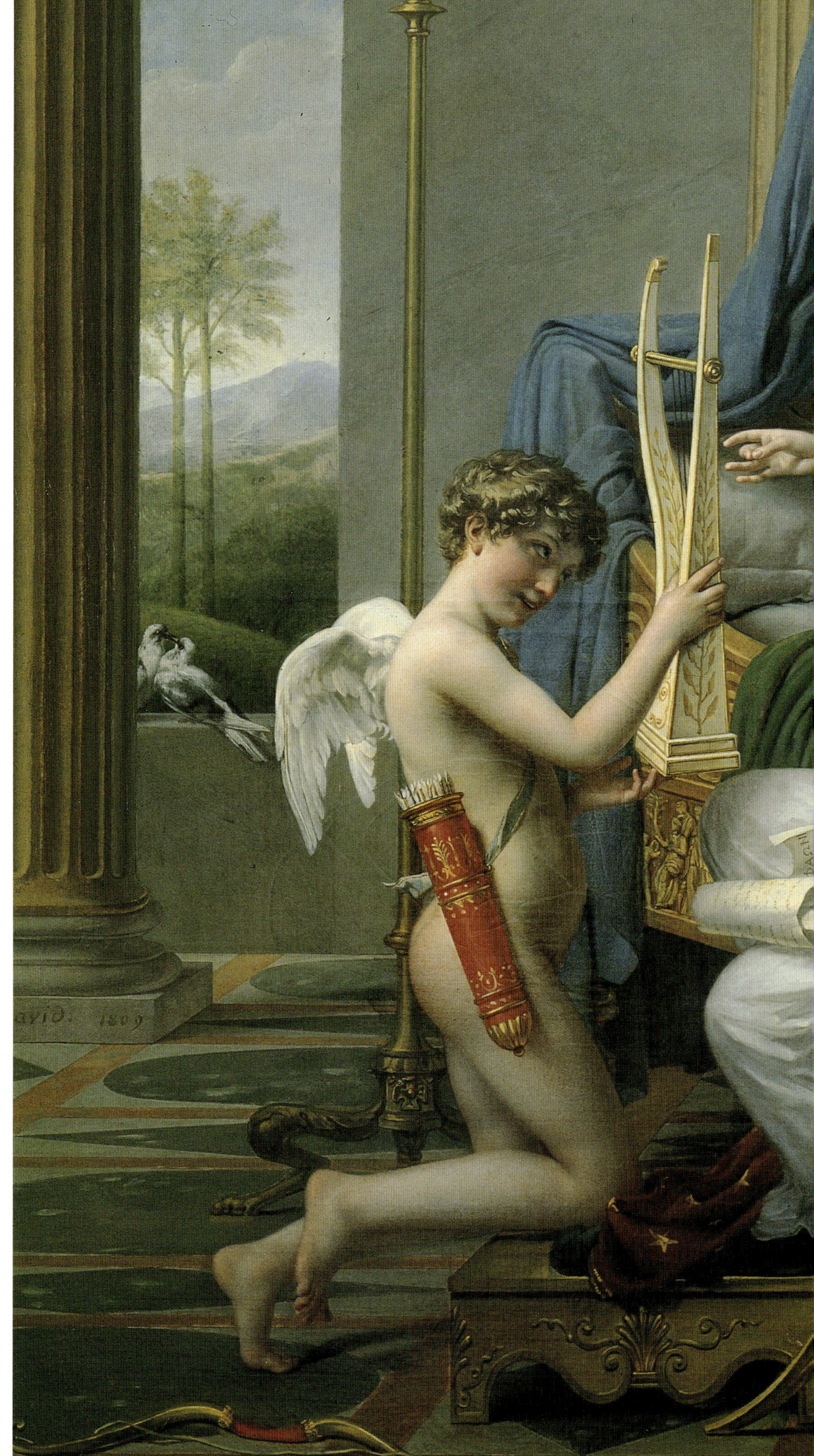

Sappho, Phaon and Cupid
Jacques-Louis David
1809
State Hermitage Museum

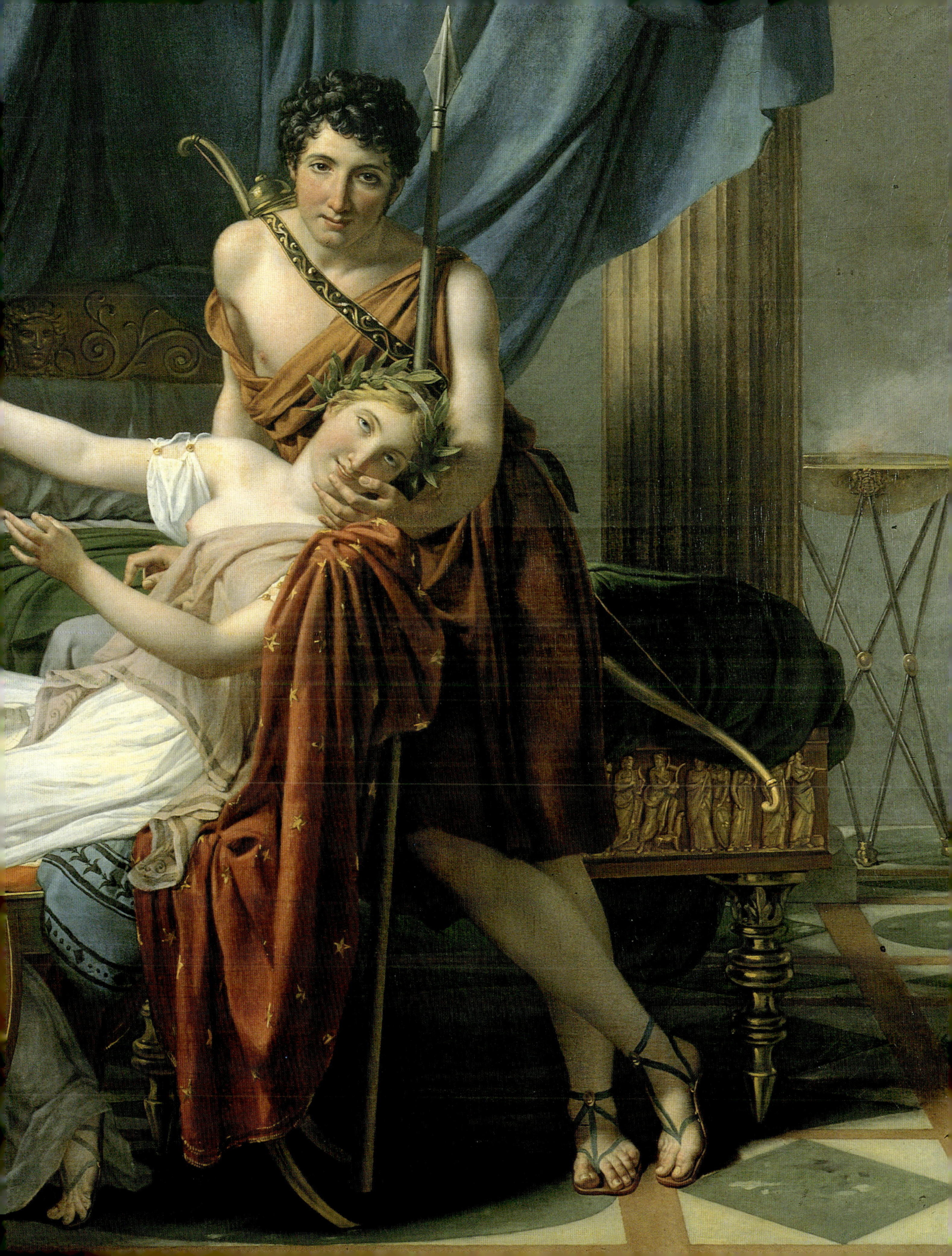

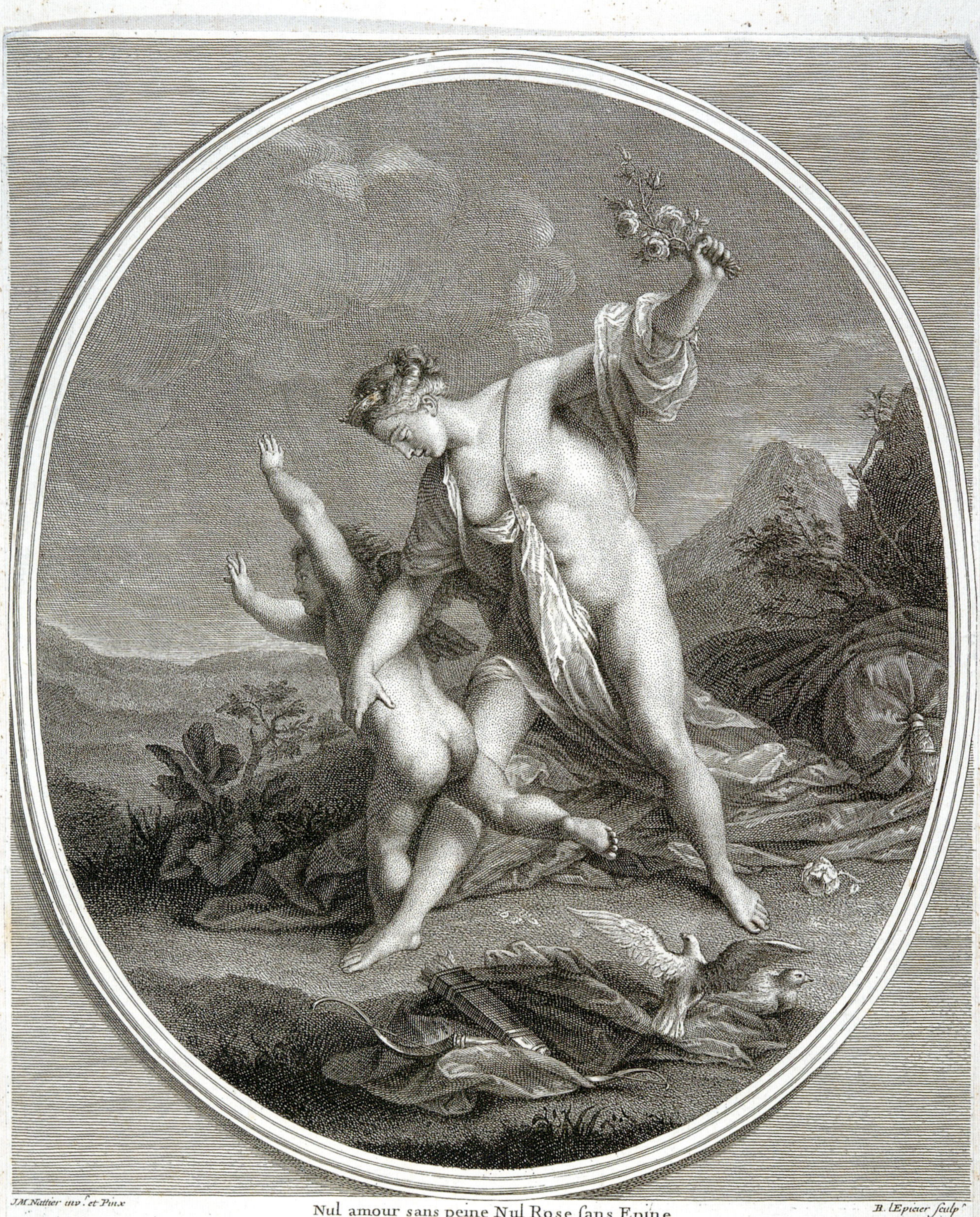

J.M. Nattier inv.t et Pinx
B. LEpicier sculp.t
Nul amour sans peine Nul Rose sans Epine
Rien n'est exempt d'amour, quand un cœur est Sévère
C'est qu'il n'a point trouvé l'Objet fait pour luy plaire.
Souvent trop tard helas, un tendre engagement
...us prouve qu'on ne peut estre heureux en aimant.
Telle est de ce Portrait la fiction badine,
Le Peintre nous fait voir par ce bizar. retour
Que jamais il ne fut de Rose sans épine,
Et que les Deplaisirs; accompagnent L'amour.
A Paris chez Duchange Graveur du Roy rue S.t Jaques 1720

Sarane Alexandrian   *Education in Love in the Age of Enlightenment*

In eighteenth-century France young people received their education in love mainly
through novels and gallant engravings. At a time when France was the model for
the whole of Europe as far as lifestyle, fashion and even philosophy of life were
concerned, all of its serious or light-hearted works on love had an impact in Europe
and came to uphold the principles of a universal art of loving.

There were two genres that dominated eighteenth-century literature and art: the
libertine genre and the sentimental genre. Consequently there were two types of
education: libertine and sentimental. The first genre corresponded with the French
Regency and the reign of Louis XV; the second to the reign of Louis XVI, when Jean-
Jacques Rousseau's followers advocated virtue and sensitivity and engaged
in verbose rhetoric about what one should aspire to in life.

The climate of austerity imposed by Louis XIV on his court when he became
devout and morose in his latter years was abolished when, upon his death in 1715,
Philippe II, Duc d'Orléans, was appointed Regent. The latter was something of
an uncontrollable playboy, throwing himself into orgies with his mistresses and
courtesans at the Palais-Royal and Saint-Cloud – a period of licentiousness which
continued under Louis XV. This monarch had but two passions: hunting and women.
His regime reflected his tastes as an insatiable seducer; lords wanted to be able to
seduce like him, and ladies of the court made it a point of honour to be seduced. As a
witness of this period, Crébillon the younger recalls in *Les égarements du coeur et de
l'esprit* (1738): 'You told a woman three times that she was beautiful, no more was
needed; upon the first she quite believed you, upon the second she thanked you, and
not uncommonly she rewarded you upon the third.' His hero is a seventeen-year-old
adolescent called Meilcourt who is introduced to life's pleasures by a forty-year-old
libertine, the Marquise de Lursay. This activity was referred to in the language of
the time as 'providing an education'.

Naturally, official education did not prepare women to be so liberal. Aristocratic
young girls were placed at seven years of age in a convent, where they received not
only religious education but also lessons in dance, music and embroidery to prepare
them for the role of the perfect housewife. The daughters of the bourgeoisie would
enter bourgeois boarding-schools at the same age where they were taught to read,
write, count and embroider over a period of five years, whilst adopting a Christian
moral code. They were married off at sixteen, sometimes earlier, to husbands they
had never met – chosen by their parents. What was important was not the husband
but the marriage: a state of emancipation where they could do as they pleased in the

No Love without Suffering,
No Rose without Thorns
Francois-Bernard Lépicié
After the painting by Jean-Marc Nattier
1720
cat. 10

company of a man they very rarely saw. As for boys of noble birth, they were
brought up in the manner of Charles Duclos's hero in *Confessions du Comte de* ***
(1741): 'As a child I had a tutor to teach me Latin, which he failed to teach me; a few
years later, I was placed under the instruction of a governor to teach me the ways of
the world, of which he knew nothing.' Instead it is women such as Mme de Valcourt
and Mme de Rumigny who each in their turn 'provide his education' and turn him
into the perfect gentleman of pleasure.

Popular novels, salon paintings, and the engravings exhibited by dealers taught
young girls everything their convents and bourgeois boarding-schools had failed
to instruct them in. These works showed them that desire was more important than
love, and that when it came to love the only thing that counted was the pleasure of
the senses. As the Goncourt brothers aptly exclaim in *La femme au dix-huitième
siècle*: 'Sensuality! It is the very essence of the eighteenth century; its secret, its
charm and its soul. The eighteenth century lives and breathes sensuality. Sensuality
is the air upon which it feeds and which brings it to life. It is its character and its
breath; its force, its inspiration, its life and its spirit.'[1] The Goncourts also
emphasized that learning about sensuality came mostly through images: 'This is the
century in which nudity surpasses the negligée, and art, dispensing with beauty's
sense of propriety, recalls Fragonard's little Cupid, laughing as he carries away the
woman's decency in the painting *La Chemise enlevée*. What mischievous, suggestive
little scenes! What mythological adulteration! Oh *Nymphs scrupuleuses*, *Balançoires
mystérieuses*! What spiritually immodest passages escaped from Baudouin and little
Queverdo, from Freudeberg and Lavreince… And the engraver is there, with his
lithe chisel, brisk and mischievous, to spread these ideas in prints sold to the public,
entering the most respectable homes and bringing these images of impurity, these
shameless coquettes, these couples draped in rows of flowers, these scenes of
tenderness, infidelity and surprise to the bedroom walls of young girls, above
their beds and in their dreams.'[2]

In Catholic France of the eighteenth century, when the religious authorities were
committing the abuses of power opposed by Voltaire, an inspired eulogy to Roman
paganism was heard as compensation. While Renaissance artists had painted
numerous works depicting the Virgin Mary clasping the infant Jesus to her breast,
those of Louis xv's reign replaced her with the figure of a nude Venus playing with
Cupid. Raphaël's *La Vierge à la chaise* and his other famous Madonnas gave way to
François Boucher's various Venuses caring for the young Cupid (Boucher was
dubbed 'the painter of voluptuousness and the Graces'). Numerous imitators from
Antoine Coypel to Louis Lagrenée represented these works in every possible way.
There was clearly no concern for realism in these images of Venus breast-feeding
Cupid, teaching him to read, kissing him better after a bee-sting, making him drink
nectar, punishing him by whipping him with a bouquet of roses, and so forth (cat.
10–14). Nobody believed that the capricious education bestowed upon Cupid by
Venus could serve as an example, nor indeed that it corresponded to its mythological
origins. These works simply provided a pretext to show a nude goddess in her role as
a mother and to suggest that the heathen religion of Antiquity was more engaging
than Christianity, since its notion of the sacred involved such voluptuous nudes.

Nonetheless, the continual representation of Cupid with or without his mother
undeniably influenced contemporary mores. This pretty little winged boy, presented

Peeping Tom
Pierre Malœuvre
After the gouache by Pierre-Antoine Baudouin
1779
cat. 74

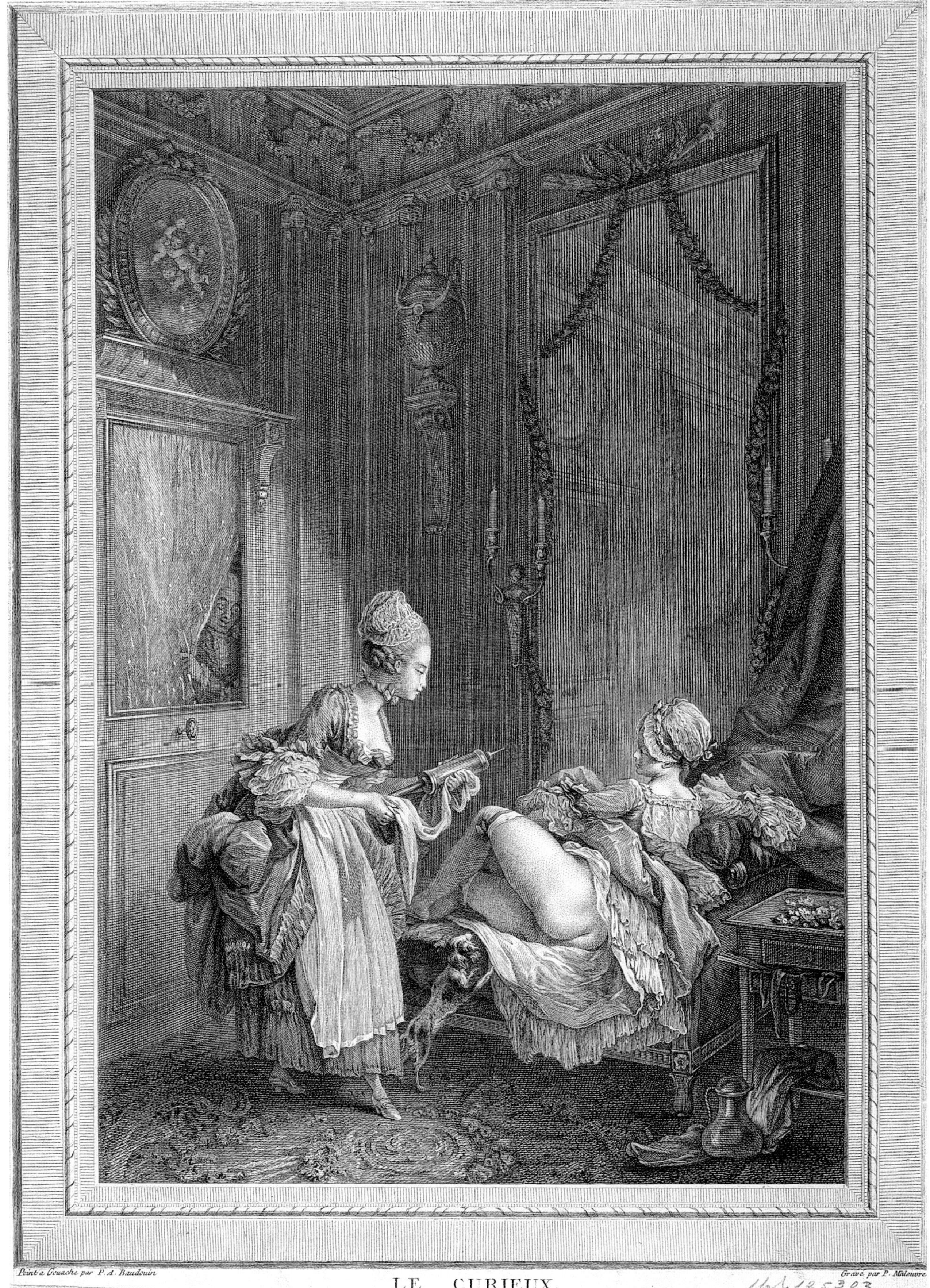

LE CURIEUX.

as 'a cunning god' amusing himself by firing arrows at mortals from his bow, seemed
to justify the worst of lovers' follies. Nobody could be held responsible for actions
that resulted from venomous wounds inflicted by a mischievous child. His image was
found everywhere – from the residency of the Duke of Praslin, Minister of Foreign
Affairs, who owned Vanloo's painting *L'Amour menaçant*, to the home of the Farmer
General de La Popelinière, where Coypel's *L'Amour menaçant* was accompanied by
Voltaire's distich: 'Whoever you are, here is your master / He was, he is, or he ought
to be.' This unruly little boy was not satisfied with his role as a tireless archer; he also
incited his victims to do foolish things with his caresses, as in Fragonard's *Le baiser
dangereux*, in which a young girl falls in love simply because she has kissed Cupid.

The role of engraving was paramount in educating young people about love,
since it made available to amateurs the unique work, painting or gouache which a
noble lord kept in his collection. Sometimes the engraving actually strengthened
the original, as a result of the engraver's vigorous line and the contrast of black
and white. Some talented engravers such as Dennel and Bonnet interpreted the
painters' compositions so well that their engravings looked like creations of their
own invention.

Education in love in the eighteenth century consisted in making both men and
women skilled in the battle of the sexes. At a time when the campaigns of Marshal
Maurice de Saxe were dubbed 'the lace war' because the opposing armies confronted
one another beautifully turned out and exchanging displays of politeness (such as the
famous line by Count Auteroche to Lord Hay during the battle of Fontenoy in 1745:
'You fire first, messieurs les Anglais!'), the battle of the sexes was a perverse and
delightful diversion for high society. It was conducted by means of compliments,
reverence, ruses and stratagems aimed at drawing the pleasure of conquest from the
pleasure of love. One did not speak of sexual relations except in terms of victory
and defeat. Conquering the opposite sex, or, if conquered by them, preparing one's
revenge, was the ultimate preoccupation for women and men alike. The novels and
iconography of the time inculcated the principles of the spirit of the amorous
conquest, setting out the rules for its success.

Three main themes of this battle of the sexes were most often used in pictures and
engravings: reconnaissance, attack and surprise. Reconnaissance (known in military
strategy as 'la guerre à l'oeil') is the action of observing the enemy from close up to
find out who they are and what they are doing. All the scenes with a man hidden in
a bush spying on a nude bather exhibit the tactics of reconnaissance. The man is
reassuring himself in advance that she is worthy of being conquered. Sometimes
reconnaissance is of a more dissolute nature – for example, when the lover pays a
maid to let him secretly take part in administering an enema to her mistress (p. 37;
cat. 74). The maid is not always so obliging; sometimes she covers the intruder's face
with a veil when he presents himself in the alcove where her mistress stands naked.

The reconnaissance of military terrain is equivalent to the anatomical
reconnaissance of the lover, eager to contemplate the behind or the sex of their
chosen one. Eisen's *Le villageois indiscret* (which he possibly engraved himself) is a
scene of voyeurism that results in an anatomical reconnaissance. A couple of young
aristocrats dressed in the latest fashion are engaged in the prelude to amorous activity
at the foot of a tree. The young woman, dressed with panache, her bare breasts
flowing from atop her corset, spreads her thighs to reveal her 'jewel' (as the female

vulva was known in the wake of Diderot's novel *Les Bijoux indiscrets*) in the fold of her dress, to the young nobleman who is crouched on bended knee. This jewel thrills her partner, who throws up an arm in exclamation, but it also excites the peasant hidden in the branches above, who is leaning forward to witness this fascinating spectacle at risk of falling. In *Aminte surprisé au bain*,[3] the voyeur's anatomical reconnaissance is thwarted by the maid, who conceals Aminte's nudity under a hand-towel; but the sexual jewel, together with its pubic hairs, is clearly revealed to us – a considerable act of daring on the part of the artist (since the Académie royale de peinture allowed only the 'chaste nude' that showed neither the vulva or hair in the lower abdomen, women being considered not to have anything in this area).

The theme of attack in the battle of the sexes is represented in the greatest number of ways without ever being rendered as a violation, as this would contradict the ideal of 'the lace war'. In *La petite Thérèse* (Couché's engraving based on Carême),[4] the attack on a peasant woman by a peasant man recalls the playful pursuit of a nymph by a satyr. Reference was made to the 'sudden attack' and the 'gallant attack' as appropriate. The sudden attack is the action of the man brought to the climax of desire as he interprets the wishes of the woman who is excited by his confession. This is the subject of *L'eventail cassé*, Bonnet's engraving after a picture by Schall.[5] The woman pushes her lover away by hitting him with her fan and stops him reaching across her skirt to rub her genitals; but we see that her defence is a stimulant for both prior to capitulation. *L'amant écouté*, by the same artists, depicts a gallant attack.[6] According to aristocratic etiquette the man gets down on bended knee to make his declaration; however, his ecstatic desire and the insinuating gesture of his right arm indicate that he is now ready for erotic action, all the more since his partner, who has become increasingly won over, is no longer offering up any resistance.

Surprise, in military terms, is all about catching the enemy unawares, while it is at rest or immersed in an activity that leaves it vulnerable. In the battle of the sexes the surprise is the danger for lovers in bed together who are caught in the act by a husband or a mother. This situation was treated by many artists in slightly different ways. Most commonly an ironic commentary inscribed under the image reveals that the 'victor' who surprises them is in fact the conquered. In an engraving by Anselin after Borel, a servant shows his master his wife sleeping naked in the arms of her lover, saying: 'You have the key... he found the lock'.

Another form of surprise is that of the secret lovers' meeting. Here it is the young girl's parents who are the enemy, and their treasure – their daughter – is the lover's target. A gouache by Baudouin that Choffard engraved for the Prince de Ligne shows the surreptitious arrival of a bold lover forcing his way through the window of the young beauty who awaits him fluttering with desire (*overleaf*; cat. 80).

The sentimental genre arose after the tremendous success of *La Nouvelle Héloïse* (1761) by Jean-Jacques Rousseau, which caused the female public to cry over the misfortunes of a thwarted affair. It was above all at the beginning of the reign of Louis XVI that Rousseau made his mark in order to please Marie-Antoinette. People were caught up less by the desires and joys of love than by its afflictions and yearnings. Jean-Baptiste Greuze became the master of this trend with his melodramatic paintings, which are less popular today than his drawings of young girls, whom he wanted to depict as 'figures of sentiment' with 'romance in their eyes' (in Greuze's own phrase). Vigée-Lebrun also illustrated the sentimental genre in her suggestive portraits, such as the one of a virgin (in *La vertu irrésolue*, cat. 62; *overleaf*) who wonders, upon reading a declaration of love, whether or not to reply in the same tone.

Education in love in the sentimental genre is conducted by looking at doves pecking one another. Greuze's adolescent in *Les premières leçons de l'amour* follows their little game with impassioned attention. Similarly the villager in *Rêver Matin*, painted and engraved by Nicolas-François Régnault, is so moved by the coupling of two doves in front of her window that she lets the milk, which is boiling in a pan, overflow.[7] The whiteness of the doves and their wings bore testimony to their celestial purity: to see doves copulating was certainly more acceptable than watching the thrust of a stallion.

The principal theme of the sentimental genre is the solitary lover's daydream: the woman dreams as she contemplates the portrait of her beloved, or else when she is reading or writing a letter, or stroking a bird or a dog in her bedroom, from where she has banished unwelcome visitors. Another theme is expressed as homage to the god of love standing upon a pedestal in a park: here a young girl approaches to adorn him with a garland, there a couple comes to offer an invocation. The attack (sudden or gallant) of the libertine genre is replaced by the supplication of the suitor on bended knee or with hands clasped before his beloved, as if she were herself divine.

The Swedish painter Nicolas Lavreince, who made a career in Paris as well as in Stockholm, produced works in the sentimental genre but with none of its vapidity. His scenes contain a discreet moral dimension, which he leaves to the viewer to discover for themselves. In *Le billet doux* he shows how a young girl is seen slipping a letter into the hand of her lover while eluding the guard of her governess.[8] But in *Le repentir tardif* he also conveys the sorrow of the virgin who has just lost her virginity and whose seducer tries in vain to console her;[9] and in *L'innocence en danger* the inevitable risk for an adolescent when a female go-between approaches a financier who is prepared to pay a large amount for her possession.[10]

The sentimental genre did not succeed in replacing the libertine genre. However there were artists like Fragonard who knew how to mix these two genres in a very natural way. Libertinism even took on a new force when Laclos made an apology through the heroes of his epistolary novel, *Les Liaisons Dangereuses* (1782). The letters by Valmont and the Marquise de Merteuil form a tactical manual for the battle of the sexes. One sees them 'providing an education' (that of the young Cécile Volanges) and laying out plans of attack. Under Louis XVI a recrudescence of erotic novels sold in secret with illustrations by first-rate engravers who did not sign them also contributed to the libertine education of young people. Engravings sold by traders never depicted the sexual act: only the preliminary or symbolic actions of the half- or fully-clothed couple.

However, within the pages of the erotic novels of André de Nerciat (for example *Félicia ou mes fredaines* (1778), illustrated with twelve free engravings by Borel after Eisen; *Monrose ou le libertin par fatalité* (1792) with twenty-four loose engravings by Queverdo; and *Les Aphrodites* (1793) with eight plates drawn by Monnet and engraved on steel) people are blatantly seen making love. Rousseau recalled that a noble lord, who wanted to go to bed with his wife Thérèse, handed her an erotic book containing illustrations aimed at arousing excitement. On that occasion he

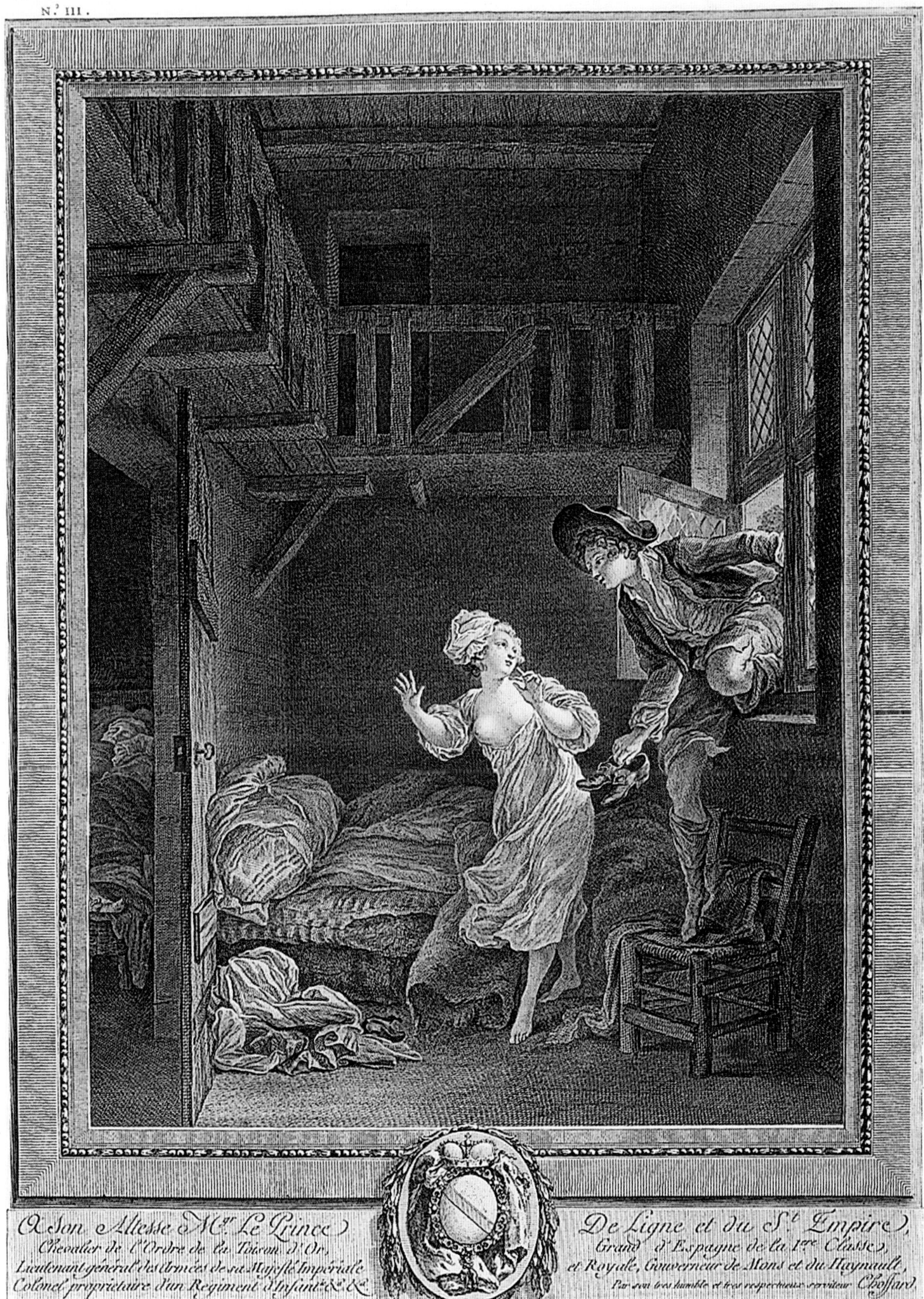

Peint a la Gouasse par P.A. Baudouin Peintre du Roi. 1765.   A Paris Quay et Batiment neuf des Théatins.   Gravé par Pt. Chossard 1782.

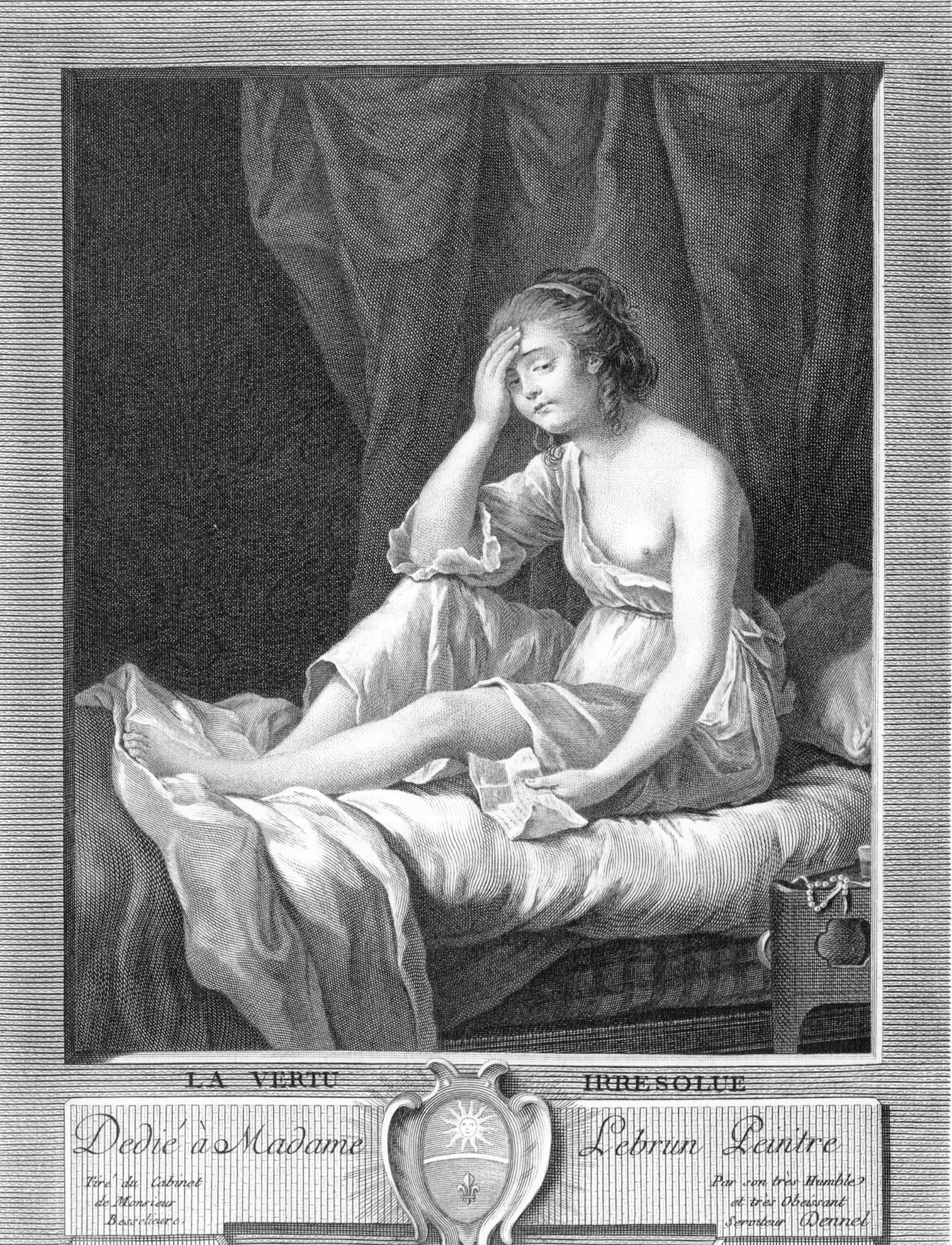

LA VERTU IRRESOLUE
Dedié à Madame Lebrun Peintre
Tiré du Cabinet de Monsieur Besseleure.
Par son très Humble et très Obeissant Serviteur Dennel
Louise Elisabeth Vigée Pinx.
Dennel Sculp.
Se trouve à Paris chez l'Auteur, rue du Petit Bourbon attenant la Foire St Germain

was out of luck, but it was nonetheless a customary procedure. The old Marquis de Sade did the same thing with the young Magdeleine Leclerc whom he lusted after at Charenton. Education in love for young women could go as far as an incitement to debauchery.[11]

Vivant Denon, who was at once a writer, painter and engraver – he published *Point de lendemain* in 1777 and became a member of the Académie in 1787 – was eccentric enough to continue up until the Empire period the libertine genre that he started to practise under Louis xv. *Point de lendemain*, the account of a night of madness in which a countess on a whim seduces the young lover of her best friend and then mocks him, reveals the light inspiration of his early years. But she is made bolder in his licentious engravings, which he pushed to the point of obscenity, such as in his *Œuvre priapique*, a collection of thirty-one engraved erotic figures, which he published around 1803.

As with the writers, the artists of the eighteenth century did their utmost to offer lessons in love, not in a didactic way, but by providing heady examples of everything that we do in connection with desire, the quest for pleasure, autoerotism, the will to seduce, and the need endlessly to conquer sexual partners or become attached to just one person. Such an education in love was clearly effective. Consulting the letters and memoirs of the time, we find that the members of the two sexes understood their shared passions far better than they might have done had they studied them through treatises on morality and psychology.

Irresolute Virtue
Antoine-François Dennel
After the painting by Louise-Elisabeth Vigée-Lebrun
1781
cat. 62

1. Edmond and Jules de Goncourt, *La femme au dix-huitième siècle* (rev. edn.), Paris, 1905, p. 151.
2. Ibid.
3. Dimitri Ozerkov, *Éducation de l'Amour*, ex. cat., St Petersburg, 2006, no. 84.
4. Ibid., no. 34.
5. Ibid., no. 56.
6. Ibid., no. 48.
7. Ibid., no. 49.
8. Ibid., no. 43.
9. Ibid., no. 75.
10. Ibid., no. 42.
11. Related works by Sarane Alexandrian: *La peinture en Europe au XVIII-ème siècle*, Paris, 1970 (on the sentimental genre); *Les Libérateurs de l'amour*, Paris, 1977 (on the libertine art of 'conducting an education'); and *Histoire de la littérature érotique*, Paris, 1989 (on the erotic illustrated novels of the eighteenth century).

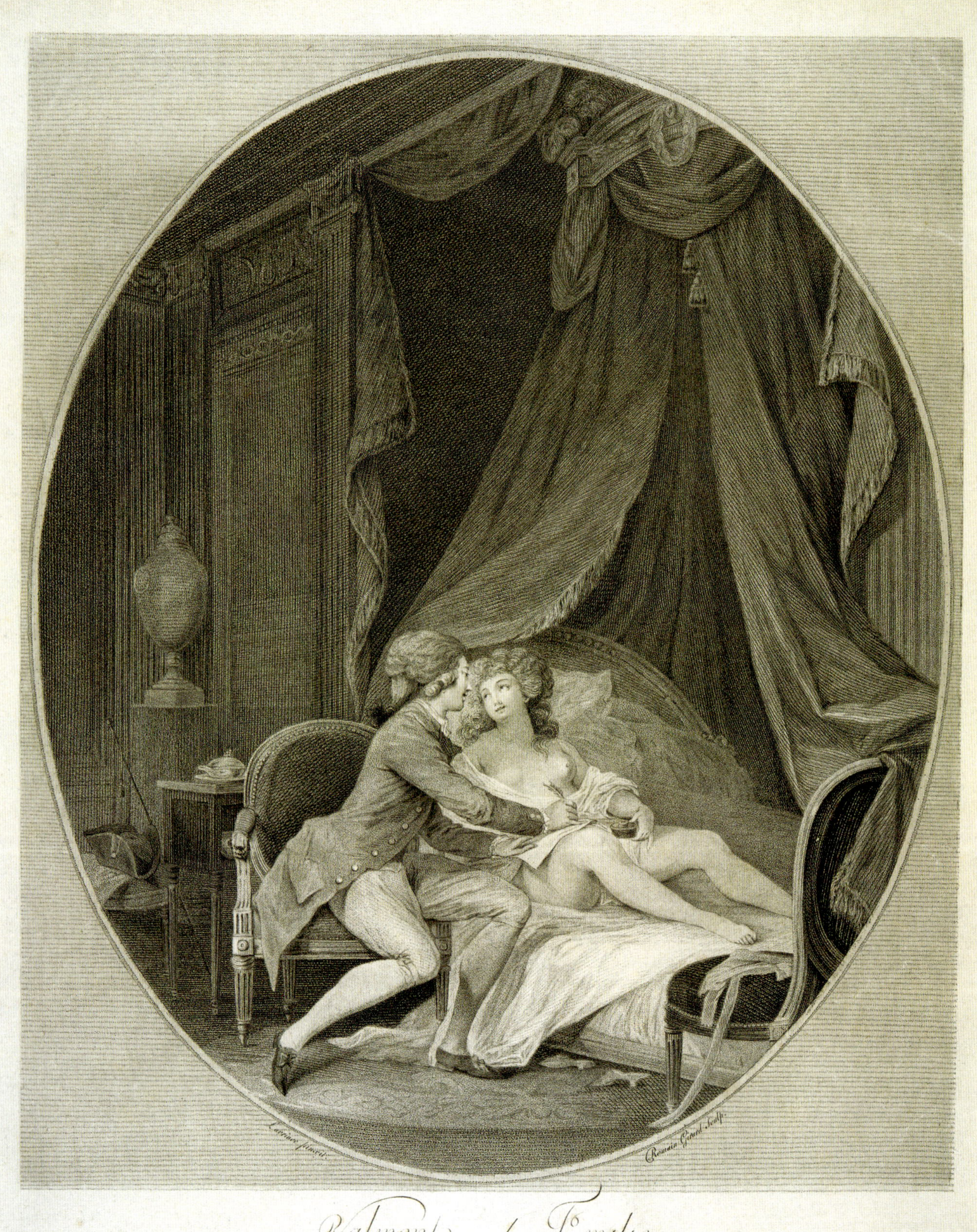

Valmont and Emilie

Cette complaisance de ma part est le prix de celle qu'elle vient d'avoir de me servir de pupitre pour ecrire a ma belle devote,
a qui j'ay trouvé plaisant d'envoyer une lettre ecrite du lit et presque entre les bras d'une fille

Liaisons Dangereuses. Tom I. Lettre XXXXVII.

A Paris chez Girard, Graveur, rue de Savoye, derriere le Quay de la Vallée, N.º 21.

Dimitri Ozerkov   *French Prints of the Gallant Age in Paris and St Petersburg*

Of all eighteenth-century art forms, prints – easy to reproduce and thus widely available – offer one of the fullest reflections of society's attitude towards materials of an amorous and sexual nature. In the gallant age, it was to the engravings in their libraries that young men and women would turn in search of answers to questions of the heart. And in response they would find not just images, but also words and verses, for eighteenth-century French prints were often accompanied by poetic texts to form an artistic whole. Found at the bottom of the sheet, these might be fashionable quotations from novels and poems by authors such as Lafontaine, Gentil-Bernard, Favart, Gacon and Lemierre, or dedications which were open to the most liberal interpretation.

Prints reached their culmination as an art form in the 1700s. In a rapidly developing world they were the principal means of recording and conveying an image. French eighteenth-century prints can be divided into several groups. First and foremost they served as reproductions: before the invention of the photograph, they were the way to bring together a collection of works by an artist, or give a general impression of an art gallery. Prints were also used to illustrate works of literature: engraved plates, bound between the pages of a book to illustrate poems and novels about love, were widely produced in Enlightenment France. Thirdly, prints were created as original works of art in their own right, using principally the technique of etching. Their intimate character encouraged collections of rare off-prints, often from slightly unfinished plates or those created before the addition of title and dedication. Such collections frequently focused on works of a gallant or erotic nature, which were destined to be kept hidden from the public eye in private cupboards and cabinets.

Eighteenth-century gallant prints were closely linked to the French romantic novel. But while romantic novels were most popular with society ladies (and, in secret, their daughters), it was the visual arts – erotic paintings and prints – that appealed to men. In the eighteenth century, as today, 'female' literature described the grand emotions of love through romantic imagery – fiery embraces, gushing torrents and so forth. Erotica and pornography are rooted in a male perception, where images traditionally have greater influence than descriptions. Engravers and printers of the gallant age naturally responded to the increased demand for such works, and soon their appearance and distribution were widespread. The works of great masters such as Watteau, Boucher and Fragonard, as well as lesser artists like Borel and Boitard, Baudouin and Schall, formed the basis for the later evolution of

Valmont and Émilie
Romain Girard
After the painting by Nicolas Lavreince
1788
cat. 69

the theme of corporeality and sexuality in European art. In the eighteenth century, erotica ceased to be taboo, and became, on the contrary, a fashionable accoutrement of enlightened society life.

In European culture the problem of censorship, both religious and moral, has always faced erotic pictures and words. Engravings were subject to censorship as early as the beginning of the sixteenth century, when copies of *I Modi*, showing sixteen sexual positions in plates by Marcantonio Raimondi from drawings by Giulio Romano, were destroyed by order of Pope Clement VII. Reprinting of this legendary work, first published in Rome in 1524 with the sonnets of Pietro Aretino, was punishable by death.[1] Despite the ban, 'Aretinian postures' achieved great popularity, and numerous echoes can be heard in French classical literature – in Brantôme's *Vies des dames galantes* (1666) and Diderot's *Les Bijoux indiscrets* (1748). The ban also gave rise to a large number of underground reprints in various European countries, with French illustrated collections of sexual positions foremost among them.

Nevertheless, in eighteenth-century France, where the problem of censorship was acute, racy novels were of secondary importance: the main targets of censorship were publications connected with the politics of the ruling classes and, in particular, the love affairs of the king, his entourage and high society. For example, *Les Bijoux indiscrets* was banned not because the author had female private parts speaking aloud, but because the main characters, the Sultan Mangogul and his favourite Mirzoza, were seen as transparent references to Louis XV and Madame de Pompadour. It was, incidentally, typical of the age that the author of similarly frolicsome gallant-erotic novels could quite legitimately seek a position as a royal censor. Thus it was that for some time the position was occupied by Claude-Prosper de Crébillon *fils*, author of *Tanzaï et Néadarné* (1734) and *Le Sopha* (1745).[2]

Official censorship did not traditionally extend to biblical and mythological subjects, which explains why such themes were often chosen by engravers.[3] 'Aretinian postures' were merrily reworked as 'loves of gods', where heroes of the Graeco-Roman pantheon illustrated various sexual positions. Often artists turned to those mythological and biblical themes which invited them to portray the naked female form: Orpheus and Euridice, Diana and Acteon, Lot and his daughters, or Susanna and the Elders. These subjects allowed the artist without fear of persecution to create pictures which were quite seductive enough to appeal to the 'amateur' (although in official circulation it was usual to conceal the most intimate parts behind a delicately positioned leaf or cloth).

Many prints, however, had a first print-run that was altogether more explicit. French laws allowed engravers and printers to produce a specified number of test prints, or *épreuves* (for example, *right*; cat. 75, 76). These were not subject to moral censorship, and although they were nominally works in progress, more often than not they were simply more explicit versions of the final work. Such so-called *épreuves avant la draperie* or *épreuves avant feuillage* were printed only in minimal runs and sold under the counter to 'connoisseurs', according to a list specially compiled in advance.[4] Nowadays these works – where no delicate ringlet or swish of cloth covers the breast or frames the bosom – are extremely rare. For if they fell into the wrong hands, they were often the victim of moral censorship. Examples are quite common where the sinewy hand of an eighteenth- or nineteenth-century 'mentor' has carefully crossed out all the genitalia.

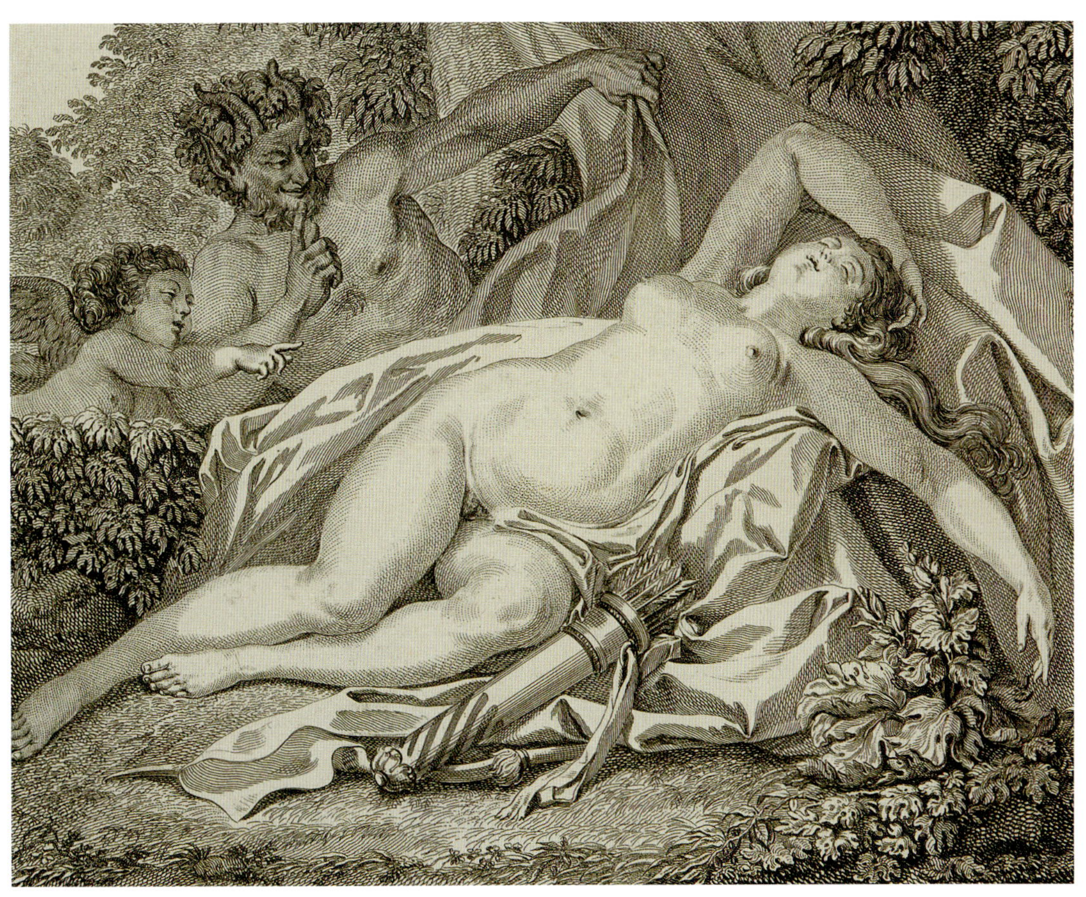

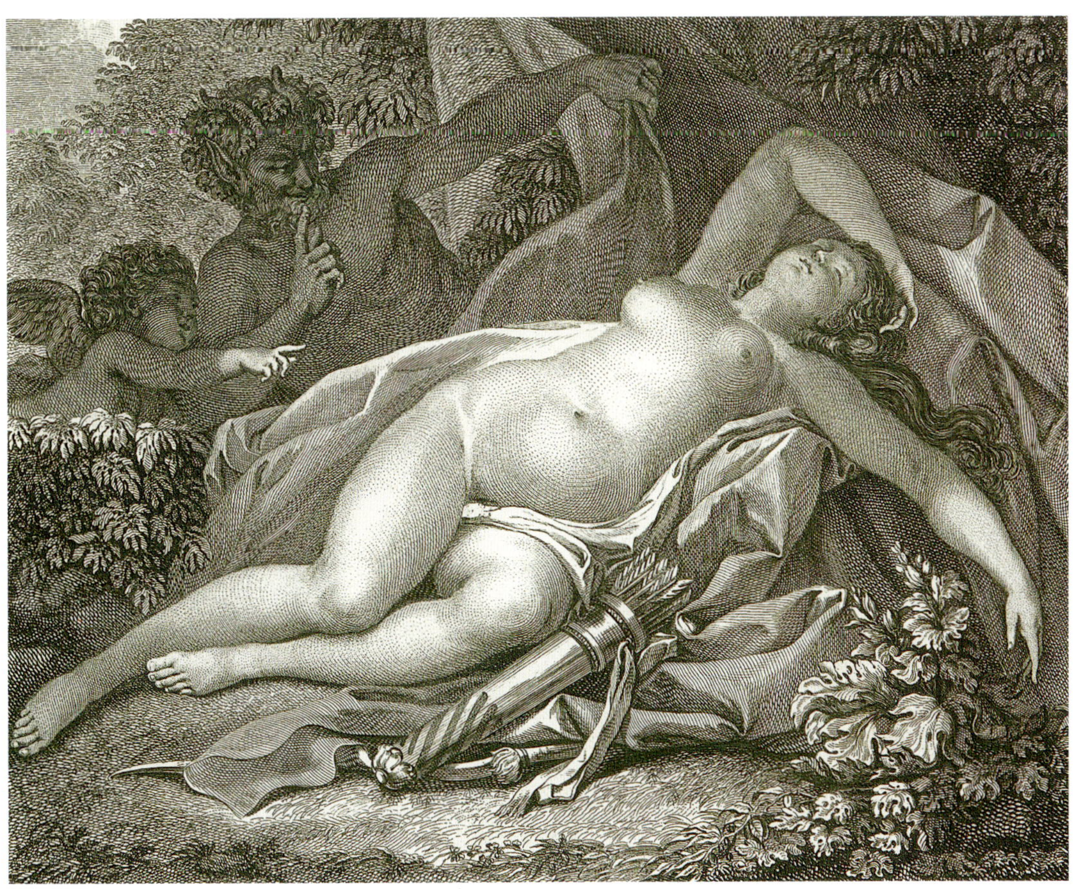

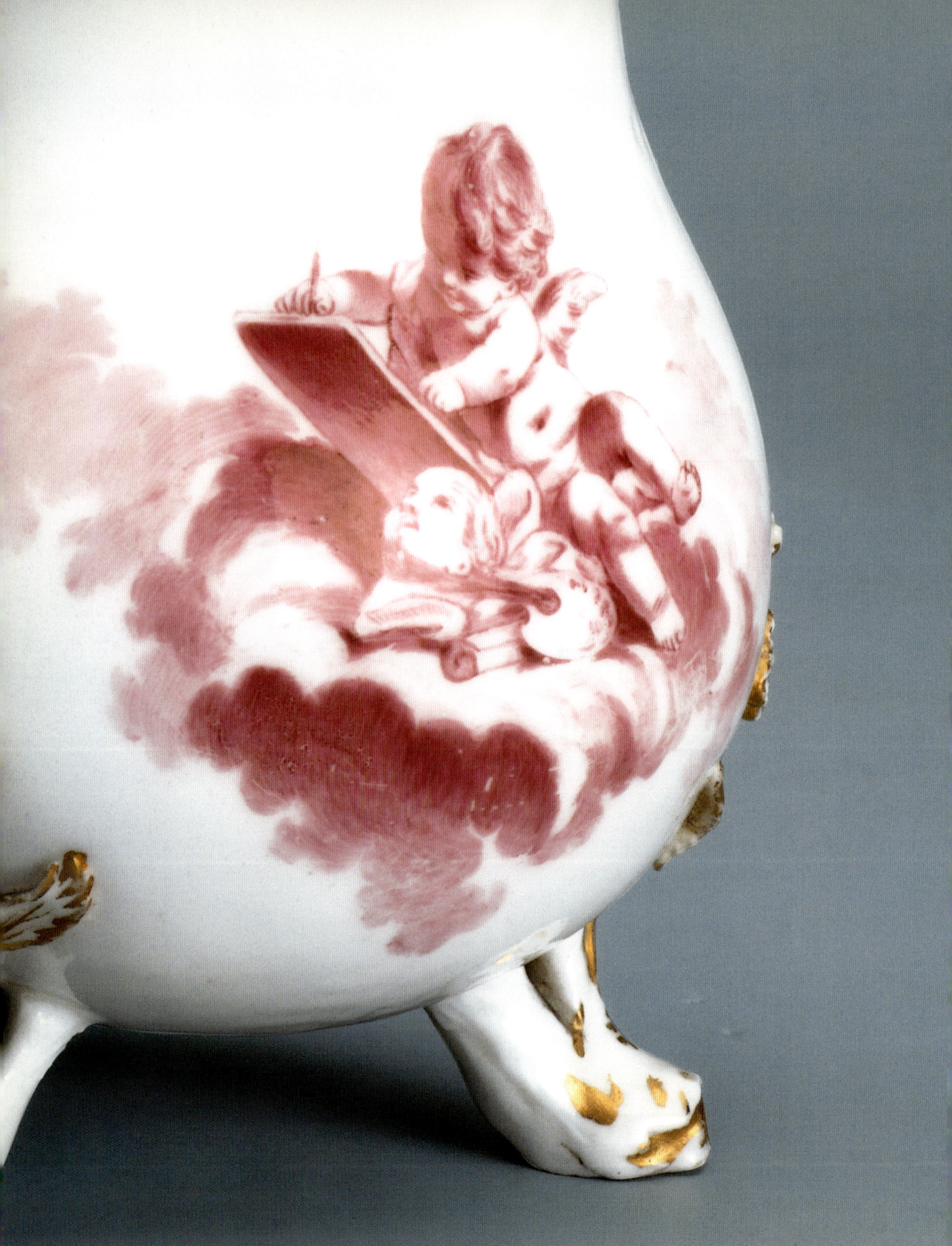

By the middle of the nineteenth century the anonymous production of obscene off-prints had turned into a genuine pornography industry with its own clientele, one of whom was a certain Prince Golitsyn. The catalogue of 'The collection of Prince G***' was published in Paris in 1887;[5] the fate of the collection itself, however, is unknown. At the same time a growth in the market and increased censorship led to a sharp fall in the artistic value of erotic and pornographic works. Today the finest collections of such books and prints are held in the Private Case of the British Library, and the Collection d'Enfer of the Bibliothèque Nationale de Paris.

French engravings were frequently used by artists as sketches for decorations on works of applied art, as is shown by grids ruled on some sheets in sanguine or graphite pencils. A number of such prints came to St Petersburg at the turn of the nineteenth century, and they are now kept in the collections of the Hermitage, the Academy of Fine Arts and the Russian National Library. Engravings were used as the basis for large paintings, *dessus-de-porte* and small decorative panels for decorating vaults, theatre valances, wall panels or fire screens. A further use of engravings in applied art was as a decorative source for fabrics, porcelain, fans, snuff-boxes, jewellery and so on. This exhibition contains a number of examples of the 're-use' of prints in this way (for example, *left*; cat. 27).

For the Russian imperial court, as well as for the libraries of a number of noble families, books and prints were specially ordered from European publishers. The inventory of books belonging to Baron P.P. Shafirov, for example, which came to the library of the Academy of Sciences in 1723, lists works by Molière, Corneille, Antoine Furetière, Alain-René Lesage and Prosper Jolyot de Crébillon, as well as Boileau's *Art Poétique* and Fénelon's *Telemache*. In 1734 the latter work was translated into Russian by A.F. Khrushchov, who also translated Fénelon's *Sur l'éducation des filles* and Trotti de la Chetardye's *Instruction pour une jeune princesse, ou l'idée d'une honneste femme* in 1738. These works, however, were only published in Russian a quarter of a century later, in the 1760s.[6] Under Empress Elizabeth the official propagandizing of everything French became ever more popular. At the beginning of her *Notes*, written towards the end of her life, Princess Dashkova (1743–1810) paints a picture of a girl reading in Elizabethan Russia: 'Books were my passion. Bayle, Montesquieu, Boileau and Voltaire were my favourite authors… Shuvalov, who was Elizabeth's lover and obviously wanted to be thought of as a fashionable merchant, found out that I was passionate about books, and offered me use of all the literary novelties that were constantly being sent him from France. This loan was a source of constant pleasure to me, especially the following year when I moved to Moscow after my marriage. Here I discovered that bookshops contained little that I had not already read, and in some cases I even had these works in my own library, which now comprised almost 900 volumes. I spent all my pocket money on this collection, and acquired Moréri's dictionary and *Encyclopédie* in the same year…' It is true, however, that Dashkova later adds: 'At the time of which I write, there can scarcely have been any other women in Russia who were such serious readers as Princess Ekaterina [later Catherine the Great] and I.'[7]

Inhabitants of the capital, St Petersburg, could obtain French books and probably engravings at a book stall opened in Gostiny Dvor in the first quarter of the eighteenth century by order of Peter the Great. In 1760 the bookseller Weitbrecht opened the city's second bookshop, the Imperial Book Stall, and soon afterwards a

number of other shops opened. In his *Description of St Petersburg* (1793) Johann
Georgi already lists a number of foreign booksellers who had stalls in the city
(Weitbrecht, the Brothers Gay, Gerstenberg, Klostermann, Logan, Miller, Rospini,
Shnorr and Evers), and records that bookshops also dealt in engravings: 'Some of
the Nürnberg and Augsburg tradesmen have significant collections of prints on sale.'
According to Georgi, each year paper worth between 44,000 and 56,300 roubles was
imported into the city, along with prints worth between 48,000 and 72,000 roubles.[8]
At the same time, the engravings sold in the 1780s and 1790s by the Parisian publisher
Pierre-François Basan state that they could be bought in St Petersburg.[9] By the end
of the eighteenth century, however, the constant tightening of censorship had left
the Russian book market in an impoverished state, where a few expensive works
available only to the wealthy stood alongside French and German novels.[10]

In Russia collections of prints began to appear from the middle of the eighteenth
century. They often accompanied major collections of paintings and books. Among
the largest print collections were those of Empress Catherine II, which later formed
the basis of the Hermitage Print-room. A whole series of large western collections
of graphic art came to Russia in the second half of the eighteenth century thanks
to Catherine's acquisitions. These included the collections of Bergholz, Brühl
and Hermann.

A detailed catalogue of the Print-room of the Imperial Hermitage was compiled
in French between 1817 and the early 1830s under the department's assistant curator
Antoine Noth, and is now known as the 'Noth Catalogue'. The drafting of the Noth
Catalogue, subdivided into sections, marked the final stage of restructuring the
Print-room using the Heinecken system, a process begun in 1806.[11] It is worth noting,
however, that notwithstanding a number of recent publications (Malinovsky 1987;
Rakova 1987; Lander 2000), the subject of Russian print collections remains
relatively little studied.

The selection of prints on display here found its way into the Print-room in the
1920s. Among these are works which were part of a collection of eighteenth-century
French erotic prints, unique in Russia. This single group of works was formed
towards the middle of the nineteenth century and numbered around 500. During the
Soviet period these works were divided up according to schools and artists, which
led to their being spread across the Hermitage's Print-room. In the 1950s the most
salacious prints were locked away in a special cupboard known as *spetskhran* ('special
archive'), and right up to the beginning of perestroika in the mid-1980s special
permission was required from the museum director in order to see them.

All the gallant and erotic prints which were originally part of this unique
collection bore the mark of the Russian Imperial Crown (in the catalogue 'RIC')
stamped in blue ink in the bottom right-hand corner of the sheet. They were part
of a large collection whose history is yet to be studied in full. In the Hermitage
collection there are portraits and landscapes from the mid-nineteenth century
bearing this mark, which are entirely mainstream and have nothing at all to do with
erotica. It has not been possible to identify the RIC symbol in any of the available
catalogues of owners' marks (Lugt; Lugt Suppl.; Vlasova-Balashova 2003; Hudoley
2004). However, the presence of the RIC mark on a number of folios from the
Hermitage collection suggests that they belonged to the library of one of the
members of the House of Romanov.

The body of erotic prints with this mark came from one of the personal libraries of the imperial family in the Winter Palace in St Petersburg. This can be deduced from a document stored in the Archive of the Hermitage Print-room, according to which the prints come from the personal libraries of Alexander II (1855–81) and Nicholas II (1894–1917) in the Winter Palace.[12] According to an act of 28 July 1927 the prints became part of the permanent collection of the Department of Engravings and Drawings of the State Hermitage, where they remain to this day.

The question of how and when this collection came to one of the palace libraries remains open. It is not clear who assembled and sold the collection to the Winter Palace, and for the moment we can only guess at probable explanations. The previous owners' marks shed some light on the situation. Two sheets show the mark of Count P. de Corneillan (Lugt 458), the majority of whose collection was sold off in 1865. A rare off-print by Fragonard (cat. 83) came from the collection of Chevalier J. Camberlyn (Lugt 514), which was sold off in 1865 and 1867. The old mounts of two sheets show the embossed symbol of the shop of A. Binant in Paris. This suggests that some of the engravings from the Winter Palace collection were acquired in Paris in the mid 1860s.

The owner's mark RIC was almost certainly applied to these prints during the reign of Nicholas II, since it is found on a large number of engravings and folios which are known to have come from his personal library. Nicholas II's diaries and

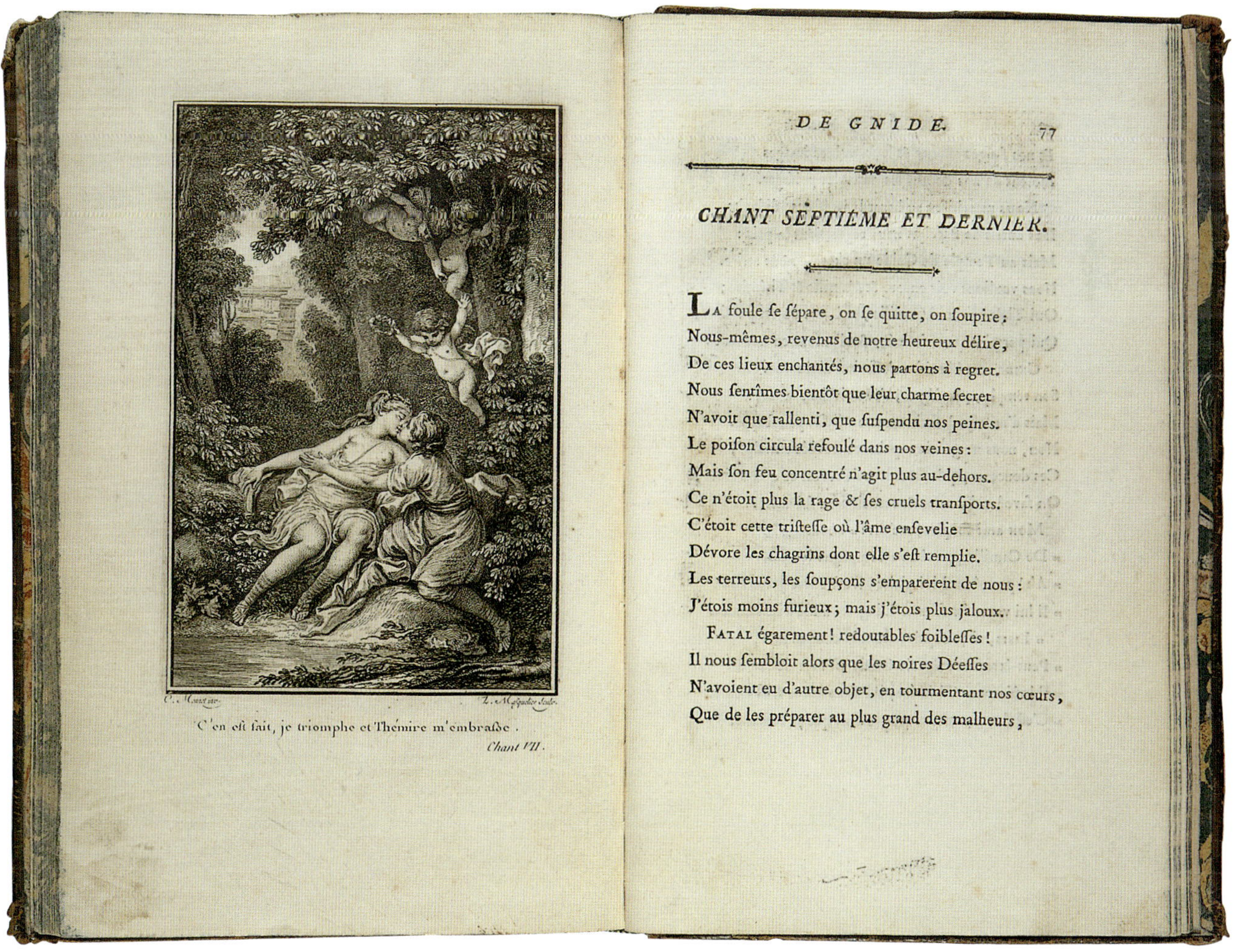

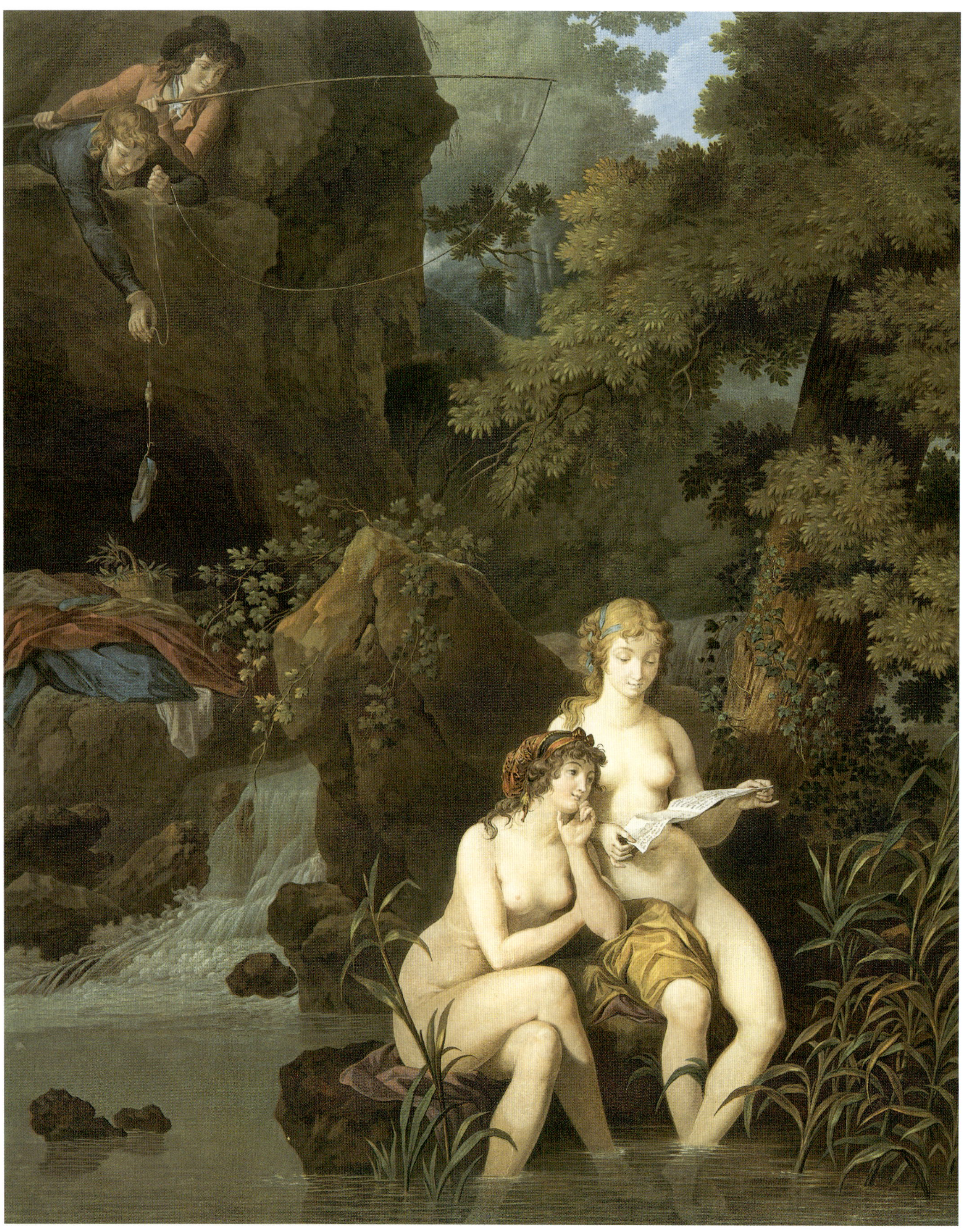

1. O. Neverov, *Liubovnye pozitsii epokhi Vozrozhdeniia*, St Petersburg, 2002.

2. O. Renault, 'Crébillon, le paradoxe du censeur', in *Censures*, June 2003, p. 55–6; J. Henric, 'De Socrate à Rushdie', in *Censures*, June 2003, p. 6.

3. Lionel Dax and Augustin Butler, *Augustin Carrache: Les Lascives*, Paris, 2003, pp. 9–10.

4. See more in A. Griffith, 'Proofs in Eighteenth-century French Printmaking', in *Print Quarterly*, vol. XXI, 2004.

5. *Catalogue du cabinet secret du Prince G***. Collection de livres et objets curieux et rares concernant l'amour, les femmes et le mariage avec les prix de vente. Première partie*, Brussels, 1887; H. Van der Kamp, 'The Trader and the Policeman. Catalogues of Nineteenth Century Erotic Art', in *Romantique. Erotic Art of the Early Nineteenth Century*, Amsterdam and Singapore, 2000, p. 67.

6. S.P. Luppov, ed., *Frantsuzskaia kniga v Rossii v XVIII v. Ocherki istorii*, Leningrad, 1986, pp. 21–40.

7. E.R. Dashkova, *Zapiski kniagini: Vospominaniia. Memuary* [1805], Minsk, 2003, pp. 9–14.

8. J.G. Georgi, *Opisanie rossiisko-imperatorskago stolichnago goroda Sankt-Peterburga* [1794], St Petersburg, 1996, pp. 181, 330–3.

9. P. Casselle, 'Pierre-François Basan marchand d'estampes à Paris (1723–1797)', in *Paris et Ile-de-France. Mémoires publiés par la Fédération des Sociétés Historiques et Archéologiques de Paris et de l'Ile-de-France*, vol. XXXIII, Paris, 1982, p. 118.

10. J. Meerman, *Reise durch den Norden und Nordosten von Europa in den Jahren 1797 bis 1800*, Weimar, 1810, p. 228.

11. *Catalogue Nominatif et Descriptif des Estampes du Cabinet de l'Hermitage Impérial, commencé au mois de Janvier 1817 par le conseiller de college Antoine Noth*, vols. I–XXXVII. The Noth Catalogue is kept in the Print-room of the State Hermitage. The introduction of the Heinecken system can be traced to an order by Count Nikolai Tolstoy to Ignatz Klauber of 14 April 1806 (Hermitage Archive, III, 1806, d. 3, l. 1). See also F. Gille, *Musée de l'Ermitage Impérial. Notice sur la formation de ce musée et description des diverses collections qu'il renferme avec une introduction historique sur l'Ermitage de Catherine II*, St Petersburg, 1860, pp. 151–2; V.F. Levinson-Lessing, *Istoriia kartinnoi galerei Ermitazha (1764–1917)*, Leningrad, 1985, p. 132.

12. *Opis' 1 by inventory. State Hermitage. Department of Engravings and Drawings. Delo 1. Deeds for submission of drawings, engravings and lithographs to the permanent collection. Begun 29 July 1919, finished 11 December 1930. On 368 sheets. Sheets 45–105.* See particularly sheets 105–105 ob.

13. A.N. Benois, *Moi dnevnik: 1916–1917–1918* (intro. J.E. Bowlt and N.D. Lobanov-Rostovsky), Moscow, 2003, p. 244.

14. L.V. Vyskochkov, *Imperator Nikolai I, chelovek i gosudar'*, St Petersburg, 2001, pp. 494, 539.

15. E. & J. de Goncourt, *La femme au dix-huitième siècle*, Paris, 1887.

16. D. Posner 'Watteau mélancolique: la formation d'un mythe', in *Bulletin de la société de l'histoire de l'art français. Année 1973*, Paris, 1974, p. 346.

17. *Liubov' XVIII veka – Frantsuzskie graviury luchshikh masterov XVIII veka* (intro. by Iu. Shamurin), Moscow, 1912, p. 4.

the observations of contemporaries, however, make it extremely unlikely that he would have initiated the purchase or deliberate collecting of erotic subject matter. It seems more likely that this collection of erotic graphic art belonged to his grandfather, Emperor Alexander II, and that the works came to the Print-room from his personal library. The liberator-tsar's passion for such works is well known. Alexander Benois, describing Alexander II's office in the Winter Palace in his diaries of 1917, refers to pictures with a 'lively content'.[13]

It is not inconceivable that this collection actually had its origins in the era of Nicholas I (1825–55). This tsar is known to have spent significant sums on risqué drawings and prints which were sent to him inside sealed envelopes and kept in a 'secret library', and which, by the end of his life, comprised a large collection. The tsar bequeathed his 'secret library' to his son, the future Alexander II; its fate, however, is unknown.[14]

It should be mentioned, of course, that the collecting of works with gallant subjects in nineteenth-century Russia was far from out of the ordinary. An interest in such works was entirely in keeping with the tastes of St Petersburg's 'male' culture of the mid-nineteenth to early twentieth century. The presence and make-up of this collection of gallant and erotic works thus gives us an insight into the collecting practices of its owner, a typical amateur collector; at the same time it offers a clear illustration of ideas inherited by the nineteenth century on sex education and love itself.

In the nineteenth century an interest in the 1700s was particularly fashionable; no doubt this, too, influenced the emergence of the Hermitage collection of French gallant works, and of erotic prints in particular. The education of young girls in eighteenth-century France was already a recognisable phenomenon by 1862, when the Goncourt brothers published their work *La femme au dix-huitième siècle*, which examined all aspects of French everyday life and etiquette from the point of view of the place and role of women in society.[15] Academic interest in the eighteenth century grew steadily from the end of the nineteenth. French academics have linked this to the return to France from the 1830s of political émigrés. For these people the pre-revolutionary era represented the good old days of their fathers, a symbol of a healthy opposition to materialism and democracy.[16] This inherently French interest in the earlier century was reflected in Russia, where it reached its height at the turn of the twentieth century with the passéist pictures and vignettes of the World of Art movement, whose artists revelled in a 'time of hedonistic parasites swarming about the volcano, which would soon swallow them and wipe them off the face of the earth'.[17]

The Hermitage's collection of prints constitutes a unified whole, and its rarest and most interesting examples are on display here. Together they represent a graphic exploration of the gallant theme of the Triumph of Eros in eighteenth-century France; it is an erotic education open to all who find these carefully collected prints in their hands.

The Imps
Charles-Melchior Descourtis
After a painting by Jean-Frédéric Schall
c. 1798
cat. 63

EDITORIAL NOTE

Titles
All works are titled in English; where an
established French title also exists, this is
given in italics beneath.

Dimensions
For prints, the first dimensions refer to the size
of the impression; the second dimensions refer
to the overall size of the sheet of paper.

Inscriptions
Inscriptions on prints are given in the original
French only. Spelling, punctuation and
capitalization follow the original.

Titles and dedicatory inscriptions are given
first; artist and production details and addresses
are given second.

Watermarks
Where applicable watermarks are referenced
to E. Heawood, *Watermarks mainly of the 17th
and 18th centuries*, Hilversum, vol. 1, 1950. 'See
Heawood' indicates that the watermark is given
in Heawood; 'cf. Heawood' indicates a close
analogy to a mark in Heawood.

Stamps
Two further marks relate to the provenance
of the prints. 'RIC' stands for 'Russian Imperial
Crown' and indicates that the print has a small
crown embossed in blue ink in the bottom right-
hand corner of the sheet. This mark suggests
that the print was part of the private library
of one of the members of the imperial family.

Lugt Suppl. 2681[a] refers to a Hermitage stamp
of the Soviet period which indicates that the
print entered the Print-room of the Hermitage
Museum before 1932.

Bibliography
In the catalogue bibliographies, a shortened
form is given for each publication (usually
author or exhibition title, page or picture
reference), while the full entry can be found in
the main bibliography – in the case of Russian
publications, first transliterated, then translated.

Russian Transliteration in the Bibliography
The Library of Congress (LC) system is used
for Russian publications in the bibliography
(both at the end of catalogue entries and in the
main bibliography) to facilitate access to works
in the original Russian.

Russian Transliteration in General Text
In the essays and catalogue entries the Russian
transliteration system used is a version of the
British Standards Institute (BSI) system, modified
to improve readability.

Catalogue introductions
Catalogue introductions on pages 59, 81, 109
and 123 are by Satish Padiyar, on page 101 by
Dimitri Ozerkov.

Catalogue contributors
Catalogue entries are by the following contributors.
Initials are given at the end of each entry.

AB Alexander Babin
AG Anna Geyko
AV Anna Vilenskaya
DO Dimitri Ozerkov
EA Ekaterina Abramova
ED Ekaterina Deryabina
GD Galina Dorofeeva
JV Jan Vilensky
NB Nina Birioukova
OK Olga Kostyuk
OT Olga Triskalo
OZ Olga Zimina
SK Svetlana Kokareva
YUK Yulia Kagan
YUZ Yuna Zek

Satish Padiyar *An Introduction to the Catalogue*

The Triumph of Eros had as its genesis the recent discovery in the Hermitage
Print-room of a collection of around five hundred eighteenth-century French
erotic engravings. These were probably collected in the nineteenth century
by Tsar Nicholas I for his private library, and had remained unseen in public.
On the site of the Winter Palace where they had first been collected, the
Hermitage displayed a selection of one hundred of these engravings in the
summer of 2006, in an exhibition entitled *The Education of Eros. French
Engravings from the Age of Gallantry.*

The revelation of the Hermitage collection of eighteenth-century French
erotic engravings has invited a fresh look at the reinvention of the figure of
Eros at a key moment in the historical formation of Western-European attitudes
to love and sexuality. For this purpose forty-four of the Hermitage engravings
have been selected for *The Triumph of Eros*, of which fourteen were not
displayed in *The Education of Eros*. These range from well-known masterpieces
of the art of eighteenth-century French engraving, such as Jean-Honoré
Fragonard's virtuosic *L'armoire* of 1778 (cat. 83), to newly discovered rarities.
In order to illuminate the complex meanings of the engravings and to position
them in the context of the wider visual culture of Eros, the curators of
The Triumph of Eros have added fifty-four of the Hermitage's other eighteenth-
century French treasures. They include Boucher's artificial *Pastoral Scene*
(cat. 86), Lancret's erotic *The Swing* (cat. 70) and Watteau's late masterpiece
The Capricious Girl (cat. 88), as well as Falconet's iconic sculpture *Menacing
Cupid* (cat. 1), porcelain, gold snuff-boxes, fans and cameos.

This was an era of tension. Around 1700 French aristocratic elites distanced
themselves from a waning martial absolutist power by turning their art
commissions away from iconographies of war to those of love. From the
middle of the eighteenth century the critical movement of the Enlightenment
began to champion 'family values', and attempted carefully — and productively
— to channel sexual desire solely towards the maintenance of the family. From
the 1750s what the eighteenth century considered to be aristocratic libertine
imagery was in turn subjected to enlightened criticism on behalf of a newly
constituted public.

In this way an engraving that depicted an upper-class woman exposing and
enjoying her body (cat. 74) could invite simple enjoyment, but it could also
incite criticism – indeed could itself be understood as harbouring criticism –
of the French aristocracy's lax morals. The era that produced Laclos's *Les
Liaisons Dangereuses*, Diderot's *Les Bijoux indiscrets*, Prévost's *Manon Lescaut*,
and the erotic canvases of François Boucher, Jean-Honoré Fragonard and
Antoine Watteau, was riven with social, political and ideological tensions.
And as the codes of aristocratic libertine behaviour were beginning to cede
to bourgeois propriety, notions of sex and gender equally became subject to
renewed scrutiny.

Eighteenth-century French art and culture continue to receive interest
and attention from scholars and public alike. Following the recent scholarly
reappraisal of François Boucher in France, Britain and America, this year,
2006, is the bicentenary of Jean-Honoré Fragonard, the rococo artist whose
work perhaps engaged most profoundly and originally with the nature of
Eros. There has also been a recent resurgence of curatorial and scholarly
interest in the decorative arts of eighteenth-century France. Decoration,
costume and architectural interiors are increasingly appreciated as areas
through which social and sexual identities were formed in eighteenth-century
France, and the strategies of seduction performed. It is thus a timely moment
to reveal the richness and depth of the Hermitage collections of French
eighteenth-century decorative and fine arts, conceived around the theme
of seduction and eroticism.

In addition to individual masterpieces of painting and sculpture, objects
have been chosen in media that through the reproductive technologies of
eighteenth-century France would have been available to a wider public.
Print culture was fundamental to the process of democratizing the libertine
erotic imagination in eighteenth-century France. It went hand in hand with
the increasingly free accessibility of the written word, and French engravers
self-consciously catered to a public that soon became familiar with the
dynamic interaction between words and images. The resulting erudite and
witty meanings – double entendres that commingled visual language and
verbal pun – are elucidated in the catalogue entries.

Alongside the democratization of culture – and of an erotic language –
that prints brought about, there was also a lively market for what one historian
of eighteenth-century commodity has designated 'populuxe' objects. This
refers to the perhaps contradictory eighteenth-century attempt to produce
elite luxury objects in numbers a broader public could afford, but which
retained requisite qualities of refinement and high finish. In this exhibition
the fascinating interaction of the new eighteenth-century French amorous
subject-matter with innovative technologies of reproduction can be seen in
the many fine examples of unglazed 'white' biscuit porcelain figure groups.
Although relatively expensive because of their time-consuming process of
manufacture, they were nonetheless produced as multiples. In their luminosity
and refined surface finish, these miniaturist objects are uncanny in their ability
to mimic marble. Such highly intricate, aesthetically innovative objects –
designed in collaboration with artists such as François Boucher and Étienne-

Maurice Falconet – enjoyed success almost from the moment of their invention by the Sèvres Porcelain Factory in 1752. They demonstrate how erotic imagery was translated across media, and became subject to novel variations of scale and textural surface quality. There are nine examples in the exhibition: Falconet's famous *Menacing Cupid* features in both its full-scale marble and reduced biscuit porcelain versions.

The catalogue is thematically divided into five sections. Within each section objects are grouped by medium: painting, engraving and decorative arts – clocks, bronzes, gold boxes, fans and cameos.

One theme that runs throughout *The Triumph of Eros* is the figure of Cupid. Section one, entitled 'The Reign of Cupid', focuses on the re-invention of the figure of Cupid in eighteenth-century French art. Eighteenth-century fine and decorative artists mobilized Cupid as an embodiment of desire that was essentially irrational; the figure of Cupid was thus a peculiar anomaly in an age that tended to see itself as ideally reasoned and self-knowing. The subject of the second section, entitled 'Touched by Love', is the way in which the female body was seen, sometimes problematically, to yield to the influence of irrational desire: in the eighteenth century the succumbing of women to the power of Eros was often visualized as occurring via the all-important, potentially dangerous, act of reading. The literary theme is continued in the third section of the catalogue, 'Le Billet Doux'. Here ten engravings have been selected to illuminate how acts of writing and reading in the eighteenth century were themselves eroticized, and especially how the reading and writing of letters featured in visual narratives of seduction. The fourth section is titled 'Encounters and Transgressions', and brings together a group of works that explore moments of breakdown in narratives of seduction, and visual tensions and unrest in amorous imagery; it presents a series of 'libertine' works of art which, if not actually obscene, tested the bounds of eighteenth-century decency. The final section of the catalogue, 'The Triumph of Eros', brings together thirteen works – by, amongst others, Watteau, Fragonard, Falconet and Boucher – that explore how Eros in eighteenth-century French art was envisioned as a transformative power, who could excite, bind bodies together and, in the painted and sculpted depictions of the figure of Pygmalion shown here (cat. 87, 97), define the excitement of making and viewing art itself.

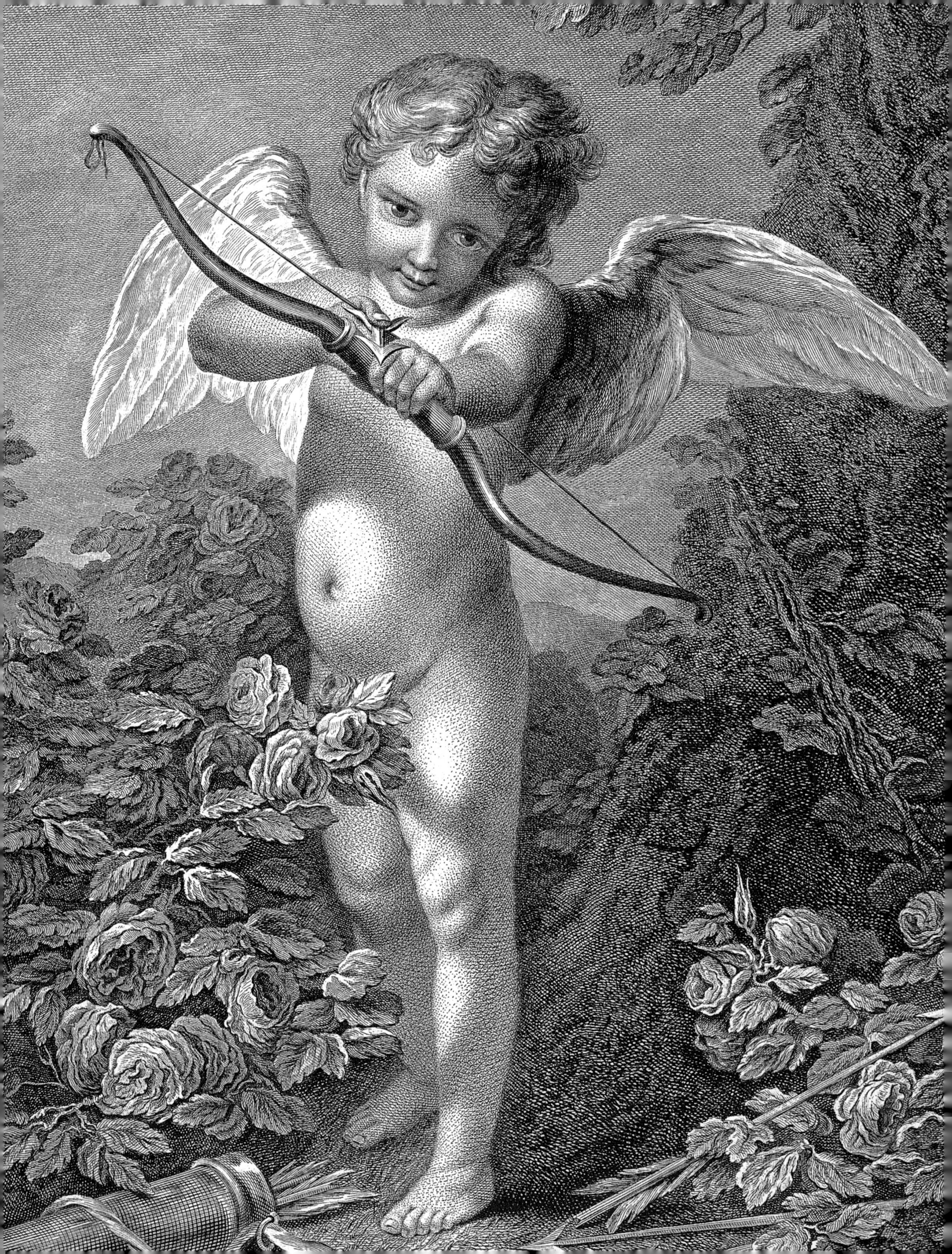

The Reign of Cupid

During the Age of Reason Cupid embodied irrepressible passion and the
failure of control and order. The classical ancient Greek figure of Eros
(or, in Latin, Cupid, meaning desire) ruled over the passions of gods and
men. From the early 1700s an extraordinary resurgence of this embodiment
of desire took place in the literary and visual culture of France. By the mid-
eighteenth century the god of love was to be seen everywhere and in a variety
of seductive forms: in sculpture and paintings, on porcelain and decorative
objects, and in widely circulated engravings. As is clear from the works
of art in this exhibition, men and women of the rococo could hardly avoid
meeting his penetrating, alluring gaze.

Eighteenth-century France considered itself to be in an age of rationality
and order. Cupid disturbed this, for he embodied the power of erotic desire
unbound by the constraints of social regulations and rules. The Enlightenment
envisaged Cupid as receiving a 'good' education from his mother, the goddess
Venus, but ultimately he was never effectively disciplined (cat. 10, 14). Small
yet powerful, Cupid is an agent of desire who is free and irresponsible.

In these paintings, prints and works of applied and decorative art, Cupid
perpetually alights upon new victims at whom to aim his darts of love.
Once struck, the victim – man or woman – will be propelled into a love-
sickness beyond their control. Cupid is therefore a menace. The most famous
'modern' representation of Cupid in eighteenth-century France was Étienne-
Maurice Falconet's boudoir-size statue *Menacing Cupid* (cat. 1). It is a
paradoxical work: Cupid's powerful gesture of silence enjoins us not to
speak about disorderly sexual desires which were nonetheless constantly
spoken of in the eighteenth century.

Menacing Cupid (detail)
Christian von Mechel
After the painting by Charles Vanloo
1763
cat. 8

1

Menacing Cupid
Amour menaçant

After 1757

Étienne-Maurice Falconet (1716–91)

Marble
Height 85 cm
INV: N.sk. 1856
PROVENANCE: 1931, from Antikvariat; previously in
the collection of the Stroganovs
BIBLIOGRAPHY: Kosareva, p. 445; Levitine, pp. 30–1;
Mme de Pompadour, ex. cat., pp. 311–12; Réau 1922,
pp. 183–8, 501

Falconet's first representation of the mythical
Cupid was in the form of a plaster cast, shown
at the Salon of 1755. Then, at the Salon of 1757,
a marble sculpture 'belonging to Madame de
Pompadour' was displayed. Falconet later made
several replicas of the work, which enjoyed
immediate success. The finest version is in the
Rijksmuseum in Amsterdam, and was originally
in the collection of the Shuvalovs. The Hermitage
statue was made for the Russian collector, Count
Pyotr Stroganov, and kept in his house on Nevsky

Prospect in St Petersburg right up until the
Revolution in 1917.

In Madame de Pompadour's collection
there was a small terracotta model representing
Harpokrates, the god of silence, with his finger
to his lips (*Falconet à Sèvres*, p. 92, nos. 4, 5).
It is possible that Falconet borrowed this gesture
for his work: Cupid's left hand reaches out for an
arrow – his usual weapon and Cupid's hallmark –
but the finger of his right hand is at his lips.
It is this gesture which made the sculpture famous
by suggesting a variety of interpretations.
Contemporaries gave the work titles such as *Soyez
discret* ('Be Discreet'), and *Garde à vous* ('Take
Care'). Can we be certain that the name generally
accepted today, *Menacing Cupid*, is entirely fitting?

In this immaculately executed marble
sculpture, Falconet succeeds in conveying the
hidden meaning and ambiguity of the ancient
myth: he gives the god the face of an ordinary
little boy, and a look perhaps best described by
the French word *gamin*. The work has genuinely
become the 'triumph of Eros': the image of
the eternally young god created by Falconet's
genius is everywhere – in paintings, drawings
and engravings, and in many replicas in bronze
and porcelain. AV

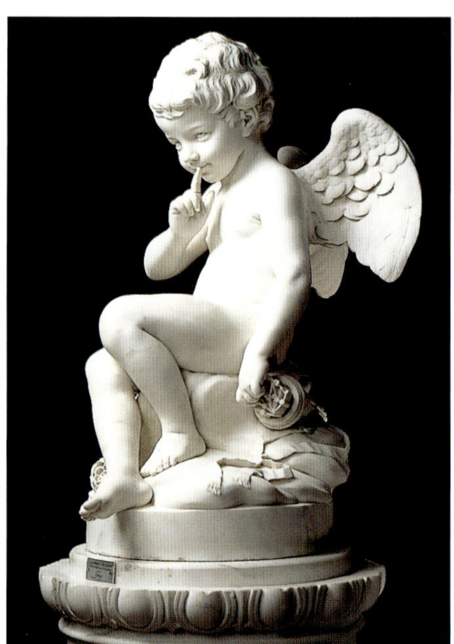

2

Cupids: Allegory of Painting

1750s

François Boucher (1703–70)

Oil on canvas
82 × 87 cm
INV: GE 7750

3

Cupids: Allegory of Poetry

1750s

François Boucher (1703–70)

Oil on canvas
82 × 87 cm
INV: GE 7751
PROVENANCE: acquired for Catherine II between 1763
and 1774
BIBLIOGRAPHY: Ananoff II, p. 170; Georgi, p. 479

Boucher's speciality was mythological subjects,
particularly on the theme of Venus, the ancient
goddess of love, and her son Cupid. He enjoyed
the ardent support and patronage of the mistress
of Louis XV, Madame de Pompadour, and through
her intervention obtained the post of first painter
to the king.

Cupids: Allegory of Painting and its pair
Cupids: Allegory of Poetry evidently belong to
a series of works representing allegories of the
arts. A similar set, devoted to art and science,
remains intact and still adorns the royal palace
of Amalienborg in Copenhagen, for which it
was painted. It includes seven canvases depicting
Sculpture, Painting, Architecture, Music, Poetry,
Geography and Astronomy. Like the Amalienborg
pictures, in the mid-nineteenth century both
Hermitage compositions began to be used as
dessus-de-porte. From 1860 to 1935 they adorned
one of the rooms of the Old Hermitage. These
works by Boucher blend organically with the
furnishings and wall-hangings of rococo interiors;
their typical rose and pink pastel tones, along
with the sketched style and sweeping brushstrokes,
are a perfect complement to the interior décor
of the age.

Several allegorical compositions very similar
to the Hermitage ones are known, which Boucher
made as artist's sketches for the Beauvais Tapestry
Factory. He was recruited to work there through
the good offices of his devoted patroness, Madame
de Pompadour. ED

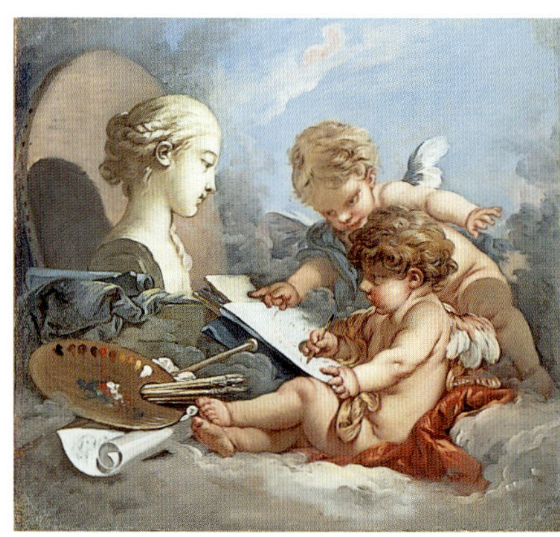

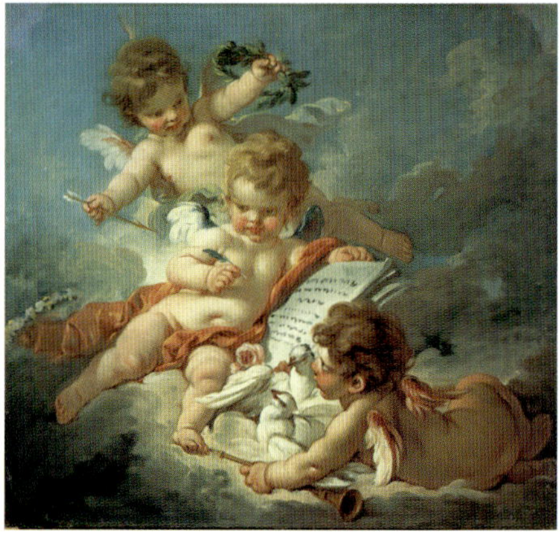

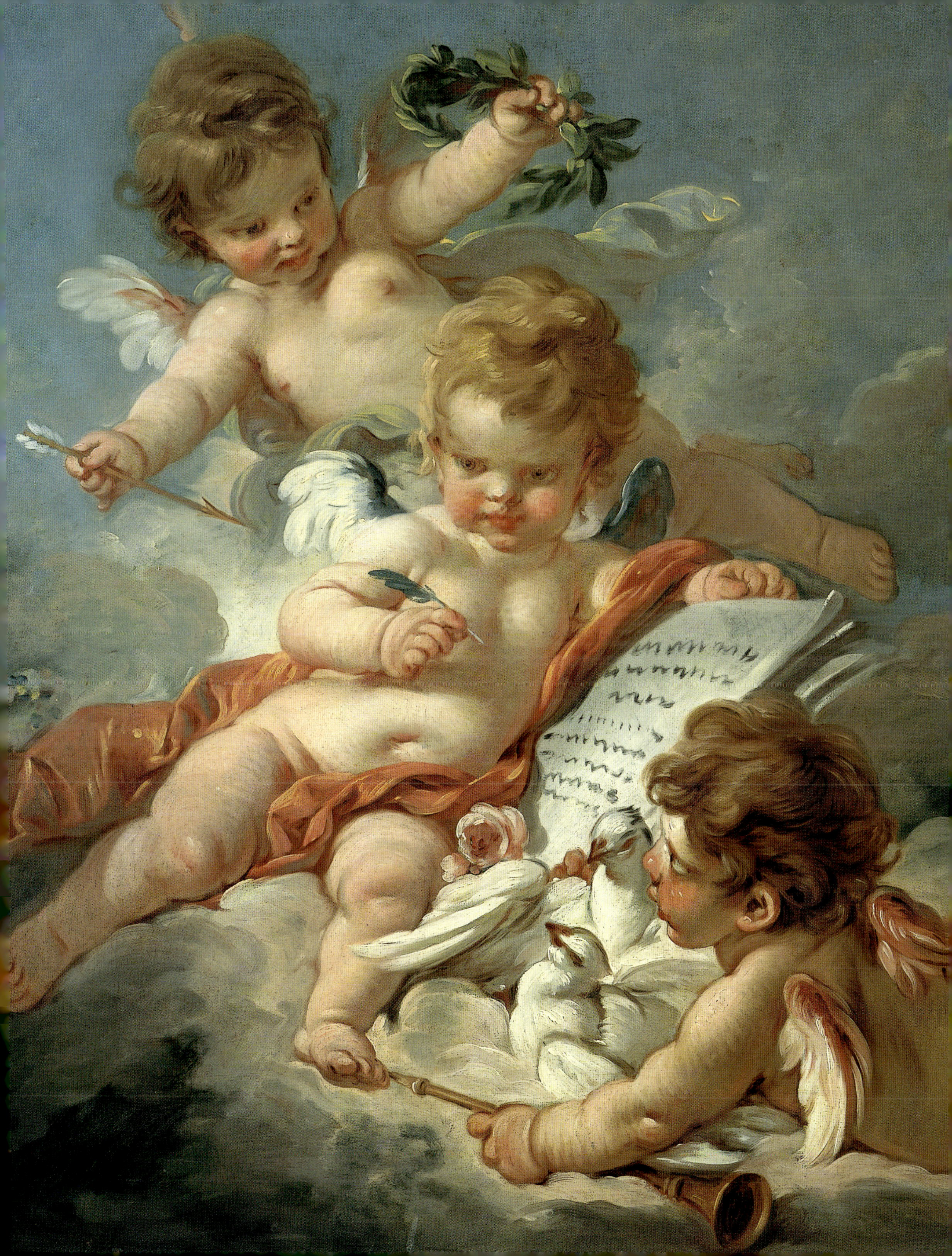

4
Venus and Nymphs

François Guérin (? – 1791/93?)

Oil on canvas
83 × 129 cm
SIGNED on the right: *F. Guérin*
INV: GE 8419
PROVENANCE: acquired in 1938 from the collection
of A.N. Tolstoy, Moscow

Very little is known about François Guérin, except
that he was in Paris from 1761 to 1791. He is
mainly known as a genre painter and portraitist.
Mythological subjects are very rare for him, which
makes the Hermitage's *Venus and Nymphs* all the
more interesting. The work, which is signed by the
artist, is an interpretation of a subject similar to
those of François Boucher, while Guérin's
portraits and genre paintings recall the style of his
other famous contemporary, Jean-Baptiste Greuze.

Like Boucher, Guérin depicted the ancient
goddess of love as young and beautiful, but
covered her nakedness with diaphanous cloth.
Venus is enjoying relaxing in the company of two
nymphs and her mischievous son Cupid, who is
armed with his bow and is always ready to pierce
the hearts of both gods and humans with the
arrows of love. Beautiful flowers are scattered
around Venus, while doves – birds dedicated to
the goddess – are cooing at her feet. ED

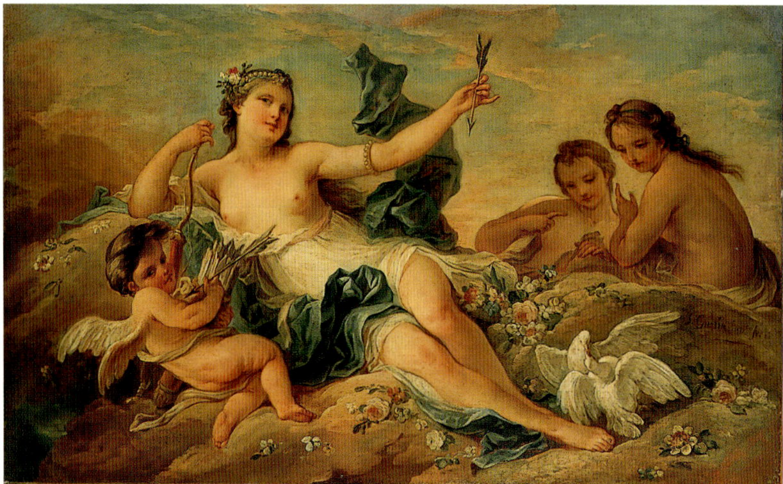

5
Cupid Sharpening his Arrow

1750

Charles-Joseph Natoire (1700–77)

Oil on canvas
55.5 × 42.5 cm
SIGNED and dated on the left, on the stand of the
grindstone: *C. Natoire 1750*
INSCRIBED on a scroll, lying next to the quiver:
Non Dum Pungit ('it doesn't prick yet')
INV: GE 7653
PROVENANCE: acquired in 1772 as part of the collection
of Pierre Crozat, Paris; 1854, sold at auction on the
instructions of Nicholas I; after 1854, collection of
B.N. and V.N. Khanenko, Kiev; State Museum of
Western and Eastern Art, Kiev; 1932, returned to
the Hermitage
BIBLIOGRAPHY: Boyer, no. 77; Cat. Crozat, p. 54;
Dussieux, no. 961; Georgi, p. 480; Livret XIX, p. 189,
no. 99; Natoire, ex. cat., p. 43; Stuffmann, p. 131,
no. 154; Wrangel, p. 129

According to some traditions Cupid, the god of
love, was the son of Venus; according to others,
her companion. In later mythology, the primary
source for European artists, he was the son of
Venus and Mars, the deity who ruled over nature
and over the moral world of mortals and gods.
Usually he was depicted as a winged infant or boy,
sometimes as a beautiful youth. The flower and
lyre, his original attributes in fine art, came to be
replaced by the arrows of love and a flaming torch.
The god of love used two kinds of arrow: gold,
for happy, mutual love, or lead, for unrequited
love. One source of inspiration for artists who
depicted Cupid was an ode by Anacreon entitled
'The Arrows of Eros' (Ode 28).

However, this scene depicting Cupid
preparing his arrows is very unusual. In a painting
by Hendrick Goltzius in the Hermitage Cupid
is tempering his arrows in the fire, while in a
composition by Francesco Guardi (Prussian
Collection, Cultural Heritage Foundation, Berlin),
two cupids forge arrows on an anvil. ED

6

Cupid Sharpening his Arrows
L'Amour aiguisant ses traits

1770

Pierre-Charles Lévesque (1736–1812)
After the painting by Pierre-Jacques Cazes
(1676–1754)

Etching
384 × 263 mm; 535 × 410 mm
INSCRIPTIONS: *L'AMOUR AIGUISANT SES TRAITS.*
Pour aiguiser une flèche cruelle
A quoi bon tant de soins, Amour, Tyran des coeurs?
Va te placer dans les yeux d'une belle;
Ils sauront te fournir des traits toujours vainqueurs.
Le Tableau Original est dans le Cabinet de M. Valade
Peintre du Roi.
Cazes Pinx / P. Car Levesque Sculp. / A Paris chés
J. Fr. Chereau rue S.! Jacques au coin de la rue des
Mathurins.
INV: OG-129477
PROVENANCE: before 1928, from main collection
(Lugt Suppl. 2681ª); acquired before 1830s
BIBLIOGRAPHY: Le Blanc II, p. 548, no. 4 (*L'Amour
aiguisant une flèche*); Ozerkov, no. 3; P.-B. II, p. 712

Since late antiquity Cupid has traditionally been
portrayed as a semi-naked boy – either an infant
with plump arms and legs, or a youth planing a
bow (from Hercules' staff) and pursuing nymphs.

Cupid is winged, for nothing is more ephemeral
than the passion brought by him (Droulers, p. 50).
'Artists give Eros wings to hint at the mobility he
possessed', writes Heliodorus (*Ethiopica*, p. 80).
With a look of concentration he is occupied with
serious business: behind a grindstone, which is
turning, and pressing on a pedal he is sharpening
the ends of his arrows. Merry pranks need careful
preparation.

Cupid is as careful when sharpening his arrows
as he is indiscriminate in selecting his target.
Moreover, in order to hit a target which has fallen
within his field of vision – a nymph, perhaps, who
has caught sight of the handsome Apollo – it costs
him nothing to select an arrow from his quiver at
random. The element of chance lies in the fact that
Cupid's quiver contains two types of arrow: 'one
banishes love and the other inspires it'. 'The one
which inspires with a hook has a sharp glinting
point; / The one which banishes is blunt and is
lead under a reed' (*Metamorphoses* I, pp. 468–71).
It is the golden arrow which inspires love and thus
requires sharpening, since it is destined to penetrate
the very depths of the heart. In French paintings
and engravings of the eighteenth century Cupid can
often be seen holding two arrows with different tips.

Pierre-Charles Lévesque was an amateur
engraver, but in Russia he was better known as a
writer. From 1773 to 1780 he worked in St Petersburg,
having come there at the recommendation of

Diderot, and there he wrote his *History of Russia*.
His engraving contains a whole range of
incongruities: a clumsily depicted grindstone belt,
unrealistic draping and background, an odd-looking
water vessel which the water enters by some unknown
means. Notwithstanding all of this, the picture is
a characteristic mid-eighteenth-century depiction of
the surroundings of the chubby, capricious little god
who distributes charms and inspires passions. DO

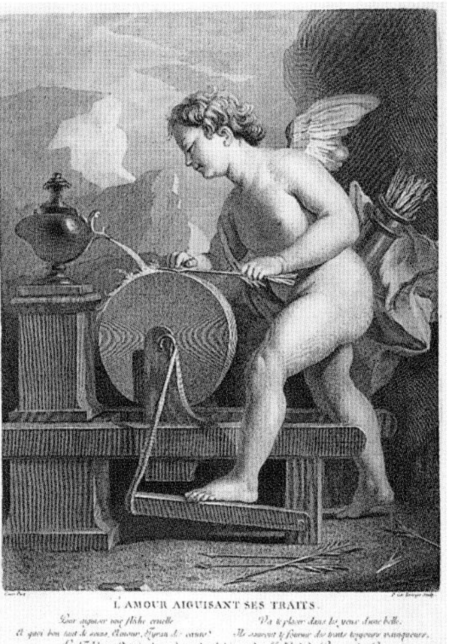

7

Menacing Cupid
L'Amour menaçant

1755

Jean Daullé (1703–63)
After the painting by Charles-Antoine Coypel
(1694–1752)

Engraving and etching
410 × 275 mm; 545 × 400 mm
INSCRIPTIONS: *Qui que tu sois, Voicy ton Maitre:*
Il le fut, il l'est, ou doit l'être.
Voltaire
Peint par C Coypel premier Peintre du Roi / Gravé par
J Daullé Gr du Roi / Le Tableau original haut de 3. pieds
et large de 2. pi. est dans le cabinet de M. De la Popliniere
/ à Paris chez l'Auteur ruë du Platre S.! Jacques à coté du
College de Cornouaille A.P.D.R.
INV: OG-128612
PROVENANCE: before 1928, from main collection
(Lugt Suppl. 2681ª); acquired before 1830s
BIBLIOGRAPHY: DE, pp. 97–8; Huber-Rost VIII, p. III,
no. 21; IFF VI, p. 112, no. 113 (state not noted: the
Hermitage impression has no date beneath the image);
Le Blanc II, p. 97, no. 9; Lefrançois 1994, p. 244A;
Ozerkov, no. 1; P.-B. I, p. 667, no. 17

Coypel's Cupid is either beckoning or – as
contemporaries of the artist supposed – wagging
his finger menacingly. The critic Lafont de Saint-
Yenne noted in 1747 the special mastery of Coypel,

who managed to combine in Cupid's face two
mutually contradictory but equally inherent
qualities: simplicity, and even tenderness, with
cunning and treachery. The critic writes, quite
justifiably, that in this face there is no beauty or
expression of divinity; the heavy cloth knotted
around his waist likewise does little to make Cupid
any more attractive. This description perfectly
corresponds to the image of Eros expressed by
Diotima in Plato's *Symposium*.

Coypel's painting *Menacing Cupid*, which was
shown at the Salon of 1746, and after which the
engraving was made, has been lost. It is known that
it was oval in shape. The engraver Jean Daullé,
who was acclaimed as a portrait painter, took
particular care over the depiction of Cupid's face.
The impression in the Hermitage collection is from
the state before inscription of a date; this state is
not recorded in the *Inventaire du fonds français*.
The Daullé engraving was exhibited at the Salon
of 1755. Cupid's crafty half-smile, half-grimace is
evidence of his essential duality, as described by
the participants of Plato's *Symposium*. 'The gesture
of Cupid's hand and his entire appearance show
that he is planning something malicious,' wrote
a critic in *Mercure* in October 1756. In this light
Voltaire's pithy couplet engraved beneath this
print looks mocking ('Inscription pour une statue
de l'Amour', *Poésies mêlées*, XI). It proclaims
Cupid to be teacher, mentor and educator from
time immemorial and for ever. For indeed it was

precisely in this capacity that the eighteenth
century considered, judged, used and ultimately
outlasted the perfidious Cupid. 'Where Cupid
is the teacher a king is nothing but a slave,
notwithstanding the lofty position which Heaven
has given him.' These are the words of Crébillon,
from his 1703 tragedy *Idoménée* (II, 3); they
beautifully characterise such attitudes towards
'Cupid the Teacher'. DO

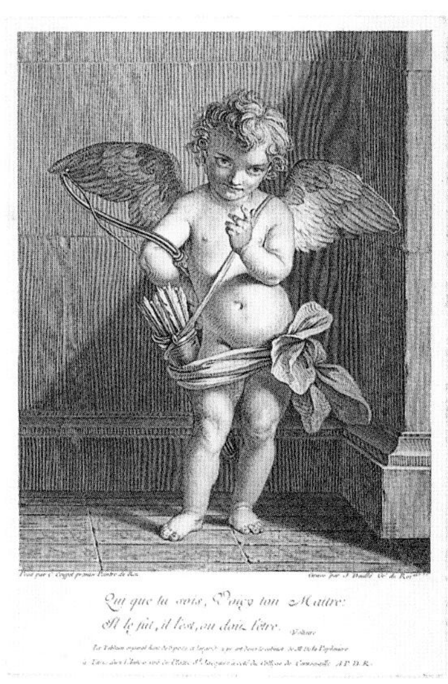

8

Menacing Cupid
L'Amour menaçant

1763

Christian von Mechel (1737–1817)
After the painting by Charles Vanloo (1705–65)

Etching
410 × 295 mm; 455 × 334 mm
INSCRIPTIONS: *L'AMOUR MENAÇANT*
   Dédié à Monseigneur le Duc de Praslin Pair de Françe,
   Chevalier des Ordres du Roy, Ministre Sécretaire d'Etat
   des Affaires Etrangeres. / Le Tableau qui a 3 pied de
   Haut sur 2 et demi de Large est tiré du Cabinet de
   Monseigneur le Duc / Par son très Humble et très
   Obeissant Serviteur C de Mechel
Peint par Charles Vanloo Premier Peintre du Roy. 1761. /
Gravé a Paris par C. de Mechel 1763 [corrected on the
   engraving to 1764]
INV: OG-147769
PROVENANCE: before 1928, from main collection
   (Lugt Suppl. 2681ᵃ); acquired before 1830s
BIBLIOGRAPHY: Le Blanc II, p. 632, no. 7; Lefrançois
   1994, p. 244; Nagler KL XIX, p. 369; Ozerkov, no. 2;
   Sahut, p. 84, no. 175; Gaz. B.-A. LV (1960),
   p. 9, pl. 27

'Young Cupid is wild, his temper obstinate,'
warns Ovid (*Ars Amatoria* I, 9). A bow and arrow
are his principal weapons. He carries a gold quiver
and full-length arrow with a bow always at the
ready. Cupid aims directly at the person looking at
the engraving. The optical effect echoes Ovid's
verse: 'The arrows from his quiver, flying straight
into my breast, burn my heart' (*Ars Amatoria* I, 22).
At the same time it is a figurative play on Virgil's
famous phrase 'love conquers all, let us yield to
love' ('Omnia vincit amor, et nos cedamus amori';
Eclogues 10, 69).

   This etching, after the painting by Charles
Vanloo, was created by the Swiss von Mechel.
The orientation is the same as the original, which
is now kept in Pavlovsk Palace Museum on the
outskirts of St Petersburg. In the State Hermitage
collection there is another state of the etching with
the address of the engraver in the lower left-hand
corner: 'Rue Sᵗ. Honoré vis à vis celle de l'Echelle
chez Mʳ. le Noir Notaire.' (inv. OG-147770). The
Vanloo painting was exhibited in the Salon of 1761.
Diderot describes what he considers to be Cupid's
incorrect pose, and launches into an argument
about how artists handle Cupid's arrows less
skilfully and naturally than do poets: 'In this
picture Cupid may threaten with his arrow, but
he does so without beauty. The victim is not a
physical presence in the picture: the artist seems
to have forgotten about allegory, and fires not a
metaphorical but an altogether real arrow at his
viewer' (*Les Salons* I, 34).

   The work contains an allegorical as well
as erotic subtext. In eighteenth-century French
gallant literature military, and particularly infantry,
vocabulary was used euphemistically: fire (*tirer*),
spear (*lance*), arrow (*flèche*) and so on. The two
vocabularies are directly combined in the title
of Jacob De Gheyn II's engraving *The Archer
and the Milkmaid* (*c.* 1610; Hollstein, De Gheyn
nr. 108; Hot Dry Men, cat. 49), which may have
been a source of inspiration for Vanloo when
he created his visual technique of 'aiming at
the audience'. De Gheyn's archer is in every
sense 'standing to attention': the string of his
bow is taut, the crotch of his trousers strained.
It is worth mentioning Vanloo's subtlety in
concealing Cupid's nudity with a rose-bush
branch, thus avoiding the forthright approach
of De Gheyn, who makes the linguistic metaphor
materially explicit.

   The nature around Cupid is fragrant and
beautiful. The eye discerns beautiful roses,
flowers of fiery passion – a passion which will
grip whomever the arrow strikes. Telling of the
accomplishments of Eros in *Symposium*, Agathon
describes him as the most beautiful and perfect
of the gods: 'And you can judge the beauty of
this god's flesh because he lives among flowers.
For Eros does not alight on what has faded or
grown pale – be it soul, body or anything else;
he stops and dwells only in places where
everything is blooming and fragrant.' DO

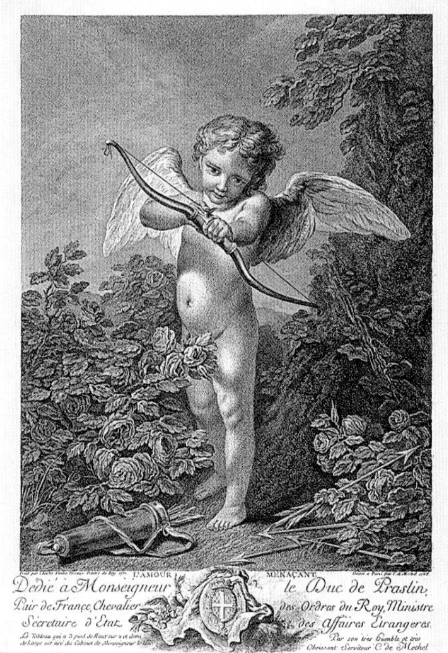

9
The Warrior Cupid
L'Amour Guerrier

1780s

Ambroise-Marguérite Bardin (1768–?)
After the composition by Jean Bardin (1732–1809)

Stipple engraving, brown-tone impression
218 × 161 mm
INSCRIPTIONS: *L'AMOUR GUERRIER / Dedié à M^r le
Comte Auguste de Louvois.* Device on the coat of arms:
Melius frangi quam flecti [Better to break than to bend]
*Bardin inv. et del. / Mlle Bardin sculp. / Se vend à Paris
chez Bardin Peintre du Roi. rue du Foin S. Jacques.*
INV: OG-123177
PROVENANCE: before 1928, from main collection;
   acquired before 1830s
BIBLIOGRAPHY: IFF II, p. 51, no. 1; Le Blanc I, p. 148,
   no. 2; Ozerkov, no. 4; Th.-B. II, p. 489

This is one of two engravings by the minor artist
Ambroise-Marguérite Bardin, engraved after
drawings by her father and teacher Jean Bardin.
Her husband, called Molière, was the director
of a porcelain factory. In the eighteenth century
engravings were often a source for compositions
on porcelain, and stylistically Bardin's works are
close to French porcelain painting.

The engraving is interesting for its
iconography, which looks back to ancient
emblems. Dressed in armour and hung with
weaponry, Cupid stands before us as an
unconquerable warrior, the personification of
the all-vanquishing power of love. The diverse
methods of love's campaign are seen as elements
of his military tactics. Thus, for example, in
Philip Ayres' *Emblemata amatoria* (1680s) the
Warrior Cupid is depicted as an adroit and
plucky fighter whose feet are adorned with little
wings similar to those of Mercury (Ayres,
emb. 8).

In Bardin's engraving the Warrior Cupid
is standing solemnly before us, fully armed with
his bow and quiver, with the tents of an army
camp visible in the background. Thus he stands
in the victor's camp in love's battlefield. His
head is adorned with feathers. His finger points
to the flames of a bonfire of rose bushes, the
flowers of Venus. This plump, clumsy little boy
is capable of saddling a menacing satyr (as in the
painting by Antoine Coypel, engraved by C.
Dupuy, 1719; Le Blanc II, p. 158, no. 3, inv. OG-
400654), cutting himself a bow from Hercules'
staff (as in the sculpture by Edmé Bouchardon,
1750; Paris, Louvre), and, freely playing with
Mars' weapons, even encroaching upon Venus's
power over love.

By his appearance the armed Cupid is
proclaiming to all that love is capable of disarming
the strong and discouraging the cunning. 'All is
fair in love and war', as the early-seventeenth-
century English proverb says. But Cupid will
always triumph: *et omnia vincit Amor.* DO

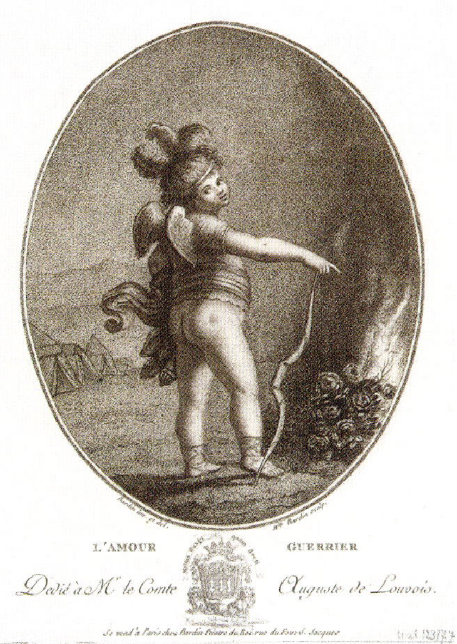

10

No Love without Suffering,
No Rose without Thorns
Nul amour sans peine,
Nul rose sans épine

1720

François-Bernard Lépicié (1698–1755)
After the painting by Jean-Marc Nattier (1685–1766)

Etching and stipple engraving
326 × 245 mm (trimmed sheet)
INSCRIPTIONS: *Nul amour sans peine Nul Rose sans Epine
   Rien n'est exempt d'amour, quand un coeur est Sévère
   C'est qu il n'a point trouvé l'Objet fait pour luy plaire.
   Souvent trop tard helas, un tendre engagement
   <No>us prouve qu'on ne peut estre heureux en aimant.
   Telle est de ce Portrait la fiction badine,
   Le Peintre nous fait voir par ce bizar retour
   Que jamais il ne fut de Rose sans épine,
   Et que les Deplaisirs; accompagnent Lamour.*
   *J.M.Nattier inv. et Pinx / B. lEpicier sculp. / A Paris chez
   Duchange Graveur du Roy rue S Jaques 1720*
WATERMARK: *IHS* (see Heawood no. 2983 [1743])
INV: OG-129747
PROVENANCE: before 1928, from main collection
   (Lugt Suppl. 2681^a); acquired before 1830s
BIBLIOGRAPHY: Delteil, p. 193; Le Blanc II, p. 538,
   nos. 53/54; Ozerkov, no. 15; P.-B. II, p. 664, no. 24;
   Salmon 1999, p. 20, fig. 8 (addressed 'A Paris chés
   Basan')

Cupid is punished for his escapades, painfully
beaten by the most beautiful flowers in the world.
The rose is the flower of Venus, the image of
perfect beauty. From late antiquity the rose was the
traditional metaphor for a beautiful woman. In his
poem 'Hero and Leander', Musaeus (AD 400–500)
describes Hero's beauty thus:

> A bright blush played on her snowy cheeks,
>   they were as two roses in bud,
> And you might perhaps have compared her
>   body to a meadow of fragrant roses,
> Thus it shone with bright beauty,
> And her delicate feet were fleetingly glimpsed
>   beneath a white tunic
> (vv. 58–62)

European culture sees the rose as a union of
contradictions: the stem of the most beautiful
flower is covered in sharp thorns which painfully
prick the unwary. The ancients believed that love,
too, was both beautiful and bitterly painful. The
scent and beauty of the rose enabled European
culture to proclaim it the flower of Venus, and
to compare the pricks from its thorns with the
wounds of love; the pain caused by love was
thus directly associated with the rose. As Venus
hastened to her wounded beloved Adonis, she
pricked her foot on a white rose, and the drops
of her blood coloured red the white petals of the
flower of love. Even today red roses symbolise
rebirth and the triumph of love over death.

Christianity resolves this paradox by
asserting that a rose without thorns did once exist.
St Ambrosius of Milan wrote that the only rose
without thorns grew in Eden and became covered
in thorns at the moment of the fall from grace.
And it is a rose which is seen by the hero of the
Divine Comedy when he enters into the heart of
Paradise: the gigantic rose of paradise becomes
a great symbol of heavenly love. DO

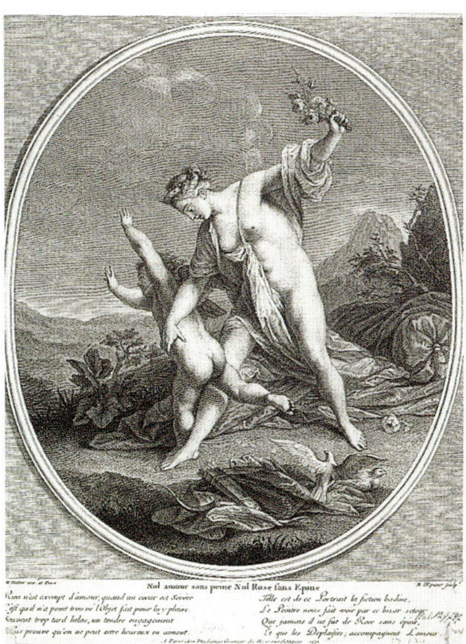

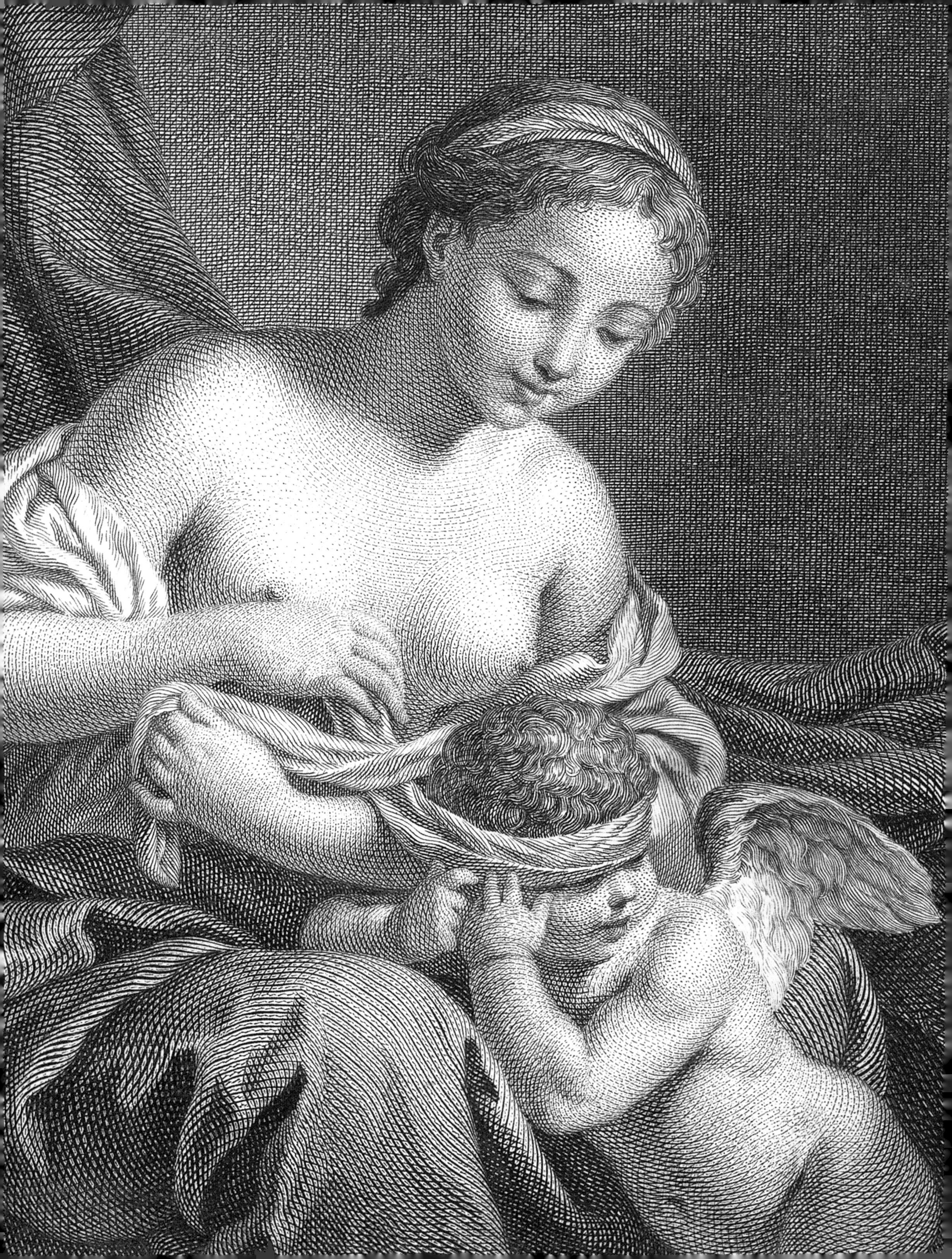

11

The Infancy of Cupid
Premier age de l'Amour

1783

Jacques Boüilliard (1744–1806)
After the painting by Louis Lagrenée (1725–1805)

Engraving and etching
315 × 250 mm; 496 × 332 mm
INSCRIPTIONS: *PREMIER AGE DE L'AMOUR /
A Monsieur le Marquis de Cossé Ancien Menin du Roy
Brigadieu de ses Armées &c. / Tiré de son Cabinet. /
Par son très Humble et Obeissant Serviteur Boüilliard.*
*Peint par L. Lagrenée / Gravé par J. Boüilliard / A Paris
chez J.Couché rue S.t Hyacinthe la 3.e porte à droite en
entrant par la Place S.t Michel.*
WATERMARK: *DUPUY FIN* (cf. Heawood no. 3309
[1752])
INV: OG-123259
PROVENANCE: before 1928, from main collection
(Lugt Suppl. 2681ª); acquired before 1830s
BIBLIOGRAPHY: IFF III, p. 301, no. 3; Ozerkov, no. 8;
Sandoz 1988 I, p. 252, no. 305 B, b (rare)

Like the Christ-child or an ordinary mortal, Cupid
is nestling against his mother's breast. Late Greek
mythology, adopted by art of the modern era,
removes sinister chthonic features from the image
of Eros, rendering his childhood as similar as
possible to that of a mortal child. Thereafter Venus
is frequently portrayed as a mother, and entire
series of 'family scenes' appear: the education and
punishment of the disobedient child, his serene
sleep and dilatory study.

This engraving, together with three others
(cat. 12, 13, 14), belongs to a series of four
engraved by Jacques Boüilliard after paintings
by Lagrenée, which were probably exhibited in
the Salon of 1779. The current whereabouts of the
paintings is unknown. Sandoz classifies this series
of engravings as rare; only two engravings out of
the four are present in the collection of the Cabinet
des Estampes, Bibliothèque Nationale de Paris.
This exhibition presents the entire series, which is
held in the collection of the Print-room of the
Hermitage. DO

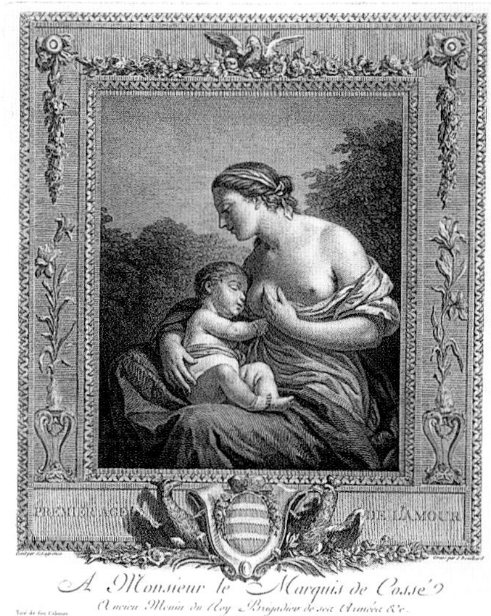

12

The Education of Cupid
Éducation de l'Amour

1783

Jacques Boüilliard (1744–1806)
After the painting by Louis Lagrenée (1725–1805)

Engraving and etching
308 × 245 mm; 402 × 278 mm
INSCRIPTIONS: *ÉDUCATION DE L'AMOUR /
A Monsieur le Marquis de Cosse Ancient Menin du Roy
Brigadieu de ses Armées &c. / Tiré de son Cabinet. /
Par son très Humble et Obeïssant Serviteur Boüilliard.*
*Peint par L. Lagrenée / Gravé par J. Boüilliard / A Paris
chez J.Couché Graveur rue S.t Hyacinthe Maison de
M.r Le Blanc.*
INV: OG-123260
PROVENANCE: before 1928, from main collection
(Lugt Suppl. 2681ª); acquired before 1830s
BIBLIOGRAPHY: Bourcard, p. 287; IFF III, p. 301, no. 2;
Ozerkov, no. 9; Sandoz 1988 I, p. 252, no. 305 B, b
(rare)

Venus is blindfolding Cupid. She at once restrains
and provokes him. The picture tells of Cupid's
blindness, his passion, which is akin to madness,
and of the notion that love is evil and perfidious.
In the central upper part of the frame, we see
Cupid's bow and arrow aimed directly at the
viewer. In the corners of the frame Cupid's altars
are laid with reeds and canes, symbols of the
grief and suffering caused by Cupid. The nymph
Syrinx turned into a reed after rejecting Pan's
advances and hurling herself into the waters
of the river Ladon in order to escape from him
(*Metamorphoses* I, 690–712).

The subject dates back to Titian's famous
painting showing Venus blindfolding Cupid
(*c.* 1565; Rome, Borghese Gallery), in which we
see a seated goddess blindfolding Cupid, who has
buried himself between her knees. At the same
time she gazes expressively upon another little boy
who is leaning against her shoulder. Two nymphs
extend a bow and arrows. Lagrenée/Boüilliard's
Cupid is craftily attempting to tweak the blindfold
in order to look at her from under it without being
noticed. DO

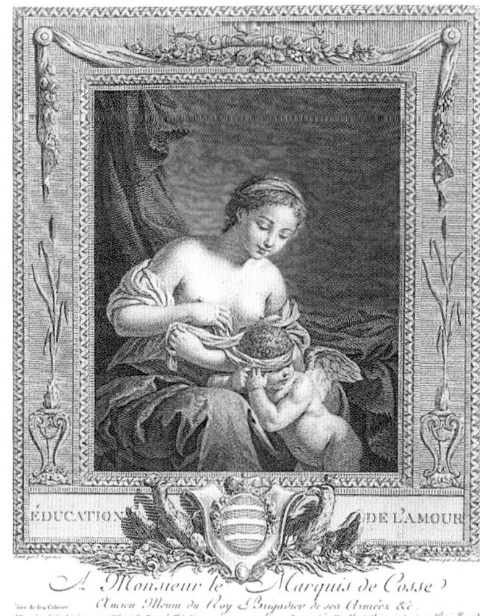

13

The Education of Cupid
Éducation de l'Amour

1783

Jacques Boüilliard (1744–1806)
After the painting by Louis Lagrenée (1725–1805)

Engraving and etching
312 × 248 mm; 402 × 277 mm
INSCRIPTIONS: *ÉDUCATION DE L'AMOUR /*
A Monsieur le Marquis de Cossé Ancien Menin du Roy
Brigadieu de ses Armées &c. / Tiré de son Cabinet. /
Par son très Humble et Obéissant Serviteur Boüilliard.
Peint par L.Lagrenée / Gravé par J.Boüilliard / A Paris
chez J. Couché rue S! Hyacinthe la 3.ᵉ porte à droite en
entrant par la Place S! Michel.
INV: OG-123261
PROVENANCE: before 1928, from main collection
(Lugt Suppl. 2681ᵃ); acquired before 1830s
BIBLIOGRAPHY: Bourcard, p. 287; IFF III, p. 301, no. 1;
Ozerkov, no. 10; Sandoz 1988 I, p. 252, no. 305 B, b
(rare)

Venus is teaching Cupid to read; the subject matter,
in all likelihood, is the *Ars amatoria*. However, the
decorative framing of the scene also contains
Mercury's caduceus, which suggests the cunning
inherent in the lover's art. Amongst the rose
branches the caduceus is combined with a burning
torch with which Cupid will inflame the hearts of
his victims. From an emblematic point of view
the caduceus appears as a sign of the deceitful
eloquence of those in love. Thus, for example,
in Ayres' *Emblemata amatoria*, the caduceus is
precisely the attribute that 'Eloquent Eros' holds
in his hands (Ayres, emb. 21).

Traditionally, it is in fact Mercury who teaches
Cupid to read. The original iconography of this
subject dates back to Italian painting – to the works
of Correggio (*c.* 1525–8; London, National
Gallery), Titian (1546; Texas, El Paso Museum
of Art), and Giovanni Francesco Romanelli (mid-
seventeenth century) amongst others. Prints
played the principal role in the spread of this
subject in French art of the eighteenth century.
In particular, Boüilliard made an engraving after a
painting by Titian which was part of the collection
of the Duc d'Orléans in the eighteenth century
(IFF III, p. 305, no. 14; P.-B. I, p. 233).

This rarer iconographic variation, in which
the principal role has been allotted to Venus, is
intended to emphasise the theme of motherhood.
Cupid is a sweet child who innocently, without
shame, grasps the subtleties of the art of love.
But as Cupid's eyes move swiftly down the scroll,
it is as if the wings that will give flight to his
cunning begin to sprout on his back. DO

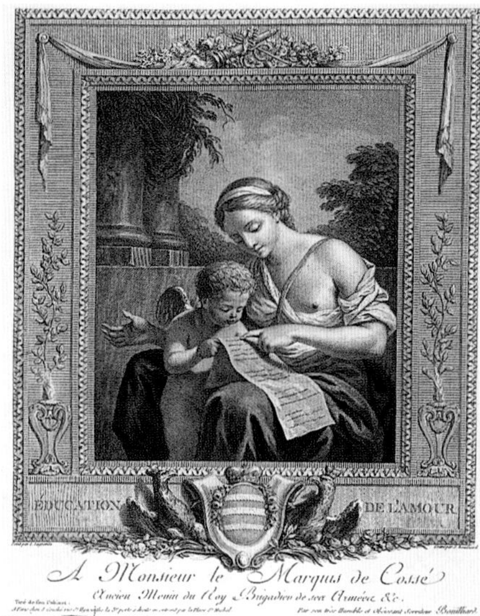

14

The Punishment of Cupid
Punition de l'Amour

1783

Jacques Boüilliard (1744–1806)
After the painting by Louis Lagrenée (1725–1805)

Engraving and etching
308 × 246 mm; 485 × 331 mm
INSCRIPTIONS: *PUNITION DE L'AMOUR /*
A Monsieur le Marquis de Cossé Ancien Menin du Roy
Brigadieu de ses Armées &c. / Tiré de son Cabinet. /
Par son très Humble et Obéissant Serviteur Boüilliard.
Peint par L.Lagrenée / Gravé par J.Bouilliard / A Paris
chez J. Couché rue S! Hyacinthe la 3ᵉ porte à droite par
la Place S! Michel.
WATERMARK: *FIN DE D♥TAMIZIER AUVERGNE*
1740 (see Heawood no. 1237, no. 1314)
INV: OG-123262
PROVENANCE: before 1928, from main collection
(Lugt Suppl. 2681ᵃ); acquired before 1830s
BIBLIOGRAPHY: Bourcard, p. 287; IFF III, p. 301, no. 4;
Ozerkov, no. 11; Sandoz 1988 I, p. 252, no. 305 B, b
(rare)

Venus is punishing Cupid for his pranks, bending
him over her knee in an altogether everyday
manner. Cupid can only plaintively beg for mercy:
the hands of Venus are holding roses. As an image
of just desserts this subject was very popular in
eighteenth-century France. Examples include
Étienne Fessard's engraving after the drawing of
Edmé Bouchardon (Le Blanc II, p. 226, no. 27, inv.
OG-123706), an engraving by François-Bernard
Lépicié after the painting by Jean-Marc Nattier
(cat. 10), and an anonymous engraving ('Peint par
E.L.S. / Gravé par ***', inv. OG-131262). DO

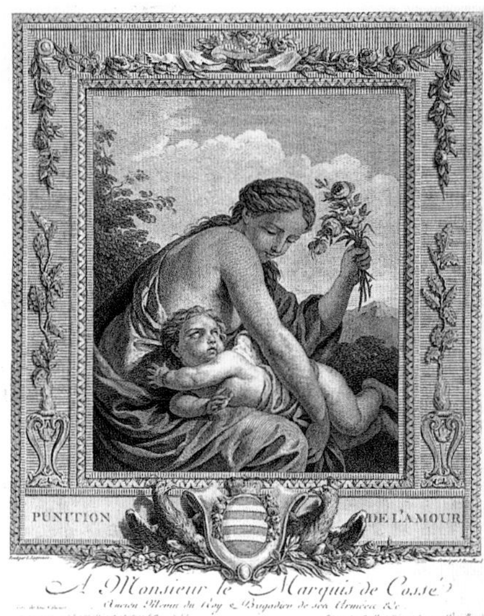

15

Sleeping Cupid
L'Amour qui sommeille

1780s

Studio of Pierre-François Basan (1723–97)
After the drawing by François-Marie-Isidore
    Queverdo (1748–97); from a series of four
    'Emblèmes d'Amour'

Etching and stipple engraving
224 × 153 mm; 262 × 192 mm
INSCRIPTIONS: *L'AMOUR QUI SOMMEILLE*
    De ce Dieu jeunes coeurs, redoutés la puissance,
    S'il r'ouvre sa paupiere à la clarté du jour.
    Le regne de la Paix, comme de l'Innocence,
    Est le tems fortuné du sommeil de l'Amour.
    Queverdo del. / Basan exc.
WATERMARK: two-line inscription (illegible)
INV: OG-275279
PROVENANCE: 1931 (Lugt Suppl. 2681ᵃ)
BIBLIOGRAPHY: Bober–Rubinstein, p. 89, no. 51;
    Huber–Rost VIII, p. 270, no. 2; IFF II, p. 98, no. 30;
    Le Blanc III, p. 263, no. 1; Œuvre de Basan VI, no. 2;
    Ozerkov, no. 5; P.-B. III, pp. 366–70

This engraving after Queverdo's drawing comes
from a series of four bearing various images of
Cupid. The iconography of Cupid asleep on a
lion-skin holding poppies dates back to antiquity,
where it is found in bronze sculpture, on marble
sarcophagi, and marble and terracotta sculptures.
The Greek marble original, *Sleeping Eros*, in which
a boy is also tightly holding poppies, symbolic of
sleep, is in the Uffizi Gallery in Florence. Vasari
refers to a 'Sleeping Cupid' ('Cupido che dorme'),
which was shipped in 1488 from Naples to Florence
as a present to Lorenzo de Medici from King
Ferdinand I and installed in the Medici garden.
He also mentions that Michelangelo produced
a copy of a sculpture of the same name in ancient
marble (Norton 1957; Brown 1993). 'Sleeping
Cupid' iconography was also much employed
in Western-European painting, notably in the
works of Caravaggio, Battistello, Guido Reni
and Elisabetta Sirani. In French art the theme
was used by Nicolas-René Jollain (1781; London,
Wallace Collection, inv. P488) amongst others.

Cupid's carefree sleep in the lap of nature is
not without cost: someone has lain in wait for him
and deprived him of his bow and arrows. In an
emblem of Andrea Alciati (1534), Death is
breaking the arrows of the sleeping Eros. Love
dies, and Eros turns into Thanatos. Nothing
remains but to mourn the love which has gone,
never to return – as in the theme of the famous
painting by one of Antoine Caron's circle, *The
Funeral of Eros* (Paris, Louvre, inv. R.F. 1954-4).

However, Cupid, wearied by mischief, is also
an eternal target for Diana's chaste nymphs. Only
while he sleeps can they harm him. The fragments
of Cupid's bow and arrows strewn in the
foreground of Queverdo's drawing are clearly
the work of their hands. As soon as Cupid begins
to fall asleep they surround him, steal away his
bow and arrows and break them or throw them
into the fire; or else they cut off his wings while
he blithely slumbers; or they weave garlands of
flowers tightly around his body; or, finally, they
simply gambol joyfully without fearing his
cunning – as in the famous *Allégorie mythologique*
by an anonymous artist of the Fontainebleau
School (c. 1580; Paris, Louvre, inv. R.F. 1946-22).
In this painting the sleeping Cupid is also
surrounded by small fauns hoping to get their
hands on some miracle-working part of his
divine armoury. In Girolamo Mazzola Bedoli's
painting *Cupid's Slumber* (c. 1555; Chantilly,
Musée Condé, inv. 51) they manage to get hold
of his miraculous arrows, and all that remains is
quietly to remove the bow from his hands, which
hang limp with sleep.

Taking Cupid unawares while he is asleep
is the only way of obtaining power over him, if
only for a short time, and momentarily turning
love's capricious web to one's own favour. This
unrealisable dream is found in French art of the
eighteenth century, for example in Joseph-Marie
Vien's painting *Greek Girls Discover Eros Asleep in
the Garden*, painted in 1773 for Madame du Barry's
pavilion in Louvecienne (Paris, Louvre, inv. 8431;
Gaehtgens–Lugand, p. 191, no. 230).

The weariness of the god turns his triumphal
procession into a triumph *over* him. In Petrarch's
Triumphs the procession of Love is replaced by
the procession of Chastity. In this print by Basan,
should the triumph of Chastity over Eros be
linked to the appearance in the left background
of a church – the embodiment of Purity, Chastity
and Mercy in the eighteenth century? There is
a striking similarity between the sleeping infant
Cupid and the traditional image of the infant
Christ meditating on symbols of passion, or
simply sleeping surrounded by the Holy Family
and angels. DO

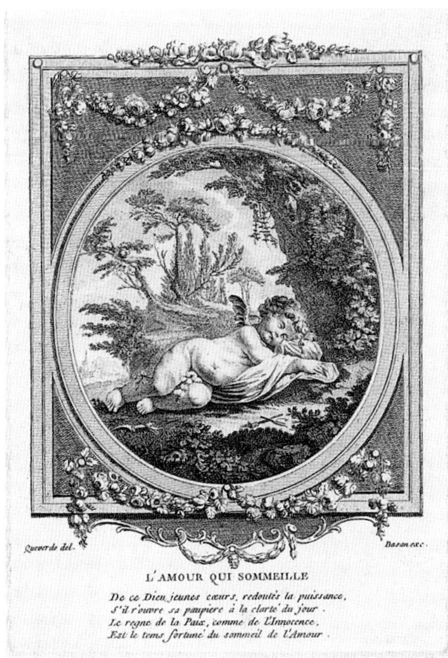

16

Venus Disarming Cupid

18th century

Circle of Corneille Van Cleve (1645–1732)

Bronze
Height 46.5 cm
INV: N.sk. 476 (pair with inv. N.sk. 477)
PROVENANCE: before 1920

Angered by her son's antics, Venus takes away Cupid's quiver and arrows, so preventing him from carrying out his insidious plans. This subject belongs to the group of works known as 'the Punishment of Cupid'. There are many famous images of Venus taking away Cupid's quiver and bow, breaking his arrow, or angrily spanking him with a bouquet of roses (cat. 10, 14).

Works similar to this pair of Hermitage bronzes – *Venus Disarming Cupid* and *Psyche Discovering Cupid* – can be found in many European collections. Although the two sculptures appear not to represent the same subject, they may have a common didactic subtext. On the one hand there is Venus, taking the quiver and arrows away from Cupid, thus preventing him from causing amorous suffering; on the other is Psyche, the symbol of the human soul, whose story teaches us that there is no love without suffering. AV

17

Psyche Discovering Cupid

18th century

Circle of Corneille Van Cleve (1645–1732)

Bronze
Height 46.5 cm
INV: N.sk. 477 (pair with inv. N.sk. 476)
PROVENANCE: before 1920

The statuette is based on the myth of Cupid and Psyche, which was first written in the second century AD by Apuleius, and retold in the second half of the seventeenth century by La Fontaine. The myth celebrates the all-conquering power of love.

In an attempt to discern the identity of her lover, Psyche has leant over the sleeping Cupid, illuminating him with the flame of her lamp. A drop of hot oil has fallen onto the forehead of the sleeping god and woken him. Cupid flees, and Psyche has to undergo a series of trials before she can find happiness again. The legend of Psyche – the human soul ready to follow a long and dangerous path in search of true love – is a common theme in works of art of the seventeenth and eighteenth centuries.

In this Hermitage bronze, there is no lamp, which has led some to suppose that it in fact depicts Venus bending over the sleeping Cupid (Kosareva, p. 15). The indisputable similarity to a statuette in the Wallace Collection in London, however, leaves little doubt that this is indeed Psyche. AV

18

Menacing Cupid
L'Amour menaçant

Model of 1755

Sculptor Étienne-Maurice Falconet
Sèvres Porcelain Factory, between 1766 and 1773

Soft-paste porcelain, biscuit
Height 23.3 cm
INV: ZF-23937
PROVENANCE: 1934, from the State Museum Fund

18a

Pedestal for Menacing Cupid

Sèvres Porcelain Factory, early 1760s

Soft-paste porcelain, polychrome painting, gilding
Height 7.5 cm
INSCRIBED ON PEDESTAL: *OMNIA VINCIT AMOR*
INV: ZF-20930
PROVENANCE: 1918, from the collection of A.S. Dolgorukov, Petrograd

The plaster model of the sly and mischievous god of love was made in 1755. In 1757 Falconet produced a marble version for Madame de Pompadour. This biscuit version was created at the factory in 1758 and reproduced countless times. The figure of Cupid reaching for his perfidious arrow, intended for some lovestruck target, while holding a finger to his lips as if appealing to the viewer not to give away his secret, achieved great popularity. Buyers were many and famous, the small god being found in almost every aristocratic home. JV

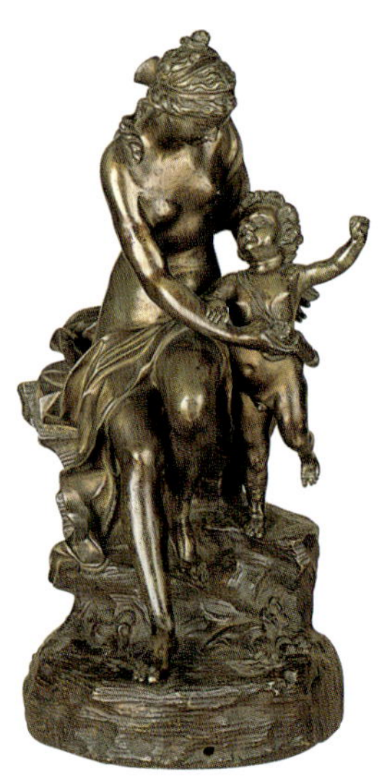

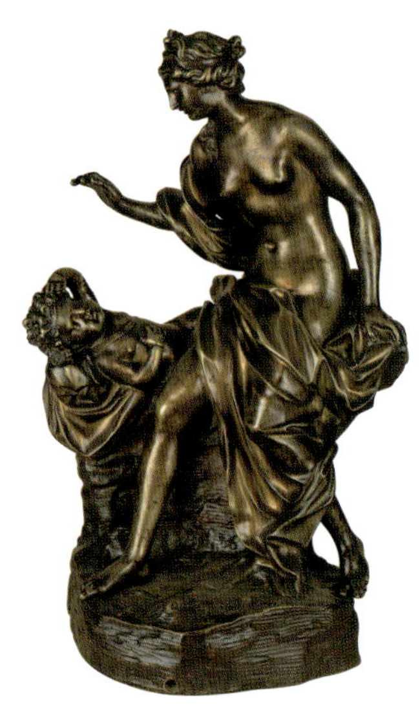

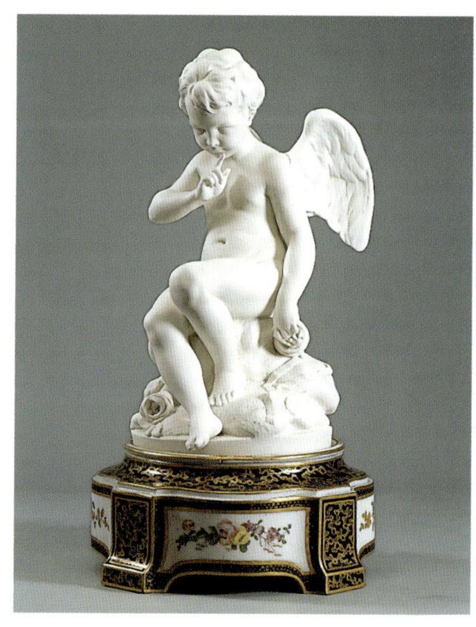

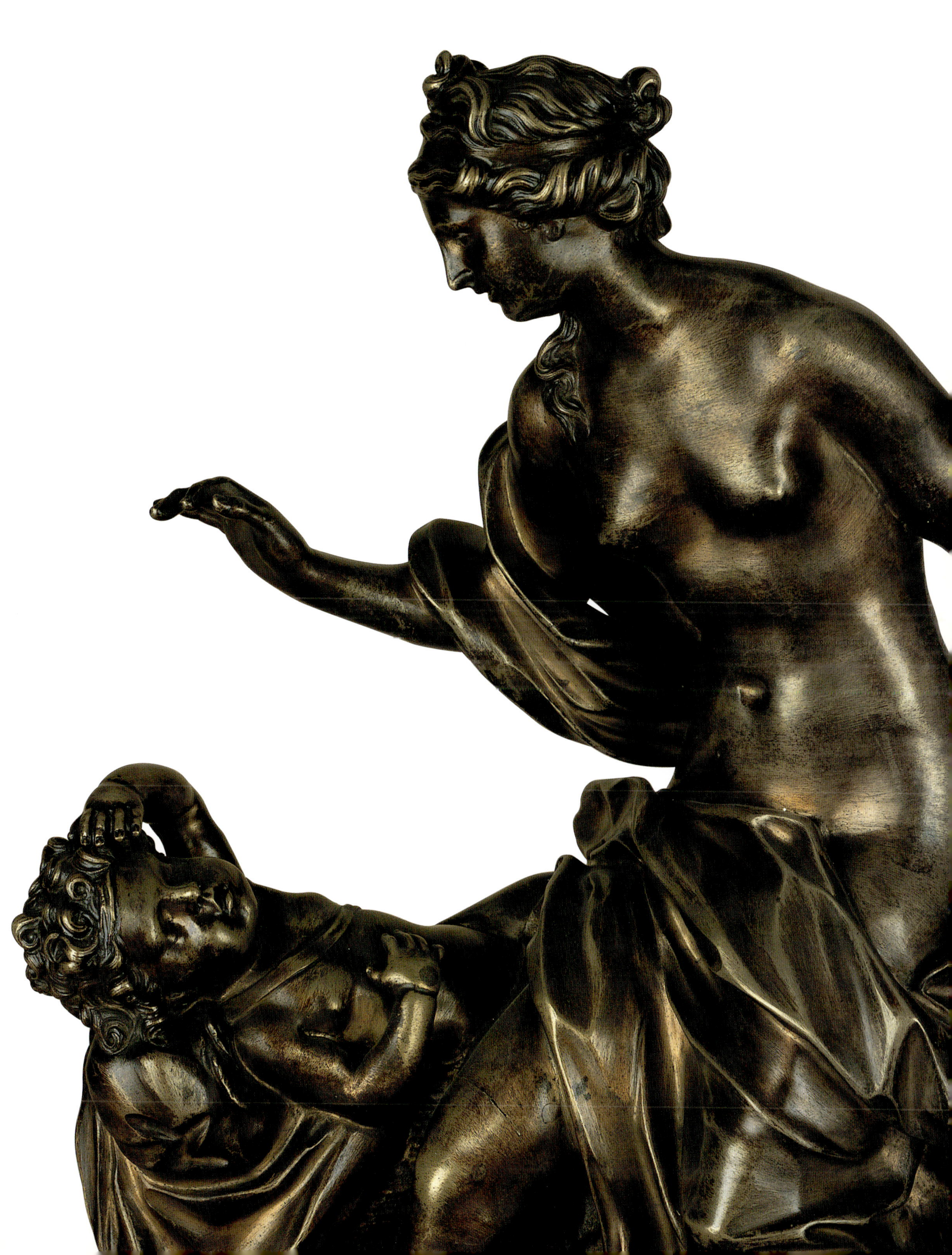

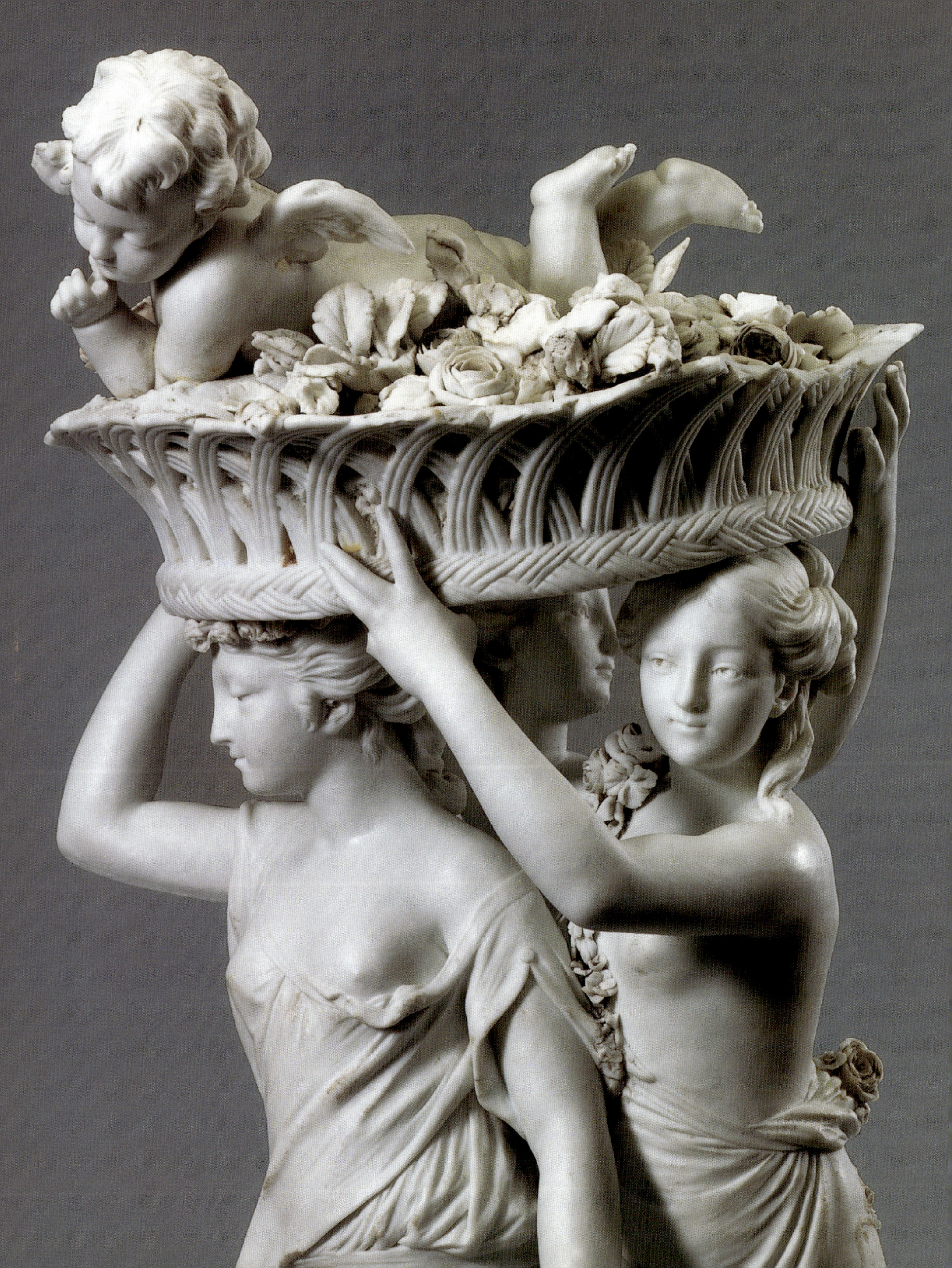

19

The Three Graces as Caryatids
Les trois Grâces Cariatides

Model of 1778

Sculptor Louis-Simon Boizot (1743–1809)
Sèvres Porcelain Factory, after 1780

Hard-paste porcelain, biscuit
Height 37 cm
INV: ZF-26619
PROVENANCE: 1959

Louis-Simon Boizot (1743–1809) was appointed
director of the sculpture studios at the Sèvres
Factory in 1773. Under Boizot, models which
copied works by outside sculptors and which were
not originally designed for biscuit were no longer
created. New models were made specially for
biscuit by Boizot himself (see also cat. 21), or by
Jossé-François-Joseph Le Riche. To judge by his
models from the early years, Boizot tried to imitate
Falconet, but these were pale imitations. Although
he lacked Falconet's mastery and talent, Boizot's
versatility and ability to adapt to the tastes of
the day or respond promptly to events that
preoccupied the court were notable. Models from
the early years are significantly better than the
later ones, which often display a superficial
prettiness or excessive sentimentality. NB

20

Cupid Sharpening his Arrow
L'Amour aiguisant une flèche

Dihl and Guérhard Factory, between 1781 and 1789

Hard-paste porcelain, biscuit
Height 16.5 cm
INV: ZF-25196
PROVENANCE: 1949, from the collection of the
    Evdokimovs

The Dihl and Guérhard Porcelain Factory
(1781–1831) was founded in Paris in 1781 by
the sculptor Christophe Dihl and the merchant
Antoine Guérhard. As well as fine tableware,
Dihl and Guérhard also made figures and groups
in high-quality biscuit. The figure of *Cupid
Sharpening his Arrow* is a fine example of the
factory's work. In the Hermitage there is most
of a service made in 1813 for the Empress
Josephine and Eugène de Beauharnais; all
the pieces and accompanying figures are richly
gilded. Some of the figures of cupids that form
part of the service were made after eighteenth-
century models, including a replica of the figure
of *Cupid Sharpening his Arrow*. NB

21

Cupid Preparing to Fire
his Arrow
*Amour se disposant à décocher
une flèche*

Model of 1774

Sculptor Louis-Simon Boizot (1743–1809)
Sèvres Porcelain Factory; replica of a marble
    figure made in 1772 for the Marquise Du Barry;
    this version a copy of the 1774 model, executed
    in 1913

Hard-paste porcelain, biscuit
Height 24.5 cm
INV: ZF-21932
PROVENANCE: after 1917, from the collection of Grand
    Duke Georgy Mikhailovich

See cat. 19. NB

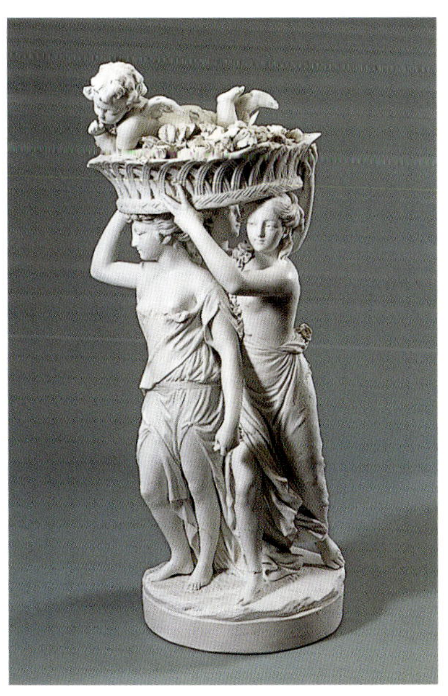

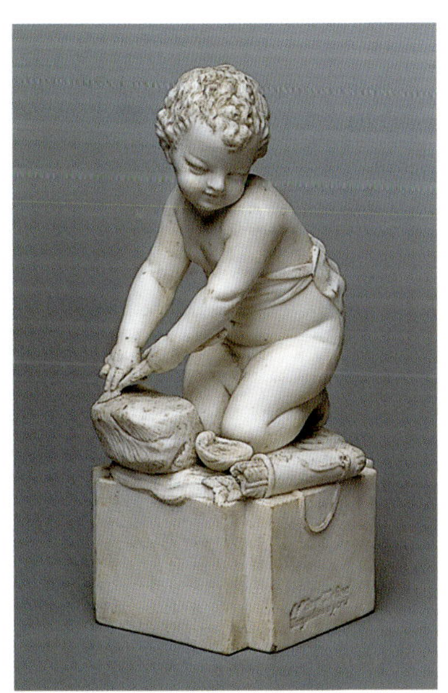

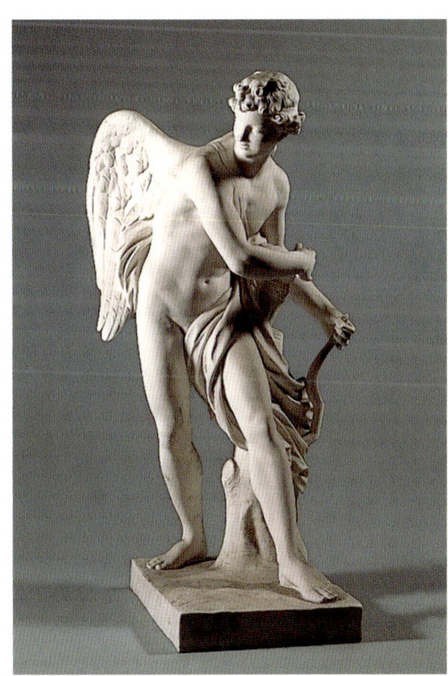

22

Blind Man's Bluff
Le petit colin-maillard

Model of 1795

Sculptor Louis-Simon Boizot (1743–1809) (?)
Sèvres Porcelain Factory

Hard-paste porcelain, biscuit
Height 20.5 cm
INV: ZF-23372
PROVENANCE: 1925, from the Museum of the Stieglitz
    School of Technical Design, Leningrad

The French Revolution undoubtedly provided
a source of inspiration for the articles produced
at Sèvres, with a succession of works showing
distinct features of neoclassicism. The subsequent
coup of 9 Thermidor (27 July 1794), which
brought about the fall of Robespierre, signalled
a marked change in the development of French
art as a whole, including porcelain modelling.
As the dominant artistic movement, neoclassicism
lost its revolutionary content, taking from
antiquity only mythological and historical subjects.
This work was created shortly afterwards; it is
not certain who the sculptor was, but stylistically
it is very similar to models by Boizot. NB

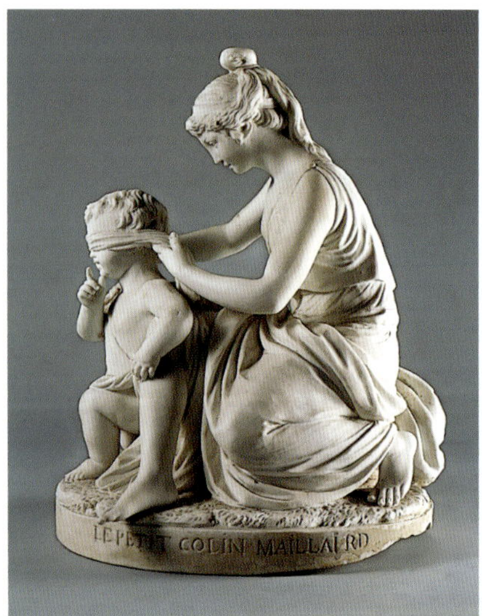

23

Tray
Plateau du roi

1755

Sèvres Porcelain Factory

Soft-paste porcelain, polychrome painting, gilding
Length 25.2 cm; width 17.7 cm
INV: ZF-23575
PROVENANCE: 1931, from the Winter Palace

The *plateau du roi* model has been known since
1753. Small trays of this type were used as stands
for two small jam dishes or were part of a déjeuner
set. Most probably this tray was part of the
déjeuner set described as 'Un déjeuner du Roy,
camayeu, enfans-pourpres, 288l' (Savill II,
pp. 590–2), which was one of the articles from the
Sèvres Factory supplied in 1757 by Louis XV
to his ambassador to Russia, the Marquis de
L'Hôpital, for use as diplomatic gifts.

A small tea or coffee service arranged on a
tray was given the name 'déjeuner' in 1753. The
composition of the déjeuner depended on the size
of the tray. It could include between one and four
cups and saucers and various other articles, most
often a milk-jug, sugar-bowl, tea- or coffee-pot,
and sometimes a tea-caddy. Crimson monochrome
painting ('camaïeu pourpre') appeared in about
1748 but did not become popular until 1752, when
Madame de Pompadour bought several pieces
with this decoration (Eriksen, p. 259). The painting
is by J.L. Morin and is an interesting example of
the artist's early work. JV

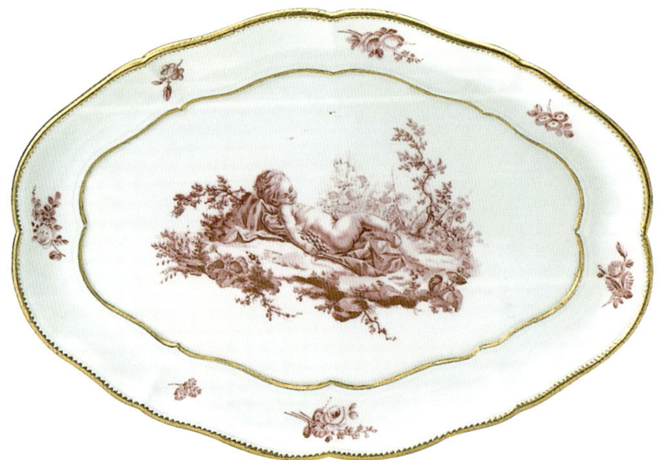

24
Tray and Sugar-bowl with Lid

Part of a breakfast service (déjeuner batcau),
missing the cup

1761

Sèvres Porcelain Factory

Soft-paste porcelain, polychrome painting, gilding
TRAY: height 5.6 cm; length 27.8 cm; width 12.4 cm
SUGAR-BOWL: height 7.2 cm; diameter 7.3 cm
INV: ZF-19884
PROVENANCE: 1918, from the collection of A.S.
    Dolgorukov, Petrograd

From 1749 the head of the painting studio at Sèvres
was the flower-painter Jean-Jacques Bachelier.
A wonderful artist, teacher and administrator, he
recruited François Boucher to work at the factory,
an artist whose pictorial subjects accorded superbly
with porcelain. Boucher's paintings and drawings
depicting landscapes, children, cupids and pastoral
scenes were distributed in large numbers as prints,
and became a primary source for Sèvres painters.

In 1736 Boucher published his *Livre de
groupes d'enfants*. The Sèvres painter of 'figures
and landscapes', André-Vincent Vieillard,
enthusiastically started to decorate porcelain with
'enfants de Boucher', using the many engravings
which the factory possessed. He also encouraged
the other artists at the factory to follow his
example. Little gardeners, mowers, bird-catchers
and cupids became extraordinarily popular. Under
Vieillard's influence, the Sèvres painters did not
always copy Boucher's subjects exactly. They
would often single out a figure they liked from the
drawing, perhaps slightly alter his or her external
attributes, and thus create a new porcelain world
of 'enfants de Vieillard'. The grace and charm
of these remarkable figures, combined with the
elegant forms of the pieces they decorate, more
than make up for drawing which is occasionally
a little inaccurate or execution which may appear
hasty (Belfort, 1976). JV

25
Cup and Saucer
Gobelet 'litron' et soucoupe

c. 1780

Sèvres Porcelain Factory

Soft-paste porcelain, polychrome painting, gilding
Height of cup 7.6 cm; diameter of saucer 14.7 cm
INV: ZF-23299
PROVENANCE: late 1920s, from the Museum of the
    Stieglitz School of Technical Design, Leningrad

The *litron* form was extraordinarily popular
throughout the eighteenth century. It was used
both for ceremonial services and for more modest
daily ware. In France the *litron* was a cylindrical
measuring glass usually made from wood, for
measuring flour, salt, grain etc. JV

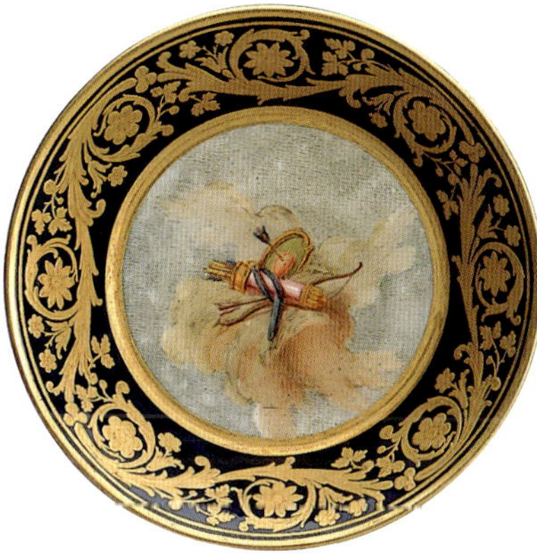
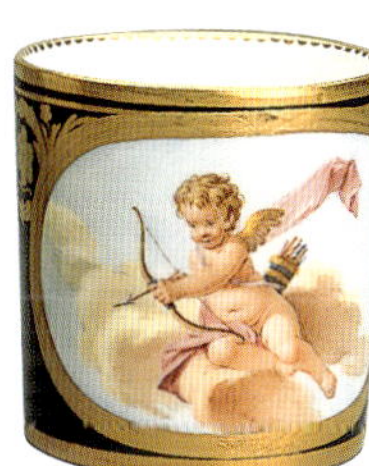

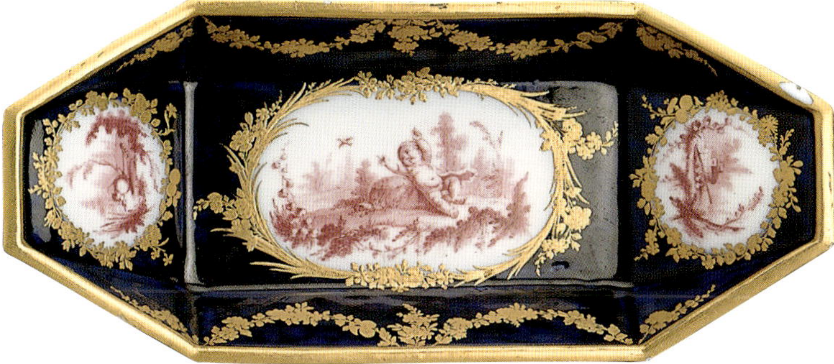
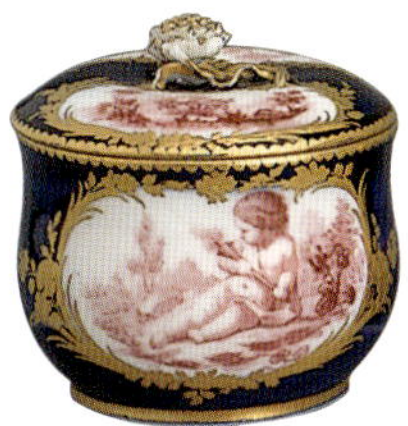
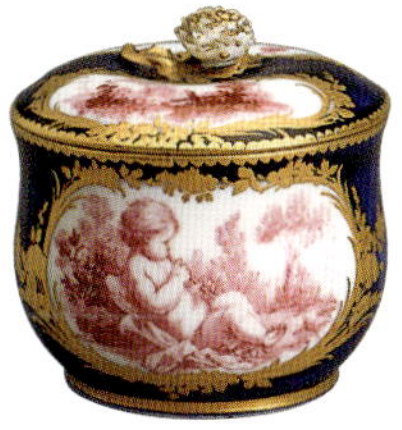

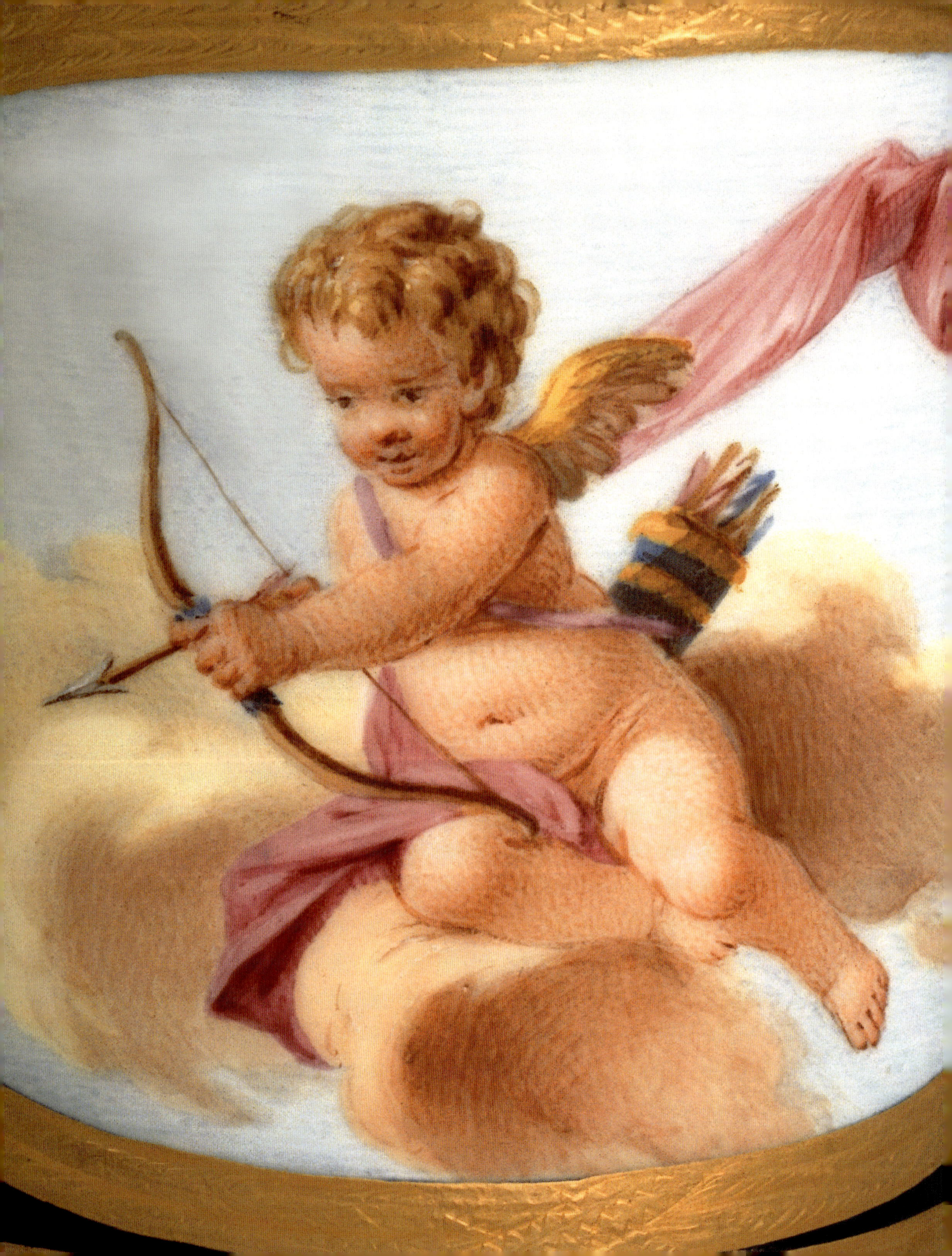

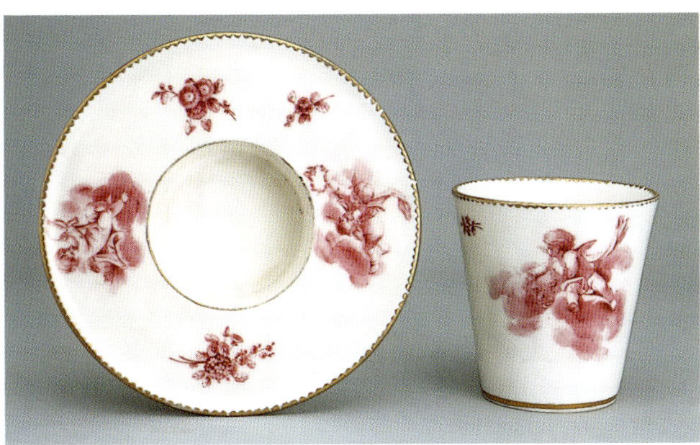

26
Cup and Saucer
Gobelet et soucoupe 'enfoncé'

1764

Sèvres Porcelain Factory

Soft-paste porcelain, polychrome painting, gilding
Height 9 cm; diameter 15.5 cm
INV: ZF-19881
PROVENANCE: late 1920s, from the Museum of the
    Stieglitz School of Technical Design, Leningrad

This form probably first appeared at the St Cloud
Factory, where the saucer was given its central
indentation. Because of their stability, cups of this
type were widely used in travelling sets. The term
enfoncé derives from the French verb meaning
'to drive into', and first appeared at Sèvres in 1759.
Madame de Pompadour's Inventory for 1764
mentions a cup with a similar name. They were
usually sold singly or, more rarely, in pairs (Savill
II, p. 675).
    In the 1760s and 1770s, cups and saucers of
this type were mostly acquired by members of the
royal family and their retinue (*La porcelaine de
Sèvres*, p. 350, cat. 1224). JV

27
Milk-jug
Pot à lait à trois pieds

1754

Sèvres Porcelain Factory (Vincennes)

Soft-paste porcelain, polychrome painting, gilding
Height 12 cm
INV: ZF-19879
PROVENANCE: late 1920s, from the Museum of the
    Stieglitz School of Technical Design, Leningrad

A plaster model of an object described in the 1752
Inventory as 'Petit Pot à lait à trois pieds' was kept
at the Sèvres Factory. The lightness, stability and
elegant details, such as the design of the rim and
the bent legs in the form of little tree trunks with
small branches in relief, made this form popular
throughout the eighteenth century (see also cat.
28). Similar milk-jugs were included in most
déjeuner sets (Brunet, Préaud, p. 150).
    The form was inspired by metal cream-jugs
from the first half of the eighteenth century.
The handles and legs in the form of branches
were borrowed from Chinese porcelain ware. The
milk-jug could be used separately or, as was most
common from the end of the 1750s, as part of a tea
service or déjeuner set (*La porcelaine de Sèvres*,
p. 324, cat. 1186). JV

28
Milk-jug
Pot à lait à trois pieds

1765

Sèvres Porcelain Factory

Soft-paste porcelain, polychrome painting, gilding
Height 8.3cm
INV: ZF-16650
PROVENANCE: 1918, from the collection of A.S.
    Dolgorukov, Petrograd

See cat. 27.

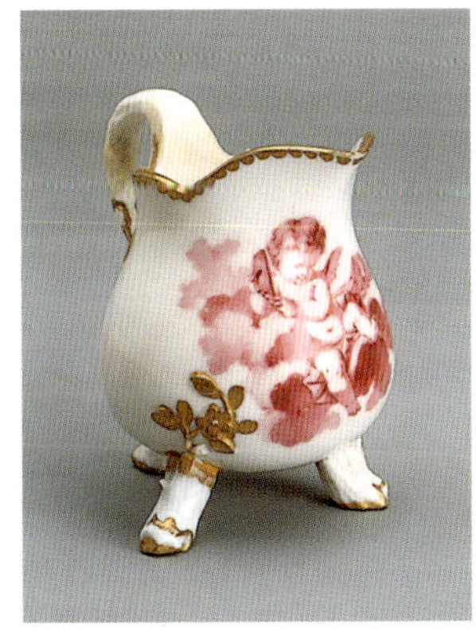

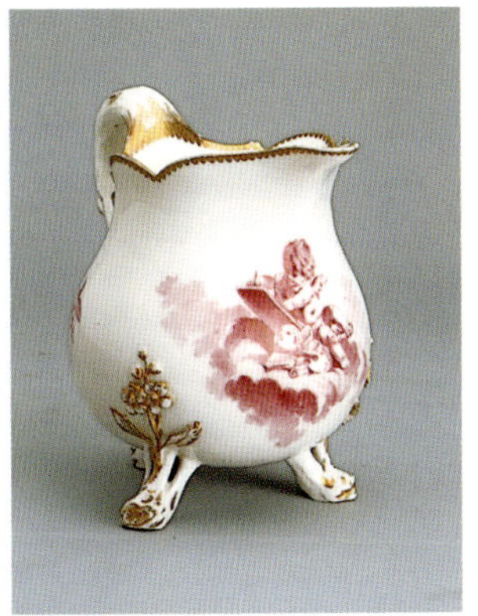

29
Ink-well
Écritoire

1774

Sèvres Porcelain Factory

Hard-paste porcelain, polychrome painting, gilding, glass
Height 13.1 cm; length 19.2 cm; width 8.5 cm
INV: ZF-21940
PROVENANCE: 1918, from the collection of A.S.
    Dolgorukov, Petrograd

A wide variety of everyday objects was produced
at the Sèvres Factory, including writing
implements. Porcelain ink-stands and ink-pots
of the most varied forms accorded perfectly with
eighteenth-century interiors. This small ink-well
with its humorous figure of a drummer-boy cupid
could very well have graced a small bureau in a
lady's boudoir. JV

30
Mantel-clock with the figure of Eros

Late 18th century

France

Gilded and patinated bronze, griotte marble
87 × 58 × 30 cm
SIGNED on the face: *Manière à Paris*
INV: Epr-910
PROVENANCE: 1924, from the State Museum of the
    Revolution; originally in the main collection of
    the Winter Palace

AG

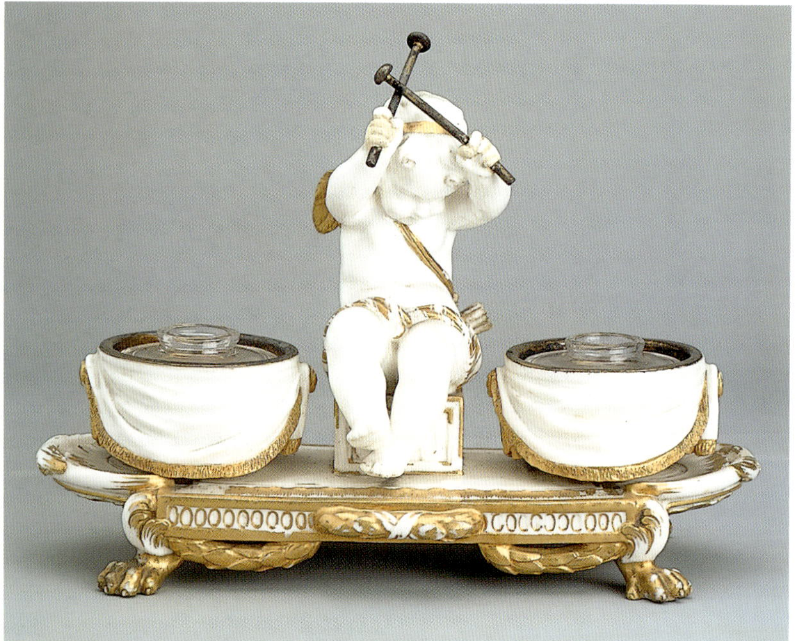

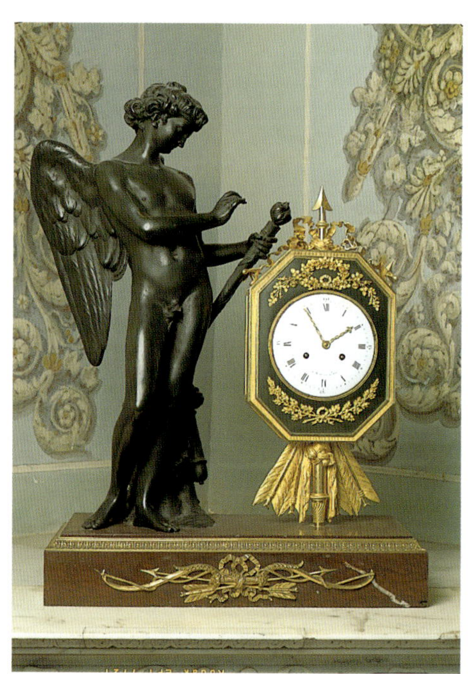

31
Mantel-clock with two porcelain groups: *La leçon d'Amour* and *La leçon à Amour*

Late 18th century

Paris
Models for the Sèvres biscuit groups made by
    Louis-Simon Boizot (1743–1809), 1794

Red marble, two medallions of Sèvres porcelain
    'in the Wedgwood style' (one renewed), Sèvres
    biscuit, gilded bronze
49 × 65 × 14 cm
SIGNED on the face: *Sauvajot a Paris. Barbichon*
INV: Epr-876
PROVENANCE: 1810s, collection of Nikolai Borisovich
    Yusupov, Moscow; September 1819, transferred to his
    Arkhangelskoe estate near Moscow; from 1850,
    Yusupov Palace, St Petersburg; 1919–24, Yusupov
    Palace Museum, Petrograd; from 1925, State
    Hermitage
YUZ

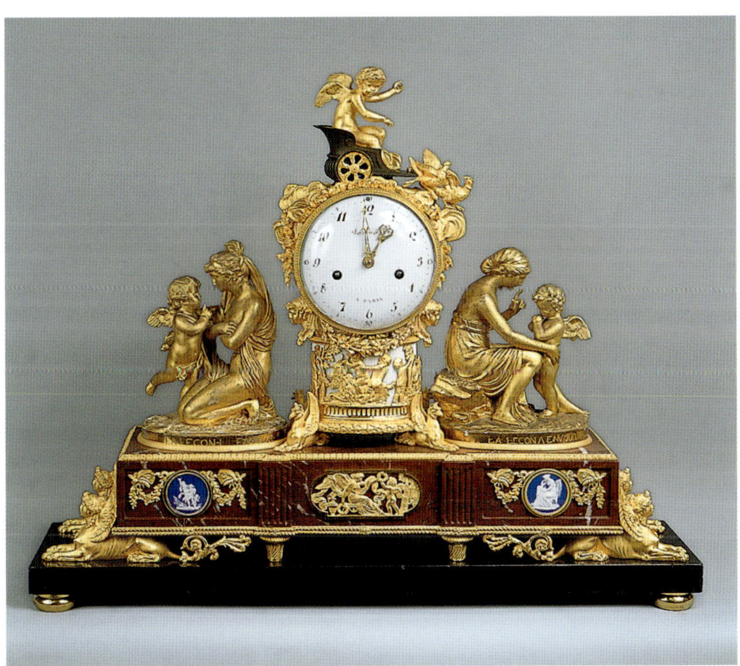

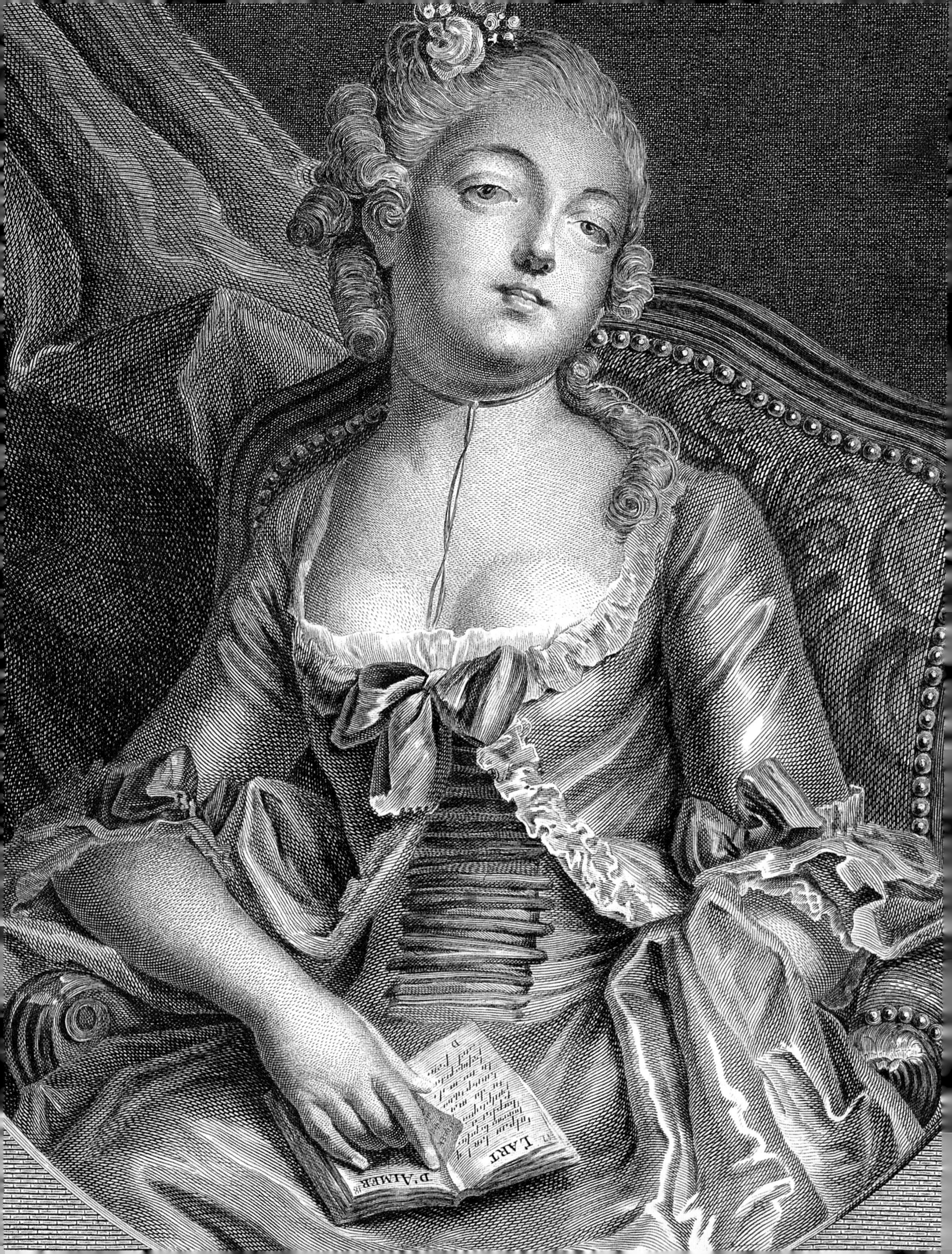
L'ART
D'AIMER

Touched by Love

What happens when Cupid touches the body and mind of a woman? In the
eighteenth century the pre-eminent space of seduction and erotic pleasure
was the 'boudoir'. The boudoir was a private, interior space within the house,
where a woman could escape the formal restrictions and role-playing of social
life; it was an erotic space of reverie for the contemplation of love. Intimate
personal possessions and embellished objects made the woman mindful of the
presence and power of Cupid (cat. 44–55). The intimate space of the boudoir
was therefore both real and symbolic.

Moralists thought that reading popular illustrated erotic novels inflamed
the imaginations of their women readers, causing them to become physically
aroused. In his *Confessions* Jean-Jacques Rousseau spoke of 'those dangerous
books… that can only be read with one hand' – an allusion to the erotically
stimulating effects that the solitary activity of reading might have on women
readers in the freedom and privacy of the boudoir (*left*; cat. 38).

For the ancient lyric poet Sappho, Eros was the 'loosener of limbs'.
Transformed through their imaginative encounters with Cupid, the
women depicted in these paintings and engravings also undergo a physical
transformation through the touch of Eros. Innocence turns into self-
consciousness, ignorance into sexual knowledge. As their bodies change
in response to what they are reading, women begin to scrutinize themselves.

But Cupid also represents threat. The boudoir is a solitary place, and the
figures of the women depicted here are propelled into a loss of self-control.
Private enjoyment is liable to turn into melancholic longing; the freedom
of sexual imagination into obsessive erotomania. Touched by love, these
eighteenth-century women are thrown into a state of precariousness:
extreme erotic abandon, or extreme melancholy.

Shame on Him who Evil Thinks (detail)
François Hubert
After the composition by Jacques-Philippe Carême
1775
cat. 38

32

Young Woman in front of a Mirror

1713

Jacques-François Courtin (1672–1752)

Oil on canvas
92 × 73 cm
SIGNED and dated on the right, on the mirror:
    Jacques Courtin. 1713
INV: GE 1171
PROVENANCE: 1772, acquired for Catherine II as part
    of the collection of Pierre Crozat, Paris
BIBLIOGRAPHY: Cat. Crozat, p. 59; Dussieux, p. 579;
    Fare, pp. 293, 300; Georgi, p. 477; Réau 1929, no. 43;
    Stuffmann, p. 128, no. 127; Th.-B. VII, p. 588

Similar three-quarter length portraits of pretty
girls engaging in innocent pursuits were very
typical of Courtin's work. They were doubtless
inspired by the era of Watteau and the charming,
elegantly dressed ladies of his *fêtes galantes*.
Unfortunately very few have survived, and they
are known only from engravings by the brothers
François and Jean-Baptiste de Poilly. In spite of
the fact that Courtin's work was shaped before the
end of the seventeenth century, he undoubtedly
expresses the world-view of the following century.
Even those of his subjects which, in the sixteenth
and seventeenth centuries, would have been
allegories – a girl with a squirrel, mask or parrot –
have a different meaning in his paintings. Whereas
before, a woman in front of a mirror would
probably have represented the idea of *vanitas*
(vanity, transience), in Courtin's work the subject
is simply admiring her beauty and youth, and
the necklace and ring lying beside the mirror no
longer represent vanity; instead there is the sense
that they have been removed in order to emphasise
that natural beauty needs no adornment.

It seems likely that the girl depicted was
the artist's regular model, since a girl of similar
appearance, even dressed the same way, is found
in a number of Courtin's compositions. To all
appearances the picture was highly esteemed
by viewers from the moment it saw the light
of day, but it was made particularly popular
by the engraving of it by François de Poilly,
with a coquettish quatrain beneath the picture:

> *Lorsque dans ce miroir, vous consultez*
>   *vos charmes,*
> *Vous préparez des fers à qui n'y pense pas;*
> *Les plus indifférents qui versent tant l'appas*
> *Se trouveront force de vous rendre les armes.*
> (While in this mirror you consider your appeal,
> You prepare chains for the unaware;
> Even those most indifferent to so much charm
> Will find themselves forced to surrender.)

ED

33

Young Woman Drawing an Arrow from Cupid's Quiver
Jeune femme retirant une flèche du carquois de l'Amour

Second half of the 1790s

François Leroy de Liancourt (1741/42–1835)

Oil on board
32 × 24 cm
INV: GE 5657
BIBLIOGRAPHY: Berezina, cat. 34; Ernst, pp. 148–9

The Hermitage painting reveals a certain stylistic
and iconographic kinship with the works of Louis-
Léopold Boilly (1761–1845) and Marguerite
Gérard (1761–1837). These artists were fond of
similar subjects with an erotic subtext. Boilly and
Gérard often depicted pretty women near a statue
of Cupid, dressed in satin or silk robes. Judging
by the dress and hairstyle of the young lady, and
likewise by the figurative style of execution, the
Hermitage work belongs to the second half of
the 1790s.

If the dating of the Hermitage painting is
not in question, its attribution has up to now been
rather problematic. When it was in the collection of
Prince Nikolai Borisovich Yusupov it was believed
to be the work of Jean-Baptiste Lallemand, as was
indicated in the Yusupov gallery catalogue of 1839.
Subsequently, for almost 100 years, the painting
was considered to be the work of an unknown
artist. Finally, in 1924, Sergei Ernst attributed
the painting to Leroy de Liancourt on the basis
of an old inscription (now missing), and a certain
resemblance to works of this artist known from
the engravings of Pierre-François Le Grand. AB

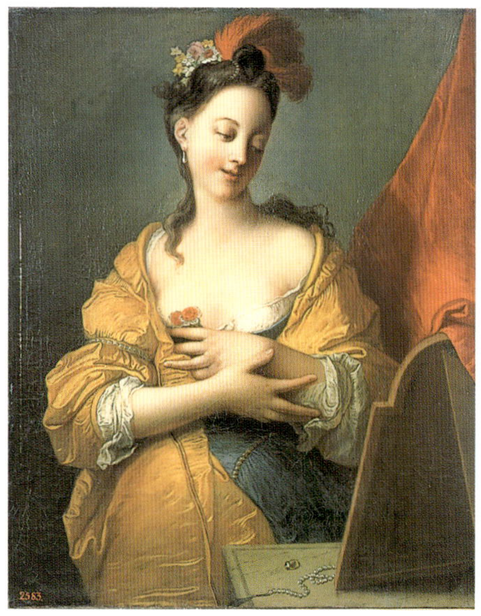

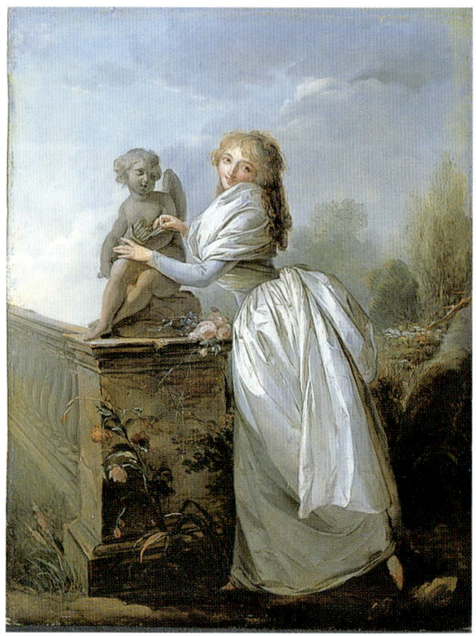

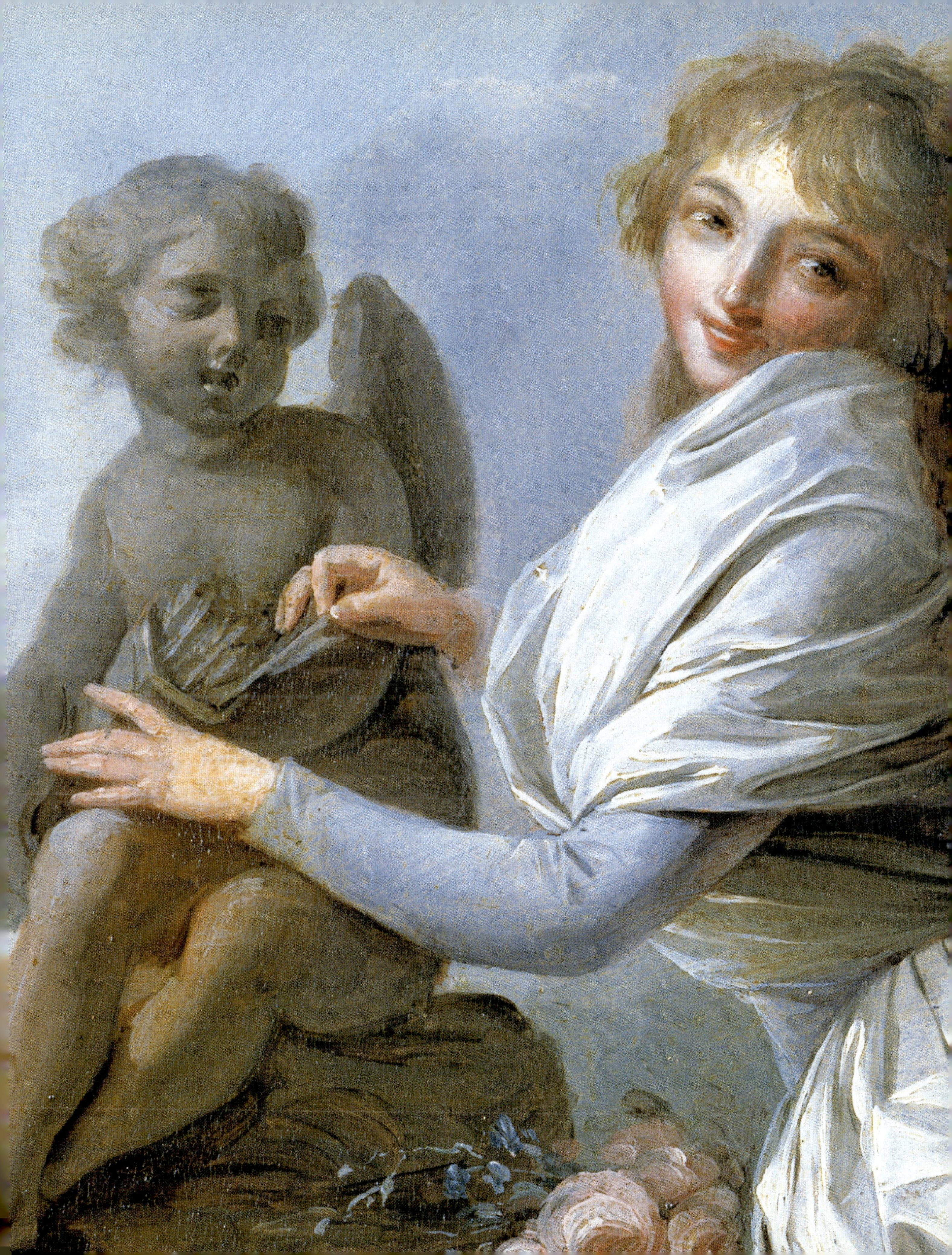

34

Portrait of an Unknown Lady with a Bird

c. 1760s

Louis-Michel Vanloo (1707–72/5)

Oil on canvas
64 × 55 cm
INSCRIPTIONS: on the reverse is a mount from an old
stretcher with the inscription: *Peint par Vanloo à l'hôtel
de Soisson en 1721, pour Monsieur de Douxmenil. NB
c'est Jean Baptiste Van Loo d'ont il s'agit né à Aix 1684
mort ibid 1745.*
INV: GE 5634
PROVENANCE: 1919, from the Ferzen collection,
Petrograd, through the State Museum Fund
BIBLIOGRAPHY: De Baye, pp. 109–12; Dezallier
d'Argenville II, p. 272; Ernst, p. 244 (as J.-B. Vanloo);
Houssaye, p. 499; Nemilova 1973, pp. 236–51;
Réau 1929, no. 359 (as J.-B. Vanloo)

Contrary to the inscription on the back of the
painting, the stylistic features and the manner in
which it is painted indicate that the work is not in
fact by Jean-Baptiste Vanloo, who was famous for
his ceremonial portraits in the seventeenth-century
tradition. Rather, the nature of the painting, the
light, bright colours, the lady's costume and
coiffure, all suggest that it was painted no earlier
than the mid-eighteenth century, by a different
member of this artistic dynasty – Jean-Baptiste's

son and pupil, Louis-Michel Vanloo. This
attribution is confirmed by an engraving by
François Chéreau the younger, which is an exact
copy of the Hermitage composition. Beneath the
engraving is the signature *Vanloo*, without initials,
but many authoritative sources link it with the
name of Louis-Michel Vanloo, which would
suggest that he painted the original work as well.
At the Salon of 1763, Louis-Michel Vanloo
exhibited his *Portrait of a Lady Holding a Dove
Leaning on a Windowsill*, which matches another
Chéreau engraving that also refers to Vanloo in
the inscription as the originator of the picture,
again without identifying which Vanloo. Judging
by the engravings, these were based on a pair of
works, one of which is this Hermitage portrait
of a lady with a bird.

The Hermitage acquired the picture under the
title *Portrait of an Unknown Lady*. In the first half
of the twentieth century, the subject was identified
as Jeanne-Agnès Berthelot de Pléneuf, Marquise
de Prie (1698–1727), as would appear to be
indirectly confirmed by the inscription on the
reverse of the picture. The Marquise de Prie was
the mistress of the first minister of France, Louis
Henri, Duc de Bourbon, Prince de Condé, and the
Hotel de Soisson mentioned in the inscription was
once given by Catherine de Medici to the Bourbon-
Condé family.

However, a more likely supposition is that
Chéreau made an engraving of two attractive

women with birds that were not necessarily
portraits. Later, in the nineteenth century, in order
to arouse interest in the engravings, the subjects
were identified with women who had enjoyed a
certain notoriety (the companion engraving, *Lady
with a Parrot*, is said to be a portrait of Madame
Sabran, mistress of the Duc d'Orléans). This kind
of composition was very typical of Louis-Michel
Vanloo, who liked to depict young ladies musing
or dreaming. ED

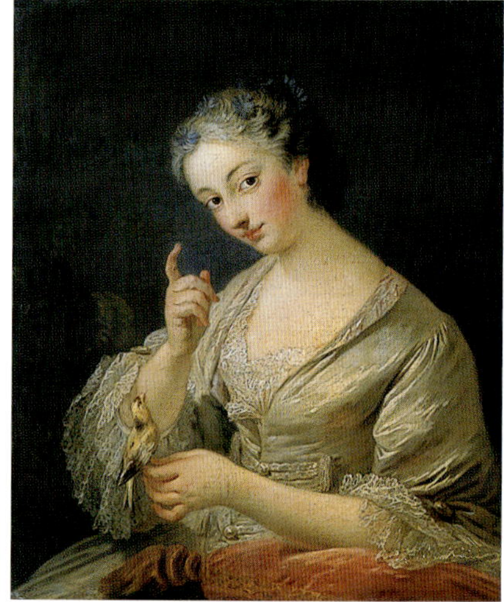

35

Comparison with a Rose Bud
La comparaison du bouton de rose

1781

Antoine-François Dennel (active 1760–1815)
After the painting by Gabriel-Jacques de Saint-
    Aubin (1724–80)

Etching and engraving
316 × 236 mm
INSCRIPTIONS: *COMPARAISON DU BOUTON DE
ROSE / Dedié à Madame de Saint Aubin / Le Tableau
Original est dans le Cabinet du Sr. Dennel / Par son
très humble et très Obeissant Serviteur Dennel.*
*G. de St. Aubin Pinx / Dennel Sculp. / Se trouve a Paris
chez l'Auteur, rue du Petit Bourbon attenant la Foire
St. Germain.*
WATERMARK: EAGLE (cf. Heawood no. 1317 [c. 1772?])
INV: OG-123886
PROVENANCE: before 1928, from main collection
    (Lugt Suppl. 2681ᵃ); acquired before 1830s
BIBLIOGRAPHY: Bourcard, p. 486 (state 'avec la lettre');
    Dacier 1914, pp. 31, 32, 168; Dacier 1929 II, no. 373;
    Delteil, p. 155; IFF VI, p. 507, no. 8; Lawrence &
    Dighton, p. 16, no. 36 (state II/II; authorship wrongly
    attributed to Louis Dennel); Ozerkov, no. 27; Stewart
    1992, pp. 90–1

An important step in a girl's education in matters of
love is when she becomes aware of her own beauty
and attractiveness. Beauty was revered in every
epoch: 'In order to catch a beauty, you must look
and look' (*Ars Amatoria* I, 44).

'The young beauty is no more than fifteen –
a real rose bud', writes the Marquise de Merteuil
about Cécile Volanges (*Les Liaisons Dangereuses*,
no. 2). In the eighteenth century the rose bud was
a common metaphor for that part of a girl's body
with which she was – quite justifiably – wont to
compare it (Le Pennec, p. 24). The comparison
of two types of bud was used in numerous French
paintings in the second half of the eighteenth
century, including: Jacques-François Courtin's
Young Woman before a Mirror (1713; State
Hermitage, inv. GE 1171, cat. 32; engraved by
F. De Paoli; Le Blanc III, p. 222, no. 104,
La Comparaison); Joseph-Marie Vien's *La toilette
d'une jeune mariée dans le costume antique* (1777;
Paris, private collection; Gaehtgens–Lugand,
p. 194, no. 238); Joseph Roque's *Rose and Bud*
(Salon of 1788; Toulouse, Musée des Augustins,
inv. Ro 249; Vie en France, p. 164, no. 67); Pierre
Alexandre Wille's *The Rose Bud* (engraved by
Nicolas Voyez; Le Blanc IV, p. 162, no. 37); and
Pierre-Antoine Baudouin's *Le léger vêtement* (cf.
the engraving by Juste Chevillet; Le Blanc II, p. 11,
no. 75). Symbolising at once heavenly perfection
and earthly suffering, the rose was the sacred
flower of Venus in ancient times ('You need fresh

flowers to give her a fresh rose,' writes Ovid in
Fasti IV, p. 138) and the attribute of the Three
Graces. In one of the Roman Myths described by
the poet Henry Peacham in his essay 'The Truth
of Our Times' (1638), Eros puts a stop to rumours
of Venus's infidelity by bribing Harpokrates, the
God of Silence, who has pushed her into a romantic
liaison, with a white rose. The rose–eros anagram
has been famous since the Renaissance. DO

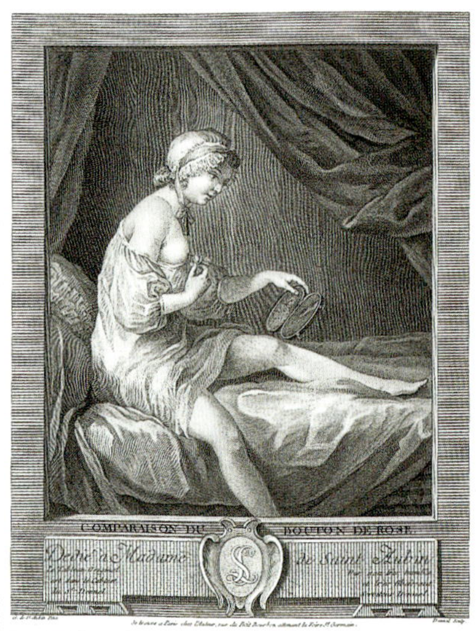

36
La Nouvelle Héloïse

1765

François Hubert (1744–1809)
After the painting by François (?) Lefèvre
  (1747–1817)

Etching
402 × 298 mm
INSCRIPTIONS: *LA NOUVELLE HELOYSE. / Dédiée
  à Madame / de Damery, Le Tableau est au Cabinet de
  M.' de Damery / Chevalier de l'ordre Royal Militaire
  de S.' Louis. / Par son très Humble et très Obeissant
  Serviteur Hubert.*
  *Le Febvre Pinx. / Hubert Sculp. Année 1765. / A Paris chez
  Beauvarlet Graveur du Roy, / Rue S.' Jacques vis-à-vis
  celle des Mathurins.*
WATERMARK: two-line inscription (illegible)
INV: OG-129245
PROVENANCE: before 1928, from main collection
  (Lugt Suppl. 2681ª); acquired before 1830s
BIBLIOGRAPHY: Le Blanc II, p. 399, no. 19; Nagler
  KL VI, p. 340, nr. 3; Ozerkov, no. 23; P.-B. II, p. 438;
  Th.-B. XVIII, p. 24

A young woman sits in her boudoir. She has put her
sewing aside and taken up some instructive reading.
Eros suddenly runs into the room with his bow and
arrow, his quiver over his shoulder. He holds a
finger to his lips, which should be taken here as a
sign that the girl is to be discreet – for this was how
the gesture was interpreted in the eighteenth and
nineteenth centuries (Droulers, p. 12).

The heading of the inside page of the book –
'Nouvelle' – refers to Rousseau's *Julie; ou,
La Nouvelle Héloïse* (1761), one of the most
fashionable and widely read novels of the second
half of the eighteenth century. Approximately
sixty editions of the book were published between
1761 and 1800. In his Preface to *Julie*, Rousseau
addresses his young female reader: 'This collection
of letters in the old style will be of more use than
philosophical works to married women. It may
even be of use to other women who have not
stopped striving for respectability, notwithstanding
their immoral way of life. The situation with
unmarried maidens is different. A wise maiden
does not read novels, and I have given warning in
this novel with a fairly clear title (*Julie; ou, La
Nouvelle Héloïse. Lettres de deux amants habitants
d'une petite ville au pied des Alpes*), in order that
all who open this book should know what is before
them. And if a girl should, despite the heading,
dare to read but one page, it means she is a lost
soul; only let her not ascribe her fall to this book,
for the evil has already taken place. But should
she start to read, let her read to the end, for she
has nothing to lose' (*Julie*, p. 26). Needless to say,
such an introduction simply fuelled the curiosity
of the female reader. The book was a huge success:
booksellers, unable fully to satisfy demand, were
forced to rent the novel out at 12 sous per hour.

Both the young girl and the society lady
constantly refer to novels for essential guidance.
As she waits for her lover, the Marquise de Merteuil
re-reads *La Nouvelle Héloïse* and La Fontaine's
Tales 'in order to remind myself of one or two
subtleties of tone' (*Les Liaisons Dangereuses*,
no. 10). Later she writes to Valmont: 'That is the
fault of novels: the author wears himself out trying
to portray ardour, while the reader remains cold.
The only exception is Héloïse' (ibid., no. 33).
Like Diderot we are impelled to cry: 'Zima, seize
the moment! Take up the book, read it, be afraid
of nothing!' (*Bijoux*, p. 33). DO

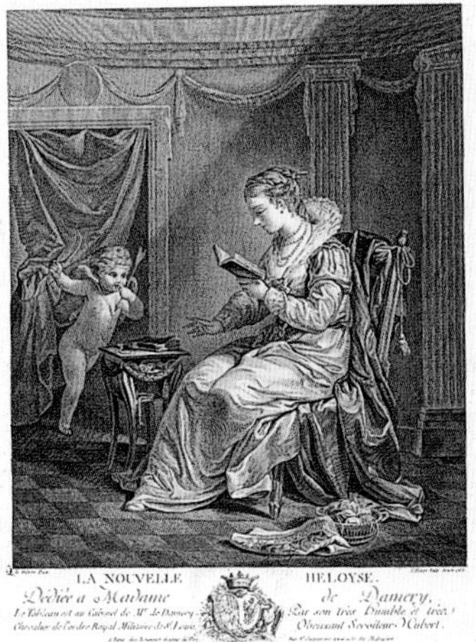

37
Even in the Merest Thing…
Jusques dans la moindre chose…

c. 1774

Louis-Joseph Masquelier (1741–1811)
After the gouache by Pierre-Antoine Baudouin
  (1723–69)

Etching
255 × 180 mm; 430 × 295 mm
INSCRIPTIONS:
  *Jusques dans la moindre chose,
  Je vois mon Amant empreint:
  Quand j'éparpille une Rose,
  Dans chaque feuille il est peint.
  Dans On ne s'avise jamais de tout*
  *Pient à Gouache par Baudouin / Gravé par L.J. Masquelier /
  Se vend à Paris ches Basan et Poignant M.ds d Estampes,
  rue et Hôtel Serpente*
INV: OG-125382
PROVENANCE: before 1830s, from main collection
BIBLIOGRAPHY: Bourcard, p. 36; Bocher (Baudouin),
  p. 28, no. 27 (state IV/IV); Delteil, p. 149; Lawrence &
  Dighton, p. 60, no. 138 (state III/III); Ozerkov, no. 36;
  P.-B. III, p. 40, no. 1

Masquelier's etching, with its affectionate dedication,
would have been suitable for a lady's album. The
Hermitage collection contains another copy of
this print from just such an album, decorated with
gouache and watercolour and set in a small frame
with an Indian ink inscription (inv. OG-126715).
The name of the plate comes from the one-act play
On ne s'avise jamais de tout with music by Monsigny
and a libretto by Sedaine, first performed at
Versailles on 2 December 1761. In Scene VIII, when
Dorval appears, Lise remembers a little song which
a love-lorn girl in her convent used to sing. The girl
sees the image of her beloved everywhere, even in
the most insignificant thing – in the cloud swept by
the wind, in her needlework, in the pages of a book.
She hears his voice coming from all around.

In Masquelier's etching, Lise dolefully plucks
off the petals of a rose, Venus's flower, and muses
over her intended. The activity is closely linked to
fortune-telling, an important part of a young lover's
yearning. People usually try and tell their future
with daisies: 'He loves me, he loves me not, he loves
me…', or in French: 'Il m'aime un peu, beaucoup,
passionnément…' And it is a daisy the girl plucks in
Greuze's painting *La simplicité*, which was painted
in 1759 for Madame de Pompadour's apartments in
Versailles (Fort Worth, Kimbell Art Museum, inv.
AP 1985.03; Salmon 2002, p. 188, cat. no. 57; p. 139,
fig. 3). Although fortune-telling is as old as love
itself, it remains formulaic to this day: what need
does one have of a daisy, if not to seek confirmation
of one's hopes; does one not pluck at a daisy
precisely because one is head over heels in love?

Fortune-telling is romantic in its innocence.
In practice, of course, in the eighteenth century
everything was sorted out a great deal more easily:
upon arranging a suitable match, parents removed
their daughter from boarding-school and married
her off, paying scant attention to the inclinations of
her heart – learn to put up with him and love will
follow! That is why guessing about the beloved bore
more of a rhetorical, literary character, perfectly
suited to the idealised world of tender pastorals.
It was rather an appeal to the beloved, a vicarious
dream, imagining oneself the beautiful heroine of
a novel whom it befits to pine for her prince. DO

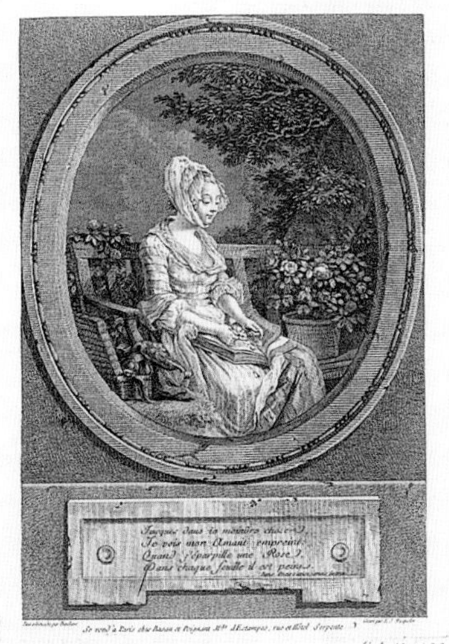

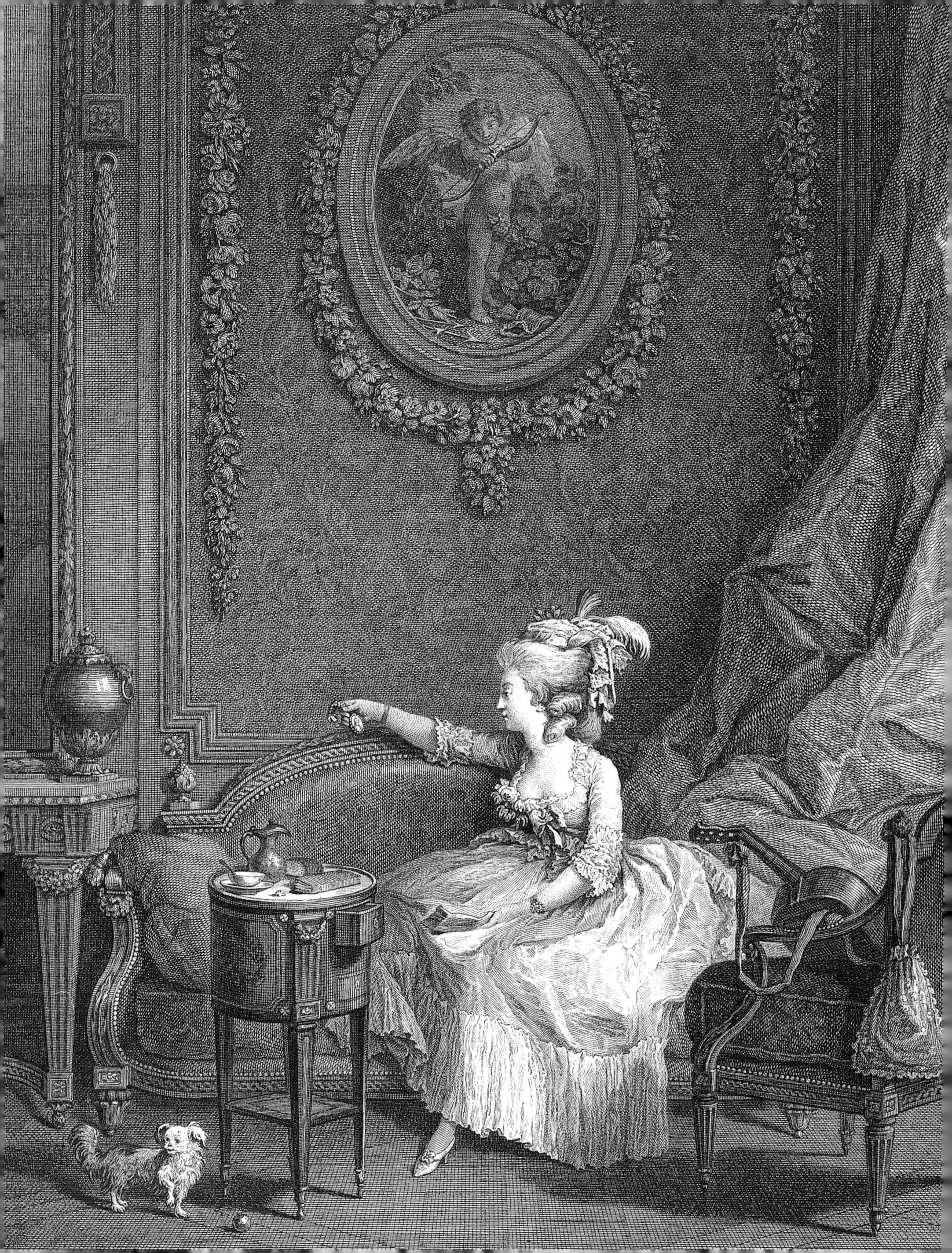

38
Shame on Him who Evil Thinks
Hony soit qui mal y pense

1775

François Hubert (1744–1809)
After the composition by Jacques-Philippe Carême
(1734–96)

Etching
427 × 301 mm; 500 × 365 mm
INSCRIPTIONS: *HONY SOIT QUI MAL Y PENSE. Dédié
et presenté a / S.A.S. Monseigneur le Duc de Chartres. /
Par son très Humble et très Obeißant Serviteur, Hubert.
Hubert Sculp. 1775. A Paris chez le Citn. Jean, rue Jean de
Beauvais. No. 32.*
INV: OG-129241
PROVENANCE: before 1928, from main collection
(Lugt Suppl. 2681ᵃ); acquired before 1830s
BIBLIOGRAPHY: Le Blanc II, p. 399, no. 17 (with incorrect
attribution to Le Febvre as the author of the original
composition); Nagler KL VI, p. 340, nr. 4 (with incorrect
attribution to Le Febvre as the author of the original
composition); Ozerkov, no. 24; P.-B. II, p. 438 (1777)

Honni soit qui mal y pense (old French; in English
'Shame on him who evil thinks') is the motto of the
English Order of the Garter. Here the artist uses the
title as an ironic justification for the scene depicted.
A girl sits before us holding Ovid's small volume,
Ars Amatoria, on her lap (*Art d'aimer*, probably the
translation by Gentil-Bernard, was published in
1775, the same year as this engraving). While one
of her hands turns the pages, the other is hidden
under the folds of her dress. Her languid look is
directed straight at the viewer. The erotic subtext
of the scene is legitimised by the ancient motto,
which demands that the viewer/reader should
'think nothing of the sort'. The engraving is paired
with one with a similar name (*Honi soit qui mal y
voit*, or 'Shame on Him who Evil Sees'), in which
a man playfully creates an unambiguous image
by pointing his index finger with two cherries
hanging either side (Ozerkov, no. 98). DO

39
A Comfort in Absence
La consolation de l'absence

1785

Nicolas Delaunay (1739–92)
After the gouache by Nicolas Lavreince (Niklas
Lafrensen) (1737–1807)

Etching and Engraving
376 × 271 mm; 391 × 289 mm
INSCRIPTIONS: *LA CONSOLATION DE L'ABSENCE.
Dédiée à Milady Comtesse de Douglas. / Par son très
Humble et très Obéissant Serviteur N. De Launay.
Peint à la Gouasse par N. Lavreince. / et Gravé par
N. De Launay, Graveur du Roi. / A Paris chez
De Launay, Graveur des Académies Royales de Paris et
de Copenhague, Rue de la Bucherie, No. 26. / A.P.D.R.*
INV: OG-228196
PROVENANCE: 1927, from the private libraries of the
Winter Palace (RIC) (Lugt Suppl. 2681ᵃ)
BIBLIOGRAPHY: Bocher (Lavreince), p. 19, no. 14
(state IV/IV); Bourcard, p. 342; Delteil, pp. 138, 142,
183; Lawrence & Dighton, p. 47, no. 106 (state IV/V);
Lundberg, p. 24, no. 114 (state V/V); Ozerkov, no. 65;
P.-B. II, p. 547, no. 24

The lady is looking at a locket containing a portrait
of her beloved. In her other hand she is holding a
letter she has just received from him. On the wall
above her, Eros takes aim at her heart. The mood is
one of anxious expectation. Two feelings towards
her lover are combined: profound irritation with
him for not being there – that he has gone away or
simply that he is late – and the fear that something
has happened to him. In *Les Liaisons Dangereuses*,
Madame de Tourvel is beside herself with worry
waiting for the slightest news from the heartless
Valmont, while in *Nina, ou La folle par amour*,
a play by Benoît-Joseph Marsollier of 1786, the
heroine Nina exclaims 'Alas! Alas! My beloved
does not return!' Expectation is the opposite of
everlasting separation, and the shorter the wait
the less painful the separation. It is during brief

periods of anticipation that mementoes linked to
the beloved are at their most precious.

'Historically separation is Woman's concern.
Woman is settled, while Man is the hunter, the
wanderer; Woman is faithful (she waits), while
Man is itinerant (he travels the world, he trails
to the side). Woman gives a form to separation,
develops its subject… From which it follows that
in every man discussing separation with another,
there appears something *feminine*: the man who is
waiting and suffering is miraculously feminised'
(Barthes, p. 314). In the twentieth century the
most striking image of a person in love was, on
the contrary, the expectant man: Humbert Humbert
awaiting Lolita's arrival from school. Indeed,
Humbert's famously theatrical line 'Am I in love? –
Yes, for I am waiting' is the essence of expectation
(Barthes, pp. 235–8, 317). DO

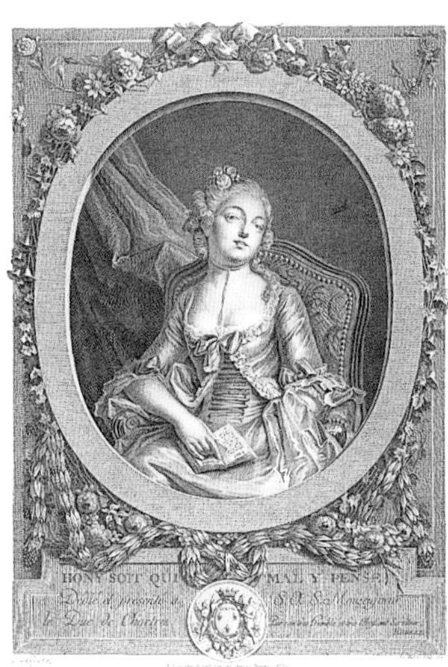

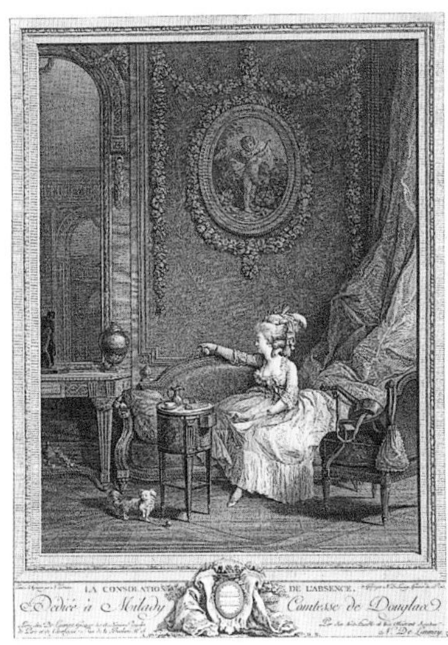

40

The Amusements of Youth
Amusemens du jeune age

1773

Juste Chevillet (1729–1802)
After the drawing by Pierre-Alexandre Wille
(1748–1821)

Etching and engraving
415 × 285 mm
INSCRIPTIONS: *Amusemens du Jeune Age / A Paris chez
Chevillet Graveur rue des Maçons, maison de M. Freville.*
on the upper right edge of the reverse: *4 Blatte
Deßiné par Wille le fils / Gravé par Chevillet*
WATERMARK: two-line inscription (illegible)
INV: OG-123544
PROVENANCE: before 1928, from main collection
(Lugt Suppl. 2681ª); acquired before 1830s
BIBLIOGRAPHY: Bourcard, p. 537 (state 'avec la lettre');
Delteil, p. 226; IFF IV, p. 353, no. 27; Le Blanc II, p. 11,
no. 61; Ozerkov, no. 21; P.-B. I, p. 292, no. 12

A little bird in a closed cage is an image of maidenly
innocence, while the little bird flying to freedom,
its cage flung open, is a symbol of a girl who has
lost her innocence. Greuze's famous painting *A Girl
with a Dead Canary* (*c.* 1765; Edinburgh, National
Gallery of Scotland) is entirely characteristic of this
notion. On the other hand, the girl who has married
becomes a caged bird again, striving for freedom just
as much. 'L'Amour est un oiseau, l'Hymen est une
cage' ('Love is a bird, and marriage a cage') begins
the poem beneath the engraving by Jacques Chéreau,
entitled *Girl Feeding a Bird* (P.-B. I, p. 381). It is a

metaphor which can easily lead to a lowering of
the tone, turning into what Boccaccio, for example,
describes in one of his novellas as 'snatching a
nightingale' (*The Decameron* V, 4). The image
of the little bird is understood in the same spirit
by J.F. Janinet in his engraving *The Captured Bird*
(*c.* 1780; Fuchs I, pp. 232–3, Farb. Bild), in which
a youth pretends he has hidden a little bird under
his hat, which he is holding on his lap, and
proposes to two girls that they try to get it out.

A girl petting a bird taken from a cage is an
image that conveys the subject's preoccupation with
her own emotions. Works on this subject enjoyed
great success in the eighteenth century: Pompeo
Batoni, *Purity of Heart* (1752; West Sussex, Uppark;
Clark, p. 256, no. 167, pl. 157); Noël Hallé, *Portrait
of E.C.J. Hallé* (*c.* 1769; private collection); Noël
Hallé, *Beloved Dove* (private collection; Willk-
Brocard, p. 427, no. 113; p. 429, no. 115); Joseph-
Marie Vien, *Sweet Melancholy* (1756; London,
private collection); Joseph-Marie Vien, *Greek Girl
with a Canary on her Finger* (1760; London, private
collection; Gaehtgens–Lugand, p. 161, no. 141,
pl. X; p. 163, no. 148); engravings of Charles Flipart
after a painting by Boucher (Boucher 1978, p. 252,
no. 1011); Jean Daullé after a drawing by Boucher
(1758; P.-B. I, p. 667, no. 11); François de Poilly after
the picture by Courtin (State Hermitage, inv. OG-
126049); Nicolas-Joseph Voyez after the picture by
Mademoiselle Castellas (*Pretty Turtle Dove*, Th.-B.
VI, p. 145); et al.

The most important thing is not to let go of
the little bird (until, of course, the moment it is
solemnly carried to the altar of Venus); because of

cunning Eros, however, this is exactly what must
happen. The bird will fly free from her hands
because she is distracted, or she will be forced to
free it herself with the arrival of spring. A young
girl reading novels and dreaming of a husband at
a tender age, inescapably becoming Eros's victim –
this is the principle heroine of the gallant epoch.
And it is she – whether portrayed as the seductive
shepherdess or the naive simple girl, depicted
'realistically' in her boudoir – who is the focus of
all the civil bows and discreet hints of suitors, and
the plans, hopes and intrigues of her family. DO

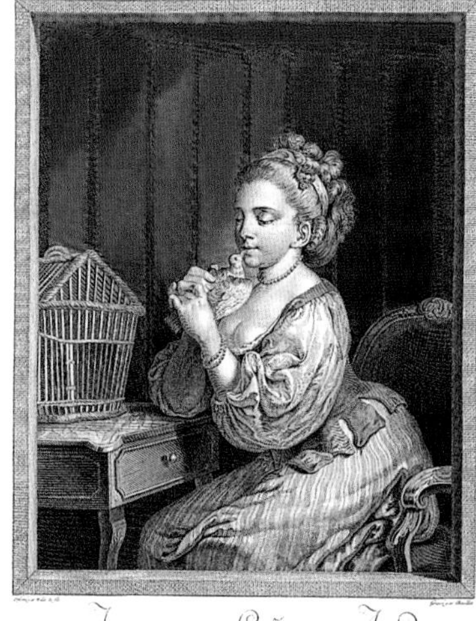

41

Tender Desire
Le tendre désir

1760s

Manoël-Salvador Carmona (1734–1820)
After the painting by Jean-Baptiste Greuze
(1725–1805)

Etching
392 × 289 mm; 526 × 384 mm
INSCRIPTIONS: *LE TENDRE DESIR / Dédié à
Monsieur Le Marquis de Veri. / Tiré du Cabinet de
Monsieur le Marquis de Veri. / Par son très humble
et très obeissant serviteur Maßard*
*Peint par J.B. Greuze / Gravé par C..... / A Paris chez
Massard Graveur, Rüe et Porte S.ᵗ Jacques.*
WATERMARK: DOVECOT (cf. Heawood no. 1237
[1784])
INV: OG-128087
PROVENANCE: before 1928, from main collection (Lugt
Suppl. 2681ª); acquired before 1830s
BIBLIOGRAPHY: Bourcard, p. 257; Delteil, p. 175;
Lawrence & Dighton, p. 10, no. 21 (with authorship
incorrectly attributed to Coron, a little-known
eighteenth-century engraver; state III/III); Nagler
MO I, p. 917, nr. 2155 (with authorship incorrectly
attributed to Juste Chevillet (1729–1802)); Ozerkov,
no. 41; P.-B. I, pp. 281–2

If passionate desire is almost inseparable from
carnal lust, then tender desire is a sign of genuine
and elevated emotion. Similar to the word *eros*
(in Greek) or *amour* (in French), which meant both
the emotion and its personification, Latin used the
word *cupido*. It was translated into French as *désir*.
Inasmuch as Cupido-Cupid is also the god Amour,
amour and *désir* effectively became synonymous.

However, in ethics, *amour* and *désir* were
separate, a distinction made clear by Descartes. The
encyclopaedia of Diderot and d'Alembert qualifies
désir as unease of the soul, experienced because of
the absence of something, which, by its presence,
would provide the pleasure sought. Whether the
desire is greater or lesser is defined by the degree
of unease (Enc. IV, pp. 885–6). For this reason
desire is always a formula for incompleteness:
'The raised hands of desire will never attain their
longed-for fulfilment' (Barthes, p. 318).

Pushkin's 'languid fire of desires' is like the
ardour aimed at the ideal lover, an ardour so strong
that reason is left far behind. Love and reason are
incompatible, proclaims the old proverb (*Proverbes*,
p. 27), and this is connected to the fact that the
organ of desire is the heart, which is uncontrollable
(Barthes, p. 337). The soul of the tender, sensitive
young woman is to be found in her heart (*Bijoux*,
ch. 29, p. 182), and the tender soul, captivated by

love, has no chance of release. From this follow
the surges of the heart and moistness of the eyes so
typical of 'Greuze's girls' (Bryson, p. 131). The eyes
begin to roll upwards or whiten, in the expression
used in Alfred Delvau's *Dictionnaire érotique moderne*
of 1864, where 'faire des yeux blancs' conveys a state
of sexual ecstasy (DŒE, p. 141).

The engraver has signed the work with a
monogram, which has led to different interpretations
of its authorship. Greuze's original painting is in
the Musée Condé at Chantilly. DO

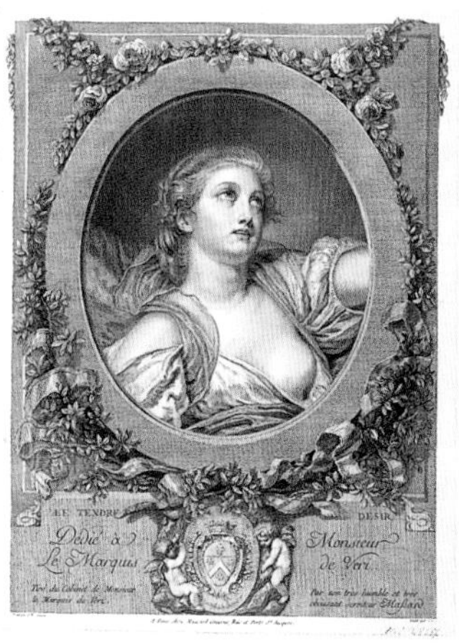

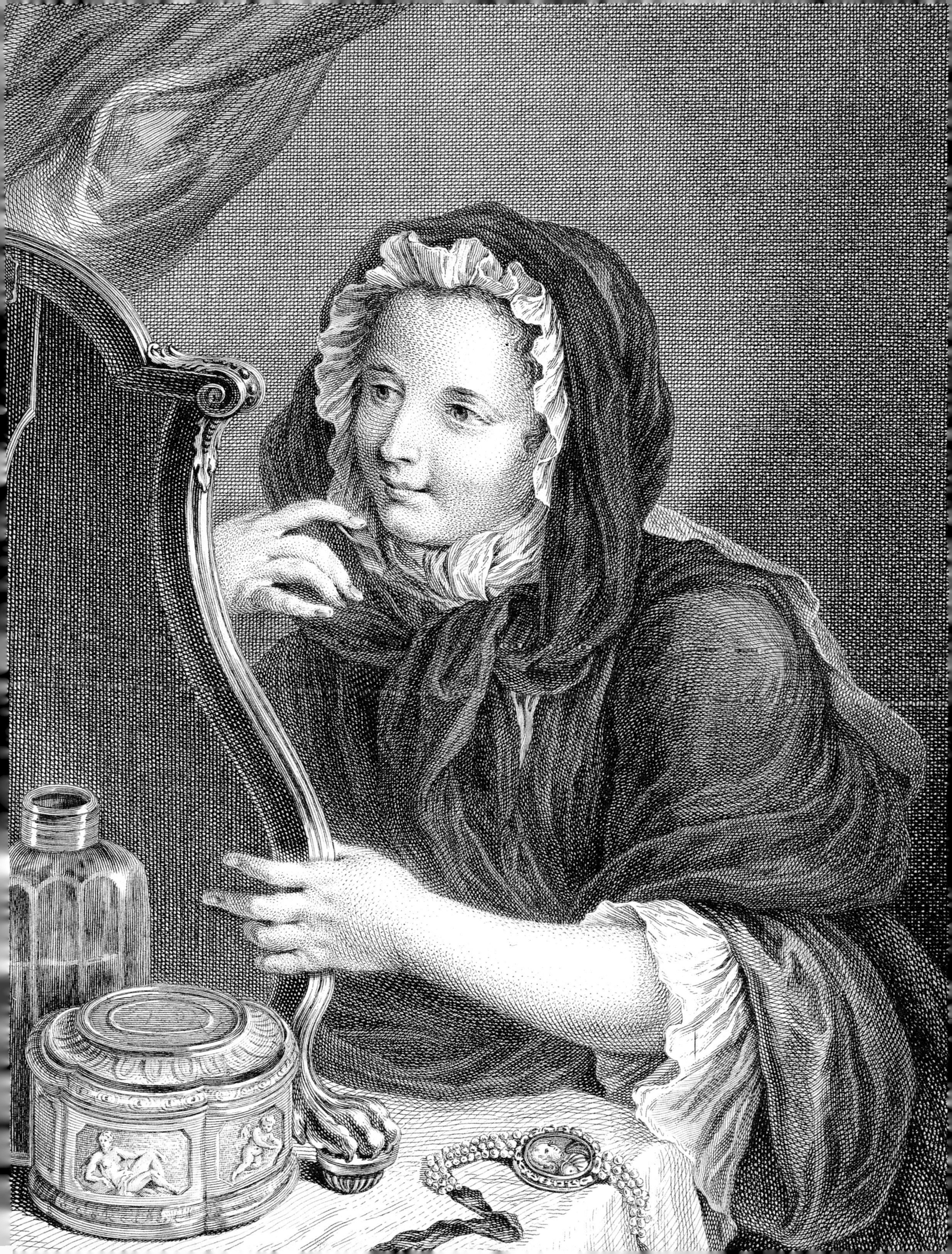

42
Young Widow in front of her Mirror

Jeune veuve devant son miroir
(*La toilette*)

Between 1730 and 1740

François-Bernard Lépicié (1698–1755)
After the painting by Charles-Antoine Coypel
(1694–1752)

Engraving
265 × 182 mm
INSCRIPTION:

Entre deux mouvements sans cesse partagée,
La veuve, en cet instant les exprime ala fois;
L'un, est la liberté de faire un nouveaú choix;
L'autre, la peúr détre changée.
Peint par C. Coypel / gravé par Lepicié:. / à Paris cheʒ
l'auteur rüe S.t Jacques au dessus des Jacobins A.P.D.R. /
Le Tableau est dans le Cabinet de Monsieur Fagon
Conseiller d'Etat Ord.re
INV: OG-129729
PROVENANCE: before 1928, from main collection
(Lugt Suppl. 2681ª); acquired before 1830s
BIBLIOGRAPHY: Bourcard, p. 118 ('La Veuve'); Le Blanc
II, p. 538, no. 60 ('Veuve coquette'); Œuvres de Basan
VI, p. 7; P.-B. II, p. 664, no. 17 ('Jeune femme se
mirant'); Lefrançois 1994, p. 113; Ozerkov, no. 78

This reverse engraving after Coypel's painting of
1730 (Salon of 1738; now at Sanssouci, Potsdam),
depicts a pretty young woman in mourning fondly
examining her features in a mirror. The mourning
locket containing her deceased husband's portrait
has been placed carelessly on the edge of the table.
Behind the mirror is a casket with reliefs on its
sides depicting Eros and Venus. There is another
less well-preserved copy of Lépicié's engraving
in the Hermitage (inv. OG-275363) with an
eighteenth-century inscription on an old mount:
'La petite veuve' ('The Little Widow'). This is
a reference to the theme, popular at the time, of
the cheerful young widow who happily has been
freed from her hateful husband. In the eighteenth
century, this was the image of a young, free,
experienced woman, seeking amorous pleasures.
La Fontaine wrote a tale entitled *La jeune veuve*,
while *La veuve coquette*, a play by Desmais
(1722–61), was performed on stage; other works,
too, portrayed this character type.

In eighteenth-century France widows often
re-married, particularly if they were young.
According to the rules of the church and etiquette,
re-marriage could take place as little as a year after
the death of a former husband. In gallant society,
however, maintaining 'widow's weeds' conferred
a certain freedom. 'A little later, as you know,
Monsieur de Merteuil died,' says the heroine of
Les Liaisons Dangereuses, 'and although really he

gave me little to complain of, nevertheless I felt the
value of the freedom accorded me by widowhood
acutely, and resolved to make use of it' (*Les Liaisons
Dangereuses*, no. 81). The widow is thus a striking
image of a temptress who will not let a single
worthy suitor pass her by. DO

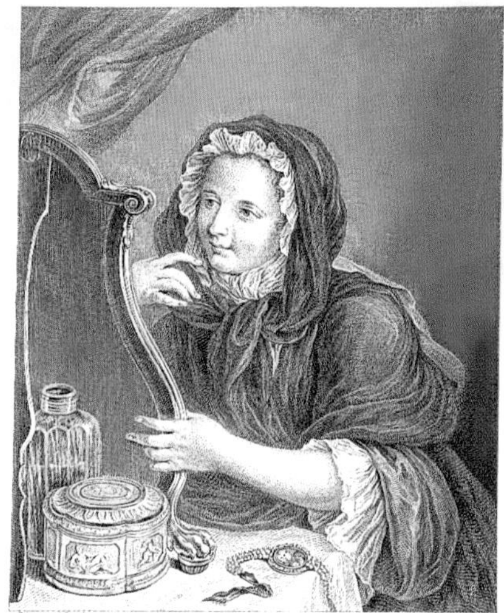

43
The Shift Withdrawn

La chemise enlevée

1787 (defacement of words 'du Roi' indicates that this
copy was printed after the French Revolution)

E. Guersant (second half of the 18th century)
After the composition by Jean-Honoré Fragonard
(1732–1806)

Etching
430 × 320 mm; 567 × 415 mm
INSCRIPTIONS: *La Chemise enlevée*
Peint par H. Fragonard, Peintre [next word deleted] /
Gravé par E.Guersant. / A Paris cheʒ Massard, Graveur
['du Roi' deleted], *rue et Porte St.Jacques No. 122.*
WATERMARK: DOVECOT (cf. Heawood no. 1238
[1793])
INV: OG-228211
PROVENANCE: 1927, from the private libraries of the
Winter Palace (RIC) (Lugt Suppl. 2681ª)
BIBLIOGRAPHY: Bourcard, pp. 193–4 (rare);
Delteil, p. 166; Lawrence & Dighton, p. 29, no. 67
(state II/II); Ozerkov, no. 50; P.-B. III, 54, no. 2;
Rosenberg, p. 161, no. 72, fig. 2; Th.-B. XV, p. 243

In this engraving, after Fragonard's famous
painting of the same name (1770s; Paris, Louvre;
Cuzin, p. 299, no. 208), Eros pulls off the girl's
blouse, thereby revealing her charms. He has
appeared from her dreams, brought to life from his

state of mythological non-existence. Captivated
by this image, she cannot resist her passionate
emotions, and helps Eros to undress her. Her
thoughts are as though paralysed by some sort of
hallucination; she moves like a sleepwalker.

In late-eighteenth- and early-nineteenth-
century perceptions, the female heart is inclined
to become captivated by an image, and to endow
its owner with qualities which he quite possibly
never possessed. Stendhal writes of a woman who
spends a whole year counting up all the meetings
with her chosen one, remembering every word
spoken by him, and never offers her hand to be
kissed by anyone else from the moment he first
inclines his lips towards them (Stendhal, p. 380).
Knowing his game, the seducer uses this quality
as a strategy, making the chosen victim fall in
love with him. Valmont is always present in La
Présidente de Tourvel's heart – through letters,
planned 'unexpected' appearances, the nobility
of his premeditated actions and the carefully
contrived stirrings of his soul. She cannot be
with him but cannot do without him; she does not
have the right to take him into her heart, but does
not have the strength to expel him from it. She
implores him for mercy but can do nothing about
the poison with which his feigned feeling has
infected her. Every meeting only deepens the effect
of the delusion: 'I implore you, we must stop
seeing each other. You must leave, but while you

are here, let us avoid these dangerous solitary talks,
when I seem to be in an incomprehensible dream,
when, unable to tell you everything I would like,
I listen all the time to things to which I should not'
(*Les Liaisons Dangereuses*, no. 90). DO

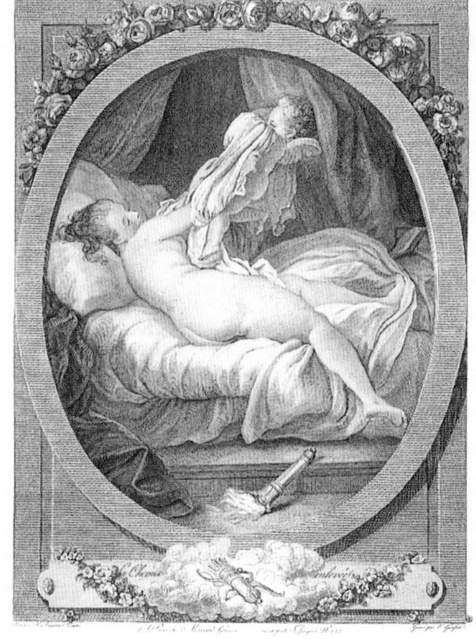

44
Snuff-box with chased medallion

1775–7

Johann Baltasar Gass
St Petersburg

Gold, silver, diamonds; chasing, engraving, pouncing
3.5 × 7.3 × 25.4 cm
ENGRAVED signature on the rabbet: *Gass à St Petersbourg*
PROVENANCE: from mid-19th century, in the Treasure
    Gallery of the Hermitage
INV: E-4485

This snuff-box was made by Johann Baltasar Gass,
a native of Germany, who moved to St Petersburg
in around 1760 and became a craftsman in the
foreign jewellers' guild. Very little is known,
however, of Gass's jewellery work; he became
renowned for being a first class medal designer
at the Petersburg Imperial Mint, where in 1772
he was awarded the rank of staff member, and
in 1773 that of imperial medal designer.

In the centre of the lid of the snuff-box is a
chased medallion with a picture of cupids framed
by a diamond garland. The subject of the
medallion, fairly common in works by craftsmen
of the second half of the eighteenth century,
can be traced back to a drawing by François
Boucher from the album *Premier livre de groupes
d'enfants*. Furthermore, one of the key features
of the decoration of the snuff-box is the use
of coloured gold. The craftsman's use of the
technique of *quatre couleurs* and the painstaking
attention to all the chased details demonstrate
his expert mastery of the material. OK

45
Oval Snuff-box

1780–1

Claude-Pierre Pottier
Paris

Gold, enamel, diamonds; polishing, chasing, pouncing,
    painting
2.4 × 7.6 × 5.8 cm
STAMPS: Paris – 1780–1781; artist's mark; charge
    Henry Clavel 1783–1789
PROVENANCE: from end of 18th century, in the Winter
    Palace; from mid-19th century, in the Treasure Gallery
    of the Hermitage
INV: E-4047

This small, elegant snuff-box is decorated with opal
glass through which the background drawing is
visible, imitating moss agate. Agates were rarities
in the eighteenth century, so genuine stones were
not always used for rings, clocks and snuff-boxes;
enamels with patterns resembling the stone's
natural pattern were also used.

The lid of this snuff-box is decorated with
a medallion of painted enamel, bordered with
a garland of chased gold. The composition in
grisaille depicting Cupid with an arrow, positioned
in the centre, was more than simply the artistic
centre of the object. Pictures like this were often
an artistic symbol which the jeweller had chosen
on purpose, having made the snuff-box to order,
as a future present. This snuff-box is the earliest
of Pottier's works in the Hermitage collection,
and is notable for the simplicity of its shape and
the restrained use of colour. OK

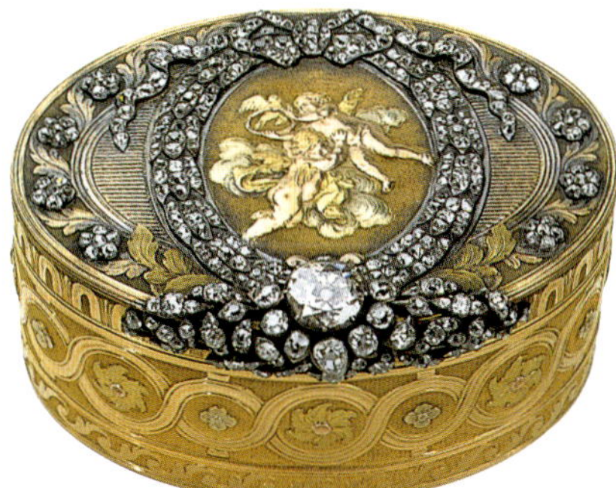

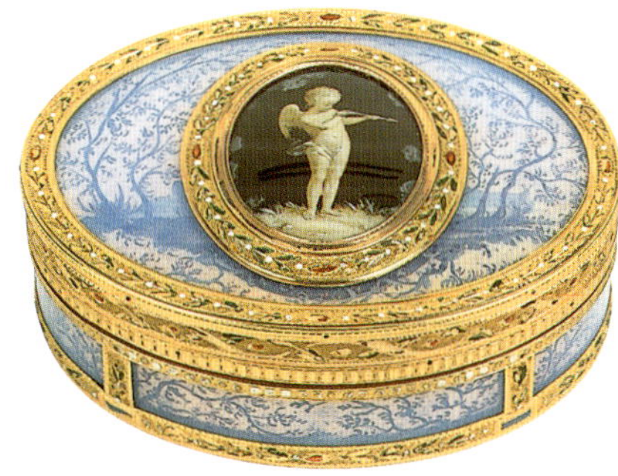

46
Snuff-box with enamel medallion

1770s

Jean-Pierre Ador
St Petersburg

Gold, silver, diamonds, enamel; chasing, engraving, painting
2.8 × 6.2 × 4.9 cm
ENGRAVED on the rabbet: *Ador St Peterbourg*
PROVENANCE: from the mid-19th century, in the Treasure
    Gallery of the Hermitage
INV: E-4496

The snuff-boxes of the gallant era were integral to
courtly etiquette. As well as being used for snuff,
they were given as rewards and presents, and their
decoration was often linked to or inspired by a
particular character or even a whole story.

   This oval snuff-box from the Hermitage is an
example of the work of Jean-Pierre Ador, one of the
best Petersburg jewellers. Born in 1724 in Switzerland,
he worked in Geneva as an enamel painter and
goldsmith, and visited London. In the early 1760s
he arrived in Petersburg, where he worked
independently, first as the owner of a workshop and
then, from 1764, taking charge of a haberdashery
factory. Ador manufactured dinner and tea services,
decorative ornaments, vases and fans; he also made
chalices, clocks, medals and ceremonial weaponry,
but in most collections his work is represented by
his snuff-boxes.

   The lid of this snuff-box has an enamel medallion
with a picture of cupids painted in grisaille set in the
centre and the bottom is decorated with a geometrical
design. The frieze-style drawing on the side and the
use of a medallion in the style of François Boucher are
typical features of Ador's work. Whether Ador himself
painted his snuff-boxes is unclear. Information about
some of the enamellists who decorated his jewellery
has been preserved – Charles-Jacques de Maine,
Barnabe-Auguste de Maine, Boutelier, Nicolas Sore
and Vezoroit – but it was extremely rare for them
to sign the miniatures on Ador's works. If at the
beginning of his Petersburg period Ador's enamels
took up almost the entire surface of the article,
towards the end of the 1770s he preferred to use
medallions set into the centre of the lid. The colourful,
bright enamels of earlier years are replaced with
monochrome grisaille compositions, in keeping with
the neoclassical aesthetic. OK

47
Pocket Watch

1760–70s

Watchmaker Lepine
Paris

Gold, silver, metal alloys, glass, enamel; chasing, painting
Diameter 4 cm
SIGNED: *Lepine a Paris*
INV: E-10996
PROVENANCE: 1922–5, from the collection of the
    Yusupovs

In the eighteenth century pocket watches were
notable for the great diversity of their decoration.
Many of them were chosen especially to go with
a particular dress and decorated with precious
stones to match. In the 1760s, Lepine began using
individual bridges in the watch mechanism, so the
processes of mounting and assembling watches
became significantly simpler. This meant that
the watches became cheaper and more widely
accessible, and at this time they were most often
decorated with painted enamel compositions.

   The lid of the Hermitage watch is decorated
with a composition showing a *fête galante* set in
a landscape. It is no accident that the seated lady
and the suitor kneeling before her have been placed
next to a pedestal with Cupid, for it is he who is
crowning this union. The delicate enamel painting
is covered with transparent enamel which makes
the romantic scene all the more enigmatic. OK

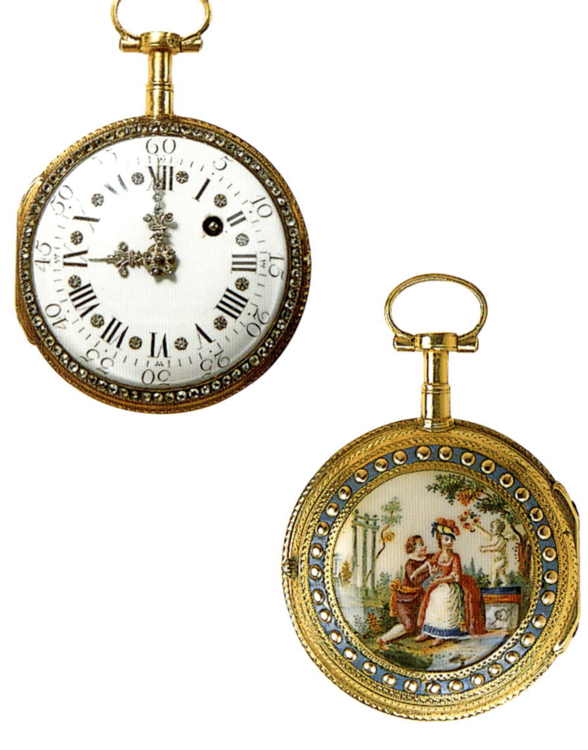

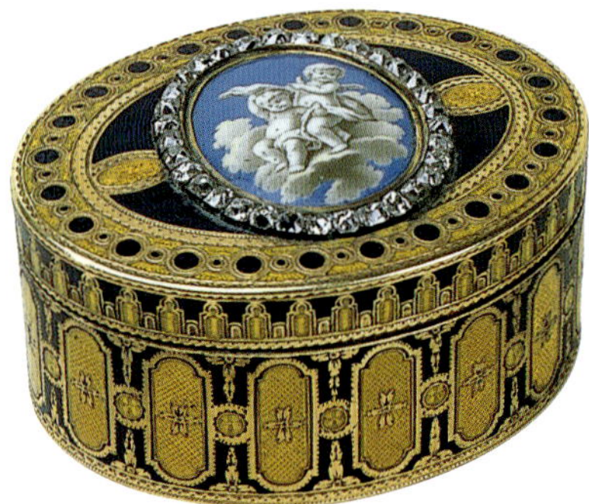

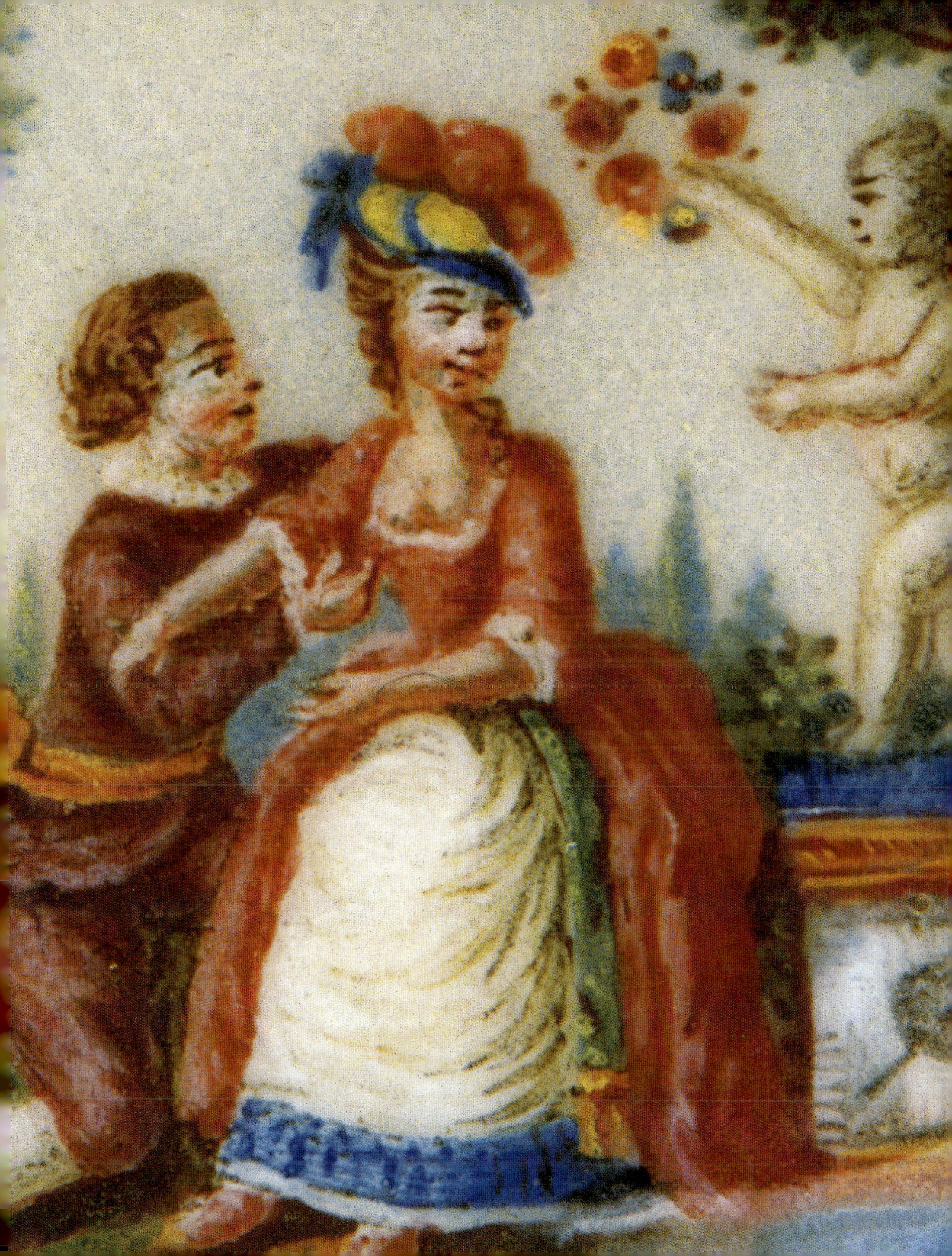

48
Cameo: Bacchus and Cupid

Second half of the 18th century

Clachant the Younger (Jean-Baptiste-Nicolas
    Glachant le Jeune [?]) (1746–1815)
France

Sardonyx, gold
4.6 × 3.8 cm
SIGNED at the bottom on the edge of the ground:
    GLA·JUN·F·
INV: K-1794
PROVENANCE: 1786, from the collection of Abraham-
    Joseph-Michel d'Ennery, Paris
BIBLIOGRAPHY: Duchamp, p. [15, 25]; Forrer, p. 437;
    Kagan 1973, no. 83; Maximova, p. 22; Raspe–Tassie,
    p. 780, no. 15248; Remi, Miliotti, p. 49, no. 229

This large cameo on double-layered sardonyx,
carved with classical works of sculpture and
glyptic in mind, depicts the god of love as an
infant asleep at the feet of the more powerful-
seeming Bacchus.

In an auction catalogue published in 1786
of the collections of tax collector and notary
D'Ennery which included carved gemstones,
the *Bacchus and Cupid* cameo was described as
the work of the engraver Clachant (in spite of
the clear inscription *GLA·JUN·F·*). Thus it was as
Clachant that the family of engravers working in
Paris in the second half of the eighteenth century,
the youngest of whom made this Hermitage gem,
entered the reference books.

The incorrect spelling of Glachant's name,
which persisted for over 200 years, not only in
the case of the *Bacchus and Cupid* cameo but also
other works in various collections by descendants
of the French engravers, was finally righted by
Michael Duchamp, who in 2000 published a
genealogy of the Glachant family and the *œuvre*
of its most gifted members. Place of honour
among the carved gemstones made by Jean-
Baptiste-Nicolas Glachant le Jeune is held by
this elegant Hermitage gem. SK

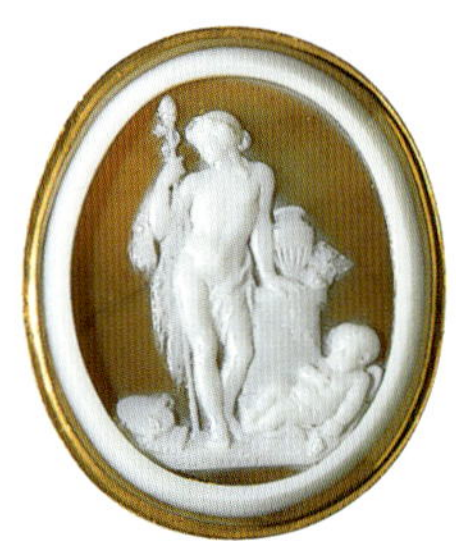

49
Intaglio: The Marriage of Cupid and Psyche

c. 1783

Charles Brown (1749–95)

Dark-yellow cornelian, gold
2.9 × 4.1 cm
SIGNED on the right: *C. BROWN*
INV: I-3950
PROVENANCE: October 1786, from the engravers'
    studio through their agent, J.J. Weitbrecht
BIBLIOGRAPHY: Kagan 1976, no. 28

In the mythology of ancient glyptic art, Cupid,
fruit of the love of Venus and Mars (in some
versions Venus and Mercury), who has himself
become the god of love while remaining forever
young, is depicted as his mother's companion or as
the youthful lover of Psyche. Most often, however,
he is alone (or sometimes transformed into a pack
of naked, winged, mischievous boys), personifying
independent strength and audaciously ruling the
fates of humans and gods. Stone engravers of the
modern era imitated the ancient models or created
their own variations on a theme which had not lost
its attraction.

Working to commissions for Catherine II over
the last ten years of her life, the brothers William
and Charles Brown sent over two hundred of their
works to Russia. The first consignment of five
gemstones included *The Marriage of Cupid and
Psyche*, the work of the younger brother Charles,
which was set in a gold bracelet (later replaced by a
museum setting) and valued at 100 pounds sterling
(Russian State Historical Archive, f. 468, op.1.
ch. 2, ed. khr. 3901, l. 322). Three years earlier,
in 1783, Londoners had had the opportunity to see
it in an exhibition at the Royal Academy of Arts
(Graves, p. 306).

The intaglio is a reproduction (minus the first
figure) of a famous cameo signed by the ancient
engraver Tryphon, which in the seventeenth
century belonged to Thomas Howard, Earl of
Arundel, and in the eighteenth century was in the
Duke of Marlborough's collection. Thanks to
casts, prints and numerous copies in a wide variety
of materials, the cameo became unusually popular
and was dubbed 'Marlborough's Cameo' (now in
the Museum of Fine Arts in Boston). YUK

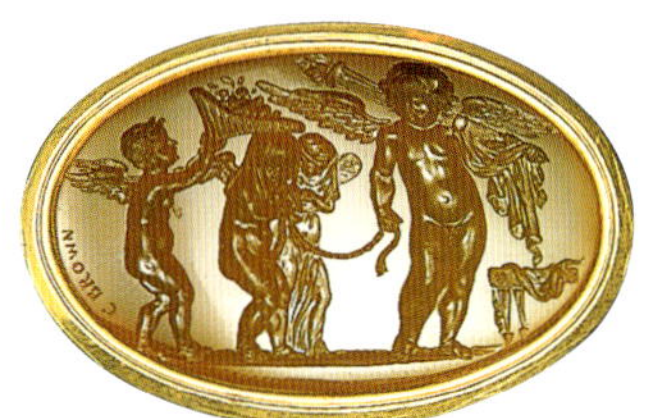

50
Cameo: Cupid with Bow

1790

William Brown (1748–1825)

Sardonyx, gold
2.0 × 2.2 cm
SIGNED on the right: *BROWN*
INV: K-1775
PROVENANCE: before 1796, from the engravers' studio
    through their agent, J.J. Weitbrecht
BIBLIOGRAPHY: Kagan 1976, no. 86

Responding to the tastes of the gallant eighteenth
century, the brothers Brown were so successful
with this subject, which they returned to
repeatedly, particularly after a short visit to France
in 1788, that they were often dubbed the 'engravers
of cupids'. The Hermitage collection of their
gems contains more than a dozen cameos dedicated
to the god of love. Cupid breaking a thunderbolt
across his knee, taming a panther or a lion,
saddling swimming dolphins or hippocamps,
making music on his lyre or flute, playing with
a butterfly or, more often, burning her delicate
wings like a cruel child (as the sufferings of the
Soul (Psyche) are depicted) – this is a far from
complete list of the subjects depicted by Charles
and William Brown on the oval surfaces of small
gems. It would be strange not to find among them
Cupid with his main attribute, the bow. Down on
one knee, he has just fired an arrow at his unseen
victim and is following its flight. In his left hand,
raised and extended forwards, he still holds the
bow, while his right arm is thrown back.

It was Rudolph Erich Raspe (author of the
famous *Adventures of Baron Münchhausen*) who
identified William Brown as the engraver when
describing the cameo in James Tassie's catalogue
of the cabinet of casts from carved stones
(Raspe–Tassie, no. 15382, with the note: 'Engraved
by W. Brown'). YUK

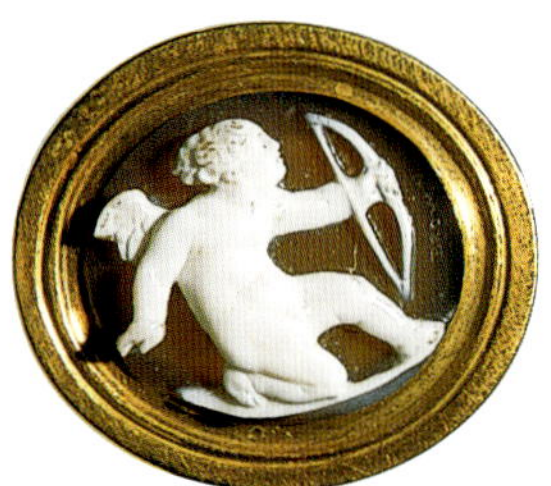

51

Cameo: Cupid Breaking Jupiter's Thunderbolt

1788 (?)

William Brown (1748–1825) & Charles Brown
    (1749–95)

Chalcedonyx, gold
3.1 × 1.8 cm
SIGNED on the left: *BROWN*
INV: K-252
PROVENANCE: September 1794, from the engravers'
    studio through their agent, J.J. Weitbrecht
BIBLIOGRAPHY: Kagan 1976, no. 87

The cameo harks back to an ancient gem which in
the earlier part of the eighteenth century was kept
in a Florentine collection (Gori II, tav. 16 (1);
Reinach, pl. 51), and which Brown may have
been familiar with from engraved reproductions.
The resourceful and omnipotent Cupid, breaking
across his chubby knee a flashing thunderbolt
which supposedly only Jupiter, god of thunder
and lord of the heavens, can command, shows how
easily, almost playfully, he can foil the fearsome
intentions of the supreme ruler of Olympus.
Here is confirmation, perhaps, of Virgil's famous
phrase, 'Omnia vincit amor' ('Love conquers all')
(*Eclogues* 10, 69). According to Brown's accounts
the cameo was valued at 30 pounds sterling
(Russian State Historical Archive, f. 468, op. 1,
ch. 2, ed. khr. 4026, l. 512). Another Brown replica
of this composition, a cast, is also known
(Raspe–Tassie, no. 6637). YUK

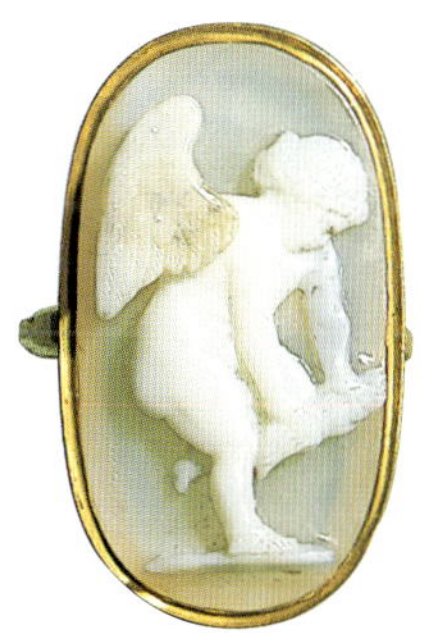

52

Cameo: Cupid Playing the Flute to a Lion

c. 1787

William Brown (1748–1825) & Charles Brown
    (1749–95)

Sardonyx, gold
2.1 × 2.3 cm
INV: K-1848
PROVENANCE: October 1787, from the engravers' studio
    through their agent, J.J. Weitbrecht
BIBLIOGRAPHY: Kagan 1976, no. 85

The ferocious lion sits submissively on its hind
legs, its front legs raised, calmed by the sounds
which Cupid coaxes from his flute. The playful
scene embodies the same idea of all-conquering
love which can tame even a wild animal. Although
the Browns' usual signature is absent, Raspe, in
James Tassie's catalogue of the cabinet of casts
from carved stones, identifies them as the
engravers (Raspe–Tassie, no. 6714), and archive
documents also show that the cameo was valued
by the engravers themselves at 60 pounds sterling
(Russian State Historical Archive, f. 468, op. 1,
ch. P, ed. khr. 3902, l. 73). YUK

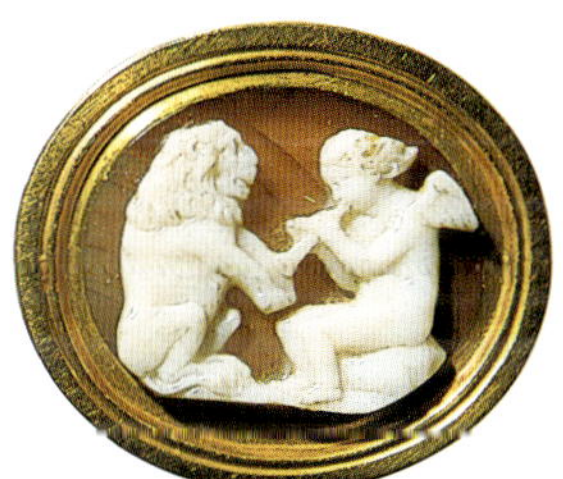

53

Intaglio: Cupid Sailing on his Quiver

Romain-Vincent Jeuffroy (1749–1826)

Sard, gold
2.2 × 2.5 cm
INSCRIBED on the left around the edge: *JEFFROY*
INV: I-3969
PROVENANCE: 1792, from the Saint-Moryce collection,
    Paris
BIBLIOGRAPHY: Maximova, p. 22; Miliotti, pl. 37

Romain-Vincent Jeuffroy, director of the Paris
mint, member of the Institut de France and knight
of the Légion d'Honneur, was one of the leading
French medal-makers and stone-engravers in the
latter part of the eighteenth and early nineteenth
century. In glyptic art he proved himself first and
foremost as a talented portraitist. Like his
contemporaries, however, Jeuffroy often copied
subjects from famous ancient Greek or Roman
gems, or created a composition 'in the spirit of
antiquity'. *Cupid Sailing on his Quiver* is one such
composition. The depiction of the god wielding
his bow as an oar and crossing the sea mounted
on his own quiver filled with arrows, one of
which serves as a mast, is to be found not only in
Jeuffroy's artistic heritage, but also that of other
European engravers. Antonio Giuliano believed
that eighteenth-century engravers took this motif
from sixteenth-century engravings (Giuliano,
p. 57). If, however, in the Renaissance era it was
often accompanied by the motto *SIC FUGA
VIOLENTA MONET* ('Thus swift flight
inspires'), by the end of the eighteenth century
this treatment of Cupid's image was seen as an
expression of his omnipotence, and the calm of
the waves as the embodiment of tender love.
Certainly this is how this intaglio was interpreted
in the catalogue of engraved stones by antiquarian
Alphonse Miliotti, who brought the collection to
Russia and in 1792 sold it to Catherine II. SK

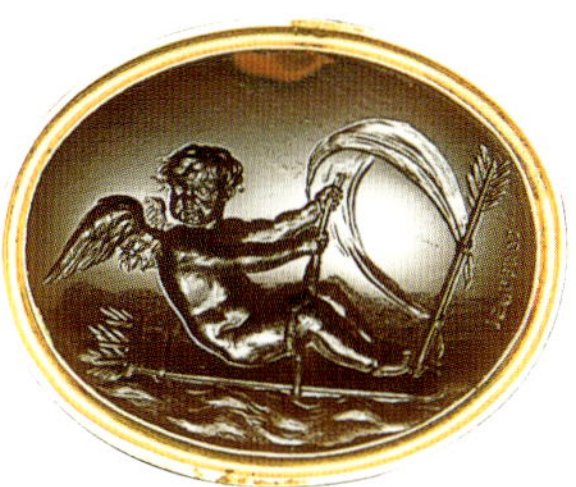

54
Fan

1780s

Germany

Mother-of-pearl, wood, parchment, metal; gilding,
    carving, watercolour
Length 28.4 cm
INV: E-15005
PROVENANCE: 1937, through the Purchasing
    Commission
BIBLIOGRAPHY: Western-European Fans, cat. 24

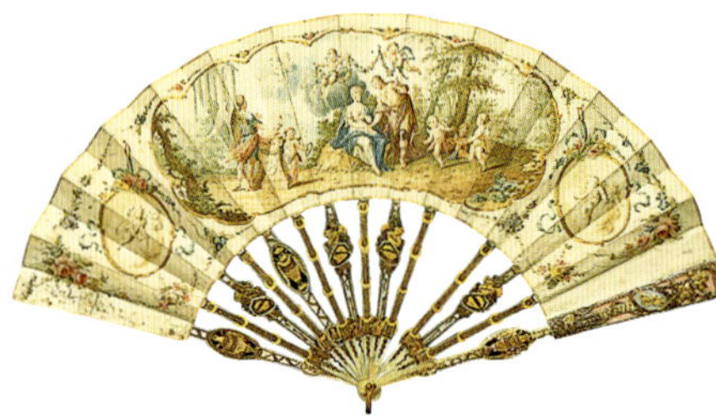

55
Fan

1770s

Western Europe

Mother-of-pearl, paper, metal, enamel; gilding, carving,
    gouache
Length 26.9 cm
SIGNED on the back, along the left edge: *B cegarg*
INV: E-15255
PROVENANCE: 1938, from the State Museum Fund
BIBLIOGRAPHY: Western-European Fans, cat. 34

As part of a lady's toilet, the fan was an
indispensable attribute of amorous interplay.
Along with the language of beauty-spots, the
figures on the fan would impart secret signs
to her admirer about the possibility of further
developments, hinting at the next 'move' from
his side. Fans were often decorated with *scènes
galantes*, and the figure of Cupid on a fan could
almost seem to be signalling to the admirer
through certain gestures of the lady's fan. EA & DO

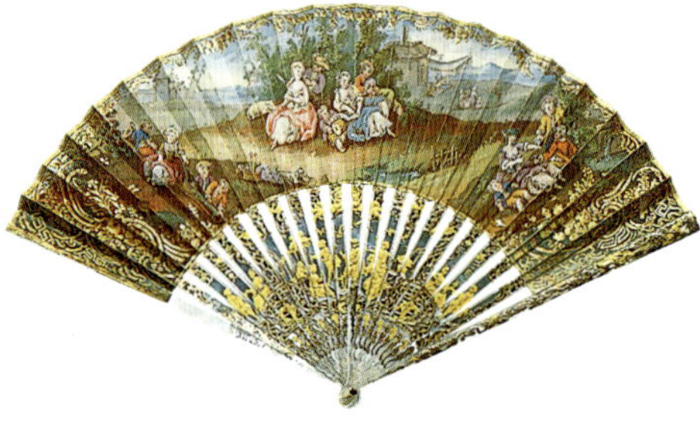

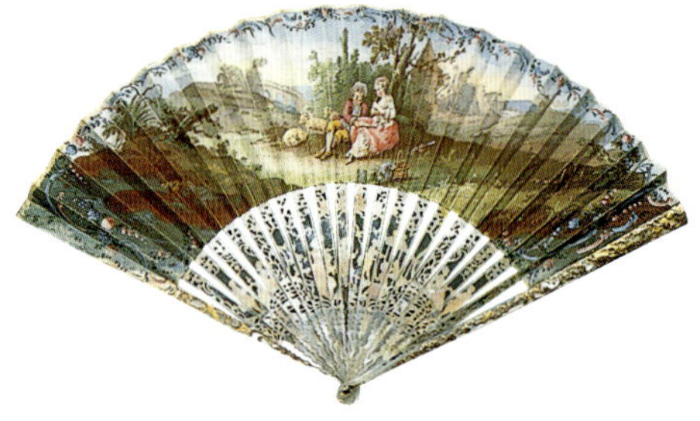

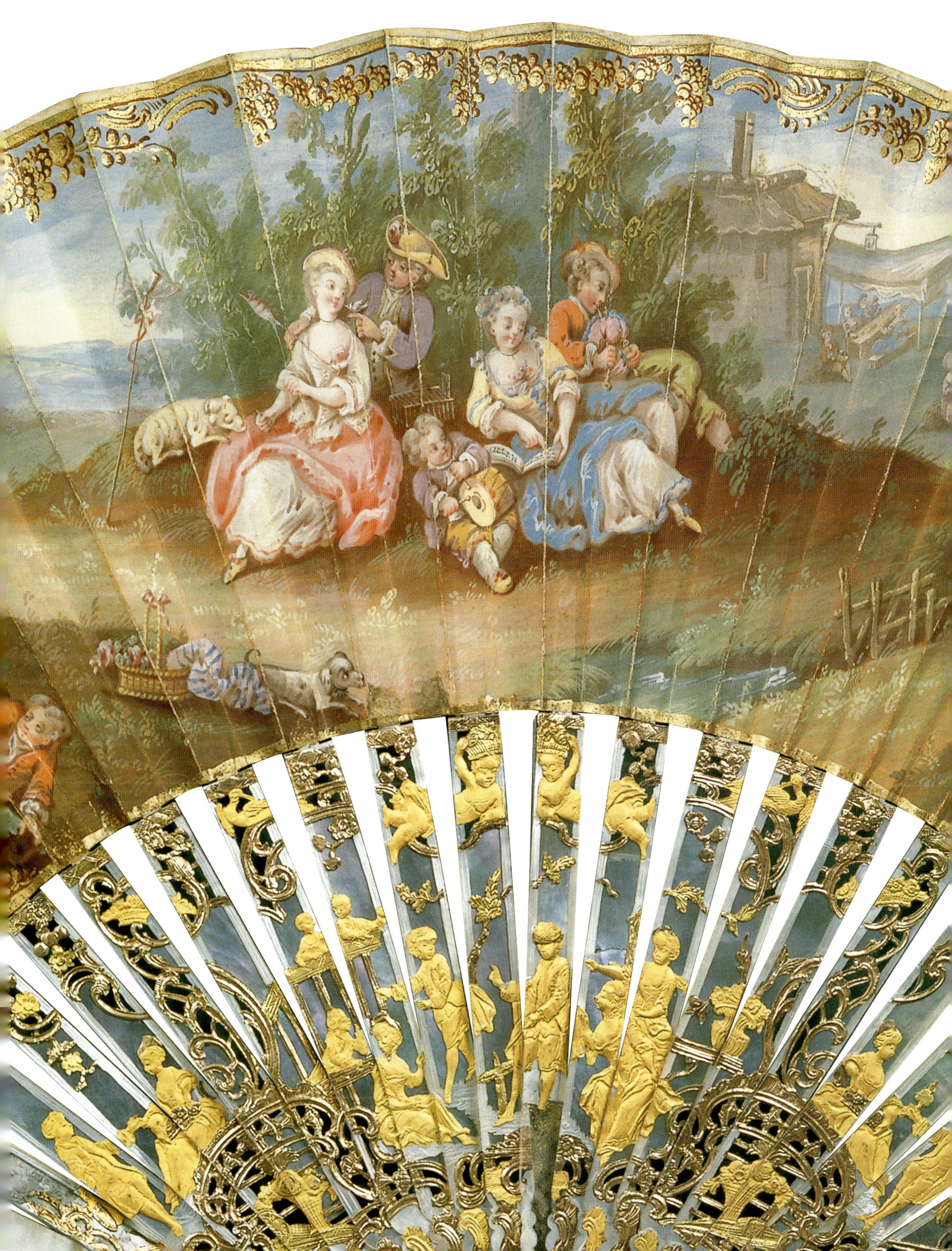

56
Chef-d'œuvres dramatiques

(vols. 1–5), vol. 3

Pierre Corneille (1606–84) & Thomas Corneille
(1625–1709)
A Londres, 1783

256 pp.

11.5 × 7.5 cm

Light-brown leather binding, triple gold-stamped border
on the covers, gold stamping on the spine; gold edge;
marbled paper fly-leaves; light-blue silk ribbon

EX LIBRIS: monogram *NA* below the imperial crown
of Emperor Nicholas II, label stuck in, round, in
light-blue paint, blind stamping

STAMP: *Bibliothèque de Tsarskoe Selo*, in black ink, oval,
in the centre the state coat of arms of Russia,
inscription along the oval

INV: 46479

PROVENANCE: after 1917, from the library of Emperor
Nicholas II; previously in the library of Tsarskoe Selo

Pierre Corneille, the seventeenth-century
playwright, is famous for his tragedies written
in the classical style, as well as comedies and
courtly verse, which were hugely popular amongst
his contemporaries, and remained influential in
Europe and Russia for many generations to come.
His younger brother, Thomas Corneille, was a
writer, translator, author of dramas, comedies and
touchingly sentimental courtly plays. He was one
of the court's favourite playwrights.

Books by the most popular authors were
often issued in a small format so that they could
be taken on journeys and walks, or put into a
pocket or under the pillow. OZ

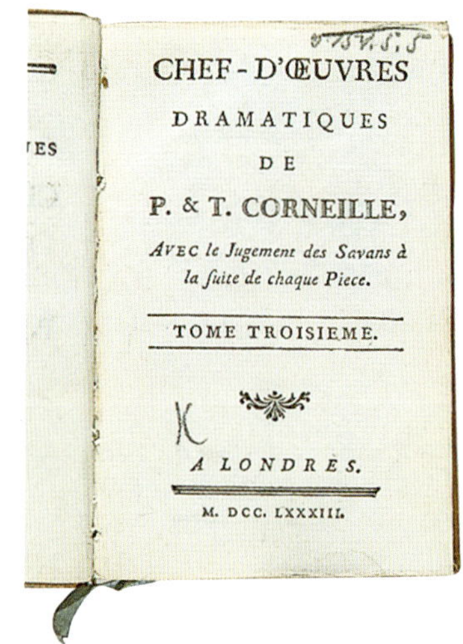

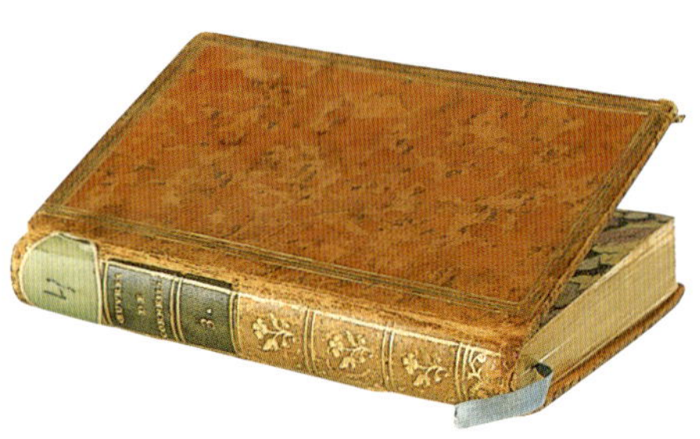

57
Les arrets d'amours, avec
L'Amant rendu Cordelier…

(vols. 1–2), vol. 1

Martial d'Auvergne (de Paris) (1460–1508)
Paris, chez Pierre Gandouin, 1731

[XLVIII] 290 pp.

16.5 × 10 cm

Engraved vignette on title page

Green leather binding, gold and blind stamping on
the covers and spine; edge decorated in imitation
marble; marbled paper fly-leaves; pink silk ribbon

EX LIBRIS: *The Imperial Hermitage. Dept of the Middle
Ages Ts. S. Ars. Cat. V. r. 33 No……*; label stuck on,
with typed and hand-written text

INV: 94987

PROVENANCE: after 1917, from the Imperial Hermitage;
previously in the Arsenal, Tsarskoe Selo

BIBLIOGRAPHY: Graesse IV, pp. 421–2

The author of the book, Martial, a French writer
from Auvergne or Paris, wrote around the second
half of the fifteenth to early sixteenth century.
His work *Les arrêts d'amours* ('Love sentences'
or 'Legal decrees concerning love') was first
published in 1528. It was extremely popular for
more than two hundred years, and was reprinted
a number of times. It is a humorous prose
composition, in which the author parodies the
courtly code of conduct surrounding love and the
tradition of 'love trials' of the twelfth century by
writing a discussion of love matters in the form
of court examinations. OZ

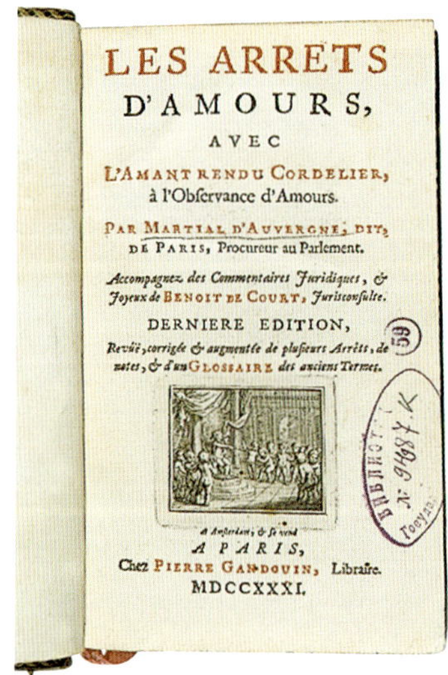

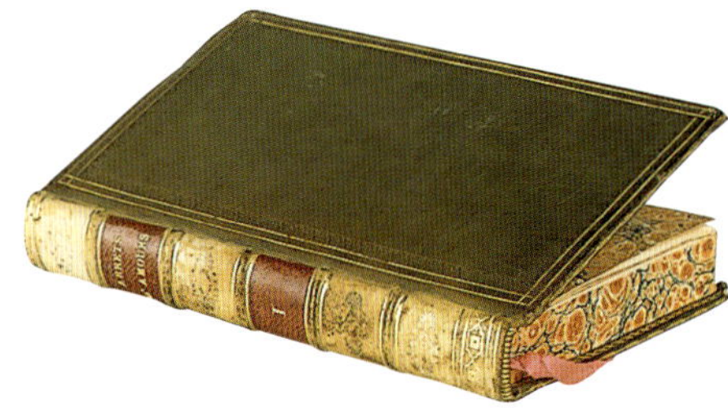

58

Œuvres de M. Dorat

vol. 2, owner's convolute

Claude-Joseph Dorat (1734–80)

Contents:

1. *Idylles de Saint Cyr, ou l'Hommage du Coeur* (*A Amsterdam, et se trouve a Paris, Chez Delalain, 1771*) 21 pp., 1 engraved frontispiece, engraved headpiece and tailpiece
INVENTORY AUTHOR: Clément-Pierre Marillier (1740–1808); frontispiece and headpiece engraver: Emmanuel de Ghendt (1738–1815); signed: *C.p. Marillier. inv. E. de Ghendt sculp*; tailpiece engraved by Antoine-Jean Duclos (1742–95); signed: *C.p. marillier. del. A. J. Duclos sculp. 1771*

2. *Ma philosophie* (*A La Haye, et se trouve a Paris, Chez Delalain, 1771*) 48 pp., 1 section l. engraving, engraved headpiece and tailpiece
INVENTORY AUTHOR: Clément-Pierre Marillier (1740–1808); engraver: Emmanuel de Ghendt (1738–1815)

3. *Epitre à Catherine II, imperatrice de toutes les Russies* (*Paris, Jorry, 1765*) 26 pp., engraved headpiece and tailpiece
INVENTORY AUTHOR: Charles Eisen (1720–78); engraver: Joseph de Longueil (1730–92); signed below the tailpiece: *Ch. Eisen. Inv. Et fec. 1765 J de Longueil sculp. 1765*

4. *Lettres d'une chanoinesse de Lisbonne à Melcour, officier François, précédées de quelques reflexions* (*A La Haye, et se trouve a Paris, Chez Lambert, Jorry, et Delalain, 1770*) 117 pp., 1 section l. engraving, engraved headpiece and tailpiece
INVENTORY AUTHOR: Charles Eisen (1720–78); engraver: Jean Massard (1740–1822)
Signed under the tailpiece: *Ch. Eisen. inv. 1770 Massard sculp.*

22 × 14 cm

BINDING: eighteenth-century in brown leather with triple gold-stamped border on the binding and gold stamping on the spine; gold edge; 'peacock-feather' fly-leaf paper

INV: 26188

PROVENANCE: 1968, from collection of G. I. Byalik

BIBLIOGRAPHY: Cohen, col. 162, 164–6

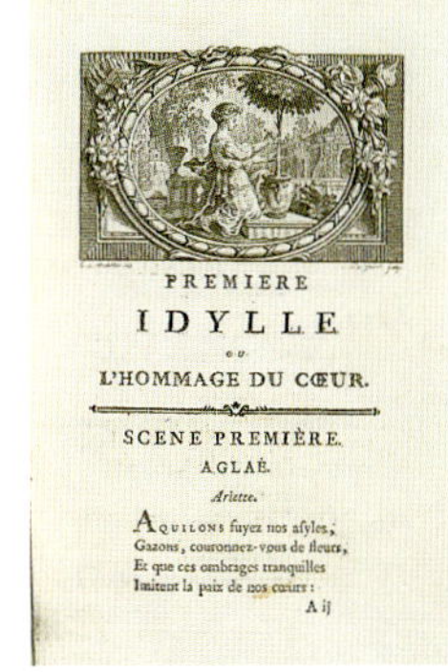

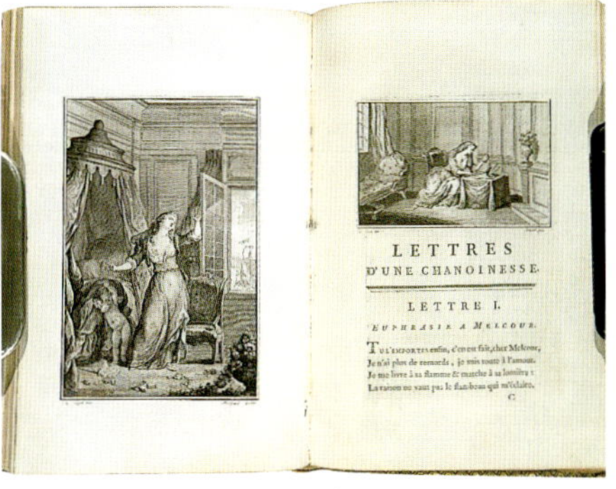

This book is the second volume of a conventional, multi-volume collected works by Claude-Joseph Dorat, compiled by the owner from separate works by the author which had been issued in different editions. The original title pages are entirely or partly (the imprint information) stuck in. GD

59

Le Temple de Gnide. Mis en Vers Par M. Colardeau

Charles-Pierre Colardeau (1732–76)
A Paris, Chez le Jay, [1773]

[6], 88 pp., [8] l. engraving

22 × 14 cm

BINDING: eighteenth-century in brown leather with triple linear gold-stamped border on the binding and gold stamping on the spine; marbled edge; 'peacock-feather' fly-leaf paper

INV: 266122

PROVENANCE: 1968, from the collection of G. I. Byalik

BIBLIOGRAPHY: Cohen, col. 120–1

This volume is an exposition in verse of the prose-poem 'Le Temple de Gnide' by Montesquieu (Charles de Secondat, Baron de la Brède et de Montesquieu, 1689–1755). The engraved title page bears a portrait of the French dramatist Pierre Corneille (1606–84), and there are seven further pages of engravings – one for each canto of the poem – from drawings by Charles Monnet (1732–after 1808). The engravers are Jean-Charles Baquoy (1721–77), Nicolas Delaunay (1739–92), Isidore-Stanislas Helman (1743–1806/10), Louis-Joseph Masquelier (1741–1811), François-Denis Née (1739?–1817) and Nicolas Ponce (1746–1831).
GD

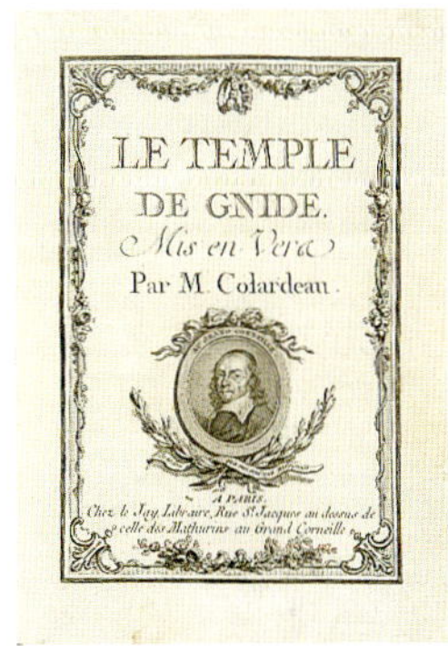

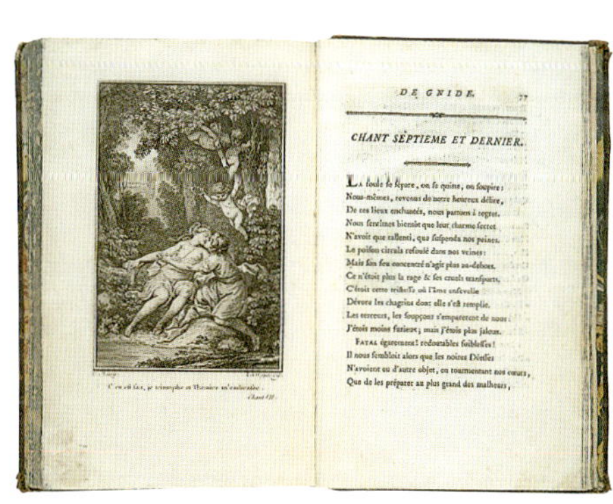

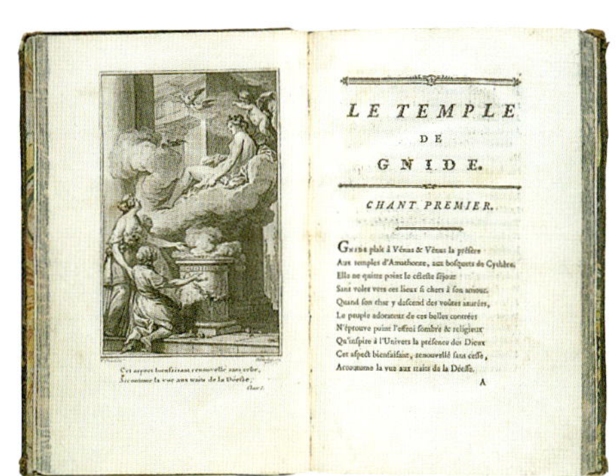

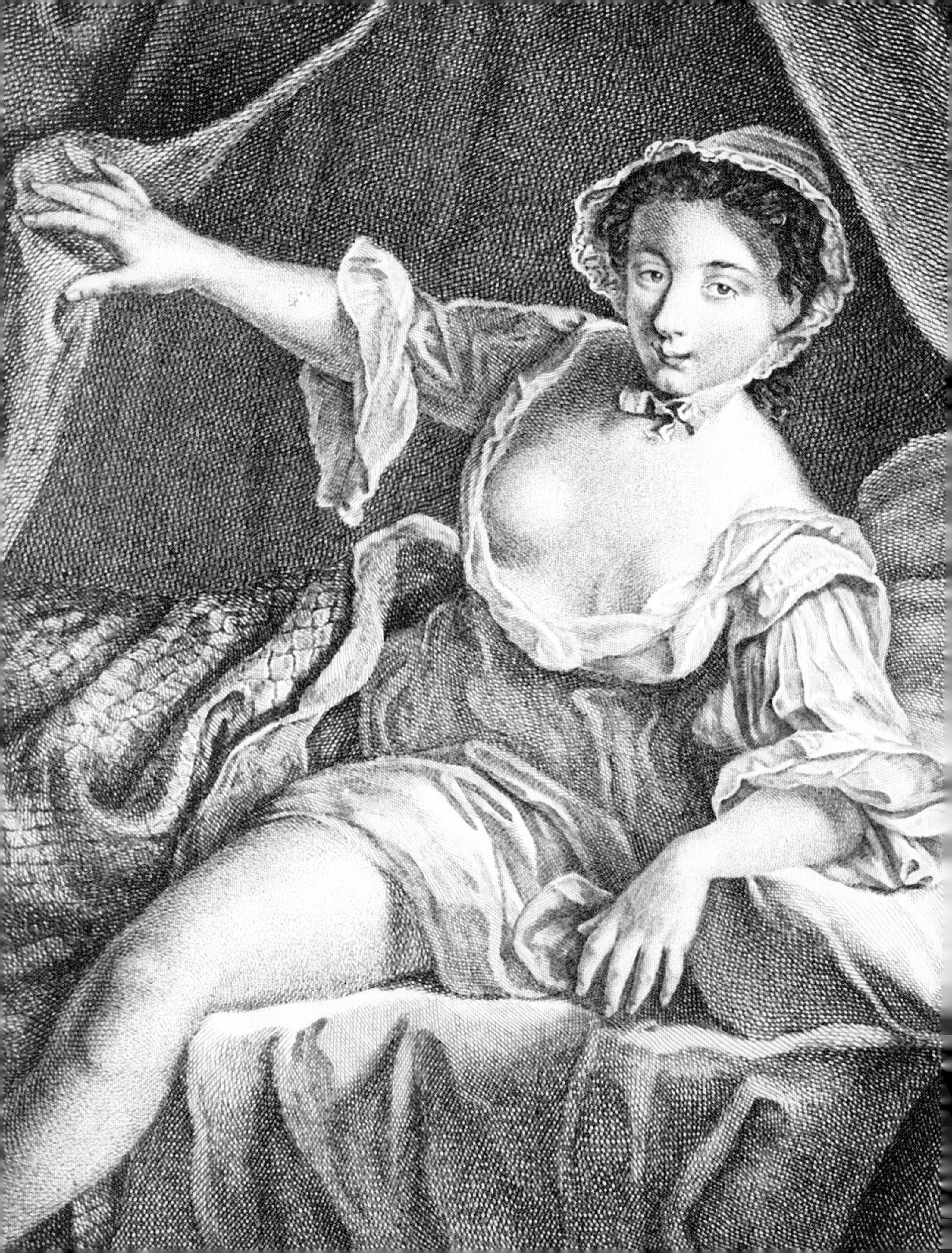

Le Billet Doux

The *billet doux*, or love letter, is the first step on the path towards union between
the beloved – the starting-point for all subsequent encounters and transgressions.
The correspondence is started by the young man, as he strives to catch the attention
of his intended. His pen uses delicate turns of phrase (often copied from romantic
novels), designed to draw her into a correspondence which will become more and
more candid. The girl always responds with more restraint, although her words
may conceal bottomless wells of passion which will capture the heart of her
beloved: surely it is Eros himself who is directing her pen (cat. 64, 65).

The letter is intended to arouse reciprocal emotions in the girl and to provoke her
towards decisive action. *Irresolute Virtue* (cat. 62) is a wonderfully clear illustration
of the feelings the girl experiences in such a situation. In the eighteenth century the
lot of the virtuous was to be deceived. This, however, is but one stage of the girl's
education in love, for which cunning and enigmatic Cupid is responsible; it is but
one step in his triumphal procession.

Like today's emails and text messages, letter-writing was a time-consuming
activity. In French pictures and engravings on pastoral themes, the heroes – peasant
shepherds and shepherdesses – would exchange letters with the help of the romantic
dove, who carried their sweet words back and forth. In reality, however, letters
were sent through a chosen manservant or a trustworthy confidante of the girl
(cat. 61, 68). The confidante might also be induced into organising the inevitable
next step – a secret meeting, perhaps, or a clandestine entry into the girl's rooms
under cover of night.

An eighteenth-century girl would wait for the love letter on tenterhooks – far
better for her to agonise over her virtue than to suffer from the thought that no one
was interested in her. For this reason it was not difficult to catch the girl on the hook
of a *billet doux*. In Descourtis's engraving after the painting by Schall, *The Imps*
(cat. 63; p. 103), two mischief-makers have distracted the young bathers with
a letter, and while the girls are immersed in reading, the lads start to reel in their
items of clothing. These are actions guided by the elusive god of love.

Pamela (detail)
Jean Heudelot
After the painting by Philippe Mercier
1770s (?)
cat. 66

60

News of the Beloved
Nouvelle du bien aimé

1780s–90s

François-Marie-Isidore Queverdo (1748–97) &
  Antoine-Louis Romanet (1748–1806)

Etching and engraving
280 × 312 mm; 281 × 313 mm
INSCRIPTIONS: *NOUVELLE DU BIEN AIMÉ /
  A Monsieur Jeofret / Par Son Serviteur et Ami Queverdo
  Dessiné et Gravé à l'eau-forte par F.M. Queverdo / Terminé
  au Burin par Romanet. / A Paris chez l'Auteur, rue
  Poupée S. André la Porte côchèr Nº 6.*
INV: OG-228054
PROVENANCE: 1927, from the private libraries of the
  Winter Palace (RIC) (Lugt Suppl. 2681ᵃ)
BIBLIOGRAPHY: Le Blanc III, p. 354, no. 53
  (state III/III); Nagler KL XIII, p. 332, nr. 41; P.-B. III,
  p. 366; p. 412, no. 4

The confidante or maid brings the girl a note from
her beloved. Having sunk to her knees she reads
her the contents, which begin 'Ma chère'. With
what tenderness and deep affection the maiden
gazes at her beloved's portrait in the small locket
lying on her lap! She has obviously just got up: on
the bedside table are washing things, and the letter,
like a morning wash, delights and refreshes her.

Beneath the oval of the main picture there is
a small emblem in a circle. It shows Eros fleeing
with a sealed love letter in one hand and an arrow
in the other. The message is intended for the eyes
of the female lover, the arrow for her heart. He
hurries towards her through rose bushes, with
a dog – Fidelity – tethered tightly to his hand.

The print was created by Queverdo using
the technique of etching, and finished by Romanet
with a burin, as can be seen from the detailed
inscription at the foot of the sheet. DO

61

The Love Letter
Le billet doux

1750s–60s

Claude-Augustin-Pierre Duflos (1700–86)
After the painting by Louis Aubert
  (active 1740–80)

Etching and engraving
381 × 265 mm; 458 × 351 mm
INSCRIPTIONS: *LE BILLET DOUX.*
  De la plus pure ardeur vôtre Amant vous assure,
  Vous vous fiez à ses sermens.
  Philis, une ardeur aussi pure
  Repond-t'elle chez vous à ses vifs sentimens? /
  S'il en doutoit, Philis, il ne seroit pas sage
  De choisir un pareil grivois
  Pour vous faire un tendre mesaage.
  Tels porteurs fort souvent se font payer deux fois.
          Jean Aubert
*Peint par L. Aubert / Gravé par Cl. Duflos. / à Paris chez
  Cl. Duflos, ruë Galande à côté de S.ᵗ Blaise.*
INV: OG-228074
PROVENANCE: 1927, from the private libraries of the
  Winter Palace (RIC) (Lugt Suppl. 2681ᵃ)
BIBLIOGRAPHY: Le Blanc II, p. 153, no. 175; Nagler KL
  III, p. 557; P.-B. II, p. 56, no. 1

The girl, called Philis, avidly reads the note she
has just received. A messenger patiently awaits
instructions for her answer, which she will clearly
now write: two quills stand ready alongside the
cup of steaming hot chocolate on the side table.

A love letter often turned into a passionate
message: from the simple conveying of
information to an ardent poem was but one step.
However, written expressions of love in the
eighteenth century followed specific formulae that
regulated the degree of intimacy and nature of
the relationship in a particular way. The pictures
on the wall, enclosed in fine rocaille cartouches,
leave no doubt that this correspondence is reaching
its culmination. For a girl's bedroom the subject
of these canvases is too risqué: the mythological
themes behind them speak of the amorous unions
between mortal women and Zeus. On the left wall
Leda is kissing the swan, while on the back wall
Danaë is looking skyward with her maidservant,
who has spread out her skirts in the naïve hope of
catching the golden rain. In Aubert's painting there
is also the alter ego of the young heroine's lover:
a black cat, the image of an insistent and flattering
lover, who tries to pull her shoe off as she reads.

Whereas in the romantic world letters are
delivered by a carrier-pigeon (its arrival or
departure – with a tender message tied to its foot –
would become a popular literary and artistic motif),
with the boudoir scene everything is simpler. The
letter is delivered by a trusted emissary – in this
case, a somewhat scruffy young man with a travel
bag in his arms and a handkerchief prosaically
sticking out of his pocket. DO

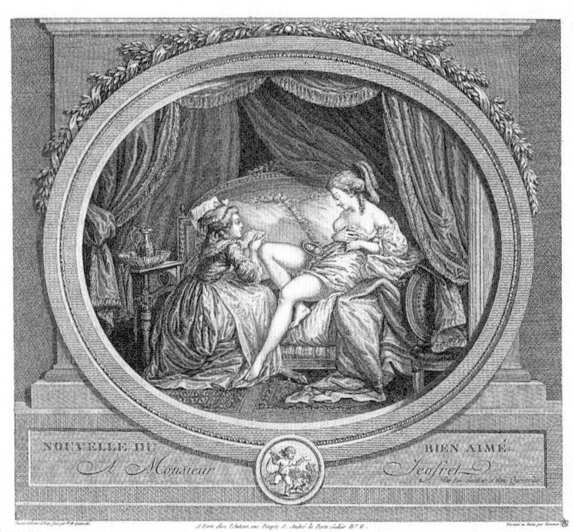

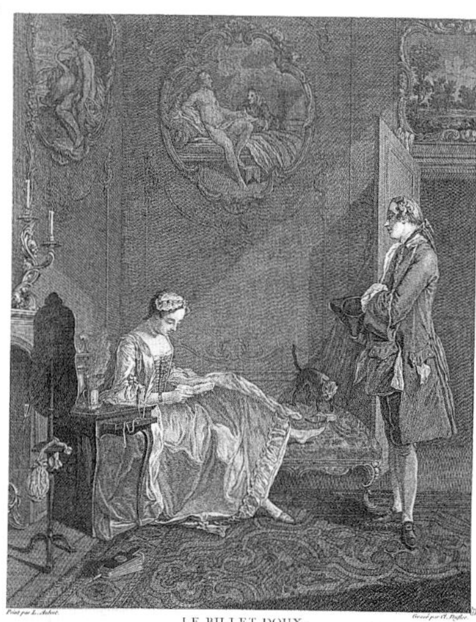

62

Irresolute Virtue
La vertu irrésolue

1781

Antoine-François Dennel (active in Paris,
   1760–1815)
After the painting by Louise-Elisabeth Vigée-
Lebrun (1755–1842)

Etching and engraving
313 × 236 mm
INSCRIPTIONS: *LA VERTU IRRESOLUE / Dedié à
Madame Lebrun Peintre / Tiré du Cabinet de Monsieur
Besselieure / Par son très Humble et très Obeissant
Serviteur Dennel*
*Louise Elisabeth Vigée Pinx. / Dennel Sculp. / Se trouve
à Paris chez l'Auteur, rue du Petit Bourbon attenant la
Foire St Germain*
INV: OG-123890
PROVENANCE: before 1928, from main collection (Lugt
Suppl. 2681ᵃ); acquired before 1830s
BIBLIOGRAPHY: Bourcard, p. 374 (state 'avec la lettre');
IFF VI, p. 507, no. 7 (pair with no. 8; cat. 27); Nagler
KL III, p. 341 (Louis Dennel nach Boucher); Le Blanc
II, p. 108, no. 19 (Louis Dennel d'après Boucher);
Ozerkov, no. 28

Virtue does not come in half measures: it either
exists or does not exist. The word *vertu* expressly
refers to the sphere of moral and ethical
expectations relating to women's behaviour,
including everything that Christian dogma
imbues in the word 'virtue'.

   In this engraving, after a painting by the
famous portraitist Louise-Elisabeth Vigée-Lebrun,
the young woman is obviously admiring a locket
containing the portrait of her lover and is silently
questioning him about a shared secret. The subject
of her question is clearly hidden in the letter,
which lies in her drooping hand. Is your vow
genuine? Can I trust you? Her onerous thoughts
lead to nothing: no conclusions can be drawn by
using logic, and she cannot act against her feelings.
She must simply pull herself together and admit
her feelings to herself. 'The first sigh of love is
the last of wisdom,' writes Antoine Bret in *L'école
amoureuse* (1670). The whole question consists
in whether or not her lover is worthy of the girl's
passionate transport. 'Only the first step is difficult,
and then there's no stopping the sanctimonious
ones! Their love is a real explosion: it only grows
stronger from resistance,' writes Valmont about
his own sanctimonious one, Madame de Tourvel
(*Les Liaisons Dangereuses*, no. 99).

   Vigée-Lebrun's painting *La vertu irrésolue*
was put up for sale at the Hôtel Drouot auction
house in Paris on 16 December 1985 (lot no. 20).
The work was not included by the artist in her own
catalogue. It is clear that it was painted in 1774–5,
that is, when she herself was no more than 20
years' old. In this connection, it is interesting that
her name is given in two different ways. In the
inscription the engraver uses her maiden name
('Louise Elisabeth Vigée') while in the dedicatory
inscription he is already using the name of her
husband ('dedicated to Madame Lebrun, artist…').
Her marriage to Jean-Baptiste-Pierre Lebrun took
place on 11 January 1776. However, just five years
later, in 1781, the picture was in the collection of
Besselieure, as shown by the inscription on
Dennel's engraving. All this information taken
together would seem to suggest that behind the
painting there is a story from the private biography
of the famous artist that she did not want to
include in her *Memoirs* (1835–7).   DO

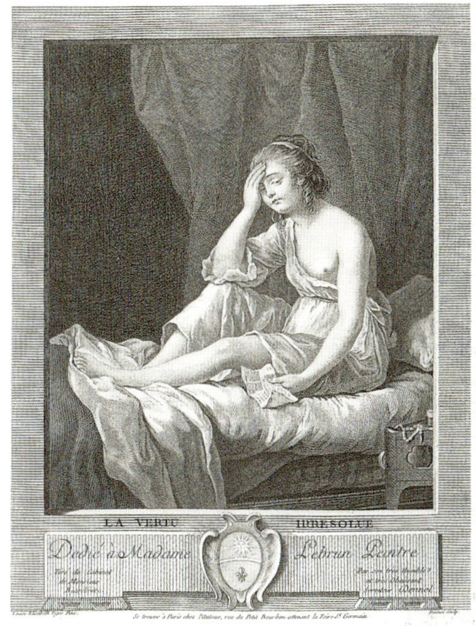

63

The Imps
Les espiègles

c. 1798

Charles-Melchior Descourtis (1753–1820)
After the painting by Jean-Frédéric Schall
   (1752–1825)

Etching, wash, colour printing
558 × 430 mm; 623 × 484 mm
INSCRIPTIONS: *Les Espiègles*
*Schall pinx. / Descourtis sculp. / A Paris chez Descourtis,
Rue des Grands Degrées No. 12.*
INV: OG-231482
PROVENANCE: 1927, from the private libraries of the
Winter Palace (RIC) (Lugt Suppl. 2681ᵃ)
BIBLIOGRAPHY: Le Blanc II, p. 116, no. 3; Nagler KL III,
p. 357; P.-B. II, p. 747, no. 3 (state II/II); Th.-B. IX,
p. 122

While the young girls are distracted by the love
note they have found, the young men use a
cunning device to pull a slipper out of their
belongings. On close inspection, the individual
words of the letter which the girls are holding
can be made out. The letter ends obsequiously,
'ton Ami'.   DO

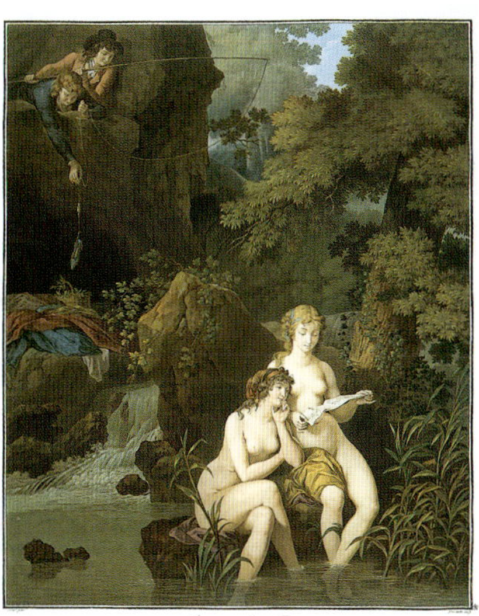

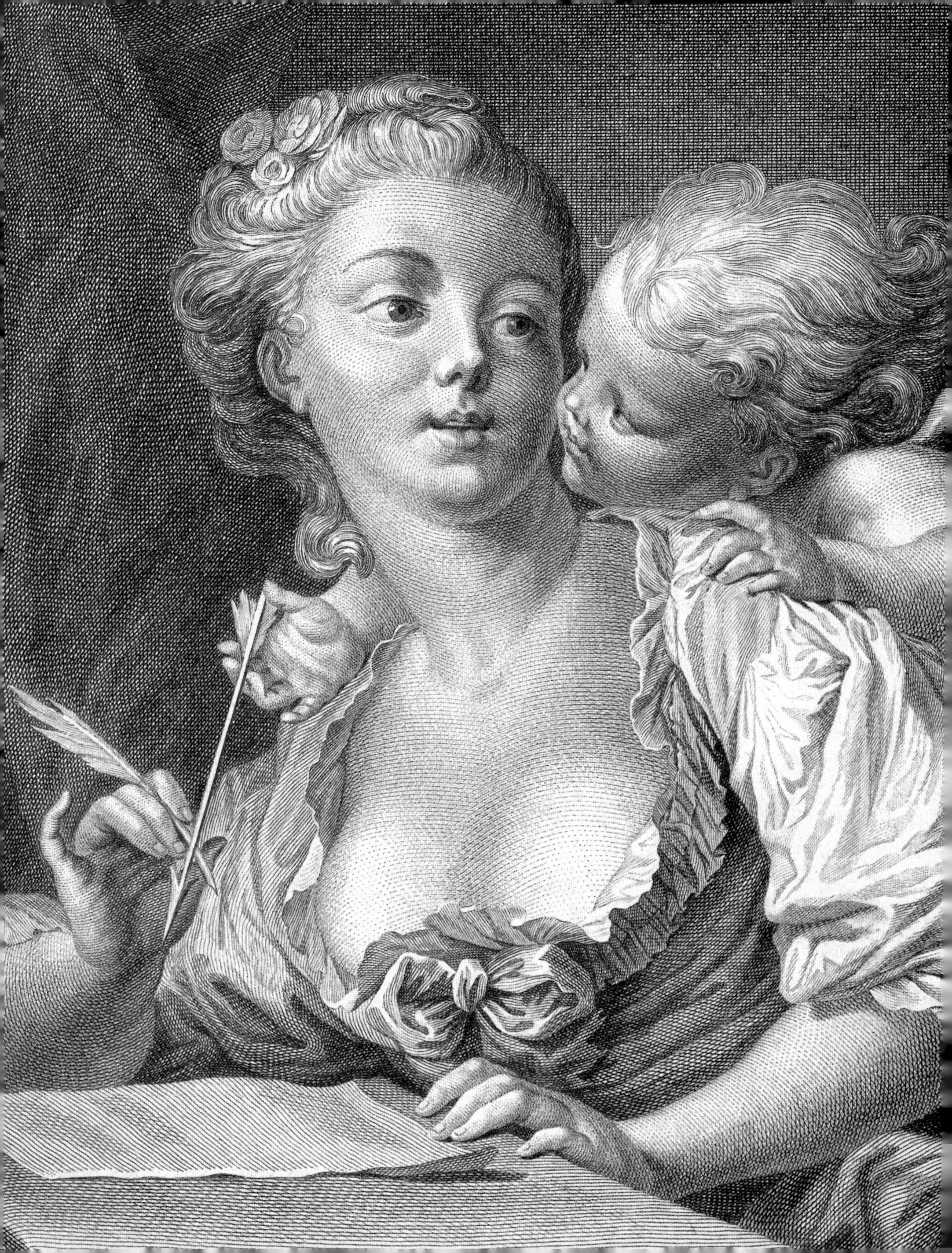

64

Favourable Inspiration
L'inspiration favorable

1783

Louis-Michel Halbou (1730–1809)
After the composition by Jean-Honoré Fragonard
(1732–1806)

Etching
400 × 294 mm
INSCRIPTIONS: *L'Inspiration Favorable*
Peint par H. Fragonard, Peintre du Roi. / Gravé par
L.M. Halbou / AParis chez l'Auteur, Rue de Fouare
Maison de Mr. Maillar, Procureur au Parlement.
WATERMARK: inscription (illegible); sheet duplicated
INV: OG-129173
PROVENANCE: from main collection; acquired before
1830s
BIBLIOGRAPHY: Bourcard, p. 211; Delteil, p. 166;
Lawrence & Dighton, p. 31, no. 70; Ozerkov, no. 68;
P.-B. II, p. 377, no. 8; Rosenberg, p. 426, fig. 21;
Th.-B. XV, p. 497

In the eighteenth century, letter-writing was a
key form of narrative, both in real life and fiction.
Indeed, it is almost impossible to distinguish
between real letters and those written by novelists;
for example, Mademoiselle de Lespinasse
(1732–76) and the heroines of Rousseau and
Laclos write in exactly the same style. The letter
is not just an outpouring of emotion, it is a
complex expression of feelings communicated
in a particular way.

The society gentleman or woman spent
a significant portion of his or her time on
correspondence. Richardson's Clarissa writes five
letters a day, and Lovelace answers her by return.
The complex etiquette surrounding the love letter
is a distinguishing feature of eighteenth-century
French culture. Special manuals on writing love
letters existed, from which letter-writers copied
whole passages. They could also take their most
passionate lines from epistolary novels. To the
eighteenth-century reader, this celebrated genre
did not seem in the least far-fetched. Thus, the
Marquise de Merteuil admonishes Cécile Volanges:
'You must understand that when you write to
someone, you are doing it for them, not for
yourself. You should therefore try to say not so
much what you think, as what he would most like
to hear' (*Les Liaisons Dangereuses*, no. 105).

The letter is a means of deferring all other
expressions of love – meetings, explanations,
physical intimacy. At the same time, it forms part
of an imaginary dialogue: it reconstructs the
presence of the beloved. Writing a letter is a way
of remaining intimate from a distance. When
distance is lost, so is the sublimation of love: in
correspondence the physical aspect disappears,
making way for an ideal world of tender feelings.
The letter is born of the hope for mutual love.
'Like desire, the lover's missive awaits a response;
implicit in it is the demand for a reply from the
other person, without which his image will be
spoilt, tarnished, altered' (Barthes, pp. 262–3).

In poetry, the love letter is idealised, and takes
on a value of its own. Love (Cupid) inspires the
poet to compose a lyrical letter and to pour out his
soul in verse. In Boileau's work, it is Cupid who
instructs poets in the art of poetry. Lyrical poetry
attains an immortality in which the object of love
and the author of the message merely provide an
occasion for composing a poem. It is the poet who
becomes the voice of love, the living embodiment
of Cupid. Such is Sappho in Fragonard's picture,
which is the basis for this print. It is characteristic
that the picture had a number of titles: *Sappho
Inspired by Cupid*, *The Muse and Cupid*, *Poetry*, and
Divine Inspiration (Cuzin, pp. 328–9, nos. 355–8).
The titles gradually move away from the image
of the poet as a human being, turning her into the
earthly intermediary of Cupid whose pen is ready
to become a carefully aimed arrow. The poet turns
out to be entirely subservient to Cupid. DO

65

The Wound without Danger
La blessure sans danger

1785

Simon-Charles Miger (1736–1820)
After the painting by François Boucher (1703–70)

Etching
448 × 342 mm
INSCRIPTIONS: *LA BLESSURE SANS DANGER*
Peint par F. Boucher Peintre du Roi / et Gravé par
S.C. Miger Graveur du Roi. / A Paris chez Miger
Place de l'Estrapade la grande Maison neuve au coin
de la Rue des Postes A.P.D.R.
INSCRIPTION on the sheet of paper the girl is holding:
Souffrez que l'Amour vous blesse / Et quittant votre fierté /
Vous scaurez que la tendresse / Est l'Ame de la Beauté
INV: OG-228147
PROVENANCE: 1927, from the private libraries of the
Winter Palace (RIC) (Lugt Suppl. 2681ª)
BIBLIOGRAPHY: Boucher 1978, no. 1427 (state I/II);
Ozerkov, no. 26; P.-B. III, 100, no. 1 (state I/II)

The brush of the arrow which does not wound its
victim is an allegory for the power of love: Cupid's
arrow does not so much wound as irritate and
awaken feelings. This is shown in the four lines of
verse held by the girl. In *Les Bijoux indiscrets*, the
'femme tendre', or sensitive woman, is a key concept
in Mirzoza's pseudo-scientific metaphysics of the
soul and her arguments for the location of the soul
in the body: 'The soul of the sensitive woman is
usually to be found in her heart, but sometimes also
in her jewels' (*Bijoux*, p. 182). And that is when the
soul turns out to be especially vulnerable to Cupid's
arrows: when the soul falls in love, the body
subjugates itself entirely (Barthes, pp. 101–3).

The second state of the engraving was entitled
Le billet doux. The sketch was used again by Boucher
– in a work entitled *L'éducation de l'Amour*, engraved
by Gilles Demarteau in the crayon manner (Boucher
1978, no. 605). DO

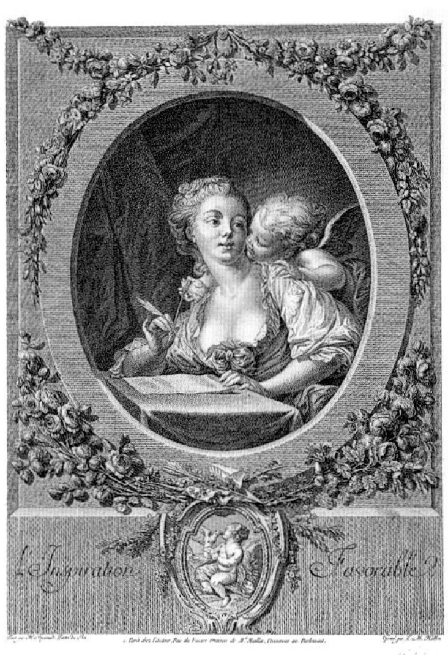

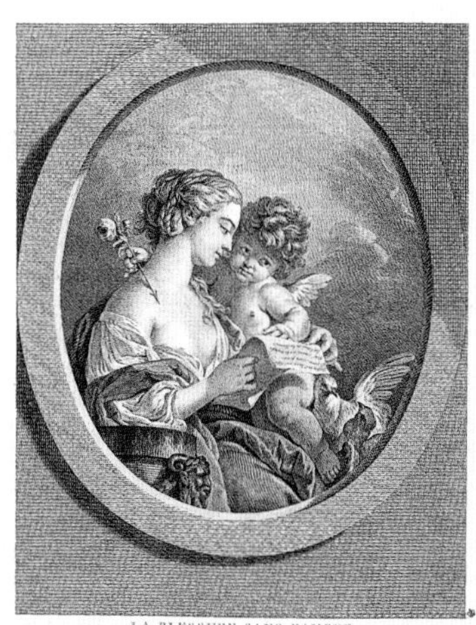

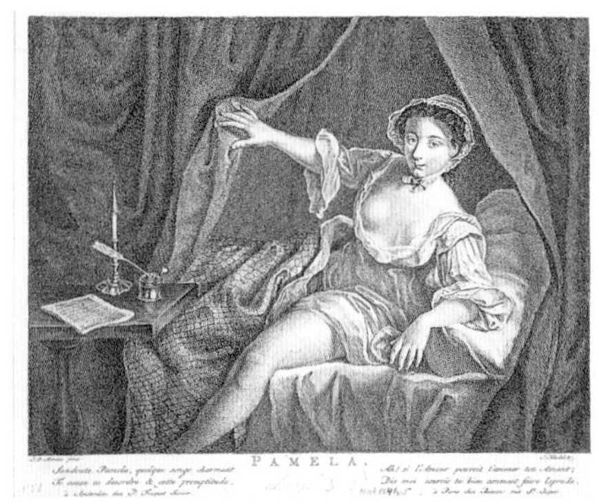

66
Pamela

1770s (?)

Jean Heudelot (1730– ?)
After the painting by Philippe Mercier (1689–1760)

Etching
242 × 290 mm
INSCRIPTIONS: *PAMELA.*
> *Sandoute, Pamela, quelque songe charmant / Te cause
> ce desordre & cette promptitude, / Ah! si l'Amour pouvoit
> t'amener ton Amant; / Dis moi saurois tu bien comment
> faire laprude.*
> *J.P. Mercier pinx. / J. Heudelot. / à Amsterdam chez
> P. Fouquet Junior. / à Paris chez Bassan ruë St. Jaques.*
WATERMARK: *FVI*
INV: OG-124665
PROVENANCE: before 1928, from main collection
> (Lugt Suppl. 2681[a]); acquired before 1830s
BIBLIOGRAPHY: Le Blanc II, p. 358, no. 5; Ozerkov,
> no. 100

Pamela, or Virtue Rewarded (1740; Russ. trans.
1787–96), the novel in letters by Samuel Richardson
(1689–1761), was the first of Richardson's novels,
and is much more optimistic than the later *Clarissa*
(1747–8), in which the heroine dies from grief at the
end of her narrative. Unlike Clarissa, the virtuous
behaviour of Pamela Andrews is finally rewarded.

The heroine of *Pamela* appears to write her
life-story herself through what seem to be real
letters, describing herself and laying bare the
depths of her soul to immortality. She writes her
autobiography, not unlike Richardson himself,
who wrote his at the age of 68. It is worth noting
that Richardson did not consider *Pamela* to be a
work of fiction. The idea for the novel came to
him when he was working on a manual of letter-
writing, using sample (genuine) letters designed to
ease the task of daily correspondence. In the first
edition of *Pamela*, the author's name was omitted,
and in the later novels Richardson was cast as the
editor of what appeared to be real letters.

The literary convention of presenting
fictional correspondence as genuine reflected
the conventions of real life. In 'a series of familiar
letters from a beautiful young damsel to her
parents… published in order to cultivate the
principles of virtue and religion in the minds of
the youth of both sexes', Richardson informed his
readers of the instructive story of a young maid
who is mercilessly pursued by her master, young
squire B. The latter, touched in the end by her high
moral qualities, offers her his hand and his heart.
In the course of the novel Pamela manages to
avoid one trap after another and follow the path
of virtue single-mindedly. She falls in love with
her pursuer and is rewarded with a happy
marriage. Richardson's readers, however, were
not always ready to espouse such Panglossian
philosophy. They saw Pamela as calculating, and
many parodies appeared: *Anti-Pamela*, *Pamela
Censured*, *Pamela's Conduct in High Life* (1741) and,
lastly, Fielding's *Joseph Andrews* (1742). However,
the impression created by Richardson's novel
remained unchanged. The author succeeded in
achieving his goal: to create a heroine who is torn
apart by contradictory feelings – the wish to
preserve her virtue and the desire not to lose the
person she had genuinely started to love. The
figure of Pamela, who combined inexperience
with the strong and sensitive nature of a person
aware of her individual rights, was seen as an
illustration of the eighteenth-century predicament.
It was precisely for this that Diderot praised the
author in his *Éloge de Richardson* (1761). DO

67
The Pretty Sleep
Le joli dormir

1760–70s

Elisabeth-Claire Tournay (1731–73)
After the composition by Étienne Jeaurat
(1699–1789)

Etching and engraving
460 × 332 mm
INSCRIPTIONS: *Le Joli Dormir*
> *Puisque d'un cher Epoux vous regrétés l'absence, /
> Ce Sommeil ne sçauroit venir d'indifference, / Sans doute
> qu'en dormant pour calmer vos soupirs, / Un rêve
> officieux le rend a vos desirs, / Ah! dirés vous bientôt,
> je n'ai vû qu'un mensonge; / Mais le plaisir est-il autre
> chose qu'un songe.*
> *Peint par. E. Jeaurat. / Gravé par Elisabeth Claire Tournay
> femme Tardieu. / A Paris chez J Tardieu Graveur du
> Roi rue du plâtre la 2e porte cochere entrant par la rue
> St. Jacques. / avec privilege du Roi*
WATERMARK: two-line inscription (illegible)
INV: OG-130862
PROVENANCE: before 1928, from main collection
> (Lugt Suppl. 2681[a]); acquired before 1830s
BIBLIOGRAPHY: Bourcard, p. 278; Delteil, pp. 124–5;
> Le Blanc IV, p. 51, no. 6; Ozerkov, no. 19

Having set the letter from her beloved aside, the
girl dozes lightly in an armchair. Her lapdog is
curled up in a ball beside her. The quiet, domestic
lifestyle of the beautiful young woman is an image
of comfort and peace. She dreams of her husband.
The beautiful romantic dream, evoked by Cupid,
softens the pain of his absence. This is exactly the
way Venus herself sleeps – for example, in the
picture by a pupil of Simon Vouet, *Venus Asleep
in the Clouds* (Budapest, Museum of Fine Arts;
Mérot, p. 413, no. R.75, fig. 544).

It was possible to escape from everyday
life in the eighteenth century through literary
creativity or by organising a salon. The subject
of this engraving is thought to be Madame Lalive
d'Epinay (née Tardieu d'Esclavelles), an
enlightened woman of her time, being both a
writer and hostess of a salon first at Montmorency
and then, from 1770, in Paris. D'Alembert,
Diderot, Marivaux, Marmontel, Montesquieu,
d'Holbach, Abbot Galiani, Baron Grimm
(a correspondent of and adviser to Catherine II)
all attended her salon. Following Rousseau's
Confessions, Madame Lalive d'Epinay published
her 'counter-confessions' (*L'Histoire de Madame
de Montbrillant*) in 1818, in which she described,
amongst other things, her reasons for being
unfaithful to her husband. This book has since
been re-appraised as a masterpiece of feminist
literature. DO

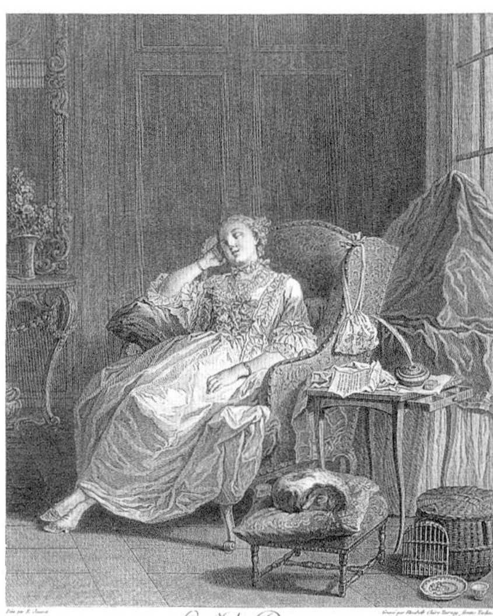

68

The Maid and Confidante
La soubrette confidente

1770s

Gérard Vidal (1742–1804)
After the painting by Nicolas Lavreince
(Niklas Lafrensen) (1737–1807)

Etching and engraving
420 × 302 mm; 455 × 335 mm
INSCRIPTIONS: *LA SOUBRETTE CONFIDENTE /
Dédié à Monsieur Boula de Nanteuil Maitre de Requêtes
Par son très humble serviteur Vidal.*
*Lavrins pinxit / G.Vidal Sculp. / A Paris ches l'Auteur rue
des Noyers, la 1ere porte côchère par la rue St. Jacques.*
WATERMARK: *FIN DE D♥TAMIZIER AUVERGNE*
INV: OG-228197
PROVENANCE: 1927, from the private libraries of the
Winter Palace (RIC) (Lugt Suppl. 2681ª)
BIBLIOGRAPHY: Bocher (Lavreince), p. 48, no. 61
(state IV/IV); Le Blanc IV, p. 120, no. 26 (state V/V);
P.-B. III, p. 615, no. 2

A girl sits at a table, holding the letter she has just
written. It is clearly a love letter: on the wall above
the girl's head is a picture entitled *Venus and Cupid*,
similar to the popular composition by Boucher. Her
maid is bending over her shoulder, appraising one
of her young mistress's first attempts at composing
a love letter.

The receipt of her first letter and the
composition of a reply was an important moment
in a girl's life. It was crucial that she should not
disgrace herself, that she should not give over-
hasty consent to a walk which might turn out to be
dangerous; but it was also important that she should
not come across as utterly sanctimonious. The
maid, traditionally her mistress's confidante in all
affairs of the heart, is experienced in such matters,
and always ready to dispense good advice. DO

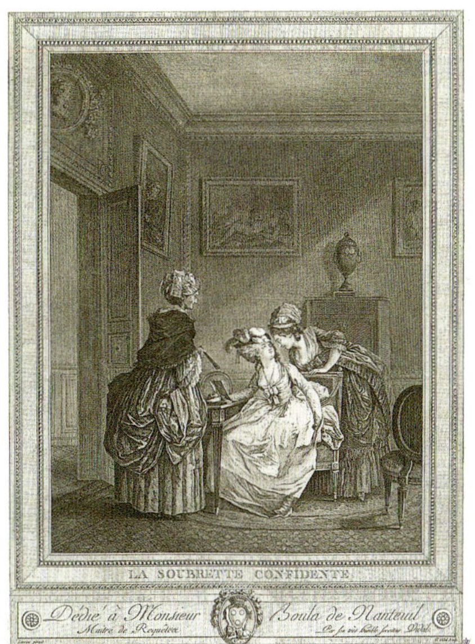

69

Valmont and Émilie
Valmont et Émilie

1788

Romain Girard (*c.* 1751–?)
After the painting by Nicolas Lavreince
(Niklas Lafrensen) (1737–1807)

Stipple engraving
421 × 354 mm
INSCRIPTIONS: *Valmont and Emilie / Cette complaisance
de ma part est le prix de celle qu'elle vient d'avoir de me
servir de pupitre pour ecrire à ma belle devote, a qui j'ay
trouvé plaisant d'envoyer une lettre ecrite du lit et presque
entre les bras d'une fille / Liaisons Dangereuses. Tom I.
Lettre XXXXVII.*
*Lavrince pinxit. / Romain Girard sculp. / A Paris chez
Girard, Graveur, rue de Savoye, derriere le Quay de
la Vallée, No 21.*
WATERMARK: two-line inscription (illegible)
INV: OG-228029
PROVENANCE: 1927, from the private libraries of the
Winter Palace (RIC) (Lugt Suppl. 2681ª)
BIBLIOGRAPHY: Bocher (Lavreince), p. 49, no. 62
(state not given); Nagler KL V, p. 208; P.-B. II, p. 318

This illustration to the novel *Les Liaisons
Dangereuses* tells of one of the adventures of
the dandy Valmont which he relates methodically
to his correspondent, the Marquise de Merteuil.
In letter number 47, he tells how, having arrived
in Paris in the evening, he ends up with friends at
a wedding supper. With the help of the bride, his
old friend Émilie, he gets the groom – a Dutch
burgomaster – drunk, and, having bundled him
into his carriage, sends him away, 'remaining the
victor on the battlefield'. In the arms of this hussy,
who is only interested in money and pleasure,
which is why she has agreed to act as his desk,
Valmont composes a sensitive letter to the
sanctimonious Madame de Tourvel – the most
innocent of all his prey. Running to her in search
of 'the spiritual rest of which I am so in need',
Valmont, to Émilie's delight, informs de Tourvel
that the position in which he is writing to her
convinces him more than ever of the omnipotence
of love. 'It is hard for me to control myself enough
to bring any order to my thoughts,' he writes,
'and I already predict that I will need to interrupt
this letter before I have finished it.'

The ambiguity of Valmont's letter derives
from both the context in which he is writing it,
and the fact that he is sending it not to de Tourvel,
but to his partner in crime, the Marquise de
Merteuil, who is to forward it to Paris, having first
perused it for her own amusement. Traditional
descriptions of lofty feelings are here turned into
straightforward images of the bedroom.

One of the artistic merits of this illustration
for the novel, in which Romain Girard uses the
delicate technique of stipple engraving, is the
artist's characteristic use of objects which are
hallmarks of French gallantry of the eighteenth
century. The hat and the cane are essential
attributes of the lover who finds himself in a
strange house, while the pen being dipped into
an ink-well is an age-old symbol of the sexual act.
The artist gives this latter attribute particular
emphasis by placing the ink-well between Émilie's
knees, as she daintily sticks out her toe. DO

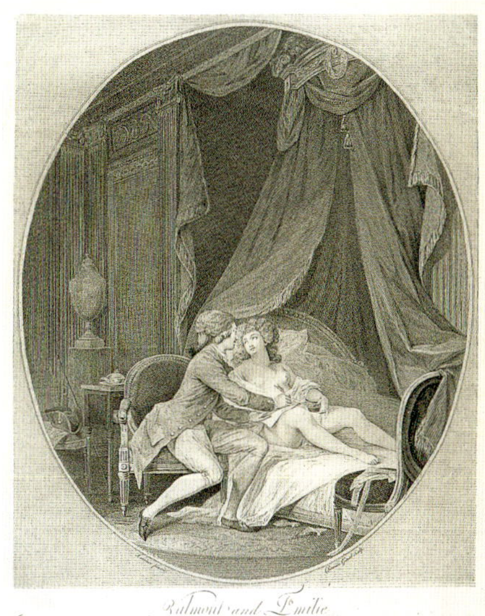

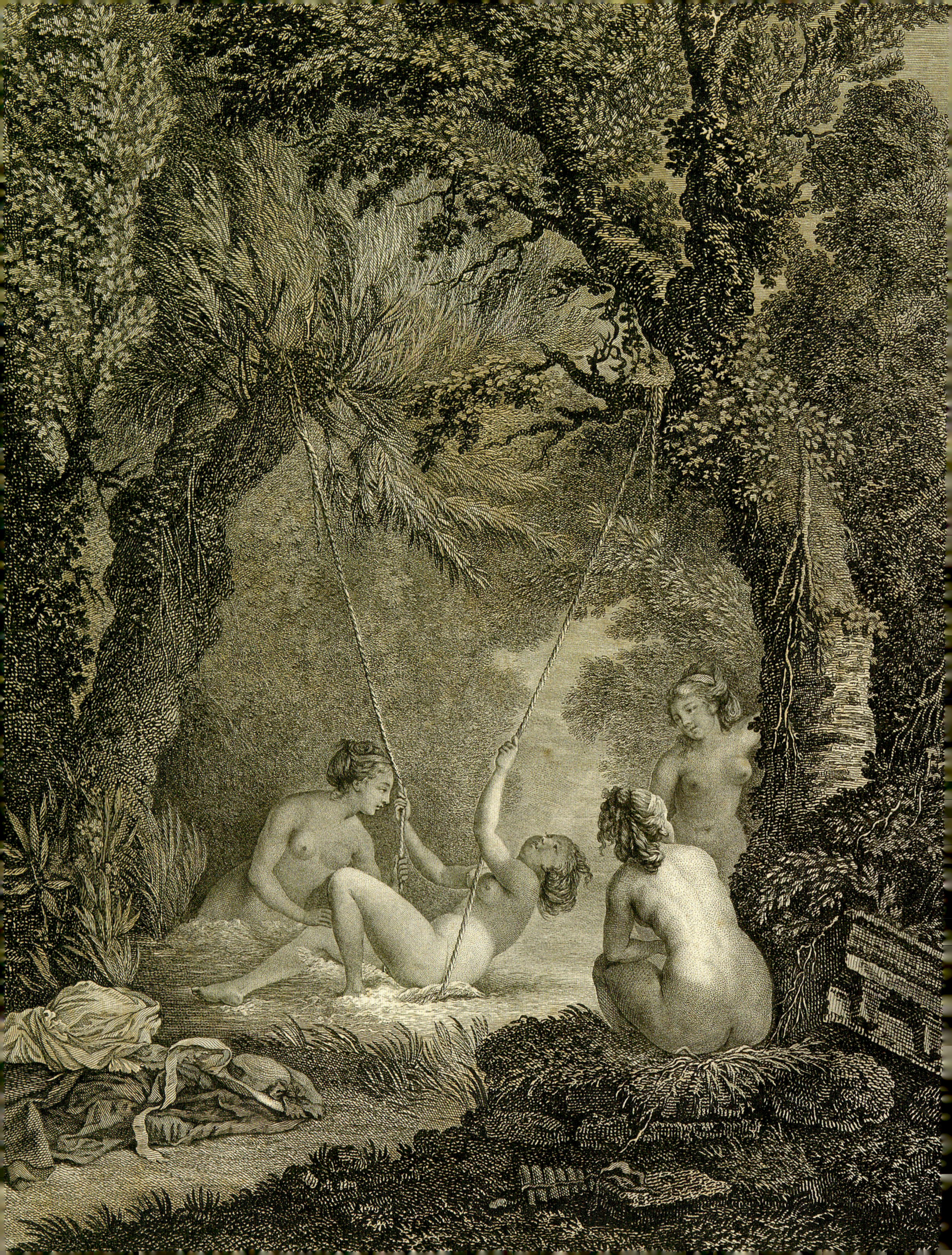

Encounters and Transgressions

The path of love was never straight. By definition seduction (Latin *seducere*, to lead aside) never follows a straight course. In charting the progress of love, eighteenth-century artists did not refrain from exploring moments of sexual tension, setback and role reversal. Jealousy, deceit and terrified flight are aspects of the darker side of rococo pleasure (cat. 83, 85).

The rococo hovers always on the brink of obscenity. Standards of public decency required that in art and poetry the artist respect 'decorum'. In order to excite without offending, and to escape censorship, celebrated artists such as Boucher, Pater and Fragonard resorted to elaborate forms of visual innuendo and sexual symbolism. Through interaction with the written word, these allusions came to be widely understood in court and popular culture. For example, the popular eighteenth-century image of the amorous couple playing on a swing was recognised, in its 'pull and push' and soaring flight, as a metaphor for sexual intercourse (*left*; cat. 70, 79).

By contrast, paintings and engravings executed for a private clientele could transgress the boundaries of decorum. Small private 'cabinet' paintings, often concealed behind curtains, revealed the forbidden parts of the object of desire. A painter such as Pierre Subleyras, better known in the eighteenth century for his religious subjects, could draw with impunity on the classic seventeenth-century *Tales* of La Fontaine to produce intimate licentious works that would never have been exhibited in public (cat. 72, 73).

Engravings of erotic mythological subjects in which the tantalising veils of decorum were lifted were produced in limited numbers for private circulation (cat. 75, 76). Such transgressive works are by definition rare; they reveal how artists of the rococo were extremely conscious of the fine line that separated high art from the forbidden works that could only be seen in secret.

The Secret Swing (detail)
Gérard Vidal
After the painting by Nicolas Lavreince
1780s
cat. 79

70

The Swing
La balançoire

1730s

Nicolas Lancret (1690–1743)

Oil on canvas
99 × 132 cm
INV: GE 7496
PROVENANCE: before 1782, collection of Madame
Lancret (?), Paris; mid-19th century, collection
of Nikolai Semyonovich Mosolov, Moscow; from
the end of the 19th century, Rumyantsev Museum,
Moscow (gift of Nikolai Semyonovich Mosolov); 1933,
acquired from the State Museum of Fine Arts, Moscow
BIBLIOGRAPHY: Art Treasures I, pp. 218–9, pl. 129;
Benois, p. 297, note 192; Rumyantsev, no. 537

In his youth Lancret spent some time working
in the studio of Antoine Watteau. Although the
great master was not Lancret's teacher for long,
he succeeded in instilling in the budding artist
his main principle – that of working from nature,
something which the latter adhered to until the
end of his days. However, there was another, less
positive, aspect to their work together: Lancret
assimilated the style of his brilliant teacher to such
an extent that he began to imitate him, and the first
works which he exhibited in the Place Dauphine
in Paris were taken to be by Watteau himself.
This scandal put an end to their relationship.

Following the exhortations of his great
teacher, Lancret either painted or sketched the
landscapes for his portraits and genre compositions
from nature. Unlike Watteau, who preferred to
depict scenes prompted by his imagination and
performed by characters from Italian or French
comic theatre, Lancret devoted himself to a
faithful reproduction of the customs and spiritual
life of aristocratic society and the bourgeois elite
of his day. Lancret, more than Watteau, was
inclined to the gallant anecdote in relating and
conveying scenes set in a real environment.

The swing is a common motif in compositions
portraying society figures at play. The majority of
artists in the Regency and rococo eras introduced
it into their work; the genre element afforded
them the opportunity to single out and direct
the viewer's attention towards one figure within
a group, who would be further accentuated by a
bright splash of colour for the clothes to introduce
life and movement into the composition. Lancret
evidently used the subject of the swing more
than once. For example, we know that a work
of a similar description figured in the sale of the
collection belonging to Lancret's widow, although
it is possible that this was the Hermitage painting.
Another surviving version is today in the Haviland
Collection.

In the mid-nineteenth century, when the
Hermitage picture entered the Moscow collection
of Nikolai Semyonovich Mosolov, it was believed
to be by another follower of Watteau, Jean-Baptiste
Pater. This attribution stuck until the beginning
of the twentieth century, when Russian researchers
questioned it, instead dating *The Swing* to the 1730s
and attributing it to Nicolas Lancret. ED

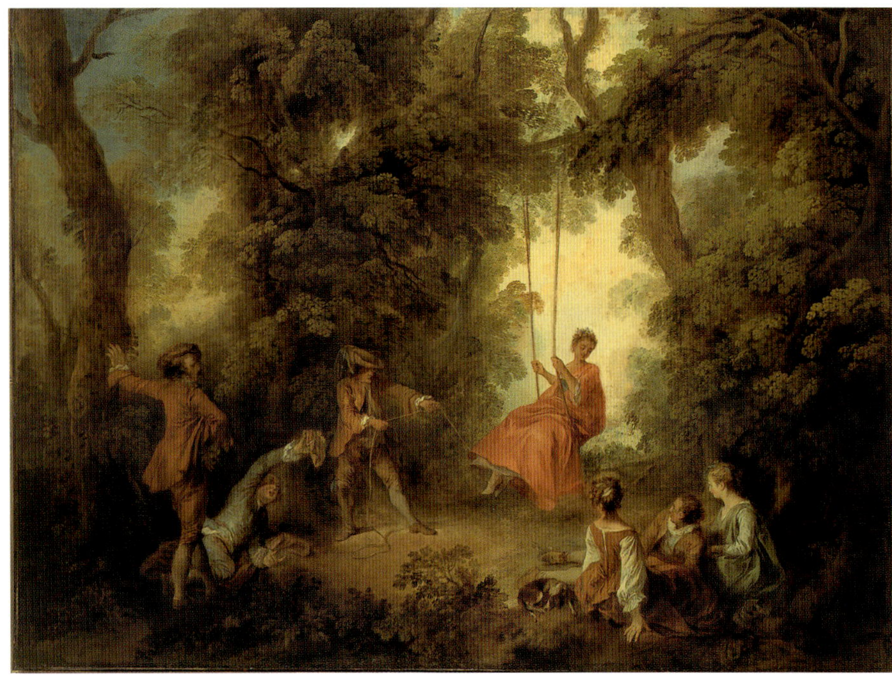

Joseph and Potiphar's Wife
Joseph et la femme de Putiphar

1711

Jean-Baptiste Nattier (1678–1726)

Oil on canvas

73.5 × 92 cm

SIGNED and dated bottom left-hand corner: *J.B. Natier fecit 1711.*

INV: GE 1268

PROVENANCE: after 1726, collection of the family of Jean-Baptiste Nattier, Paris; collection of Damery, Paris; before 1764, collection of the artist Jean-François de Troy, Paris; 1764, acquired at auction of de Troy's collection

BIBLIOGRAPHY: Clement de Ris, p. 269; Garshin, p. 434 (as Jean-Marc Nattier); Georgi, p. 480; Mantz, p. 100; Nolhac, p. 19; Réau 1929, no. 254; Th.-B. xxv, p. 356; Waagen, p. 304

The subject is taken from the Book of Genesis (39: 6–20), which tells how Joseph, son of Jacob, was sold by his brothers into Egypt, where he was bought by Potiphar, an officer of Pharaoh and captain of the guard. Because of Joseph's diligence and pleasing disposition, Potiphar warmed to him, entrusting him with important affairs and making him overseer in his house. But Potiphar's wife fell in love with the handsome youth and began to importune him. One day when her husband was out, she tried to lure Joseph into her bed, but he fled in horror, leaving her holding his garment.

The perfidious woman, rebuffed, accused Joseph of an attack on her honour. The youth was banished and incarcerated in a dungeon.

The subject of Joseph and Potiphar's Wife was very popular among artists. They usually chose a scene in the bedchamber, which afforded the most artistic opportunities. Nattier places Potiphar's wife in the foreground, glowing in all her alluring nakedness. The bright, angled light-source casts patches of light and shade on the young woman's beautiful form. The figure of Joseph, on the contrary, is plunged in shadows; all that is illuminated is part of his face and his arm as he wards her off. The swirl of his garment emphasises the swiftness of his movements.

This composition was a set piece painted by Nattier in order to be accepted into the Académie Royale de peinture et de sculpture. The minutes of the assembly of the Académie give a detailed record of the dates of the work. On 31 December 1710 Nattier applied to be admitted as a member of the Académie. The meeting, led by its director, the painter François de Troy, accepted his application and set the subject for the painting. On 25 April 1711 Nattier submitted a sketch to a meeting of the Académie, which was accepted by a majority of votes, and he was given six months to complete the final version. However, by all indications Nattier found the work hard going, as six months later he was given permission to extend the deadline by as much again. Finally, on 29 October 1712, the minutes record: 'Today [...] Jean-Baptiste Nattier [...] brought before the assembly [of the Academy] the painting commissioned from him for his election, representing Joseph being importuned by the wife of Potiphar. By a majority of votes his work was accepted, in consequence of which he was elected Academician, with all the privileges the position enjoys. He took the oath before Monsieur Van Cleve, now the president; the financial reward was moderated to the sum of one hundred livres as a son of an Academician' (*Procès Verbaux* V, 1881, pp. 156–7). A version of this composition was known prior to this; it was at Sanssouci in Potsdam until 1769, and may have been in the sale at the Hôtel Drouot in Paris in 1864. It is possible that this may have been the sketch mentioned in the minutes of the Académie.

In 1725 Nattier found himself embroiled in the scandalous Deschauffours affair, and was found guilty and imprisoned in the Bastille. This led to his rights as a member of the Académie being revoked, and the picture which had been submitted to the Académie in 1712 was returned to his family. Nattier committed suicide in prison by cutting his throat. ED

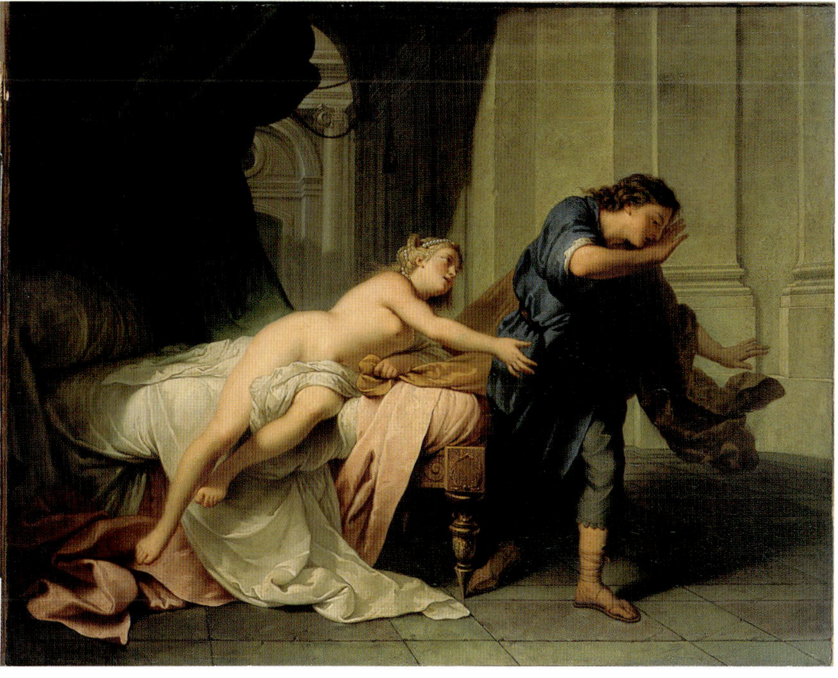

72

Scene from La Fontaine's tale
'The Mare of Peasant Pierre'
'La jument de compère Pierre'

1740s

Pierre Subleyras (1699–1749)

Oil on canvas
30.5 × 24.5 cm
INV: GE 4703
PROVENANCE: 19th century, collection of the Yusupov
    princes, St Petersburg; 1925, acquired from the
    Yusupov Palace Museum
BIBLIOGRAPHY: Arnould, p. 57

This fable by La Fontaine tells the story of a priest,
Father Jean, who takes a fancy to the wife of his
poor neighbour Pierre.

> *Il avait femme et belle et jeune encore*
> *Ferme surtout: la hâle avait fait tort*
> *à son visage et non à sa personne.*
> (He had a wife, beautiful and still young,
> He above all reliable: sunburn had damaged
> His face but not his person.)

Father Jean promises Pierre that within 24 hours
he will turn his wife Magdeleine into a mare to help
him in his work, but in order to do so he needs to
undress her. When the priest begins to caress the
peasant's wife, supposedly to achieve the desired
result, Pierre, somewhat surprised by Jean's
actions, cannot restrain himself; he breaks his
vow to remain silent, to which the priest replies:

> *Foin de toi!*
> *T'avais-je pas recommandé, gros âne,*
> *de ne rien dire et de demeurer coi?*
> *Tout est gâté...*
> (Curse you!
> Did I not tell you, you great ass,
> To say nothing and stay silent?
> Now everything is lost...)

(La Fontaine, éd. La Pléiade, 1954, pp. 589–94)
ED

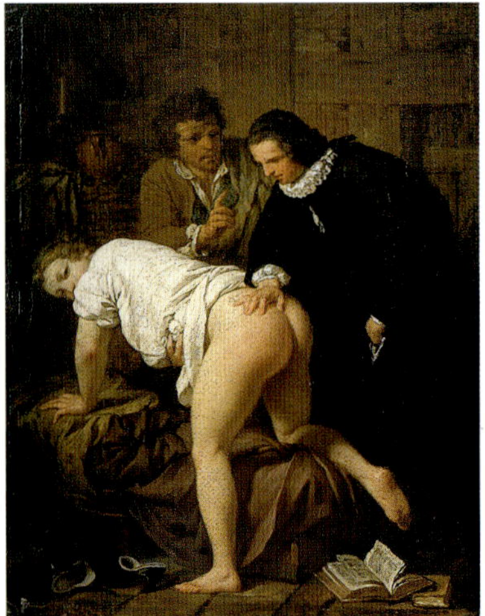

73

Scene from La Fontaine's tale
'The Pack-Horse'
'Le bât'

1740s

Pierre Subleyras (1699–1749)

Oil on canvas
30.5 × 24.5 cm
INV: GE 4704
PROVENANCE: see cat. 72
BIBLIOGRAPHY: Arnould, p. 57

This painting forms a pair with the illustration
for La Fontaine's tale *La jument de compère Pierre*
(cat. 72). Nineteenth-century tradition has it that
Subleyras, whose talents were primarily dedicated
to religious art, for unknown reasons between
1732 and 1741 painted four pictures with frivolous
subjects taken from La Fontaine's tales, based on
novellas by Boccaccio: *Faucon, Les Oies de Frère
Philippe, L'Ermite, ou Frère Luce* and *La Courtisane
Amoureuse* (Paris, Louvre). Later two more
paintings were added to this series – the ones
now in the Hermitage. It is not known for whom
they were painted.

Paintings and engravings based on La
Fontaine's tales are found in the works of many
French artists from the eighteenth century
onwards, including Pater, Lancret, Boucher,
Fragonard, the director of the Académie de
France in Rome Nicolas Vleughels, and others.
In La Fontaine's tale *Le bât* the subject is
introduced as follows:

> *Un peintre était, qui, jaloux de sa femme,*
> *Allant aux champs, lui peignit un baudet*
> *Sur le nombril, en guise de cachet.*
> *Un sien confrère, amoureux de la dame,*
> *La va trouver, et l'âne efface net,*
> *Dieu sait comment; puis en autre en remet*
> *Au même endroit, ainsi que l'on peut croire.*
> *A celui-ci, par faute de mémoire,*
> *Il mit un bât; l'autre n'en avait point.*
> *L'époux revient, veut s'éclaircir du point:*
> *"Voyez, mon fils, dit la bonne commère,*
> *L'âne est témoin de ma fidélité.*
> *—Diantre soit fait, dit l'époux en colère,*
> *Et du témoin, et de qui l'a bâté!"*
> (There was a painter, who, jealous of his wife,
> Before going out to the fields painted an ass
> On her navel as a seal.
> A friend of his, being in love with the lady,
> Came to find her and wiped the ass clean away,
> God knows how; then he put another back
> In the same place, as far as he could tell.
> But his memory failed him,
> And he painted a pack-horse; not what the other
>   had painted at all.
> The husband returned, and wanted to dispel
>   his doubts.
> 'Look, my boy,' said his excellent wife,
> 'The ass bears witness to my fidelity.'
> 'The devil it does!' cried the husband in anger,
> 'It bears witness to the one who saddled it!')

(La Fontaine, éd. La Pléiade, 1954, p. 527)

The story takes place in the studio of the deceived
husband, in his absence. On the floor stands an
open book from which his colleague is copying the
ill-fated ass. The woman is depicted in Subleyras's
favourite manner, with dark hair covered by a
headdress on the back of her head, a straight nose
and prominent forehead. This subject was an
undoubted success in the eighteenth and nineteenth
centuries, with at least four versions of the
composition circulating on the art market. ED

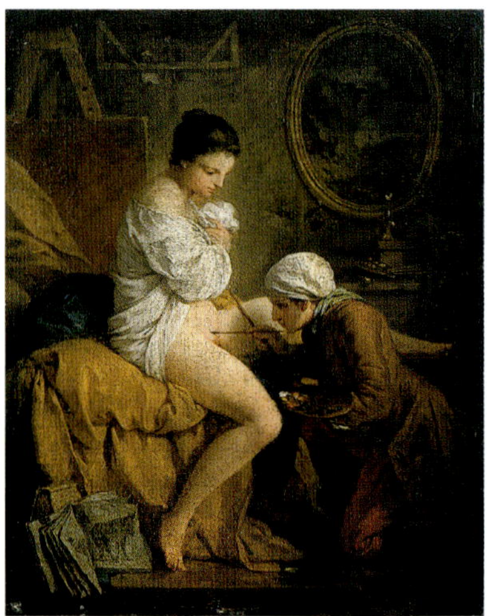

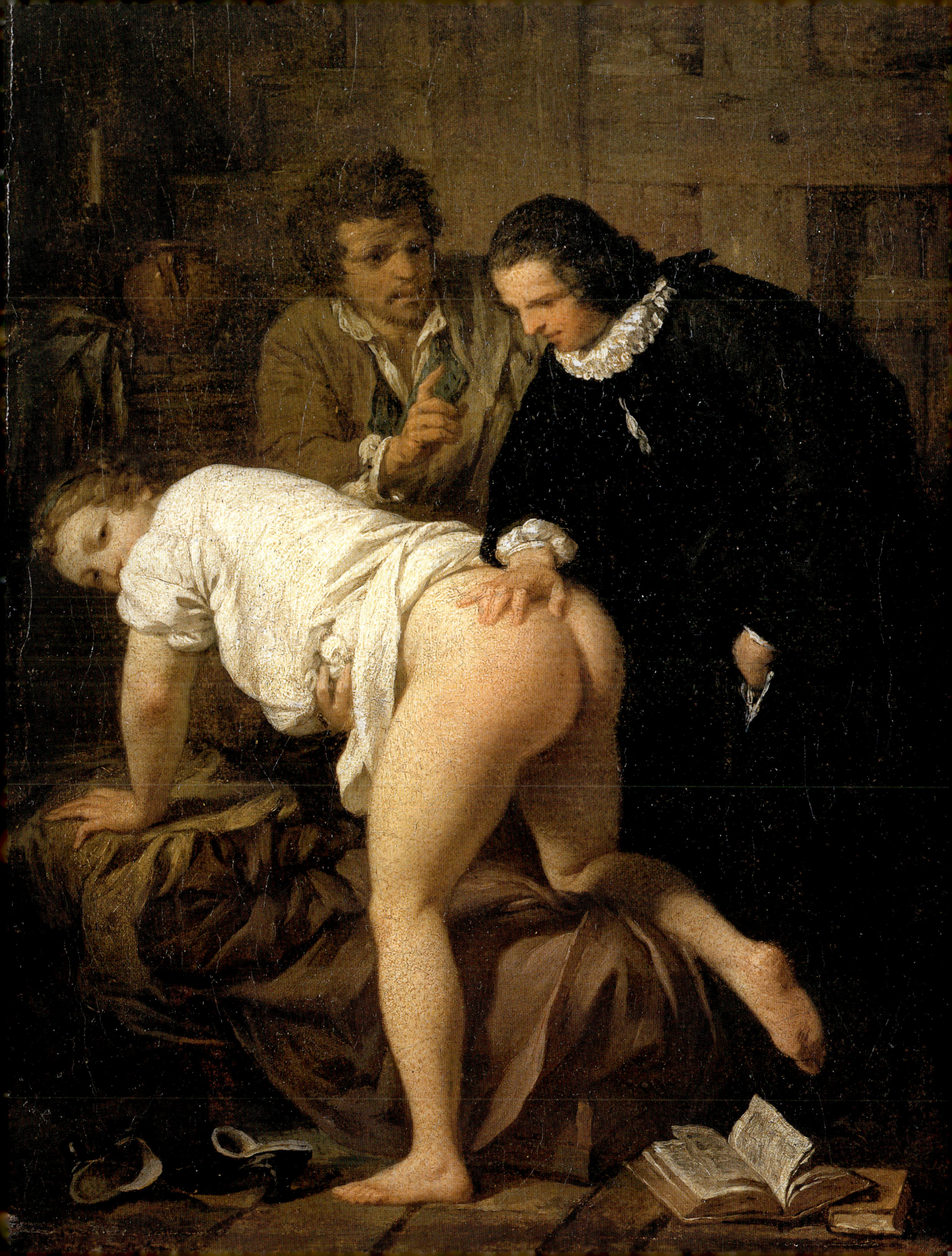

74
Peeping Tom
Le curieux

1779

Pierre Malœuvre (1740–1803)
After a gouache by Pierre-Antoine Baudouin
(1723–69)

Etching
365 × 263 mm (trimmed sheet)
INSCRIPTIONS: *LE CURIEUX.*
Peint a Gouache par P.A. Baudouin / Gravé par
P. Maleuvre
INV: OG-125303
PROVENANCE: before 1928, from main collection (Lugt
Suppl. 2681ª); acquired before 1830s
BIBLIOGRAPHY: Bocher (Baudouin) p. 20, no. 17
(states IV, V, VI/VI: trimmed sheet); Bourcard, pp.
47–9; Lawrence & Dighton, p. 58, no. 133; Le Blanc II,
p. 593, no. 13; Nagler KL VIII, p. 220, nr. 13; Ozerkov,
no. 90; P.-B. II, p. 765, no. 4; Stewart 1992, p. 172;
Wagner, p. 273, ill. 66

The servant girl is giving her mistress an enema.
This process allows her impatient guest to satisfy
his curiosity and examine parts of her body which
might normally be less accessible. Traditionally, an
enema tube was used for washing or for medicinal
purposes. Sometimes, in preparation for a long
late-night party, coffee or tobacco was added to
the liquid, enabling the recipient to stay alert for
a long time, without being left with a bad taste in
the mouth. Tobacco enemas were thought to help
those who were prone to fainting fits.

In the eighteenth century, the administering
of an enema was part of a complicated ritual.
Often, the society lady would continue to talk
to her visitors from behind a screen while having
an enema inserted. Françoise d'Aubigné, the
Marquise de Maintenon, describes the following
incident in her memoirs: 'I remember how one
evening when they were putting on a comedy at
Versailles, she [the Duchess of Burgundy], in her
evening gown and with her hair already done,
called Nanon and, continuing to chat to us, got up,
her back to the fireplace, went behind a screen, and
then got down on her knees. The king [Louis XIV],
who initially thought that the princess was simply
warming herself by the fire, asked what they were
doing down there. The duchess sprinkled herself
with water, and said she was doing what she
usually did on days when plays were shown. The
king persisted. "Well, if you really want to know,"
she said, "I am having an enema." I glanced at
the king so as to coordinate my reaction with his.
"What!" he cried in a fit of laughter. "Right now,
this minute, you are having an enema?" "Yes, right
now," answered the duchess. "But how?" And all
four of us burst out laughing: it turned out that
Nanon had brought a prepared clyster in her
pocket, had lifted up the princess's skirts, which
the latter then held up as if warming herself by the
fire, and had administered the enema, something

we did not see because of the screen. "I find it
refreshing," added the duchess. "Now I won't feel
the heat." We had not noticed anything at first: we
thought Nanon was simply adjusting the duchess's
dress. We were utterly amazed. The king, who was
often easily offended, found it all very amusing,
however' (Chandernagor, p. 473).

Inserting an enema (clyster, syringe) was
a traditional euphemism for the sexual act (Le
Pennec, p. 97). A relevant early literary source
worth noting is Jacob de Villiers' story,
'L'Apothicaire de qualité' (1670). It was translated
into English and published in 1739 under the title
'The Surprize: or Gentleman Turn'd Apothecary.
A Tale written originally in French Prose;
afterwards translated into Latin; and from thence
now versified in Hudibrastics' (London, 1739).
The story begins with a discourse on how Parisian
ladies use the enema tube in the interests of
beauty and health. The heroine of the story,
Amarinta/Araminta, asks her servant girl to insert
an enema for her; the latter, suddenly remembering
something, leaves her mistress waiting in the
required position; Timant enters the house and
finds her, and can think of no better solution than
to set to work himself (Wagner, pp. 178–80).

In Malœuvre's engraving, the curiosity of the
viewer-voyeur gives rise to fantasies in him which
are suggested by the little cupids making merry in
the oval *dessus-de-porte*. The spectator's presence is
essential for the erotic image to have full effect. It
is as if this secret voyeur 'opens up' the picture to
allow the eighteenth-century viewer (who holds the
engraving in his hands) to come in, turning it from

an abstract illustration into a scene which is really
taking place. Examining the forbidden scene just
as secretly, the viewer identifies with the spectator-
voyeur, as if he were himself in his place, fantasizing
in the same way.

The theme of the peeping Tom watching the
act of inserting an enema is not uncommon in French
graphic art of the eighteenth century. Bocher (Bocher
(Baudouin), p. 20) notes the special popularity of this
subject, giving as an example Chaponier's engraving,
The Officious Waiting Woman (P.-B. I, p. 356, no. 2),
a work which is in the Hermitage collection (inv.
OG-228129). There is also a fairly poor copy of
Malœuvre's engraving on the back of this one. The
signature is given as Bonnet's ('Gravé par Bonnet
1782'), but it is clearly not his work (inv. OG-358889).
Bourcard suggests that this imitation was composed
in Germany (Bourcard, p. 49). DO

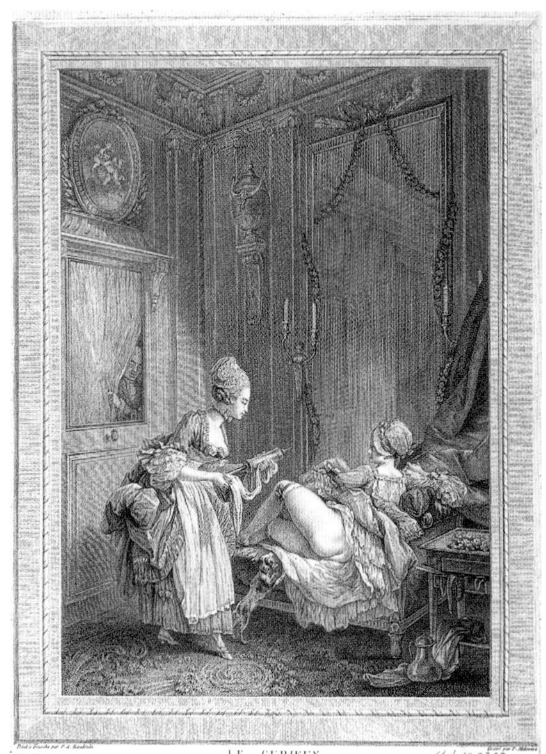

75
Jupiter and Anthiope
Jupiter et Anthiope
first state

1770s

Gérard Vidal (1742–1804)
After a drawing by Charles Monnet (1732–1816)

Etching and engraving
412 × 304 mm; 430 × 314 mm
INV: OG-228037
PROVENANCE: 1927, from the private libraries of the
  Winter Palace (RIC) (Lugt Suppl. 2681[a])
BIBLIOGRAPHY: Le Blanc IV, p. 121, no. 31 (state I/II);
  P.-B. III, p. 615, no. 13

Jupiter and Anthiope belongs to a series of
illustrations which Gérard Vidal composed for an
edition of Ovid's *Metamorphoses*. The impressions
of the two states of the engraving show the
progress of the artist's work on the plate: the plain
etching was supplemented by engraving with a
burin. The first state shows the plate before any
inscriptions were added. The position of the drape,
which does not conceal Anthiope's modesty as it
does in the following state, is also different. The
mount on which the engraving has been placed has
preserved the old title written in pen: 'Jupiter et
Anthiope. Épreuve d'eau forte avant la draperie.'
('Jupiter and Anthiope. Etching proof before
drapery.') A limited number of similar impressions
from the unfinished plate were printed and
distributed semi-legally. DO

76
Jupiter and Anthiope
Jupiter et Anthiope
second state

1770s

Gérard Vidal (1742–1804)
After a drawing by Charles Monnet (1732–1816)

Etching and engraving
412 × 304 mm; 428 × 320 mm
INV: OG-228036
INSCRIPTIONS: *JUPITER ET ANTHIOPE*
Monnet inv. del. / Vidal sculp. / A Paris chez l'Auteur rue
  Desnoyers la 1ere Porte cochere a droite en entrant par
  celle St. Jacques. / A.P.D.R.
PROVENANCE: 1927, from the private libraries of the
  Winter Palace (RIC) (Lugt Suppl. 2681[a])
BIBLIOGRAPHY: Le Blanc IV, p. 121, no. 31 (state II/II);
  P.-B. III, p. 615, no. 13

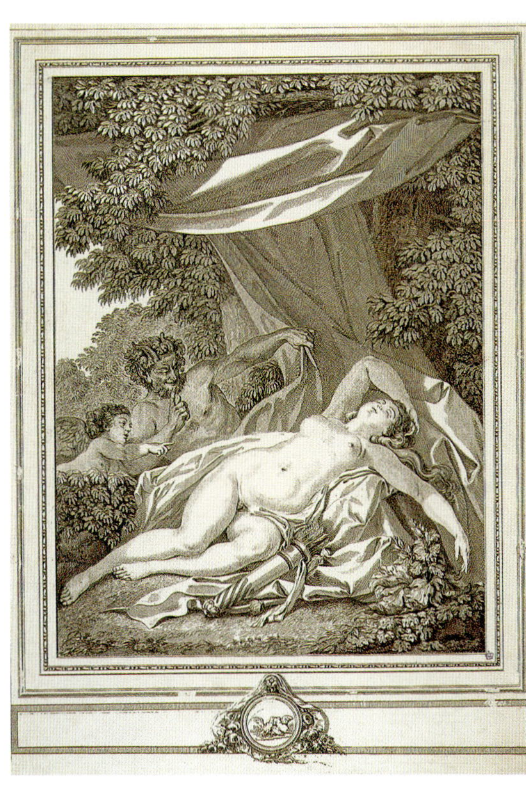

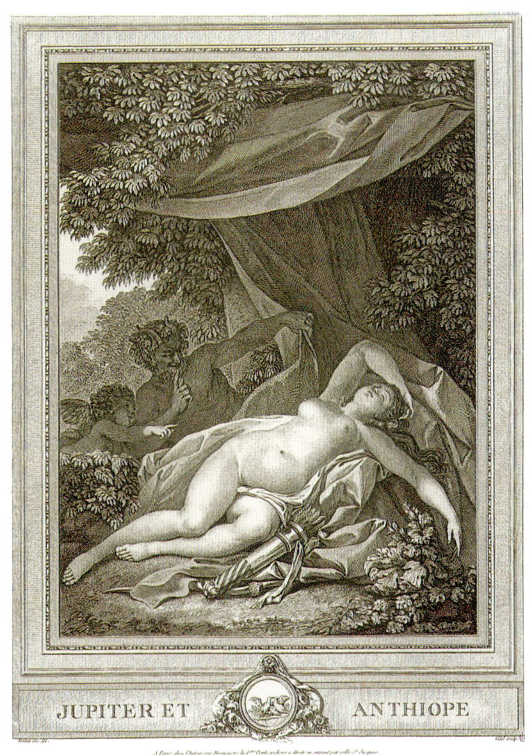

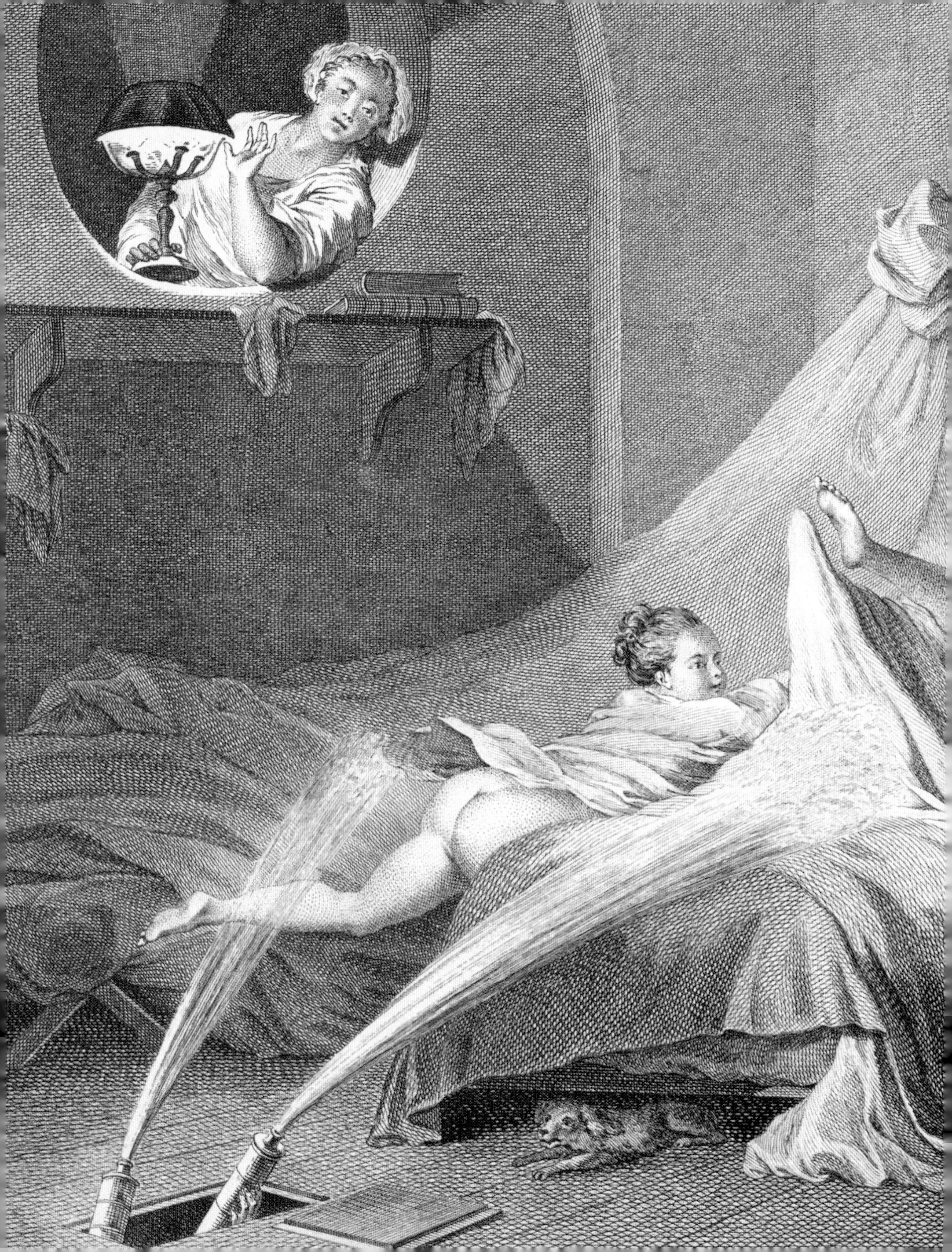

77
The Comparison
La comparaison

1760s–70s

Jacques Boüilliard (1744–1806)
After the painting by Jean-Frédéric Schall
(1752–1825)

Etching
423 × 490 mm
INV: OG-228130
PROVENANCE: 1927, from the private libraries of the
Winter Palace (RIC) (Lugt Suppl. 2681ᵃ)
BIBLIOGRAPHY: IFF III, p. 305, no. 5 (state not recorded)

Two girls are frozen in a charming pose on either side of a statue of Aphrodite Kallipygos ('of the beautiful buttocks'). The viewer is left in doubt: their bodies are so perfect that they are almost indistinguishable from the marble original. A device is found, however: a third girl touches one of the beauties with a reed, causing her to move.

Marcel Roux believes that this engraving, like the original canvas, recalls a ritual erotic ceremony involving girls known as Janettes, which was held by the Société des Aphrodites, a society of libertines founded in the Regency era and which existed until 1791. The society owned extensive grounds with gardens and forests at Montmorency, where its followers engaged in indescribable orgies (IFF III, p. 305).

This work is a rare impression made from a plate before inscriptions. Evidently this is the version of the plate before it was finished by Duprèel, as is confirmed by the inscription on another known version of the engraving (the state shown here is not listed in the *Inventaire du fonds français*). From 1898 Schall's original canvas belonged to Baron A. Oppenheim. In the Louvre (inv. R.F. 1961-75) is a canvas depicting the more beautiful right half of this print, though in the painting it appears on the left. DO

78
Jets of water
Les jets d'eau

Before 1779 (?)

Pierre-Laurent Auvray (1736–?)
After the drawing by Jean-Honoré Fragonard
(1732–1806)

Etching
270 × 312 mm; 282 × 326 mm
INSCRIPTIONS: *LES JETS D'EAU*
*Fragonard del. / Auvray sc. / Se vend chez Alibert
Mᵈ d'Estampes, au Palais Royal. Et chez le Sʳ Chevin
Peintre, rue Neuve d'Orléans, près la Porte Sᵗ Denis.*
WATERMARK: *T RICHARD / AUVERGNE 177<5> /
FIN* (cf. Heawood no. 3411 [1778])
INV: OG-228206
PROVENANCE: 1927, from the libraries of the Winter
Palace (Lugt Suppl. 2681ᵃ)
BIBLIOGRAPHY: Ananoff IV, pp. 48–9, no. 2012;
Bourcard, pp. 199–200; Delteil, p. 163; IFF I, p. 269,
no. 5; Lawrence & Dighton, p. 3, no. 5 (state not
recorded, I or II/II); Le Blanc I, p. 108, no. 9 (pair
to no. 12; plate known: 'La pl. existe encore' [1854]);
Ozerkov, no. 95; P.-B. I, p. 54; Rosenberg, p. 242,
no. 116

Auvray's print shows a sweet prank in the spirit of the eighteenth century. The lovers are aided by water pumps which they use to aim jets of water from beneath the floor at the sleeping girls. The god of love, out of sight, directs proceedings. Auvray's prints represent the revenge of young men, enflamed by Cupid's arrows, over girls: it is as if they are taking revenge over those same beautiful nymphs who, profiting from the fact that Cupid is asleep, steal or spoil his weapons. This is the subject of *Sleeping Cupid and Venus with the Graces* by Nicolas Vleughels (1723; Chicago, private collection; Hercenberg, p. 119, no. 187*; Marandel, p. 442, fig. 85) and Louis Lagrenée's *Graces Taking their Revenge* (pair to *Graces Taken Unawares by Cupids*, 1779, Scotland, private collection; Sandoz 1988, p. 259, no. 322, pl. XXXIV; cf. pair of engravings by Louis-Simon Lempereur: Le Blanc II, p. 532, nos. 12–13).

The girl 'victims' also contribute to the general playfulness of the scene, since their confusion is at least partly feigned. They are showing off their charms rather than trying to hide them, all of which enables the viewer to admire their beauty from an unexpected angle. One impression of this engraving is accompanied by an inscription which speaks of a different turmoil – that produced by the girls' charms in the hearts of their beaux. The jets of water may not be particularly devastating, but this other turmoil is much stronger: no water can quench this inner fire. DO

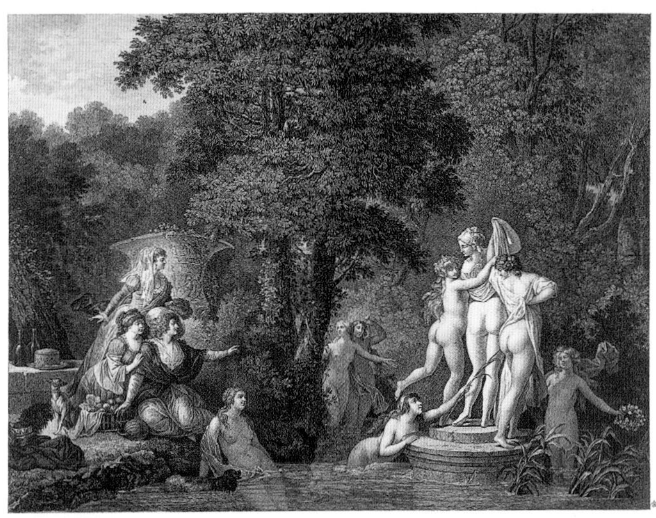

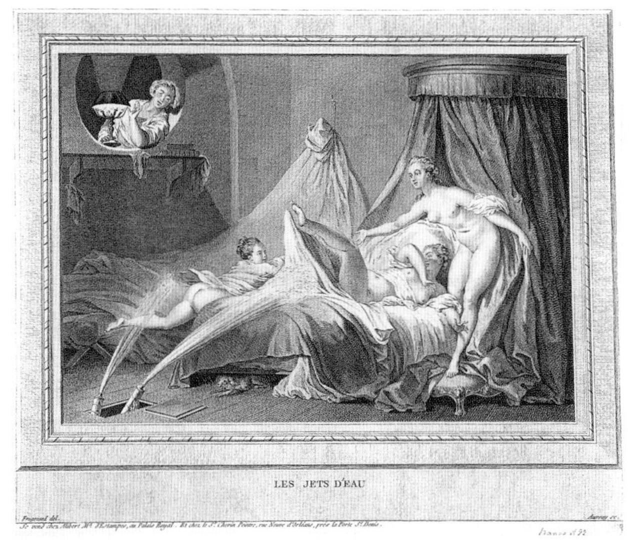

The Secret Swing
La balançoire mystérieuse

1780s

Gérard Vidal (1742–1804)
After the painting by Nicolas Lavreince
   (Niklas Lafrensen) (1737–1807)

Etching and engraving
414 × 294 mm; 414 × 306 mm
INSCRIPTIONS: *Lavrince. pin. / Vidal. Scl. / Peint par
   Lavrince, Peintre du Roi de Suede et de l'Academie
   Royale de Stokolme. / Gravée par Vidal*
WATERMARK: *FIN DE D♥TAMIZIER AUVERGNE
   17<8...>*
INV: OG-228028
PROVENANCE: 1927, from the private libraries of the
   Winter Palace (RIC) (Lugt Suppl. 2681ª)
BIBLIOGRAPHY: Bocher (Lavreince), p. 16, no. 9
   (state VI/VII); Le Blanc IV, p. 120, no. 27 (state V/VII);
   P.-B. III, p. 614, no. 1

The secret swing is an innocent game by girls who
have decided to play at being wood nymphs. To
play this game they have gone deep into the woods
where, leaving their clothes on the bank, they
have given themselves over to merriment. But
is their insouciance ill-advised? The architrave of
the ancient temple and the Pan-pipes lying on the
ground suggest that the place is in the control of
Cupid, and at any moment the shaggy head of
a satyr might peep out of the thicket.

   At least seven different states are known of
the plate from which the print was made. As it was
worked on, inscriptions appeared in the lower part
of the picture, while in the final state the nakedness
of the girl on the swing is covered by ripples of
water. DO

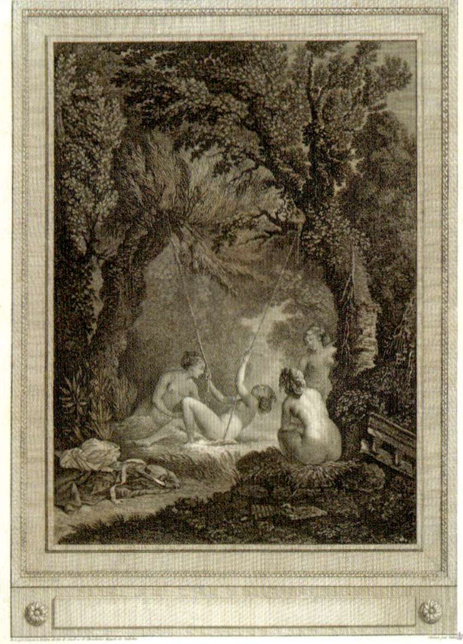

Step Softly, Speak Quietly
Marchez tout doux, parlez tout bas

1782

Pierre-Philippe Choffard (1730–1809)
After the gouache by Pierre-Antoine Baudouin
   (1723–69)

Etching and engraving
395 × 276 mm; 570 × 430 mm
INSCRIPTIONS: *A Son Altesse Mgr Le Prince De Ligne
   et du S^t. Empire, Chevalier de l'Ordre de la Toison d'Or,
   Grand d'Espagne de la 1ere Classe, Lieutenant général des
   Armées de sa Majesté Impériale et Royale, Gouverneur de
   Mons et du Haynault, Colonel proprietaire d'un Regiment
   d'Infant^ie. &^a. &^a. / Par son tres humble et tres respectueux
   serviteur Choffard.* at top: *N.º III. B
   Peint a la Gouasse par P.A. Baudouin Peintre du Roi. 1767.
   / AParis Quay et Batiment neuf des Théatins. / Gravé
   par PP.Choffard 1782.*
WATERMARK: *FIN DE D♥TAMIZIER AUVERGNE
   1740* (see Heawood nos. 1314, 1320a)
INV: OG-128204
PROVENANCE: before 1928, from main collection (Lugt
   Suppl. 2681ª); acquired before 1830s
BIBLIOGRAPHY: Bocher (Baudouin), p. 31, no. 30 (state
   III/III); Bourcard, p. 39; Delteil, p. 146, pl. XLIV; IFF
   IV, p. 447, no. 374; Lawrence & Dighton, p. 8, no. 18
   (state IV/IV); Ozerkov, no. 30; P.-B. I, p. 428, no. 3

Love affairs or liaisons (*aventures*) are a necessary
part of a person's amorous education, offering
practical experience in the lessons of Eros. In his
play *Les précieuses ridicules* of 1659, Molière
expresses the common view of love affairs through
the lips of a daughter protesting to her father:
'Enough, father, my cousin will tell you the same
as I: one should marry only after other liaisons.'

   The simplest *aventure* is that most banal of
risky ventures: to steal unobserved into the house
of one's sweetheart at night. This is the subject
of Choffard's print after the gouache by Baudouin.
The pupil and son-in-law of Madame de
Pompadour's protégé Boucher, Baudouin gained his
place in the history of French graphic arts through
his gouaches, which were masterfully executed and
usually on a somewhat frivolous subject. Here a
shepherd boy, wearing a hat and with his shoes in
his hand, steals through the window into the room
of his sweetheart, who urgently signals him to be
quiet. Behind the half-open door, her parents can
be seen sleeping peacefully.

   The title of the engraving comes from the
refrain to a folk song popular in the mid-eighteenth
century. Its words were first published in 1714
under the title *Le rendez-vous de nuit*, and two
versions are known with similar choruses: 'Step
softly, speak quietly' (Coirault, p. 157; Millien,
p. 94). Dying of love, the shepherd boy Colin,
unable to bear the torment any longer, rises from
his bed and sets off for the house of his sweetheart,
the beautiful shepherdess Catin. He knocks three
times and, as she opens the door wearing only her
nightgown, he asks whether she is ready to fulfil

the promise she made the day before. The refrain
Catin sings as she lets him in goes as follows: 'Step
softly, speak quietly, my gentle one. If my father
hears you, I am undone'. She repeats these words
at dawn when parting from her lover, who leaves
with the singing of the lark.

   Aventures do not happen of their own accord:
normally one must seek them out, contrive them.
Etymologically the word 'aventure' means that
which lies in store, that which has yet to happen
(*adventura, advenire*). Its outcome is unpredictable:
the affair may be successful or unsuccessful, its
ending happy or sad; therein lies its attraction.
But when there are conflicting interests in an affair,
who will win? In *Les Liaisons Dangeureuses*,
Madame de Merteuil appears to give hope to the
inveterate seducer de Prévan. He reciprocates by
starting an affair, wishing to make her a laughing-
stock, but the Marquise contrives things so that
the adventurer himself falls into a trap. When he
comes to her bedchamber as agreed, the Marquise
suddenly calls the servants, who are ready and
waiting, and the affair becomes a public scandal.

   Above all, a successful *aventure* is also a
pretext for whispered gossip in the salons. 'In order
for the most banal venture to turn into an *aventure*,
it must be made known' (Sartre). The *aventure* is
of interest as a whole, in all its reversals of fortune,
its piquancy, its intrigues, which can be told and
retold with ever more fantastic embellishments.
Without pausing for reflection, gallant society
discusses the affairs of the famous. The *esprit
d'aventure* which reigned in society added a vital
piquancy to eighteenth-century French life. DO

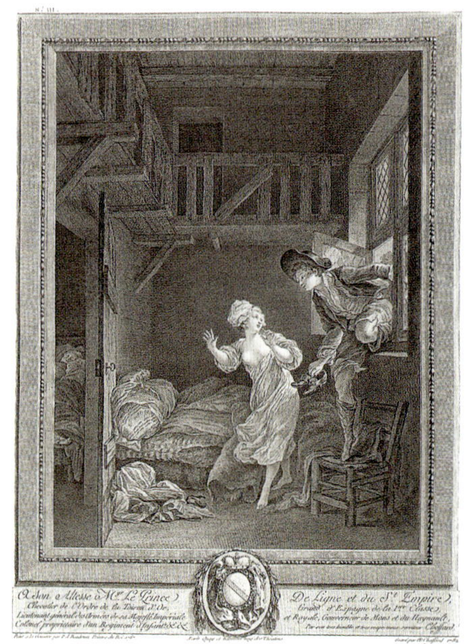

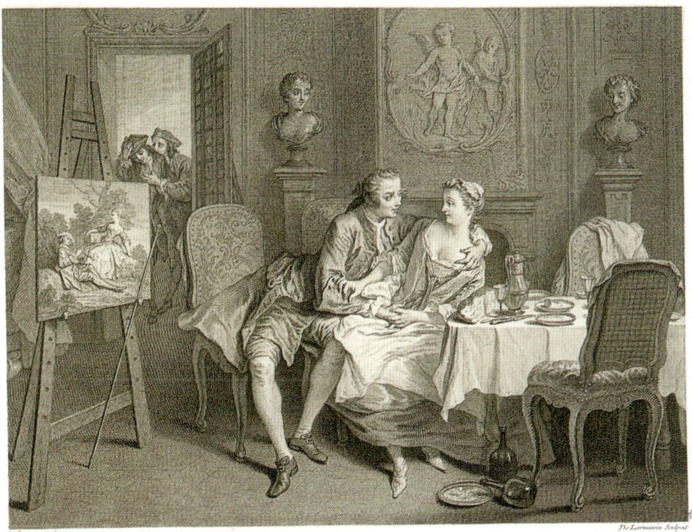

81

The Rhemese
Les Rémois

1742

Nicolas de Larmessin III (1684–1755)
After the painting by Nicolas Lancret (1690–1743)

Etching and engraving
325 × 370 mm; 379 × 433 mm
INSCRIPTIONS: *LES REMOIS.*
  A la femme du Peintre ils aspiroient tous deux
  Il leur rend tour a tour ce qu'il auroit craint d'eux,
  Trahis et prevenus les Galants temeraires,
  Sont auteurs de leur peine et temoins oculaires.
  Mr Roy
N Lancret pinxit / De Larmessin Scupsit / aParis chez
  DeLarmessin graveur du Roy ruë des Noyers a la 2^e. porte
  Cocher a gauche entrant par la ruë S^t. Jacques. A.P.D.R.
INV: OG-228239
PROVENANCE: 1927, from the private libraries
  of the Winter Palace (RIC) (Lugt Suppl. 2681^a)
BIBLIOGRAPHY: Bocher (Lancret), p. 52, no. 69;
  Le Blanc II, p. 494, no. 23; P.-B. II, p. 534, no. 7

The subject of *Les Rémois* ('The Rhemese') is
taken from the tale of the same name by Jean
de La Fontaine. It tells the story of a painter and
his young wife who has caught the eye of two
neighbours. She persuades them to come to her
house in the evening when her husband will be
away on business. All is ready for supper, the
visitors have arrived and are looking forward to
a pleasant evening, when suddenly there is a knock
at the door. The wife hastily hides her guests in
the study. Finding his wife with a table laden with
victuals, the artist is delighted and suggests that
they invite none other than the wives of her
hapless visitors to the feast. The feast commences
under the very noses of the husbands concealed
behind the door, the artist and the three women
drinking their fill and making merry. When the
wine runs out, the artist's wife with first one, then
the other, of the ladies, go out for replenishments.
While they are out, the artist, before the very
eyes of the husbands concealed behind the door,
enjoys the charms of the remaining lady.

In 1742 Larmessin's illustrations to La
Fontaine's tales were shown at an exhibition at
the Louvre. This engraving appeared under the
title *Le Remords* ('Remorse'). DO

The Beautiful Cook
La belle cuisinière

1735

Pierre Aveline (1702–60)
After the painting by François Boucher (1703–70)

Engraving with etching and drypoint
462 × 359 mm; 503 × 370 mm
INSCRIPTIONS: *LA BELLE CUISINIERE*
  Vos oeufs s'échapent Mathurine
  Ce présage est mauvais pour vous,
  Ce grivois dans votre cuisine
  Pouroit bien vous les casser tous.
  Lépicié
F. Boucher pinxit / P. Aveline Sculp. / a Paris chez Jacob
  rue S^t. Jacques chez M^r. Simart Libraire attenant la rue
  du Plâtre. / avec Privilege du Roy.
INV: OG-296226
PROVENANCE: 1927, from the libraries of the Winter
  Palace (RIC); 'ERM 1928' (Lugt Suppl. 2681^a)
BIBLIOGRAPHY: Andresen I, p. 45, no. 7; Boucher 1978,
  p. 79, no. 206; Le Blanc I, p. 110, no. 94

This work is a typical Boucher interior, with the
composition deliberately accentuated by large
objects in differing styles. The original canvas is
in the Cognacq-Jay Museum in Paris. In the
kitchen chaos reigns: the cauldron is boiling over,
the cat, unnoticed, has seized the chicken, while
the beautiful cook stands entranced in her suitor's
tentative but persistent embrace. He holds her
hand and embraces her, while she, coquettishly
revealing a foot in its stylish shoe, tries not to drop
the eggs which she holds in her skirt. The artist
makes explicit the erotic metaphor of the lap as a
bird's nest, which the man will certainly destroy.
One broken egg already lies on the floor, a second
slips from her hand. The poet's warnings to the
modest girl are in vain: on the hearth is a copper
mortar with a pestle protruding from it – one of
the most common symbols of sexual intimacy. DO

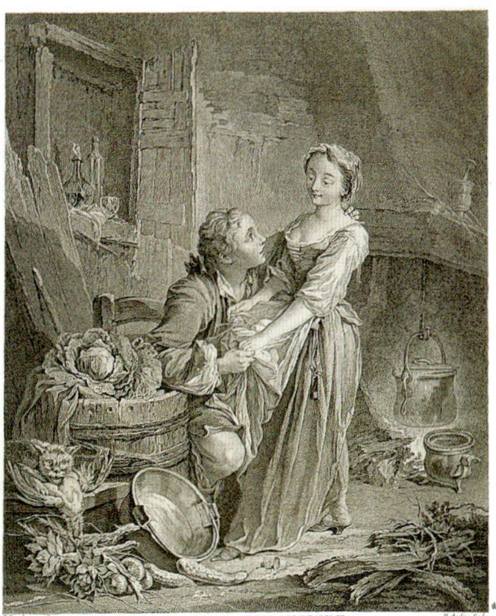

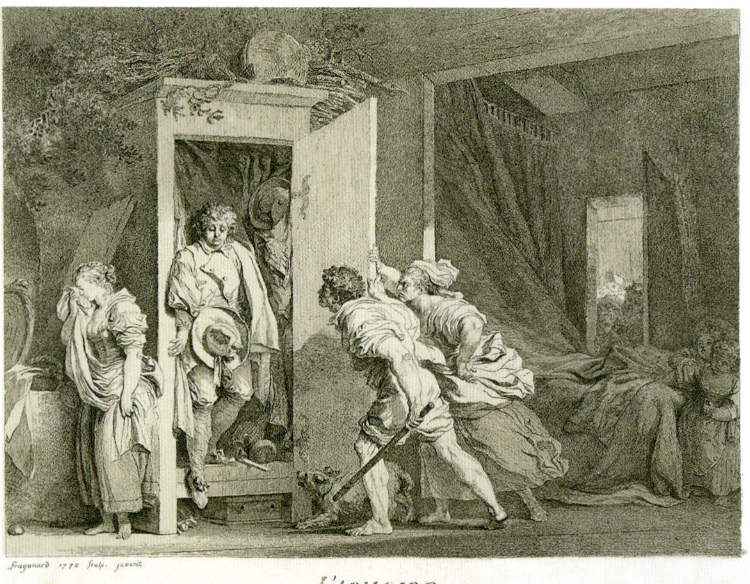

83
The Cupboard
L'armoire

1778

Jean-Honoré Fragonard (1732–1806)

Etching
419 × 549 mm; 471 × 570 mm
INSCRIPTIONS: *L'ARMOIRE*
fragonard 1778 sculp. jnvenit
INV: OG-228227
PROVENANCE: before 1865, collection of Chevalier
   J. Camberlyn (Lugt 514); acquired in 1927 from
   the libraries of the Winter Palace (RIC) (Lugt Suppl.
   2681ª)
BIBLIOGRAPHY: Andresen I, p. 519, nr. 7 (state II/III);
   Baudicour I, p. 159, no. 2 (state II/III); Le Blanc II,
   p. 249, no. 23; P.–B. II, p. 210, no. 2 (state II/III);
   Wildenstein 1956, no. XXIII (state II/IV)

This engraving was made by Fragonard after
his own drawing, of which at least two states
are known (in mirror image: Rosenberg, p. 486,
no. 238).

The unfortunate lover is caught unawares.
His sweetheart can only sob in despair. The
children crowding behind her await the inevitable
outcome in trepidation. The furious pursuers,
the girl's parents, are ready to tear the cupboard's
occupant to pieces. The latter's situation is both
awkward and comic: his eyes innocently lowered,
he tries to hold his hat in the most natural
position possible. DO

84
The Underside of a Leaf
La feuille à l'envers

Model of 1760

Sculptor Étienne-Maurice Falconet
Sèvres Porcelain Factory, between 1760
   and 1767

Soft-paste porcelain, biscuit
Height 20.2 cm
INV: ZF-27684

The subject of this group was inspired by one of
La Fontaine's tales and has an erotic undertone.
In order to see the underside of the leaf, the girl
must lie down. The factory's archives contain
a description of a subject previously attributed
to Falconet, where a young man offers a peach
wrapped in vine leaves, which also accentuates
the frivolity of the subject (*Falconet à Sèvres*,
p. 133, no. 67 a, b; *La porcelaine de Sèvres*, p. 417,
cat. 1309). NB

85
Jealousy
Le jaloux

Model of 1752

Sculptor Van de Voorst, after a drawing by Boucher
   on the subject of Charles-Simon Favart's comedy
   Vallée de Montmorency
Sèvres Porcelain Factory (Vincennes), between 1752
   and 1757

Soft-paste porcelain, biscuit
Height 22.5 cm
INV: ZF-22812
PROVENANCE: 1925, from the Museum of the Stieglitz
   School of Technical Design, Leningrad

Among the first models that were made at Sèvres
after Boucher's drawings are three groups on the
subject of Favart's popular comedy *Vallée de
Montmorency*. One of these, known as *Le jaloux*,
appeared in 1752. Its creator, the sculptor Van de
Voorst (dit Vandervolle), was rector of the Accademia
di San Luca, but very little is known about his life
and work. The Hermitage piece is a fine example of
this soft-paste porcelain group made using the biscuit
technique. Coridon declares his love on bended
knee to Lisette, who pushes him away. Behind her,
Coridon's father Mathurin, who is also in love with
Lisette, looks on jealously.

Although the subject and compositional idea
were Boucher's, no less a contribution was made by
the sculptor. The facial expressions are conveyed
with great artistic feeling: Lisette's charming, slyly
coquettish face and the angry, scowling visage of the
jealous Mathurin. The clothes are skilfully depicted
in all their detail, right down to the seams of the
youth's shirt, yet at the same time without creating
an impression of naturalism. The fine quality soft-
paste porcelain and impeccable moulding make this
group a true masterpiece of Vincennes plastic art. JV

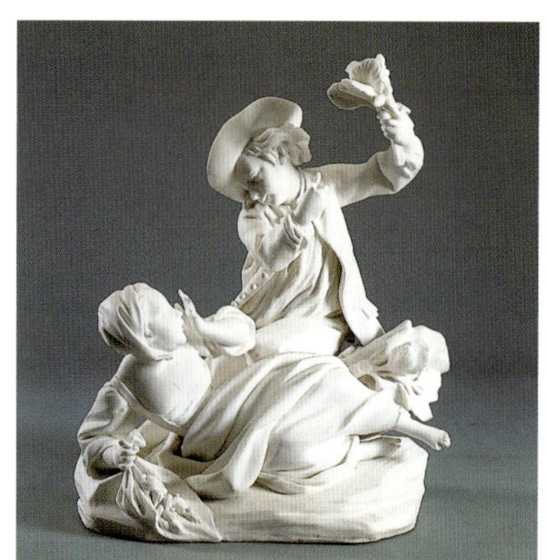

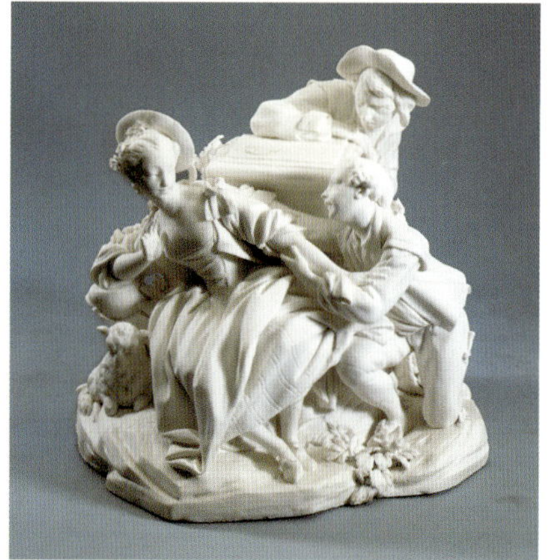

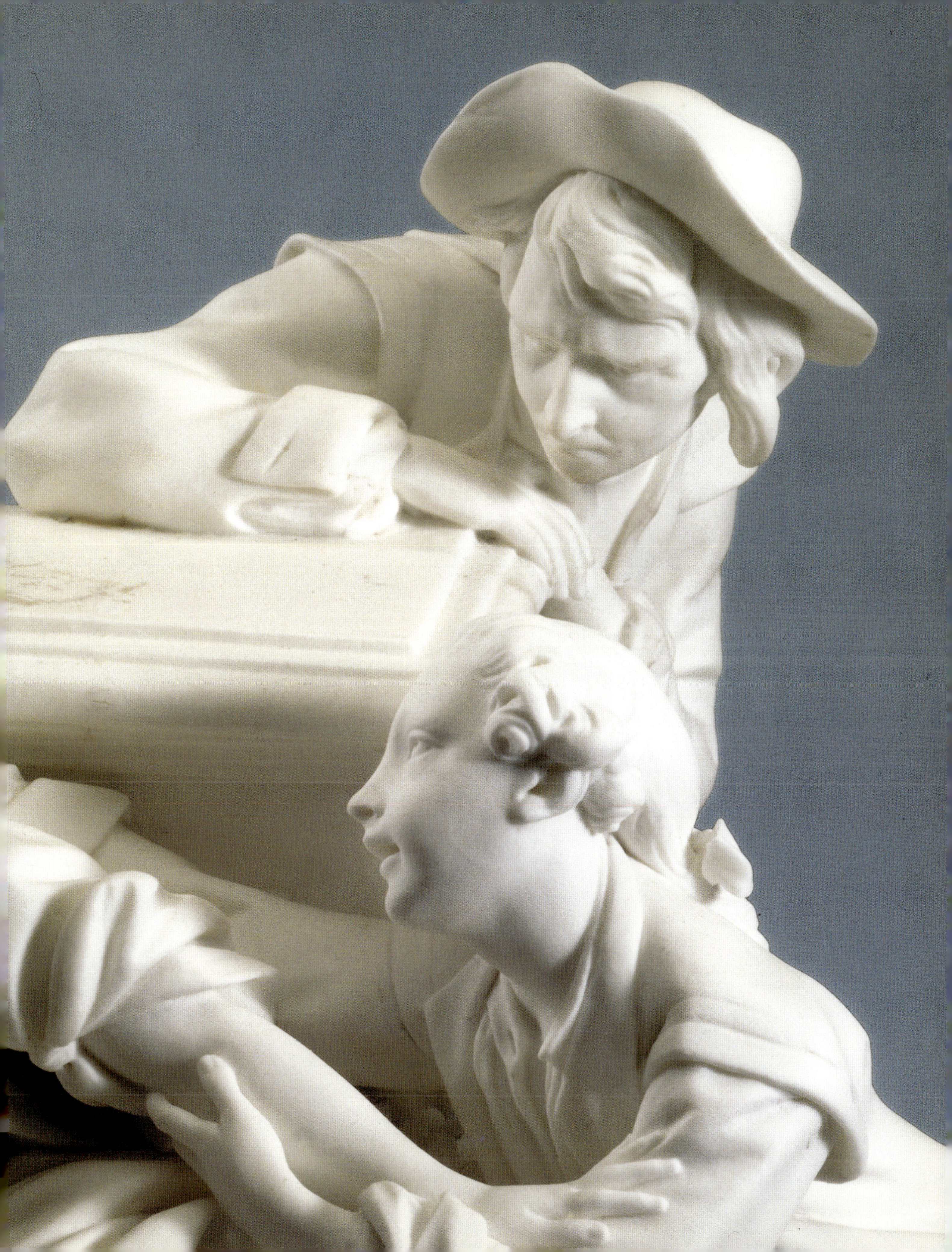

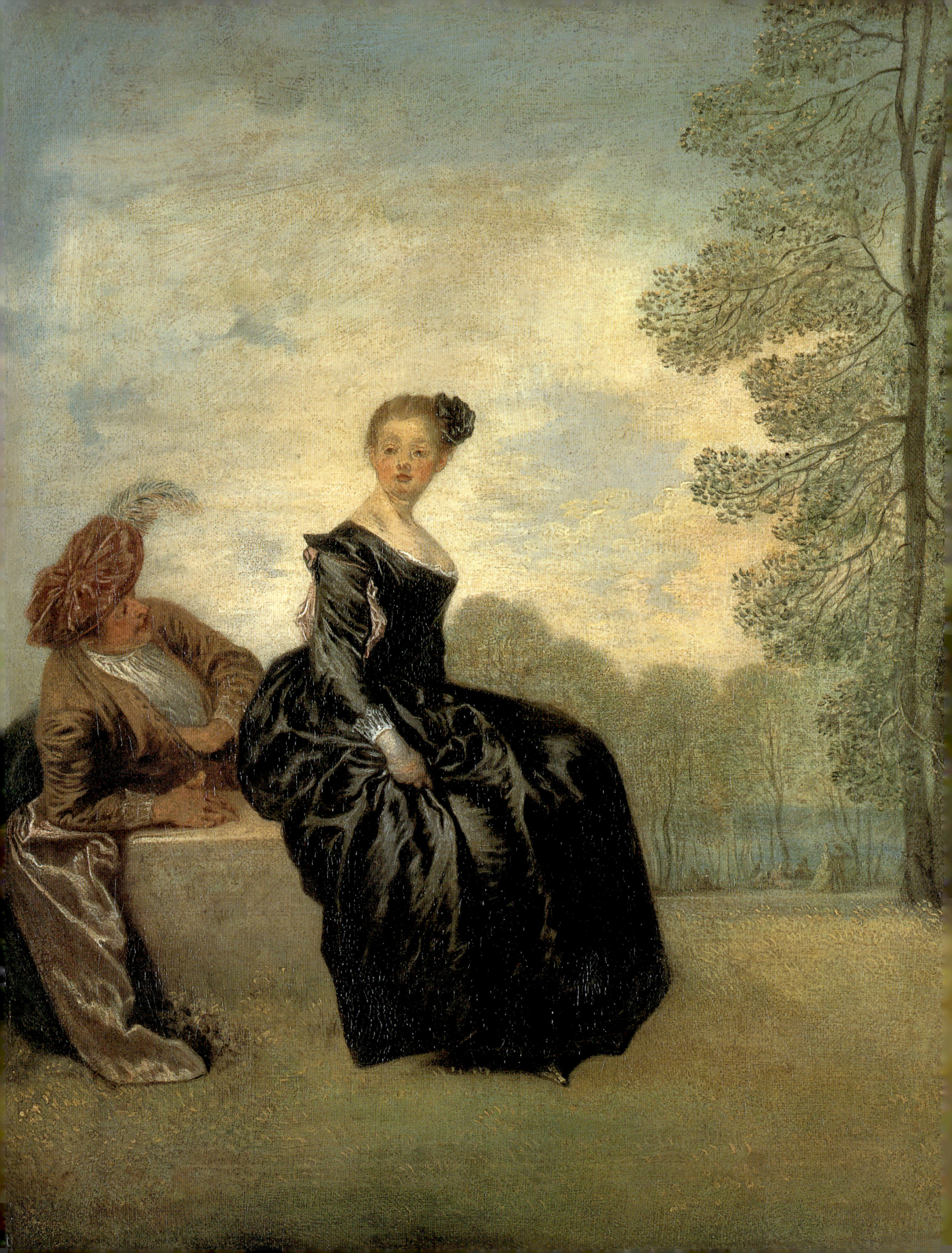

The Triumph of Eros

In the narrative of seduction Eros's triumph is inevitable. But what does it entail? The kiss: the longed-for moment of union and erotic bliss. Rococo culture was fascinated by the kiss, as embodying a shared submission to the power of Cupid. 'Two heads leaning together, the meeting of two pairs of lips, rapidly delineated on the canvas': this was the Goncourt brothers' description of all 'that sufficed for a picture' (referring to the artist Fragonard). And nowhere is this triumph of the kiss more graphically illustrated than in Jean-Antoine Houdon's voluptuous *Kiss*. This iconic sculpture was widely reproduced in a variety of gleaming materials, and especially prized by collectors (cat. 98).

But it is not just the kiss. The triumph of Eros courses through *everything*. As conclusion to the progress of love, the bodies of men and women are transformed as they begin to come together; even the landscape seems to vibrate with this erotic melancholia or thrill of sexual arousal.

In the favourite eighteenth-century theme of Pygmalion bringing to life his sculpture of Galatea, Cupid succeeds in enlivening art itself (cat. 87). Cupid is enrolled in a male sexual daydream of vivifying the depicted object of desire; erotic excitement is here confused with the delectation of the work of art (cat. 89).

This power of Eros continually to transform things and bodies means that seduction is never brought to an end. Cupid unceasingly traverses the world, claiming one victim before moving on to disturb the next. In this way the couple in Antoine Watteau's psychologically complex *Capricious Girl* (*left*; cat. 88) is imagined in a permanent state of expectancy and irresolution: flirtation without end, where the man is permanently fumbling, and the woman is left in a state of bemusement – as if haunted by Cupid.

The Capricious Girl (detail)
Antoine Watteau
1718
cat. 88

86
Pastoral Scene

1740s

François Boucher (1703–70)

Oil on canvas
61 × 75 cm (oval)
SIGNED at the bottom of the picture on a stone: *Boucher. f*
INV: GE 1275
PROVENANCE: acquired for Catherine II between 1763 and 1774
BIBLIOGRAPHY: Georgi, p. 479; Réau 1929, no. 444; Livshits; Nemilova 1961, p. 306; Nemilova 1975, p. 438

From its stylistic features, the free manner in which the subject is interpreted and the broad, light style of painting, this composition can be dated to the 1740s, when the artist created his best pastoral works. Some French researchers are inclined to ascribe it to an earlier period, the 1730s, when Boucher had only just begun to master what was for him a new genre. The painting was originally oval in form. In 1856 it was mounted in an ornamented frame above a mirror and reshaped accordingly. In 1902 the canvas was restored to its original shape, with necessary adjustments being made.

The influence of the theatre can often be felt in similar compositions by Boucher. It is assumed that the artist was inspired by the plays of his friend Charles-Simon Favart, written for the Théâtre de la Foire. Moreover, his pastoral subjects accorded perfectly with the tastes and philosophical views of the era. In the *Encyclopédie française* of 1765 the genre is described thus: 'The tranquillity of rural life, the freedom, peace, charming merriment, the innocent joy… Not all that occurs in a rural setting is worthy of the pastoral: all that is coarse or bleak, tragic events and rural passions, must be excluded.' In the catalogue for a Paris exhibition of Boucher's work, the authors see a certain symbolic meaning in this composition: 'The symbolism springs from the fact that this picture does not just show a couple, consisting of a shepherd and shepherdess, as was customary in pastoral works of the mature period […]. The raised glass represents in a unique sense a celebration of the delights of nature' (*François Boucher. 1703–1770*, Galeries Nationales du Grand Palais, Paris, 1987; Paris, 1986, p. 102). ED

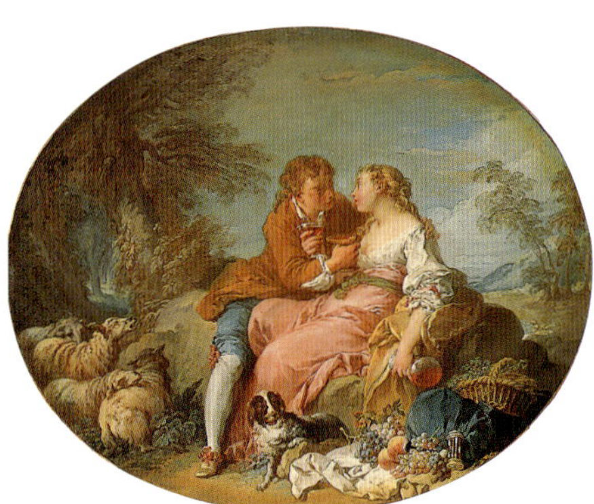

87
Pygmalion and Galatea

1784

Laurent Pécheux (1729–1821)

Oil on canvas
132 × 107 cm
SIGNED and dated bottom right:
Pecheux Tourini 1784
INV: GE 7568
PROVENANCE: 1784, commissioned by Prince Nikolai Borisovich Yusupov in Turin; Yusupov estate, Arkhangelskoe, near Moscow; from 1837, Yusupov Palace, Petersburg; 1919–24, Yusupov Palace Museum, Petrograd; from 1924, State Museum Fund; 1928, transferred to the Hermitage
BIBLIOGRAPHY: Ernst, p. 116; Prakhov, p. 43; Youssoupoff, no. 90; Yusupov, no. 363

The subject is taken from an ancient myth (Ovid, *Metamorphoses*, X, 243–97), dedicated to the story of the love of Pygmalion, the legendary king of Cyprus, for the statue of a beautiful girl which he had carved himself from ivory:

> Pleas'd with his idol, he commends, admires,
> Adores; and last, the thing ador'd, desires.
> A very virgin in her face was seen,
> And had she mov'd, a living maid had been:
> One wou'd have thought she cou'd have stirr'd, but strove
> With modesty, and was asham'd to move.
> Art hid with art, so well perform'd the cheat,
> It caught the carver with his own deceit:
> He knows 'tis madness, yet he must adore,
> And still the more he knows it, loves the more:
> The flesh, or what so seems, he touches oft,
> Which feels so smooth, that he believes it soft.

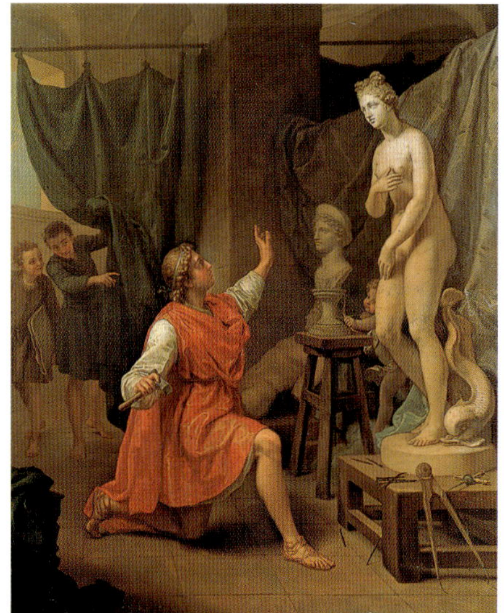

Aphrodite, goddess of love, heeded the prayers of the enamoured sculptor and brought the beautiful statue to life.

The figure of Galatea replicates the famous statue of the Venus de Medici, while the bust of the goddess which stands on a table is a smaller version of the giant bust of the Roman goddess Juno Ludovisi, which Pécheux could have sketched in Rome at the Villa Ludovisi.

The French artist Laurent Pécheux was more famous in Italy than in his homeland. After training in Paris with the famous historical painter, Charles Natoire, he soon left France and in 1753 set off to study and work in Italy. He spent 45 years of his life there, visiting the studio of the German artist Anton Raphael Mengs in Rome and becoming friends with Pompeo Batoni, with whom he often shared commissions from French clients. He became a member of the Accademia di San Luca in Rome and the Accademia di Belle Arti in Parma (1762), where he painted portraits of the reigning dynasty, and, two years later, became a member of the Accademia Clementina in Bologna. In 1774 Pécheux received a commission from Catherine II to paint portraits of the Duke and Duchess of Parma and Pope Clemens XIV for the portrait gallery of the Chesme Palace in Petersburg. Finally, in 1776, the king of Sardinia, Vittorio-Amedeo III (r. 1773–96), invited the French master to become first painter to the king of Piedmont. Pécheux was appointed director and professor at the Turin academy in 1778. By the end of the 1770s Pécheux and Batoni had become, in the eyes of their foreign clients, the leading painters of portraits and historical scenes.

This picture was commissioned by the famous collector and connoisseur of French painting, Prince Nikolai Borisovich Yusupov, the year he arrived in Turin as Russian ambassador extraordinary and plenipotentiary minister at the court of the Sardinian king. ED

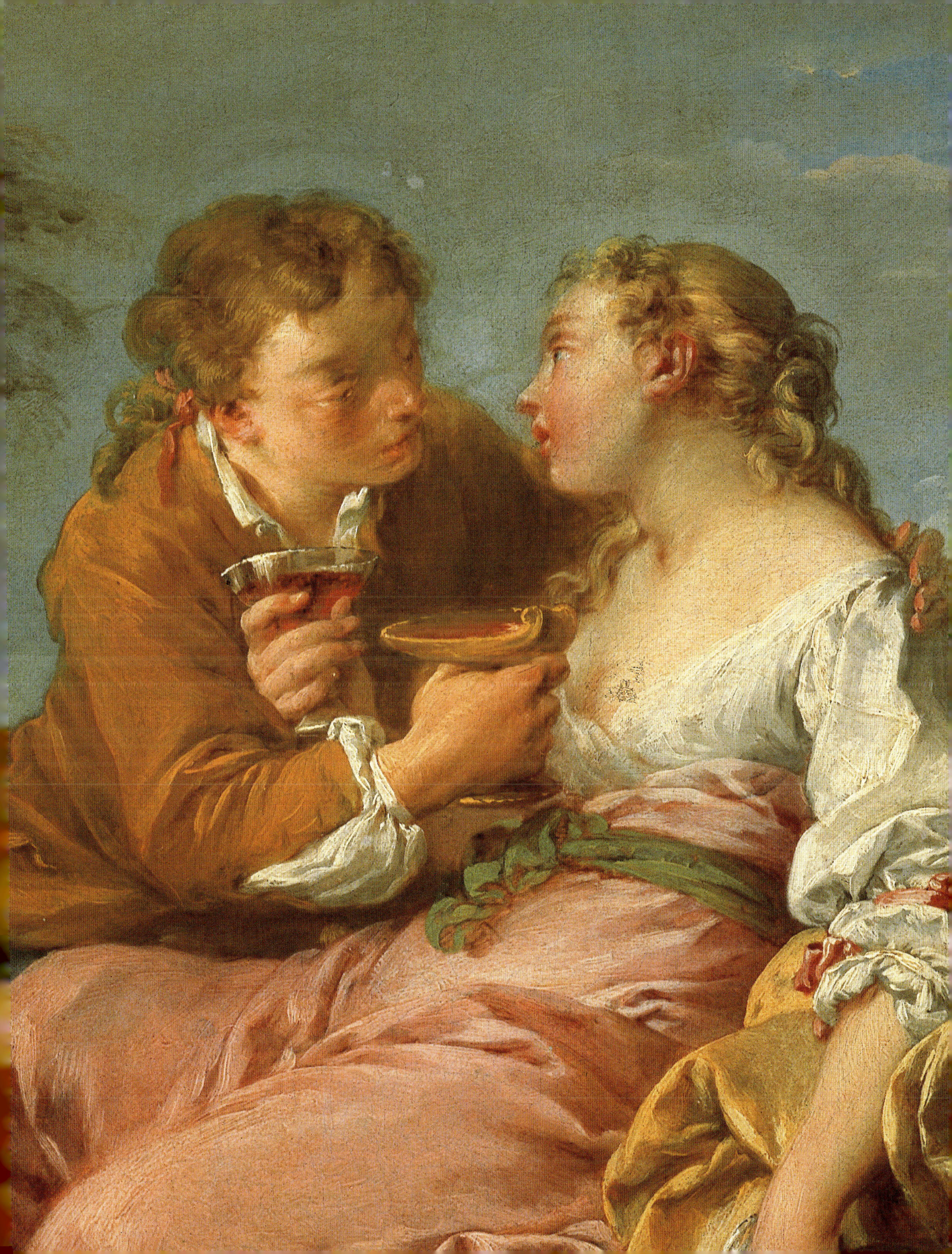

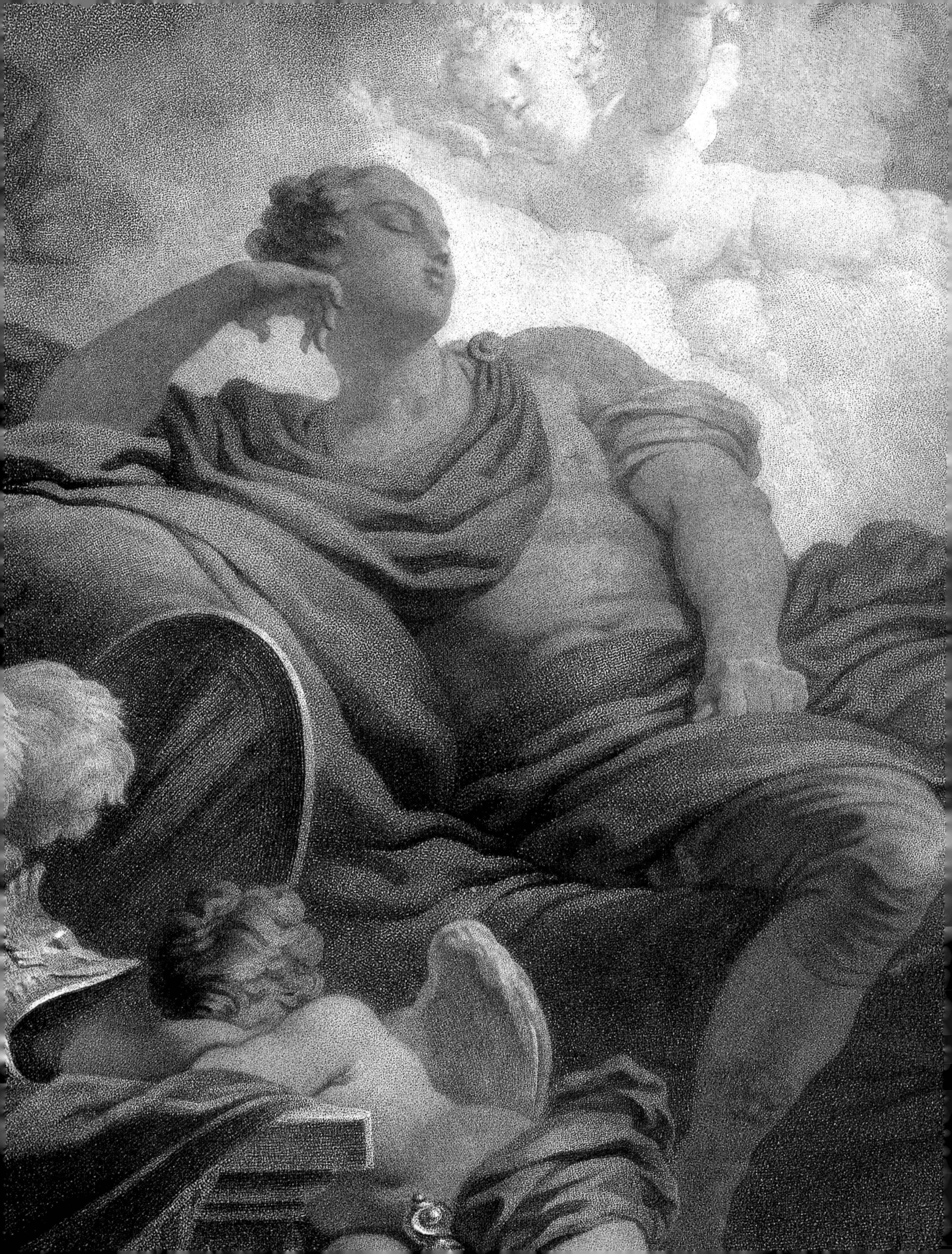

88

The Capricious Girl
La capricieuse (La boudeuse)

1718

Antoine Watteau (1684–1721)

Oil on canvas
42 × 34 cm
INV: GE 4120
PROVENANCE: 18th century, collection of Robert
Walpole; before 1842, collection of Horace Walpole,
Strawberry Hill, England; 1859, acquired by Count
Pavel Sergeevich Stroganov from Meffré in Paris;
in Stroganov's collection first at Znamenskoe, then
Petersburg; 1923, acquired from Stroganov's collection
BIBLIOGRAPHY: Adhémar 1950, no. 220 (as F. Mercier);
Baroque Masters, no. 69; Chegodayev, no. 31; D.-V.,
no. 303; Eidelberg, pp. 275–8; Ernst, p. 172; Ferre I,
pp. 149–51; III, pp. 958–9, 982, B. 24; Fourcaud,
p. 356; Goncourt 1875, no. 114; Goncourt 1914 I,
p. 86; Guerman, pp. 52, 169–71, 183; Livshits, no. 122;
L'Opera Completa, no. 116; Miller, p. 59; Nemilova
1961, p. 9, pl. 11; Nemilova 1964, pp. 145–51, cat. 7;
P.-M. II, no. 749; Posner, pp. 111, 283; Réau 1928–30 I,
no. 101; Réau 1929, no. 411; Th.-B. xxxv,
p. 193; Volskaya, p. 27; Watteau, no. 116; Watteau
1684–1721, ex. cat., pp. 354–5, no. 46; Zimmermann,
no. 84; Zolotov and Nemilova, pp. 144–5, no. 10

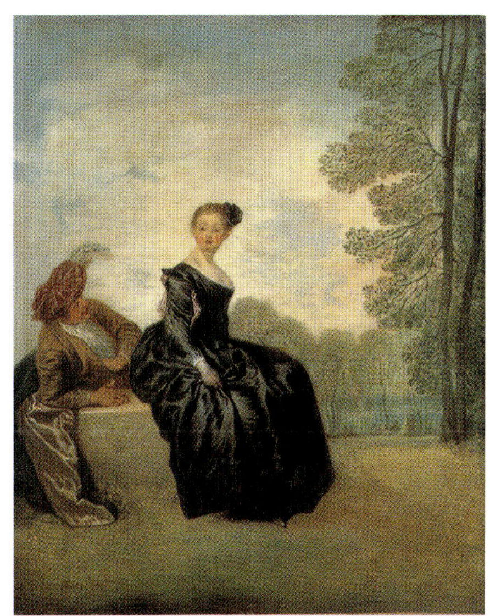

The painting is acknowledged as one of the best
examples of a *fête galante* from Antoine Watteau's
late period. Both its stylistic features and the style
of painting suggest that it can be dated to 1718.
In the eighteenth century it was probably in the
collection of British prime minister Sir Robert
Walpole, later belonging to his son Horace
Walpole: the painting features in a watercolour
by an anonymous artist depicting one of the rooms
of Walpole's house at Strawberry Hill. After
Horace Walpole's collection was sold in 1842, the
canvas changed hands several times in London and
Paris in less than two decades, until it was acquired
by count Pavel Sergeevich Stroganov, the famous
Petersburg collector of the second half of the
nineteenth century. A manuscript catalogue of
his art collection (1864) indicates that the picture
was acquired from Meffré in Paris in 1859 for 5,000
francs. At first Stroganov's collection was housed
at his Znamenskoe estate near Tambov; after the
count built his house in Petersburg, he transferred
much of his collection there. This was the only
work by Antoine Watteau in the extensive
collections of the Stroganov family. By contrast,
the picture gallery of Empress Catherine II had
acquired, by the mid-1770s, at least seven works
by the famous artist. ED

89

The Dream of Cupid
Le songe d'Amour

1791

Nicolas-François Regnault (1746–*c.* 1810)
After the painting by Jean-Honoré Fragonard
(1732–1806)

Etching and stipple engraving
630 × 480 mm; 772 × 555 mm
INSCRIPTIONS: *LE SONGE D'AMOUR / L'Amour et la
Volupté Charment le Sommeil du Guerrier par la douce
illusion des Plaisirs*
*Gravé d'Apres le Tableau d'H.Fragonard, Peintre du Roi,
par N.F. Regnault. / A Paris chez l'Auteur, Rue de
Montmorency, N⁰ 22.*
WATERMARK: *EAGLE* (cf. Heawood no. 1240)
INV: OG-132229
PROVENANCE: before 1928, from main collection
(Lugt Suppl. 2681ª); acquired before 1830s
BIBLIOGRAPHY: Le Blanc III, p. 292, no. 7 (state II/II);
P.-B. III, p. 386, no. 1 (state II/II); Rosenberg, p. 546,
no. 283

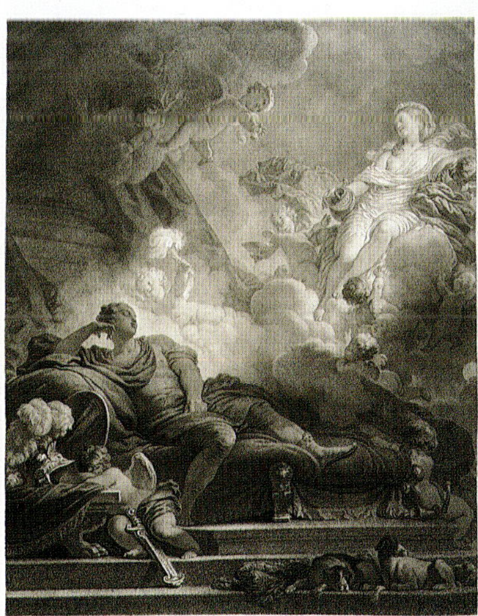

Using tender illusions of pleasure, Eros and
Volupté lead the hero into a dream. His armour
lies on the steps and his dogs are asleep at his
feet. The erotic dream is a major component
of amorous discourse. The dream is akin to
something mysterious, divine, its fabric filled
with many different creatures, both hellish and
divine. It is not clear whether he is dreaming of
Venus, Cupid and the multitude of putti depicted
by the artist, or whether they have really appeared
to the sleeping hero to make his dream pleasurable.
One thing is evident: the sleeping warrior is in a
state of perfect bliss.

Regnault was one of the first French engravers
who, in the latter part of the eighteenth century,
began to use the technique of stipple engraving,
which had been imported from England and was
now fashionable. The engraving is almost the same
size as the original canvas, but in mirror image.
Fragonard's original painting hangs in the Louvre
(inv. R.F. 2149). DO

90

The Vow of Love
Le serment d'Amour

1786

Jean Matthieu (1749–1815)
After the painting by Jean-Honoré Fragonard
(1732–1806)

Etching
585 × 445 mm; 596 × 460 mm
INSCRIPTIONS: *LE SERMENT D'AMOUR*
Gravé par J.Mathieu d'après le Tableau d'H.Fragonard P^{tre}
du Roi. / AParis chez l'Auteur Cloitre S^t. Benoit Maison
de M^r. Demarteau
WATERMARK: *DOVECOT*
INV: OG-129969
PROVENANCE: before 1865, collection of the Comte
de Corneillan (Lugt 458); 1927, from the libraries
of the Winter Palace (RIC) (Lugt Suppl. 2681^a)
BIBLIOGRAPHY: Le Blanc II, p. 624, no. 15 (state I/II);
P.-B. III, p. 69; Rosenberg, p. 428, fig. 27

In a shady park before a statue of Cupid, a young
man and woman vow to love and be true to each
other for ever, sealing the vow with a kiss. The
vow of love is something solemn and eternally
sacred. At their feet are sculptures of dolphins,
ancient symbols of love and devotion.

The Vow of Love after Fragonard's painting
is considered Jean Matthieu's finest engraving
(P.-B. III, p. 69). Fragonard's painting formed a
pair with another, oval, canvas, *The Good Mother*
(Rosenberg, p. 428), which was also engraved
by Matthieu (Le Blanc II, p. 624, no. 11). DO

91

The Cage Concealed
La cage d'Erobée

1769

Louis-Marin Bonnet (1736–93)
After the painting by Noël Hallé (1711–81)

Etching and engraving, crayon manner, printed in two
colours on blue paper
335 × 263 mm; 346 × 273 mm
INSCRIPTIONS: *La Cage d'Erobée*; in upper right-hand
corner: *No 22*
Hallée pinx. / L. Bonnet sculp. / AParis chés Bonnet rue
Galande la porte Cochere entre un Chandellier et un
Layetier vis a vis la rue du Fouard.
INV: OG-298586
PROVENANCE: 1932, from the Central Library of the
State Hermitage
BIBLIOGRAPHY: Hérold, pp. 20, 68, no. 22$^{2)}$; Ozerkov,
no. 57; Willk–Brocard, p. 408, no. N83

Bonnet's pastoral scene, executed using a complex
technique combining etching and two-colour
crayon manner, explores a metaphor popular in the
eighteenth century: innocence as a bird in a cage.
Loss of innocence is an open cage from which
the bird has flown. Works by French eighteenth-
century artists often depict a girl crying over an
empty cage or over a dead bird, or a young man
trying to capture a girl's interest with a bird in a
cage: with one careless movement the girl could
allow the bird to escape (for example in paintings
by Lancret; Wildenstein, p. 100, nos. 455–6,
458–60, figs. 111–13, 115, 116; p. 120, no. 735,
fig. 189). Noël Hallé makes the metaphor literal
by placing the cage beneath the skirt of the
shepherdess's outer garments. The shepherd's
gesture is also clear as he reaches confidently
towards the cage despite her feigned, weak
resistance. The essence of innocence is to be
in permanent danger.

The ultimate innocent, of course, is the
convent girl Cécile Volanges. 'In appearance this
girl is artlessness and innocence incarnate', writes
the perfidious Madame de Merteuil. 'Her little
head is uncommonly easily agitated, whereupon
she becomes even more amusing as she knows…
absolutely nothing of what she would so like to
know. She is seized by a quite absurd impatience:
she laughs, cries, becomes angry, then with quite
captivating artlessness asks me to enlighten her'
(*Les Liaisons Dangereuses*, no. 38). The innocent
girl remains in a happy languor of sweet
ignorance: 'Long did she not know, filled with the
most innocent spirit, whether children were really
born from the ear' (Molière, *The School for Wives*;
see also Ariès, 1962).

The print, from Hallé's now lost painting,
uses a combination of techniques which highlights
Bonnet's brilliant mastery and was made much
of in announcements of its publication and sale.
It was published in 1769 by *Mercure de France* and
L'Avant-Courier. DO

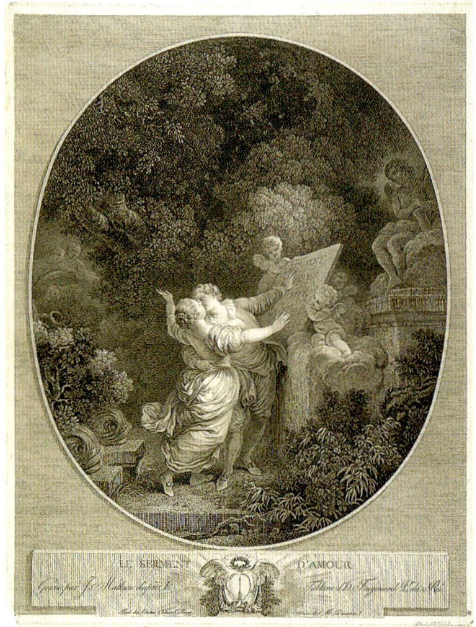

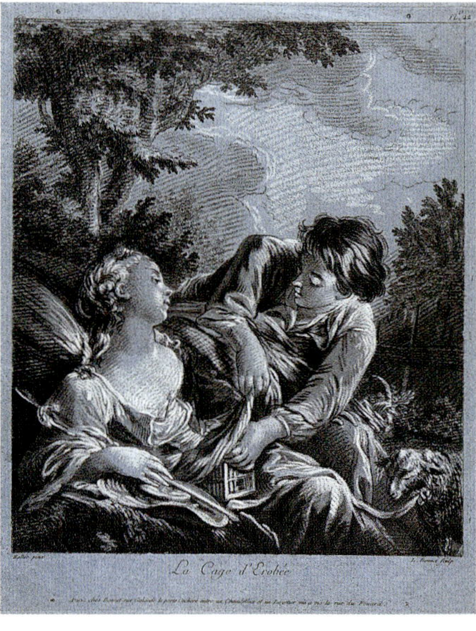

92
Night
La nuit

c. 1778

Emanuel de Ghendt (1738–1815)
After the gouache by Pierre-Antoine Baudouin
(1723–69)

Etching and engraving
374 × 270 mm; 442 × 355 mm
INSCRIPTIONS: in upper right-hand corner, above
border, *fes de plate*
INV: OG-197977
PROVENANCE: 1925, from the Yusupov collection (?)
(Lugt Suppl. 2681ª)
BIBLIOGRAPHY: Bocher (Baudouin), p. 35, no. 33
(state II/III); Bourcard, p. 30; Dresden 2005,
nr. 164c; Lawrence & Dighton, p. 27, no. 63
(state I/II); Ozerkov, no. 88; P.-B. II, p. 306, no. I

This print is from a series entitled 'The Four Times
of Day'. A romantic moon illuminates a secluded
corner of the park, where a lady has retired with
her beau. The night-time tryst holds pure pleasure
in store for Baudouin's heroine. A little Falconet
cupid has cunningly concealed himself and casts
sly glances in anticipation of a diverting spectacle.
The print is a rare state 'before lettering'. DO

93
Yes or No?
Oui ou non

1781

N. Thomas (*c.* 1750–*c.* 1812)
After the composition by Jean-Michel Moreau
le Jeune (1741–1814)

Etching
412 × 321 mm; 491 × 334 mm
INSCRIPTIONS: *Oui ou Non*
J.M. Moreau le Jeune inv. / N. Thomas sculp. 1781. /
No. 31. / A. P. D. R.
WATERMARK: three-line inscription ('D. TAMIZIER'?)
INV: OG-126406
PROVENANCE: before 1928, from main collection
(Lugt Suppl. 2681ª); acquired before 1830s
BIBLIOGRAPHY: Bourcard, pp. 421–2; Cohen–De Ricci,
p. 354; Delteil, p. 207; Lawrence & Dighton, p. 100,
no. 237 (state III/IV); Le Blanc IV, p. 31, no. 13
(state III/III); Ozerkov, no. 71; Rothschild, pp. 193–4

This print, made in 1781, was part of the third and
last series of prints illustrating a publishing project
(1775–83) entitled *Troisième suite d'estampes pour
servir à l'histoire des modes et du costume en France,
dans le dix-huitième siècle* (Paris, Prault, 1783).
In this publication each print was accompanied
by a text by the famous writer Nicolas-Edmé Rétif
de la Bretonne (1734–1806), written after the prints
were made. For this one he composed a short,
entertaining story about a poor girl who succeeds
in getting her admirer to propose to her and marry
her, when he had only intended to amuse himself.

The print depicts the tale's denouement, a
passionate scene where he declares his love on a
garden bench. A fan and a torn letter lie at their
feet, thrown on the ground in a surge of emotion.
The decisive moment has come: yes or no? The
gentleman begs for the girl's reply. Her mother,
who is hiding behind the bench, also awaits her

reply. Meanwhile Falconet's Cupid, finger to his
lips, reaches for his quiver, for it is now that true
passion stirs in the young man's breast.

Conversation in the gallant century took the
most whimsical forms and used the most refined
imagery. When preparing to venture forth into
society, ladies and gentlemen chose the tone and
genre of their behaviour for the coming evening
and night, dressing in significant colours and
applying beauty-spots to their faces and necks.
Public conversations were conducted using refined
formulae and imagery. The most eloquent of
these were, however, reserved for outpourings
of emotion in amorous tête-à-têtes, and no better
pretext could be found for such a conversation
than a walk in the garden that led to a secluded,
shady path. DO

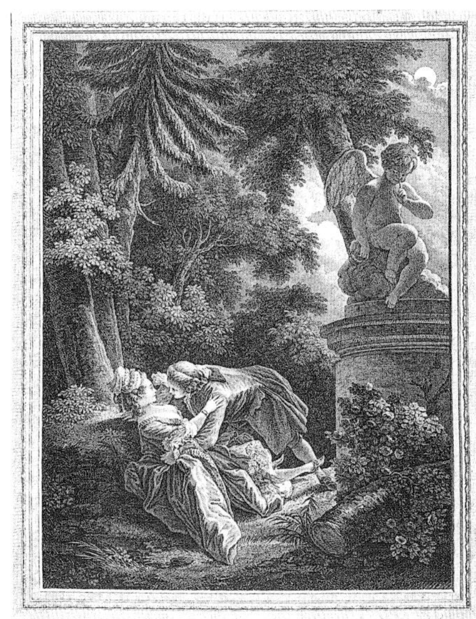

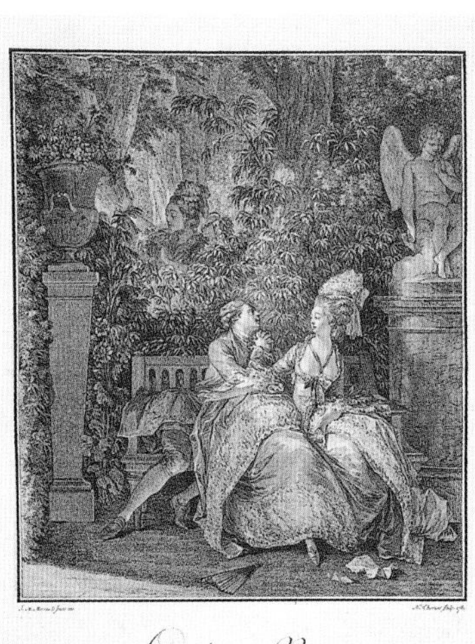

94
Vertumnus and Pomona
Vertumne et Pomone

Mid-18th century

François Chéreau le Jeune (1717–55)
After the composition by François Marot
(1666–1719)

Etching
334 × 265 mm (part of sheet cut off)
INV: OG-124634
PROVENANCE: before 1928, from main collection
(Lugt Suppl. 2681ᵃ); acquired before 1830s
BIBLIOGRAPHY: Le Blanc II, p. 8, no. 11 (indicating
that the print is by François Chéreau *l'aîné* working
together with Audran: 'gravée avec Audran');
Ozerkov, no. 47

The poem by François Gacon which accompanies
the engraving explains the meaning of the scene:

> *Cette vieille aux discours perfideʒ,*
> *Pomone, en veut a vôtre cœur.*
> *L'Amour s'est caché dans ses rides,*
> *Pour vous porter un trait vainqueur.*
> *S'en est fait, je vois vôtre perte;*
> *Vous vous plaiseʒ a l'ecouter,*
> *Quand il attaque a force ouverte,*
> *L'Amour est moins a redouter.*
> (This old woman with her cunning talk
> Wants your heart, Pomona.
> Eros is hidden in her folds,
> Ready to strike you with his victorious arrow;
> The deed is done, I see you are lost;
> You are listening to her with pleasure,
> When Cupid attacks openly,
> There is less to fear from him.)

The gullible Pomona falls straight into the
trap; she is not immediately suspicious, but noone
can avoid the cunning and perfidy of Cupid.
Cupid knows better than anyone how to adopt
other guises – any guise, in fact, as long as it leads
him to achieving his goal, which is why the mask
is one of Cupid's traditional attributes. It is found
in the painting *Venus and Cupid* by the school of
Michelangelo (London, Hampton Court; Lucie-
Smith, p. 53, ill. 51); and in Claude Mellan's famous
engraving *The Mousetrap*, and others. Pomona
must avoid falling into the trap, but Vertumnus,
by turning into an old woman, still manages to
achieve his aim.

The story of Vertumnus and Pomona
illustrates the nature of gullibility and obstinacy.
Gullibility is similar to illusion, and both are
based on obstinacy and imagination. Vertumnus,
Pomona's husband, is the god of all that changes:
the seasons, the course of rivers, people's moods,
ripening fruit (*Metamorphoses*, XIV, 623–97 and
767–71). The Hermitage collection contains a
second copy of the engraving in an album, with
the lower part of the page intact and bearing the
following inscriptions: *Peint par F. Marot. Gravé
par Chereau le jeune. / A Paris Cheʒ F. Chereau
Graveur du Roy rue Sᵗ. Jacques aux deux Piliers d'Or.
/ avec Privilege du Roy et de l'Academie.
VERTUMNE ET POMONE.* DO

95
Vertumnus and Pomona
Vertumne et Pomone

Model of 1704

Robert Le Lorrain (1666–1743)

Bronze
Height: 47 cm
INV: N.sk. 1844
PROVENANCE: 1931, from the Museum of the Academy
of Arts, Leningrad

Works by Le Lorrain are fairly rare. His most
famous is the large relief, *The Horses of Apollo*
(1736–7; Paris, Hôtel de Rohan). He preferred to
create small figures and compositions on classical
themes for private clients. A group of bronzes
similar to the Hermitage group and its pair, *Venus
and Adonis*, was exhibited in the Salon of 1704
as Le Lorrain's work. The Hermitage group is
in keeping with the sculptor's style and employs
his favourite subjects (Kosareva, p. 28).

According to the legend, Pomona, the goddess
of fruits and fruit trees, rejected the affections of
numerous suitors. Vertumnus alone was able to
inspire love in her. God of the changing seasons,
he could change himself too, and take on any form.
One day, appearing to Pomona in the form of
an old woman, he persuaded the goddess to turn
her attentions to Vertumnus. He then cast off his
unattractive guise and appeared before Pomona
in all his glory.

The bronze statuette depicts Vertumnus
turning back into himself, the change shown by
the wrinkled mask he is holding. The mask, the
traditional symbol of deception and reincarnation,
is a sign of Vertumnus's fickleness. Cupid is
present in the foreground as evidence that, once
again, it is only with his help that love is born. AV

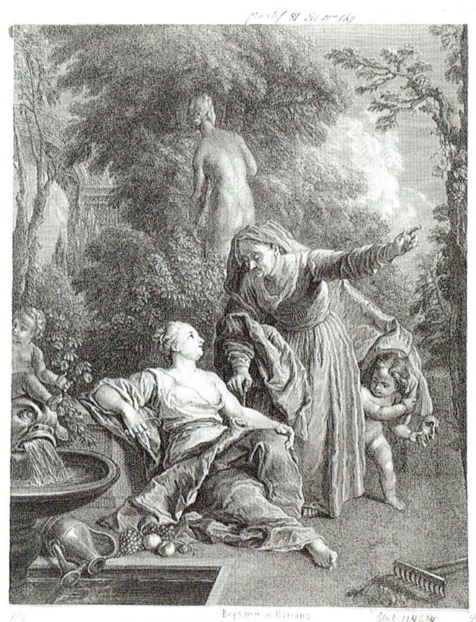

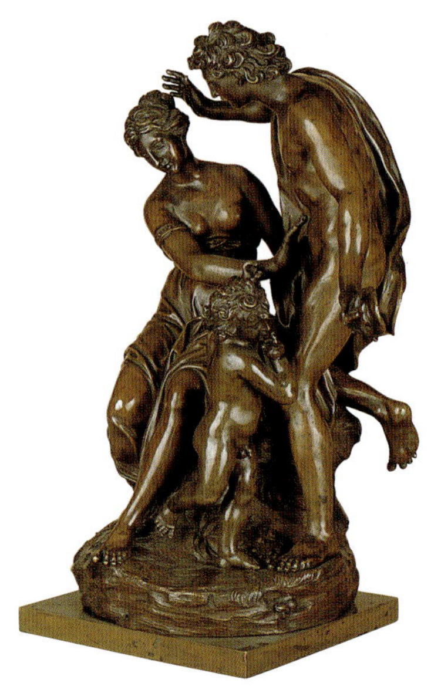

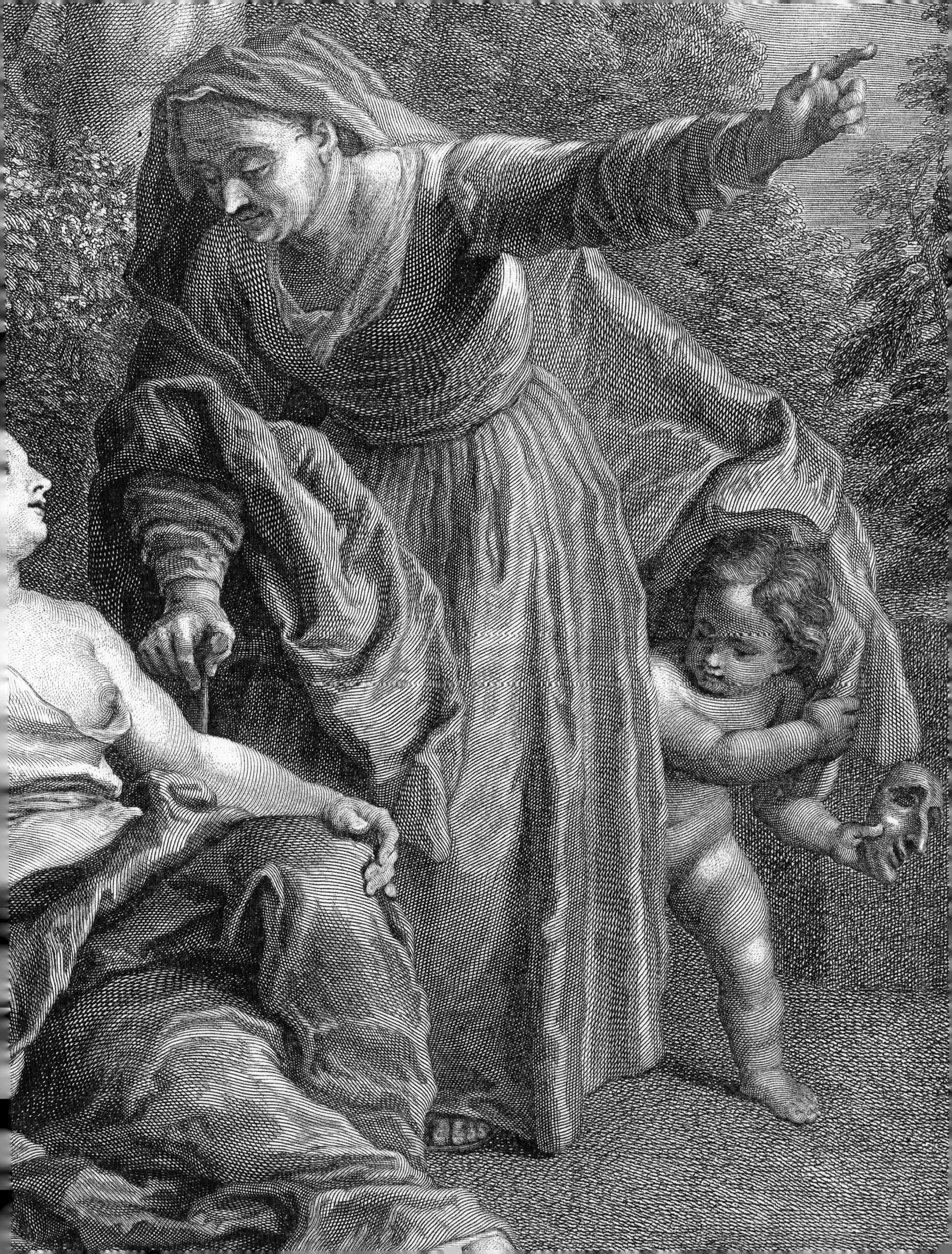

96
The Grape Eaters
Les mangeurs de raisins

Model of 1752

Sculptor unknown (Van de Voorst?), after a
    drawing by Boucher on the subject of Favart's
    comedy *Vallée de Montmorency*
Sèvres Porcelain Factory (Vincennes)

Soft-paste porcelain (?), biscuit
Height 20.7 cm
INV: ZF-25814
PROVENANCE: 1953, from the collection of M.I. Slonime,
    Leningrad

No information has survived to tell us who was the
sculptor of *The Grape Eaters*, but it seems probable
that it was the work of Van de Voorst, who created
Le jaloux (see cat. 85). JV

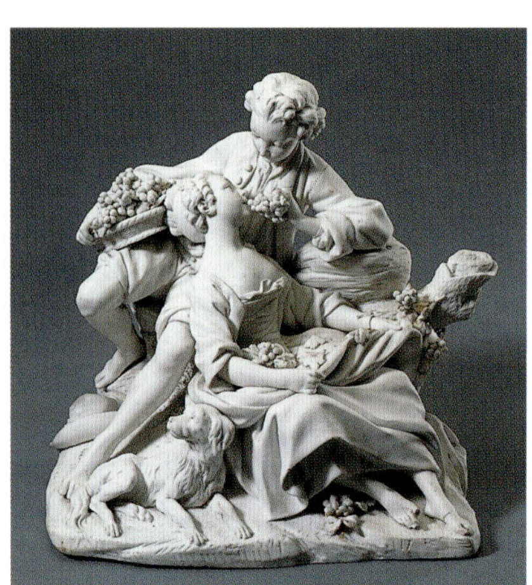

97
Pygmalion and Galatea
Pygmalion admirant Galatée

Model of 1763

Sculptor F.-C. Duru, after the marble group by
    Étienne-Maurice Falconet
Sèvres Porcelain Factory, between 1766 and 1773

Soft-paste porcelain, biscuit
Height 36.9 cm
INV: ZF-24161
PROVENANCE: 1932, from Pavlovsk Palace Museum

97a
Stand for Pygmalion and Galatea

Between 1773 and 1780

Sèvres Porcelain Factory

Hard-paste porcelain, biscuit
Length 27.6 cm; width 21.9 cm; height 9.8 cm
INV: GCh-7168

This group stands on a pedestal of hard-paste
porcelain, originally part of a similar group (now in
Pavlovsk Palace Museum) presented to Catherine II
by the Swedish King Gustav III in 1780. On the
pedestal is a poem by Jean-François Marmontel:

> *Creatrice des moeurs, avec le don sublime*
> *De se faire obeir et de se faire aimer,*
> *Elle n'a qu'a vouloire que le marbre s'anime*
> *Et le marbre va s'animer.*
> (Creator of morals with the sublime gift
> Of making herself obeyed and loved,
> She has only to wish the marble to life
> And the marble will come to life.)

By the mid-eighteenth century, Sèvres masters
were remarkably skilled in their production of
porcelain groups and figures. The properties of the
material – so-called biscuit (white matt, unglazed,
unpainted porcelain) – were perfectly suited to
the ideals of classical art. The lack of polychrome
glaze, the precision of the modelling and the
marble-like whiteness of the biscuit imbued these
pieces with an elegant modesty and beauty that
accorded with the ideals of Ancient Greek art.
    The marble group *Pygmalion and Galatea* was
exhibited at the Paris Salon in 1763. Its creator,
Étienne-Maurice Falconet, was the first director
of the sculpture studios at the Sèvres Porcelain
Factory (1757–66) and he was the first to introduce
elements of classicism into porcelain modelling.
    In the same year that Falconet exhibited his
marble sculpture, 1763, a model appeared for a
Pygmalion and Galatea in biscuit, made by his pupil,
the sculptor Duru. The only change Duru made
was to add a second cupid, behind Galatea; with this
addition, however, his porcelain work lost none of
the remarkably life-like qualities of Falconet's
marble original, and the whole was accomplished in
accordance with all the canons of the Greek ideal of
beauty combined with emotional expressiveness. JV

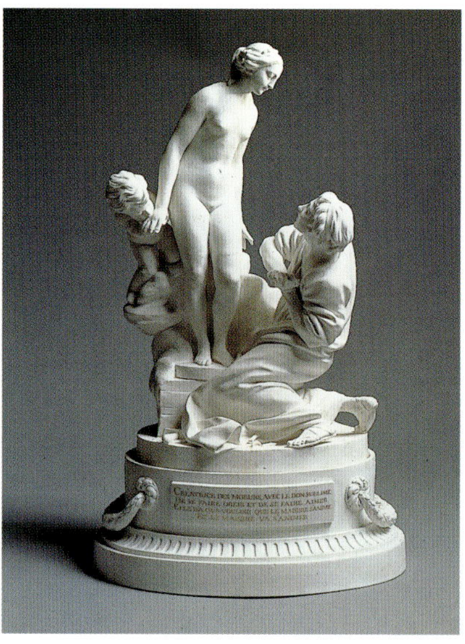

98
Mantel-clock: The Kiss

1780s

Paris

Gilded ormolu and patinated bronze, marble
44 × 27 × 15.5 cm
SIGNED on the face: *Nel Bourret à Paris*
INV: Epr-6193
PROVENANCE: from the main collection of the
    Winter Palace

The sculptural group *Le baiser donné* by Jean-
Antoine Houdon was created in 1774; its subject
was taken from one of La Fontaine's tales (J. de
La Fontaine, *Contes et Nouvelles*, Amsterdam, 1762,
vol. I, p. 231). This popular composition was
repeated many times in terracotta, Sèvres porcelain
and bronze. AG

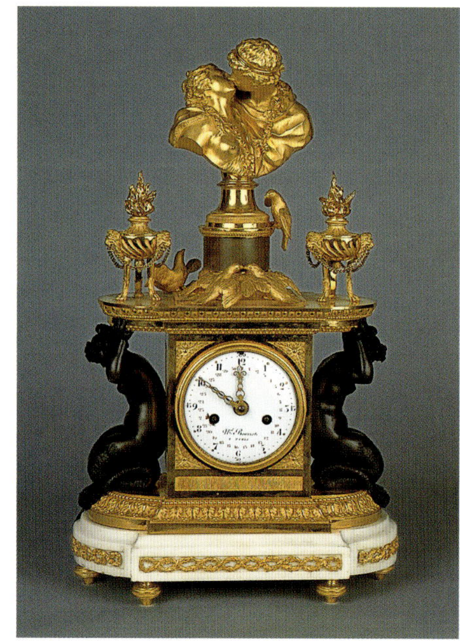

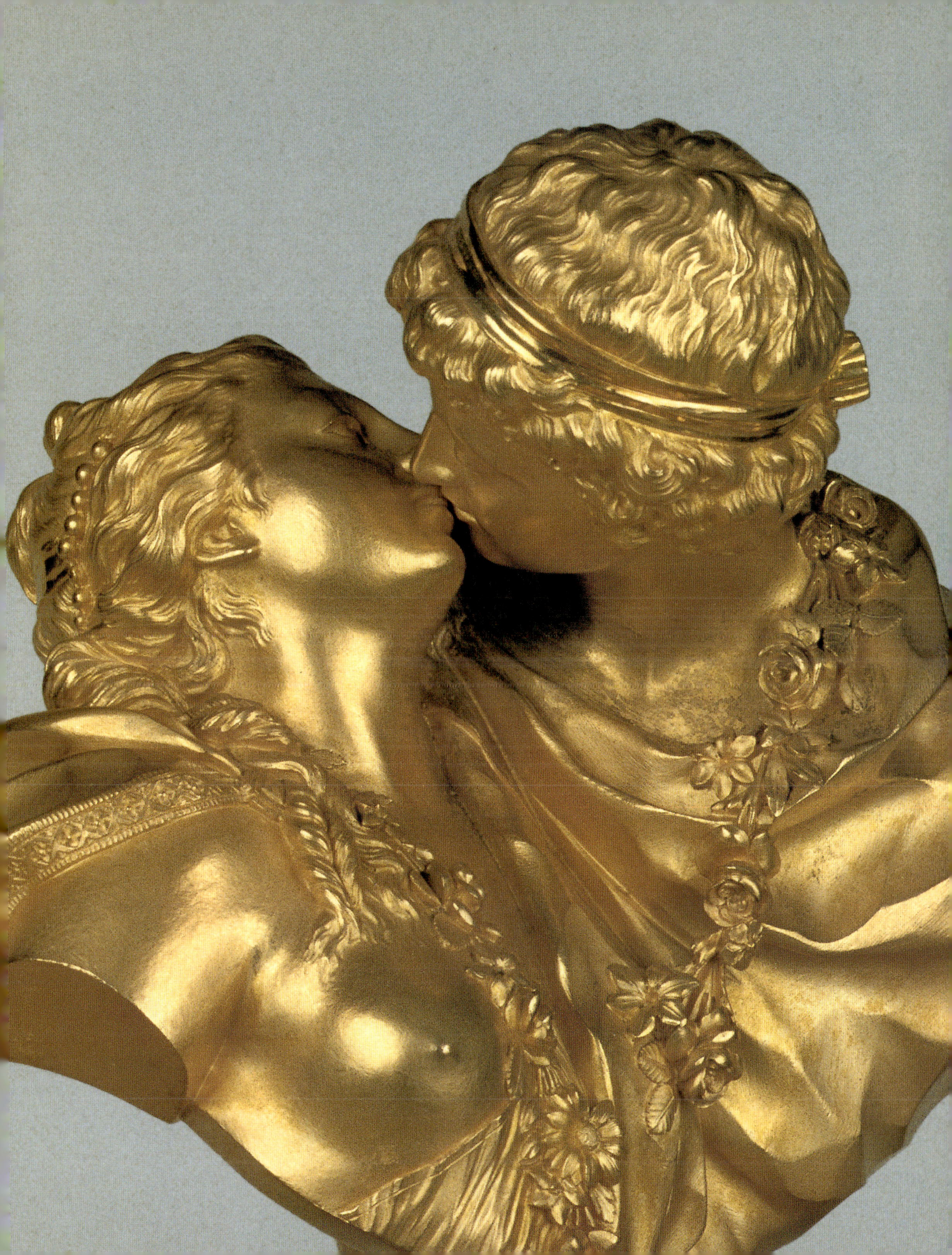

Bibliography

ADHÉMAR 1950: J. Adhémar, *Watteau, sa vie, son œuvre* (intro. R. Huyghe, 'L'Univers de Watteau'), Paris, 1950

ADHÉMAR 1963: J. Adhémar, *La gravure originale au XVIIIe siècle*, Paris, 1963

ALEXANDRIAN 1970: S. Alexandrian, *La peinture en Europe au XVIIIe siècle*, Paris, 1970

ALEXANDRIAN 1977: S. Alexandrian, *Les libérateurs de l'amour*, Paris, 1977

ALEXANDRIAN 1989: S. Alexandrian, *Histoire de la littérature érotique*, Paris, 1989

ANANOFF: A. Ananoff, *L'Œuvre dessiné de Jean-Honoré Fragonard (1732–1806)*, Catalogue raisonné, 4 vols, Paris, 1961–70

ANANOFF 1976: A. Ananoff (with Daniel Wildenstein), *François Boucher*, 2 vols, Paris and Lausanne, 1976

ANDRESEN: A. Andresen, *Handbuch für Kupferstichsammler oder Lexicon der Kupferstecher, Maler-Radirer und Formschneider aller Länder und Schulen nach Massgabe ihrer geschätztesten Blätter und Werke*, 2 vols, Leipzig, 1871–2

ANTH: J.J. Pauvert and M. Pauvert, *Anthologie historique des lectures érotiques*, vol. I (De Gilgamesh à Saint-Just: De −2000 à 1790), Paris, 1995–6

ARNOULD: O. Arnould, 'Pierre Subleyras', in *Dimier*, vol. II, 1928–30

ARIÈS: P. Ariès, *L'enfant et la vie familiale sous l'Ancien Régime*, Paris, [1960]

ARS AMATORIA: Ovid, *Ars amatoria* ('Thomas Heywood's Art of Love: the first complete English translation of Ovid's *Ars amatoria*') (ed. M.L. Stapleton), Ann Arbor, *c.* 2000

ART TREASURES: *Khudozhestvennye sokrovishcha Rossii* [The Art Treasures of Russia], 7 vols, 1901–7

AYRES: P. Ayres, *Emblemata amatoria. Emblèmes d'amour en quatre langues*, London, [1680s]

B.: A. von Bartsch, *Le Peintre-Graveur*, 21 vols, Vienna, 1803–21

BACKSBACKA: L. Backsbacka, *St. Peterburg juwelerare, gult-och silversmedek 1714–1870*, Helsingfors, 1951

BARBIER: Edmond-Jean-François Barbier, *Chronique de la Régence et du règne de Louis XV*, Paris, 1857

BAROQUE AND ROCOCO MASTERS: *The Hermitage, Leningrad. Baroque and Rococo Masters*, Leningrad and Prague, 1965

BAUDICOUR: P. de Baudicour, *Le peintre-graveur français continué, ou catalogue raisonné des estampes gravées par les peintres et les dessinateurs de l'école française nés dans le XVIIIe siècle*, 2 vols, Paris, 1859–61

BAUDRILLARD: Jean Baudrillard, *Seduction* (trans. Brian Singer), London, 1990

BELFORT: A.M. Belfort, 'L'œuvre de Vieilliard d'après Boucher', in *Cahiers de la céramique*, 1976, No. 58, pp. 6–7

BELLHOUSE: Mary Bellhouse, 'Erotic "Remedy" Prints and the Fall of the Aristocracy in Eighteenth-Century France', in *Political Theory*, vol. XXV, October 1997

BENOIS 1902: A.N. Benois, 'Galereia dragotsennostei Imperatorskogo Ermitazha' [Gallery of Treasures of the Imperial Hermitage], in *Khudozhestvennye sokrovishcha Rossii* [Art Treasures of Russia], vol. XII, St Petersburg, 1902

BENOIS 1912: A.N. Benois, *History of Painting*, vol. IV, St Petersburg, 1912

BENOIS 2003: A.N. Benois, *Moi dnevnik: 1916–1917–1918* [My Diary] (intro. J.E. Bowlt and N.D. Lobanov-Rostovsky), Moscow, 2003

BEREZINA: V.N. Berezina, *French Painting of the Nineteenth Century in the Collection of the State Hermitage*, Moscow, 1980

BIJOUX: Denis Diderot, *Les Bijoux indiscrets* [1748], in *Œuvres complètes de Diderot revues sur les éditions originales*, vol. IV, Paris, 1875

BLÜHM: Andre Blühm, *Pygmalion. Die Ikonographie eines Künstlermythos zwischen 1500 und 1900*, Frankfurt am Main and New York, 1988

BOBER–RUBINSTEIN: P.P. Bober and R.O. Rubinstein, *Renaissance Artists and Antique Sculpture: A Handbook of Sources*, London, 1987

BOCCACCIO: Giovanni Boccaccio, *The Decameron* (trans. Richard Aldington), 2 vols, London, 1954–5

BOCHER (BAUDOUIN): E. Bocher, *Pierre-Antoine Baudouin*, Paris, 1875 ('Les gravures françaises du XVIIIe siècle ou Catalogue raisonné des estampes, eaux-fortes, pièces en couleur, au bistre et au lavis, de 1700 à 1800. IIe fascicule')

BOCHER (LANCRET): E. Bocher, *Nicolas Lancret*, Paris, 1877 ('Les gravures françaises du XVIIIe siècle ou Catalogue raisonné des estampes, eaux-fortes, pièces en couleur, au bistre et au lavis, de 1700 à 1800. IVe fascicule')

BOCHER (LAVREINCE): E. Bocher, *Nicolas Lavreince*, Paris, 1875 ('Les gravures françaises du XVIIIe siècle ou Catalogue raisonné des estampes, eaux-fortes, pièces en couleur, au bistre et au lavis, de 1700 à 1800. Ier fascicule')

BOCHER (MOREAU LE JEUNE): E. Bocher, *Jean-Michel Moreau le Jeune*, Paris, 1882 ('Les gravures françaises du XVIIIe siècle ou Catalogue raisonné des estampes, vignettes, eaux-fortes, pièces en couleur, au bistre et au lavis, de 1700 à 1800. VIe fascicule')

BOCHER (SAINT-AUBIN): E. Bocher, *Augustin de Saint-Aubin*, Paris, 1879 ('Les gravures françaises du XVIIIe siècle ou Catalogue raisonné des estampes, vignettes, eaux-fortes, pièces en couleur, au bistre et au lavis, de 1700 à 1800. Ve fascicule')

BOHLIN: Diane De Grazia Bohlin, *Prints and related drawings by the Carracci family: A Catalogue Raisonné*, National Gallery of Art, Washington DC, 1979

BOILEAU: Nicolas Boileau Despréaux, *L'art poétique*, Paris, 1963

BOKOBZA-KAHAN: M. Bokobza-Kahan, *Libertinage et folie dans le roman du 18e siècle*, Louvain-Paris-Sterling, Virginia, 2000

BOUCHER 1978: *L'Œuvre gravé de François Boucher dans la collection Edmond de Rothschild* (General inventory of engravings) (ed. P. Jean-Richard), vol. I, Paris, 1978

BOURCARD: G. Bourcard, *Dessins, gouaches estampes et tableaux du dix-huitième siècle: Guide de l'amateur*, Paris, 1893

BOYER: F. Boyer, 'Catalogue raisonné de l'œuvre de Charles Natoire Peintre du roi', in *Archives de l'art français, nouvelle periode*, vol. XXI, 1949

BROWN: C.M. Brown, 'The Erstwhile Michelangelo *Sleeping Cupid* in The Turin Museo di Antichità and the drawings after antiquities in the collection of Tommaso della Porta', in *Journal of the History of Collections*, 5, No. 1, 1993, pp. 59–63

BRUNET, PRÉAUD: M. Brunet and T. Préaud, *Sèvres. Des origines à nos jours*, Fribourg, 1978

BRYSON: N. Bryson, *Word and Image: French painting of the Ancien Régime*, Cambridge, 1981

CARSON: Anne Carson, *Eros, the bittersweet: an essay*, Princeton, 1986

CASSELLE: P. Casselle, 'Pierre-François Basan, marchand d'estampes à Paris (1723–1797)', in *Paris et Ile-de-France. Mémoires publiés par la Fédération des Sociétés Historiques et Archéologiques de Paris et de l'Ile-de-France*, vol. XXXIII, Paris, 1982, pp. 97–185

CAT. CROZAT: [Lacurne de Saint Palaye], *Catalogue de tableaux du cabinet de M. Crozat, Baron de Thiers*, Paris, 1755

CATALOGUE DU PRINCE G***: *Catalogue du cabinet secret du Prince G***. Collection de livres et objets curieux et rares concernant l'amour, les femmes et le mariage avec les prix de vente. Première partie*, Bruxelles, 1887

CERVANTES: Miguel de Cervantes, *Don Quixote* (trans. Edith Grossman; intro. Harold Bloom), London, 2004

CHANDERNAGOR: Françoise Chandernagor, *Korolevskaia alleia. Vospominaniia Fransuazy d'Obin'e, markizy de Mentenon, suprugi korolia Frantsii* [Allée du roi. Recollections of Françoise d'Aubigné, Marquise de Maintenon, wife of the king of France] (trans. I. Volevich), Moscow, 1999

CHEGODAYEV: A.D. Chegodayev, *Watteau. Album*, Moscow, 1963

CHESNEAU: E. Chesneau, *Les estampes en couleurs du XVIIIᵉ siècle*, Paris, 1887

CLARK: A.M. Clark, *Pompeo Batoni: A Complete Catalogue of his Works with an Introductory Text*, New York, 1985

CLEMENT DE RIS: L. Clement de Ris, 'Les Musées du Nord. Le musée imperial de l'Ermitage à Saint-Péterbourg', in *Gazette des Beaux-Arts*, vol. XXI, 1880

COHEN: H. Cohen, *Guide de l'amateur de livres à gravures du XVIIIᵉ siècle* (5th edn), Paris, 1886

COHEN–DE RICCI: H. Cohen, *Guide de l'amateur de livres à gravures du XVIIIᵉ siècle* (6th edn, rev. by S. de Ricci), Paris, 1912

COIRAULT: P. Coirault, *Formation de nos chansons folkloriques*, Paris, 1953

CORTEY: M. Cortey, *L'invention de la courtisane au XVIIIᵉ siècle. Dans les romans-mémoires des "filles du monde" de Madame Meheust à Sade (1732–1797)*, Paris, 2001

CROW: Thomas Crow, *Painters and Public Life in Eighteenth-Century Paris*, New Haven and London, 1985

CUZIN: J.-P. Cuzin, *Jean-Honoré Fragonard. Life and Work. Complete Catalogue of the Oil Paintings*, New York, 1988

D.-V.: E. Dacier and A. Vauflart, *Jean de Jeulliene et les graveurs de Watteau au XVIII siecle*, vol. III, Paris, 1922

DACIER 1914: E. Dacier, *L'Œuvre gravé de Gabriel de Saint-Aubin. Notice historique et catalogue raisonné*, Paris, 1914

DACIER 1929: E. Dacier, *Gabriel de Saint-Aubin, Peintre, dessinateur et graveur (1724–1780)*, Paris, 1929

DANTE: Dante Alighieri, *The Divine Comedy* (ed. and trans. Robert M. Durling), 2 vols, New York and Oxford, 1996–2003

DARNTON: Robert Darnton, *The Forbidden Best-Sellers of Pre-Revolutionary France*, New York, 1995

DASHKOVA: E.R. Dashkova, *Zapiski kniagini: Vospominaniia. Memuary* [Notes of a princess: Recollections; memoirs] [1805], Minsk, 2003

DAX & BUTLER: Lionel Dax and Augustin de Butler, *Augustin Carrache: Les Lascives*, Paris, 2003

DE BAYE: De Baye, 'Les portraits de la Marquise de Prie', in *Gazette des Beaux-Arts*, vol. I, 1926, pp. 109–12

DE LEYMARIE: L. De Leymarie, *L'Œuvre de Gilles Demarteau l'Aîné, graveur du Roi* ('catalogue descriptif précédé d'une notice biographique'), Paris, 1896

DE: *Dictionnaire des éditeurs d'estampes à Paris sous l'Ancien Régime* (by M. Préaud, P. Casselle, M. Grivel, C. Le Bitouzé), Paris, 1987

DELAPLANCHE: J. Delaplanche, *Noël-Nicolas Coypel (1690–1734)* (intro. N. Willk-Brocard), Paris, 2004

DELTEIL: L. Delteil, *Manuel de l'Amateur d'Estampes du XVIIIᵉ siècle*, Paris, 1910

DEMPSEY: Charles Dempsey, *Inventing the Renaissance Putto*, Chapel Hill and London, 2001

DERRIDA: Jacques Derrida, *The post-card, from Socrates to Freud and beyond* (trans. Alan Bass), Chicago and London, 1987

DEZALLIER D' ARGENVILLE: [A.-N. Dezallier d'Argenville], *Abrégé de la vie des plus fameux peintres avec leurs portraits gravés en taille-douce*, 3 vols (par M***), Paris, 1745–52

DIDEROT: Denis Diderot, *The Nun* (trans. Russell Goulbourne), Oxford, 2005

DOBRITSYN: A.A. Dobritsyn, '"Devich'ia igrushka" i "Cabinet satirique". O frantsuzskikh istokakh russkoi obstsennoi epigrammy' ['Girl's toy' and 'Cabinet satirique': On French sources of Russian obscene epigrams], in I.A. Pil'shchikov and M.I. Shapir (eds), *A.S. Pushkin, Ten' Barkova* [Shadow of Barkov], Moscow, 2002, pp. 375–87

DŒE: *Dictionnaire des œuvres érotiques. Domain français* (intro. Pascal Pia), Paris, 1971

DÖPP: H.J. Döpp, *Eros: Die Lust in der Kunst*, Cologne, 2004

DRESDEN 2005: *Mannes Lust & Weibes Macht. Geschlechterwahn in Renaissance und Barock*, ex. cat., Staatliche Kunstsammlungen Dresden, Kupferstich-Kabinett (26 February – 11 July 2005), Dresden, 2005

DROULERS: E. Droulers, *Dictionnaire des attributs, allégories, emblèmes et symbols*, Turnhout, n.d.

DUCHAMP: M. Duchamp, 'Autour d'une fausse bague de Louis XVI', in *Bulletin de l'association Louis XVI*, No. 18, 2000, [11–43]

DUNAND: L. Dunand, 'Les estampes dites *découvertes* et *couvertes*', in *Gazette des Beaux-Arts*, vol. LXIX, 1967, pp. 225–38

DUSSIEUX: L. Dussieux, *Les Artistes français a l'étranger*, Paris, 1856

EIDELBERG: M. Eidelberg, 'Watteau's *La Boudeuse*', in *The Burlington Magazine*, May 1969, pp. 275–8

ENC.: *Encyclopédie ou Dictionnaire raisonné des sciences, des arts et des métiers*, vol. I, Paris, 1741; vol. IV, Paris, 1754

ERIKSEN: S. Eriksen and G. de Bellaigue, *Sèvres porcelain: Vincennes and Sèvres 1740 – 1800*, London and Boston, 1987

ERNST: S.R. Ernst, 'L'Exposition de la peinture français de XVII et XVIII siècles au Musée de l'Ermitage a Petrograd. 1922–1925', in *Gazette des Beaux-Arts*, vol. XVII, 1928

ERNST 1924: S.R. Ernst, *The Yusupov Gallery: French School*, Leningrad, 1924

ÉROS GREC: *Éros Grec: amour des dieux et des hommes*, ex. cat., Grand Palais, Paris, 1989

FAIRCHILDS: Cissie Fairchilds, 'Populuxe Goods in Eighteenth-Century Paris', in John Brewer and Roy Porter (eds.), *Consumption and the World of Goods*, London and New York, 1993, pp. 228–48

FALCONET À SÈVRES: *Falconet à Sevres 1757–1766 ou l'art de plaire*, ex. cat., Musée national de Céramique, Sèvres (6 November 2001 – 4 February 2002)

FARE: M. Fare, 'Un peintre indépendent: Jacques Courtin de l'Académie royale (1672–1752)', in *Gazette des Beaux-Arts*, May–June 1966, pp. 293–300

FARGE-REVEL: Arlette Farge and Jacques Revel, *The Rules of Rebellion: child abductions in Paris in 1750* (trans. Claudia Miéville), Cambridge, 1991

FASTI: Ovid, *Fasti* (trans. and ed. A.J. Boyle and R.D. Woodard), London, 2000

FEL'KERZAM: A.E. Fel'kerzam, *Alfavitnyi ukazatel' sanktpeterburgskikh zolotykh i serebrianykh del masterov, iuvelirov, graverov i prochikh. 1714–1814* [Alphabetical directory of St Petersburg's gold- and silversmiths, jewellers, engravers etc.], St Petersburg, 1907

FORRER: L. Forrer, *Biographical dictionary of medallists coin-, gem-, and seal-engravers, mint-masters, &c*, vol. I, London, 1904

FOURCAUD: L. Fourcaud, 'Antoine Watteau', in *Revue de l'art ancient et moderne*, vol. XVI, July–December 1904

FR. KNIGA: S.P. Luppov (ed.), *Frantsuzskaia kniga v Rossii v XVIII v. Ocherki istorii* [The French book in Russia in the eighteenth century: Historical essays], Leningrad, 1986

FRANCE ET RUSSIE: *La France et la Russie au Siècle des Lumières. Relations culturelles et artistiques de la France et de la Russie au XVIIIᵉ siècle*, ex. cat., Galeries Nationales du Grand Palais (20 November 1986 – 9 February 1987), Paris, 1986

FUCHS: E. Fuchs, *Geschichte der erotischen Kunst*, 3 vols, Munich, 1922–6

GAEHTGENS–LUGAND: Th.W. Gaehtgens and J. Lugand, *Joseph-Marie Vien. Peintre du Roi (1716–1809)*, Paris, 1988

GARNIER: N. Garnier, *Antoine Coypel (1661–1722)*, Paris, 1989

GARSHIN: Y.M. Garshin, 'Jean-Marc Nattier in His Relations with Russia', in *Herald of the Fine Arts*, vol. VI, 1888

GEORGI: J.G. Georgi, *Opisanie rossiisko-imperatorskago stolichnago goroda Sankt-Peterburga i dostopamiatnostei v okrestnostiakh onago* [Description of the imperial Russian capital St Petersburg and places of interest in its environs] [1794], St Petersburg, 1996

GILLE: F. Gille, *Musée de l'Ermitage Impérial. Notice sur la formation de ce musée et description des diverses collections qu'il renferme avec une introduction historique sur l'Ermitage de Catherine II*, St Petersburg, 1860

GIRODIE: A. Girodie, *Un peintre de fêtes galantes: Jean-Frédéric Schall (Strasbourg 1752 – Paris 1825)*, Strasbourg, 1927

GIULIANO: A. Giuliano, 'Antonio Pazzaglia, incisore genovese', in *Paragone. Arte. Anno XXI*, No. 241, March 1970, pp. 51–63

GOETHE: Johann Wolfgang von Goethe, *Novels and Tales* (including 'The Sorrow of Werther'), London, 1901

GOFFEN: R. Goffen, 'Renaissance Dreams', in *Renaissance Quarterly*, vol. XL, No. 4 (Winter 1987), pp. 682–706

GONCOURT 1875: E. Goncourt, *Catalogue raisonné de l'œuvre peint, dessiné et gravé d'Antoine Watteau*, Paris, 1875

GONCOURT 1887: E. and J. de Goncourt, *La femme au dix-huitième siècle* (new edn), Paris, 1887

GONCOURT 1914: E. and J. de Goncourt, *L'Art du XVIII siècle*, 3 vols, Paris, 1914

GORDON: Katherine K. Gordon, 'Madame de Pompadour, Pigalle, and the Iconography of Friendship', in *Art Bulletin 50*, no. 3 (September 1968)

GORI II: A.F. Gori, *Gemmae antiquae ex thesauro medicio et privatorum dactyliothecis Florentiae*, vol. II [of *Museum Florentinum*, 12 vols], Florence, 1732; reprinted in Reinach, 1895, pp. 12–71, pls. 5–74

GRAESSE: J.G.T. Graesse, *Trésor de livres rares et précieux*, vol. IV, Dresden, 1863

GRASSELLI: *Colorful Impressions: The Printmaking Revolution in Eighteenth-Century France* (ed. M.M. Grasselli, with essays by I.E. Phillips, K. Smentek, J.C. Walsh), ex. cat., National Gallery of Art, Washington DC, 2003

GRAVES: A. Graves, *The Royal Academy of Arts. A Complete Dictionary of Contributors and their Work from its foundation in 1769 to 1904*, 8 vols, London, 1905–6; reprinted in 4 vols, London, 1970

GRIFFITH: A. Griffith, 'Proofs in Eighteenth-century French Printmaking', in *Print Quarterly*, vol. XXI, 2004, No. 1, pp. 3–17

GUERMAN: M. Guerman, *Antoine Watteau*, Leningrad, 1980

GUICCIARDI: Jean-Pierre Guicciardi, 'Between the Licit and the Illicit: The Sexuality of the King', in Robert Parks Macubbin (ed.), *'Tis Nature's Fault: Unauthorized Sexuality during the Enlightenment*, Cambridge, 1987

GUIRAUD 1978: P. Guiraud, *Sémiologie de la sexualité. Essai de glosso-analyse*, Paris, 1978

GUIRAUD 1993: P. Guiraud, *Dictionnaire érotique. Précédé d'une introduction sur les structures étymologiques du vocabulaire érotique*, Paris, 1993

HALLAM: J.S. Hallam, 'The Genre Works of Louis-Léopold Boilly', PhD dissertation, University of Washington, 1979

HARRISSE: H. Harrisse, *Louis-Léopold Boilly. Peintre, dessinateur et lithographe. Sa vie et son œuvre, 1761–1845*, Paris, 1898

HAUMANT: E. Haumant, *La culture française en Russie (1700–1900)*, Paris, 1913

HEAWOOD: E. Heawood, *Watermarks mainly of the 17th and 18th centuries*, Hilversum, 1950, vol. 1

HEDLEY: Joe Hedley, *François Boucher. Seductive Visions*, London (Wallace Collection), 2004

HELIODORUS: Heliodorus, *Ethiopian Story (Ethiopika)* (trans. Sir Walter Lamb, intro. John Morgan), London, 1997

HENRIC 2003: J. Henric, 'De Socrate à Rushdie', in *Art Press, «Censures»* (out of series), June 2003, pp. 5–7

HERCENBERG: B. Hercenberg, *Nicolas Vleughels. Peintre et Directeur de l'Académie de France à Rome, 1668–1737*, Paris, 1975

HÉROLD: J. Hérold, *Louis-Marin Bonnet (1736–1793). Catalogue de l'œuvre gravé*, Paris, 1935

HESIOD: Hesiod, *Theogony* (ed. M.L. West), Oxford, 1966

HIGONNET: Anne Higonnet, *Pictures of Innocence. The History and Crisis of Ideal Childhood*, London, 1998

HOLLSTEIN: F.W.H. Hollstein, *Dutch and Flemish Etchings, Engravings and Woodcuts. Ca. 1450–1700*, 69 vols, Amsterdam, 1949–2004

HOT DRY MEN: *Hot Dry Men, Cold Wet Women: The Theory of Humors in Western European Art, 1575–1700* (by Z. Filipczak), ex. cat., Joslyn Art Museum (September 13 – November 2 1997); Arkansas Arts Center (November 20 1997 – February 6 1998); John and Mable Ringling Museum of Art (February 27 – April 24 1998)

HOUSSAYE: A. Houssaye, 'Les Vanloo', in *Revue des deux mondes*, July–September 1842

HUBER–ROST: M. Huber and C.C.H. Rost, *Manuel des curieux et des amateurs de l'art*, 8 vols, Zurich, 1797–1804

HUDOLEY: V. Hudoley, *Knizhnye znaki i sem'ia Romanovykh* [Book marks and the Romanovs], St Petersburg, 2003

HUISMAN: P. Huisman, *L'Aquarelle française au XVIIIe siècle*, Paris–Fribourg, 1968

HUNT: L. Hunt, 'Obscenity and the Origins of Modernity, 1500–1800', in *The Invention of Pornography, Obscenity and the Origins of Modernity, 1500–1800* (ed. L. Hunt), New York, 1993

HYDE–LEDBURY: Melissa Hyde and Mark Ledbury, *Rethinking Boucher*, Getty Research Institute, 2006

IDOMÉNÉE: C.P. Crébillon, *Idoménée*, in *Œuvres complètes de Crébillon, nouvelle édition, augmentée et ornée de belles gravures*, vol. 1, Paris, 1785

IFF: *Inventaire du Fonds Français. Graveurs du XVIIIe siècle* (by M. Roux), Bibliothèque Nationale de France, Département des estampes, 14 vols, Paris, 1930–77

IOFFE: I. Ioffe, *Frantsuzskoe iskusstvo epokhi razlozheniia feodalizma i burzhuaznoi revoliutsii. Ocherk k vystavke* [French art in the era of the breaking down of feudalism and the bourgeois revolution. Essay accompanying exhibition (State Hermitage)], Moscow–Leningrad, 1932

JEANNERET: M. Jeanneret, *Éros rebelle. Littérature et dissidence à l'âge classique*, Paris, 2003

JULIE: Jean-Jacques Rousseau, *Julie: ou, La nouvelle Héloïse*, Paris, 1963

KAGAN 1973: Iu.O. Kagan, *Zapadnoevropeiskie kamei v sobranii Ermitazha* [Western-European cameos in the Hermitage collection], Leningrad, 1973

KAGAN 1976: Iu.O. Kagan, *Reznye kamni Uil'iama i Charl'za Braunov* [Carved stones of William and Charles Brown], ex. cat., State Hermitage, Leningrad, 1976

KODA: Harold Koda, Andrew Bolton and Mimi Hellman, *Dangerous Liaisons: Fashion and Furniture in the 18th Century*, New Haven, 2004

KOSAREVA: N. Kosareva, *Frantsuzskaia khudozhestvennaia bronza XVIII veka v sobranii Ermitazha* [French eighteenth-century bronze in the Hermitage collection], Leningrad, 1988

KOSTIUK 1987: O.G. Kostiuk, 'Zhan P'er Ador i ego raboty v Ermitazhe' [Jean-Pierre Ador and his work in the Hermitage], in *Zapadnoevropeiskoe iskusstvo XVIII veka* [Western-European art of the eighteenth century], Leningrad, 1987

KOSTIUK 2000: O.G. Kostiuk, *Peterburgskie iuveliry XVIII–XIX veka* [Petersburg jewellers of the eighteenth and nineteenth centuries], St Petersburg, 2000

LA FONTAINE: Jean de La Fontaine, *The fables of La Fontaine* (trans. Elizur Wright), London, 1892

LA PORCELAINE DE SÈVRES: *La porcelaine de Sèvres du XVIII siècle. Catalogue de collection* (Editions du Musée de l'Ermitage), St Petersburg, 2005

LANDER: I.G. Lander, 'Khudozhestvennye sobraniia Petra Kornil'evicha Sukhtelena' [Art collections of Peter Kornil'evich Sukhtelen], in *Sud'by muzeinykh kollektsii: Materialy VI Tsarskosel'skoi nauchnoi konferentsii* [The fate of museum collections: materials of the sixth Tsarskoe selo conference], St Petersburg, 2000, pp. 104–16

LAUNAY–MAILHOS: M. Launay and G. Mailhos, *Introduction à la vie littéraire du XVIIIe siècle*, Paris, 1984

LAWRENCE & DIGHTON: Lawrence & Dighton, *Les plus belles gravures françaises du dix-huitième siècle*, Paris, 1912

LE BLANC: C. Le Blanc, *Manuel de l'amateur d'estampes*, 4 vols, Paris, 1854–89

LE CORBEILLER: C. Le Corbeiller, *European and American Snuff-Boxes 1730–1830*, London, 1966

LE PENNEC: M.-F. Le Pennec, *Petit glossaire du langage érotique aux XVIIe et XVIIIe siècles* (*Collection La parole debout dirigée par G. Lely*), Paris, 1979

LEFRANÇOIS 1981: T. Lefrançois, *Nicolas Bertin (1668–1736). Peintre d'histoire*, Paris, 1981

LEFRANÇOIS 1994: T. Lefrançois, *Charles Coypel. Peintre de roi (1694–1752)* (intro. P. Rosenberg), Paris, 1994

LERIBAULT: C. Leribault, *Jean-François de Troy (1679–1752)* (intro. A. Laing), Paris, 2002

LES LIAISONS DANGEREUSES: Choderlos de Laclos, *Les Liaisons Dangereuses*, Paris, 1964 (references are to numbered letters)

LEVINSON-LESSING: V.F. Levinson-Lessing, *Istoriia kartinnoi galerei Ermitazha (1764–1917)* [History of the picture gallery of the Hermitage (1764–1917)], Leningrad, 1985

LEVITINE: George Levitine, *The Sculpture of Falconet*, Greenwich, Conn., 1972

LIEFDE: *Liefde uit de Hermitage*, ex. cat., De Nieuwe Kerk, Amsterdam (12 December 2003 – 18 April 2004), Amsterdam 2003

LIMC: *Lexicon Iconographicum Mythologiae Classicae* (LIMC), vol. 1–, Zürich and Munich, 1981–

LIUBOV' XVIII VEKA: *Liubov' XVIII veka. Frantsuzskie graviury luchshikh masterov XVIII veka* [Love in the Eighteenth Century: French engravings of the best artists of the eighteenth century] (intro. Iu. Shamurin), Moscow, 1912

LIVEN: G.E. Liven, *Putevoditel' po Kabinetu Petra Velikogo i Galeree Dragotsennostei* [Guide to the Cabinet of Peter the Great and the Gallery of Treasures], St Petersburg, 1902

LIVRET: [F. Labensky], *Livret de la Galerie impériale de l'Hermitage de Saint Pétersbourg*, St Petersburg, 1838

LIVSHITS: N.A. Livshits, *A Pastoral Scene by François Boucher*, Leningrad, 1948

L'OPERA COMPLETA: Giovanni Macchia and E.C. Montagni, *L'Opera completa di Watteau*, Milan, 1968

LOSEV 1982: A.F. Losev, *Estetika Vozrozhdeniia* [Aesthetics of the Renaissance], Moscow, 1982

LOSEV 1993: A.F. Losev, *Ocherki antichnogo simvolizma i mifologii* [Essays on ancient symbolism and mythology], Moscow, 1993

LOVES OF THE GODS: *The Loves of the Gods. Mythological Painting From Watteau to David* (by C.B. Bailey with C.A. Hamilton), ex. cat., Galeries Nationales du Grand Palais, Paris (15 October 1991 – 6 January 1992); Philadelphia Museum of Art (23 February – 26 April 1992); Kimbell Art Museum, Fort Worth (23 May – 2 August 1992)

LUCIE-SMITH: E. Lucie-Smith, *Sexuality in Western Art*, London, 1991

LUGT: Frits Lugt, *Les marques et collections de dessins & d'estampes*, Amsterdam, 1921

LUGT SUPPL: Frits Lugt, *Les marques et collections de dessins & d'estampes. Supplément*, The Hague, 1956

LUNDBERG: *Lavreince. Nicolas Lafrensen. Peintre Suédois. 1737–1807* (comp. G. Lundberg), Paris, Bibliothèque Nationale, May–June 1949

LUPPOV: S.P. Luppov, *Kniga v Rossii v pervoi chetverti XVIII veka* [The book in Russia in the first quarter of the eighteenth century], Leningrad, 1973

MAGGS: *L'Œuvre gravé de A.-J. Duclos*, Paris–London (Maggs Bros.), 1939

MAKARENKO: N.E. Makarenko, *Khudozhestvennye sokrovishcha Imperatorskogo Ermitazha* [Art treasures of the Imperial Hermitage], Petrograd, 1916

MALINOVSKII: K.V. Malinovskii, 'Pis'ma F.-V. Bergkhol'tsa k Ia. Shtelinu o kollektsionirovanii graviur. K istorii sobraniia graviur Ermitazha' [The letters of F.-V. Bergholz to J. von Stahlin on collecting engravings. Towards a history of the Hermitage collection of engravings], in *Muzei 7: Khudozhestvennye sobraniia SSSR* [Museum 7: Art collections of the USSR], Moscow, 1987, pp. 253–62

MANON: Antoine-François Prévost, *Manon Lescaut*, Paris, 1999

MANTZ: P. Mantz, *Cent dessins de Watteau gravés par Boucher, précédes d'une préface de P. Mantz*, Paris, 1892

MARANDEL: J.P. Marandel, 'A New Painting by Nicolas Vleughels', in *The Burlington Magazine*, June 1977, p. 442

MASTERY & ELEGANCE: *Mastery & Elegance. Two Centuries of French Drawings from the Collection of Jeffrey E. Horvitz* (ed. A.L. Clark, Jr.; foreword P. Rosenberg), Cambridge, MA, 1998

MAXIMOVA: M.I. Maximova, *Reznye kamni XVIII i XIX vekov. Putevoditel' po vystavke* [Carved stones of the eighteenth and nineteenth centuries. Exhibition guide], Leningrad, 1926

MCALLISTER JOHNSON: W. McAllister Johnson, '"Serviteur, elève et ami": Some Print Dedications and Printmakers in 18th-century France', in *Gazette des Beaux-Arts*, vol. CXI, January–February 1988, pp. 49–54

MEERMAN: J. Meerman, *Reise durch den Norden und Nordosten von Europa in den Jahren 1797 bis 1800*, Weimar, 1810

MÉROT: A. Mérot, *Eustache Le Sueur (1616–1655)*, Paris, 1987

MET: Ovid, *Metamorphoses* (trans. A.D. Melville), Oxford, 1986

MILIOTTI: A. Miliotti, *Description d'une collection de pierres graveés qui se trouvent au Cabinet Imperial de St. Pétersbourg*, vol. I, Vienna, 1803

MILLER: M. F. Miller, 'French Paintings of the Seventeenth and Eighteenth Centuries in the New Rooms of the Hermitage', in *The City*, vol. I, 1923

MILLIEN: A. Millien, J.G. Pénavaire G. Delarue, *Chansons populaires du Nivernais et du Morvan*, Grenoble, 1977

MIRIMONDE: A.-P. de Mirimonde, 'Les sujets musicaux chez Antoine Watteau', in *Gazette des Beaux-Arts*, vol. LVIII, 1961, pp. 249–88

MME DE POMPADOUR: *Madame de Pompadour et les arts*, ex. cat., Musée national des châteaux de Versailles et de Trianon, Versailles, 2002

MUNHALL: E. Munhall, *Greuze the Draftsman* (with essay by I. Novosselskaya), London, 2002

NAGLER KL: *Neues allgemeines Künstler-Lexicon oder Nachrichten von dem Leben und den Werken der Maler, Bildhauer, Baumeister, Kupferstecher, Formschneider, Lithographen, Zeichner, Medailleure, Elfenbeinarbeiter, etc* (ed. Dr. G.K. Nagler), 22 vols, Munich, 1835–52

NAGLER MO: *Die Monogrammisten und diejenigen bekannten und unbekannten Künstler aller Schulen, welche sich zur Bezeichnung ihrer Werke eines figürlichen Zeichens, der Initialen des Namens, der Abbreviatur desselben &c. bedient haben* (ed. Dr. G.K. Nagler), Munich, 5 vols, 1858–79

NATOIRE: *Charles-Joseph Natoire*, ex. cat., Troyes, Nimes, Rome, 1977

NEMILOVA 1961: I.S.Nemilova, 'Painting by Francois Boucher', *Papers of the State Hermitage: Western European Art*, vol. I, 1961

NEMILOVA 1964: I.S.Nemilova, *Watteau and His Work in the Hermitage*, Leningrad, 1964

NEMILOVA 1975: I.S. Nemilova, 'Contemporary French Art in Eighteenth-Century Russia', *Apollo*, June 1975, pp. 428–42

NEMILOVA 1985: I.S. Nemilova, *Frantsuzskaia zhivopis' v sobranii Gosudarstvennogo Ermitazha* [French painting in the collection of the State Hermitage], Leningrad, 1985

NEVEROV: *Liubovnye pozitsii epokhi Vozrozhdeniia* [Love positions of the Renaissance epoch] (comp. O.Ia. Neverov), St Petersburg, 2002

NOLHAC: P. de Nolhac, *J.M. Nattier, Peintre de la cour de Louis XV*, Paris, 1912

ŒUVRE DE BASAN: *Œuvre de Basan*, vols I–IV, VI (BNF Est. SNR-1 BASAN (Pierre-François))

OMNIA VINCIT AMOR: *Omnia Vincit Amor. Erotische Darstellungen in der Graphik von der Reformation bis zum Rokoko*, Kunstsammlungen der Veste Coburg (14 April – 12 June 2000) [booklet]

ON LOVE AND DEATH: *On Love and Death. Drawings and Prints in the Biblioteca Nacional*, ex. cat., Fundació Caixa Catalunya, Barcelona (July–October 2001); Biblioteca Nacional, Madrid (February–April 2002)

ORTEGA: José Ortega y Gasset, *On Love: aspects of a single theme* (trans. Tony Talbot), London, 1959

OZERKOV: Dimitri Ozerkov, *L'éducation de l'Amour. La gravure française du siècle galant dans la collection de l'Ermitage*, ex. cat., State Hermitage, St Petersburg, 2006

P.-B.: Le Baron Roger Portalis and Henri Béraldi, *Les graveurs du dix-huitième siècle*, 3 vols, Paris, 1880–2

P.-M.: K. T. Parker and J. Mathey, *Antoine Watteau. Catalogue complet de son œuvre dessiné*, 2 vols, Paris, 1957–8

PANOFSKY: E. Panofsky, 'Blind Cupid', in *Studies in Iconology. Humanistic Themes in the Art of the Renaissance*, New York, 1939, pp. 95–128

PLATO: Plato, *Phaedrus* (trans. and intro. R. Hackforth), Cambridge, 1952

PLINY: Pliny the Elder, *Natural History* (trans. H. Rackham), 10 vols, London and Cambridge, MA, 1938–62

POSNER: D. Posner, 'Watteau mélancolique: la formation d'un mythe', in *Bulletin de la société de l'histoire de l'art français. Année 1973*, Paris, 1974, pp. 345–61

PRAKHOV: A. Prakhov, 'Treasures of the Yusupov Collection', *The Art Treasures of Russia*, 1907

PROVERBES: *Dictionnaire des proverbes, sentences et maximes* (comp. M. Maloux), Paris, 1980

R.-D.: A.-P.-F. Robert-Dumesnil, *Le peintre-graveur français ou catalogue raisonné des estampes gravées par les peintres et les dessinateurs de l'école française*, 11 vols, Paris, 1835–71

RAKOVA: A.L. Rakova, 'Ob istorii kollektsii ornamental'noi graviury' [On the history of the collection of ornamental engraving], in *Muzei 8: Khudozhestvennye sobraniia SSSR* [Museum 8: Art collections of the USSR], Moscow, 1987, pp. 222–8

RASPE–TASSIE: R.E. Raspe, *A descriptive catalogue of a general collection of ancient and modern engraved gems, cameos as well as intaglios, taken from the most celebrated Cabinets in Europe, and cast in coloured pastes, white enamel, and sulphur by James Tassie, modeller*, vol. II, London, 1791

RAYNAUD: Ernest Raynaud, 'La Mort de J.-B. Nattier', *Mercure de France*, 15 July 1928

RÉAU 1922: Louis Réau, *Étienne-Maurice Falconet*, Paris, 1922

RÉAU 1928–30: Louis Réau, 'Antoine Watteau', in *Dimier*, vol. I, no. 101, 1928–30

RÉAU 1929: Louis Réau, *Catalogue de l'art français dans les musées russes*, Paris, 1929

REGENCY TO EMPIRE: *Regency to Empire. French Printmaking 1715–1814*, ex. cat., Baltimore Museum of Art and The Minneapolis Institute of Arts (10 November 1984 – 6 January 1985)

REINACH: S. Reinach, *Pierres gravées des collections Marlborough et d'Orléans; des recueils d'Eckhel, Gori, Lévesque de Gravelle, Mariette, Millin, Stosch, reunies et réédités avec un texte nouveau*, Paris, 1895

REMI, MILIOTTI: Remi, Miliotti, *Catalogue des tableaux des trois ecoles; Du Cabinet de feu M. d'Ennery, écuyer*, Paris, 1786

RENAULT: O. Renault, 'Crébillon, le paradoxe du censeur', in *Art Press*, «*Censures*» (out of series), June 2003, pp. 55–8

ROMANOVS: *The Collections of the Romanovs: European Art from the State Hermitage Museum*, ex. cat., St Petersburg, 2003

ROSENBERG: Pierre Rosenberg, *Fragonard*, ex. cat., Galeries nationales du Grand Palais, Paris (24 September 1987 – 4 January 1988); Metropolitan Museum of Art, New York (2 February – 8 May 1988)

ROTHSCHILD: *Dessins et Estampes du XVème au XVIIIème siècles de la collection Edmond de Rothschild*, ex. cat., Fundación Juan March (6 February – 30 May 2004; 7 October 2004 – 10 January 2005)

ROVINSKII: D.A. Rovinskii, *Podrobnyi slovar' russkikh gravirovannykh portretov* [Detailed dictionary of Russian engraved portraits], 4 vols, St Petersburg, 1886–9

RUMYANTSEV: *The Imperial Moscow Rumyantsev Museum. Department of the Fine Arts. Catalogue of the Picture Gallery*, Moscow, 1915

SADE: Marquis de Sade, *Juliette* (trans. Austryn Wainhouse), New York, [1968]

SAHUT: *Carle Vanloo. Premier peintre du roi (Nice, 1705 – Paris, 1765)*, ex. cat. (intro. P. Rosenberg; cat. M.-C. Sahut), Musée Chéret, Nice (21 January – 13 March 1977); Musée Bargoin, Clermont-Ferrand (1 April – 30 May 1977); Musée des Beaux-Arts, Nancy (18 June – 15 August 1977)

SAINT-AMAND: Pierre Saint-Amand, *The Libertine's Progress: Seduction in the Eighteenth-Century French Novel* (trans. Jennifer Curtiss Gage), Hanover and London, 1994

SALMON 1999: Xavier Salmon, *Jean-Marc Nattier: 1685–1766*, ex. cat., Musée national des châteaux de Versailles et de Trianon (26 October 1999 – 30 January 2000), Paris, 1999

SALMON 2002: *Madame de Pompadour et les arts* (ed. Xavier Salmon), ex. cat., Musée national des châteaux de Versailles et de Trianon (14 February – 19 May 2002); Kunsthalle der Hypo-Kulturstiftung, Munich (14 June – 15 September 2002); National Gallery, London (16 October 2002 – 12 January 2003), Paris, 2002

SALONS: Denis Diderot, *Salons* (comp. Jean Seznec and Jean Adhémar), 4 vols, Oxford, 1957–67

SANDOZ 1979: M. Sandoz, *Nicolas-Guy Brenet. 1728–1792*, Paris, 1979

SANDOZ 1988: M. Sandoz, *Les Lagrenée*; vol I: *Louis, Jean, François Lagrenée, 1725–1805*, Paris, 1983; vol. II: *Jean-Jacques Lagrenée, 1739–1821*, Paris, 1988

SANDSTRÖM: B. Sandström, *Bénigne Gagneraux. 1756–1795: éducation, inspiration, œuvre*, Stockholm, 1981

SAVILL: R. Savill, *The Wallace Collection: Catalogue of Sèvres Porcelain*, London, 1988

SAVINSKAÏA: Lioubov Savinskaïa, 'La Collection de Peintures de Nicolaï Borrissovitch Youssoupov', in *Hubert Robert et Saint-Pétersbourg. Les Commandes de la Famille Impériale et des Princes Russes entre 1773 et 1802*, ex. cat., Musée des Beaux-Arts, Valence, 1999

SCHOLTEN: Frits Scholten, *L'Amour Menaçant or Menacing Love: a statue by Falconet*, Rijksmuseum, Amsterdam, 2005

SCOTT: Katie Scott, 'Framing Ambitions: The Interior Politics of Mme de Pompadour', in Katie Scott and Deborah Cherry (eds.), *Between Luxury and the Everyday: Decorative Arts in Eighteenth-Century France*, London, 2005

SCOTT: Katie Scott, 'Under the sign of Venus: the making and meaning of Bouchardon's *L'Amour* in the age of the French rococo', in Caroline Arscott and Katie Scott (eds.), *Manifestations of Venus: art and sexuality*, Manchester and New York, 2000

SEKRET DVORTSOVOI TABAKERKI: *Sekret dvortsovoi tabakerki* [The secret of the court snuff-box] (text L. Bardovskaya), St Petersburg, 2002

SHERIFF: Mary D. Sheriff, *Moved By Love. Inspired Artists and Deviant Women in Eighteenth-Century France*, Chicago and London, 2004

SNOWMAN 1966: K. Snowman, *Eighteenth-century Gold Boxes of Europe*, London, 1966

SNOWMAN 1990: K. Snowman, *Eighteenth-century Gold Boxes of Europe*, London, 1990

SONGE DE POLIPHILE: *Le tableau des riches inventions couvertes du voile des feintes amoureuses, qui sont representées dans le Songe de Poliphile. Desvoilées des ombres du Songe, et subtilement exposées par Beroalde*, Paris (chez Matthieu Guillemot, au Palais, en la gallerie des prisonniers), 1600

STENDHAL: Stendhal (Henry Beyle), *On Love* (trans. Philip Sidney Woolf and Cecil N. Sidney Woolf), New York, [1915]

STEWART 1973: Philip Stewart, *Le Masque et la parole. Le langage de l'amour au XVIIIe siècle*, Paris, 1973

STEWART 1992: Philip Stewart, *Engraven Desire: Eros, Image & Text in the French Eighteenth Century*, Durham and London, 1992

STUFFMANN: M. Stuffmann, 'Les Tableaux de la collection de Pierre Crozat. Historique et destinée d'un ensemble célèbre établi en partant d'un inventaire après décès inédit (1740)', in *Gazette des Beaux-Arts*, July–September 1968

TH.-B.: *Allgemeines Lexikon der bildenden Künstler von der Antike bis zur Gegenwart* (comp. Ulrich Thieme and Felix Becker), 36 vols, Leipzig, 1907–50

THOMAS: Donald Thomas, *The marquis de Sade*, London, 1992

VAN DER KAMP: H. van der Kamp, 'The Trader and the Policeman. Catalogues of Nineteenth Century Erotic Art', in *Romantique. Erotic Art of the Early Nineteenth Century*, Amsterdam and Singapore, 2000, pp. 65–8

VAN KLEY: Dale van Kley, *The Damiens Affair and the Unravelling of the Ancien Régime 1750–1770*, Princeton, 1984

VASARI: Giorgio Vasari, *Lives of the painters, sculptors and architects* (trans. Gaston du C. de Vere; intro. and notes by David Ekserdjian), London, 1996

VIE EN FRANCE: *La vie en France autour de 1789. Images et représentation 1785–1795*, ex. cat., Château de Biron, Dordogne (24 June – 1 September 1989); Musée des Beaux-Arts, Nancy (15 September – 15 November 1989)

VIE FR.: F. Trassard, D. Casali and A. Auger, *La Vie des français au temps du Roi-Soleil*, Paris, 2002

VIRGIL: Virgil, *Bucolics and Georgics*, London, 1918

VLASOVA–BALASHOVA: O.V. Vlasova and E.L. Balashova, *Vladel'cheskie znaki na graviurakh i litografiiakh. Na materiale otdela graviury Gosudarstvennogo Russkogo muzeia* [Owners marks on engravings and lithographs. Works of the engravings department of the State Russian Museum], gen. ed. M.A. Alekseeva, St Petersburg, 2003

VOLSKAYA: V. N. Volskaya, *A. Watteau*, Moscow, 1933

VOLTAIRE 35: *Les Œuvres Complètes de Voltaire*, vol. XXXV, Oxford (Voltaire Foundation), 1994

VOLTAIRE: François-Marie Arouet de Voltaire, *Candide, or Optimism* (trans. Norman Cameron), London, 1947

VYSKOCHKOV: L.V. Vyskochkov, *Imperator Nikolai I: chelovek i gosudar'* [Emperor Nicholas I: the man and the sovereign], St Petersburg, 2001

WAAGEN: G.F. Waagen, *Die Gemaldesammlung in der Kaiserlichen Ermitage zu St. Petersburg, nebst Bemerkungen über andere dortige Kunstsammlungen*, Munich, 1864

WAGNER: P. Wagner, *Eros Revived: Erotica of the Enlightenment in England and America*, London, 1988

WALD LASOWSKI: P. Wald Lasowski, *Libertines*, Paris, 1980

WATELET–LÉVESQUE: M. Watelet and M. Lévesque, *Dictionnaire des arts de peinture, sculpture et gravure*, vol. I, Paris, 1792

WATTEAU: Pierre Rosenberg and Ettore Camesasca, *Tout l'œuvre peint de Watteau*, catalogue raisonné, Paris, 1970

WATTEAU 1684–1721: Margaret Morgan Grasselli and Pierre Rosenberg, *Watteau, 1684–1721*, ex. cat., National Gallery of Art, Washington DC, 1984

WESTERN-EUROPEAN FANS: *Zapadnoevropeiskie veera XVIII–XIX vv. iz sobraniia Gosudarstvennogo Ermitazha* [Western-European fans of the eighteenth and nineteenth century in the collection of the State Hermitage], Leningrad, 1970

WILDENSTEIN 1924: G. Wildenstein, *Lancret*, Paris, 1924

WILDENSTEIN 1956: G. Wildenstein, *Fragonard aquafortiste. Études et documents pour servir à l'histoire de l'art français du dix-huitième siècle*, Paris, 1956

WILLK-BROCARD: N. Willk-Brocard, *Une dynastie: Les Hallé. Daniel (1614–1675), Claude-Guy (1652–1736), Noël (1711–1781)* (intro. Y. Bottineau), Paris, 1995

WIND: E. Wind, *Pagan Mysteries in the Renaissance* (rev. and enlarged edn), New York, 1968

WORLEY: M.P. Worley, 'The Image of Ganymede in France, 1730–1820: The Survival of a Homoerotic Myth', in *The Art Bulletin*, December 1994, vol. LXXVI, No. 4, pp. 630–43

WRANGEL: N.N. Wrangel, *The Hermitage of Grand Duchess Maria Nikolaievna*, St Petersburg, n.d.

YOUSSOUPOFF: *Musée du prince Youssoupoff contenant les tableaux, marbres, ivories et porcelains qui se trouvent dans son hôtel a Saint-Pétersbourg*, St Petersburg, 1839

YUSUPOV: *The State Museum Reserve. Catalogue of Works of Art from Former Yusupov Gallery*, Petrograd, 1920

ZABABUROVA: N.V. Zababurova, 'Kniga Stendalia "o liubvi" v svete psikhologicheskikh traditsii frantsuzskoi kul'tury XVII veka' [Stendhal's book 'on love' in the light of the psychological traditions of French seventeenth-century culture], in *XVII vek v dialoge epoch i kul'tur* [Seventeenth century in the dialogue of eras and cultures], Symposium (8), St Petersburg, 2000, pp. 91–3

ZIMMERMANN: E.N. Zimmermann, *Watteau, Klassiker der Kunst*, Stuttgart, Leipzig, 1912

ZOLOTOV AND NEMILOVA: *Antoine Watteau* (intro. Iu. Zolotov; notes on plates I. Nemilova, I. Kuznetsova, T. Kamenskaia, V. Alexeeva), Leningrad, 1973

Index

Page numbers in *italic* refer to the illustrations